This, the first complete edition of Carew's writings in half a century, supplies a critical test based on the early printed versions and many manuscripts. The principal variants are given in full. Two poems which may be Carew's are printed for the first time, and the traditional canon has been reconsidered throughout. The introduction includes a life of Carew derived in part from newly discovered documents. A systematic commentary presents what is known about the composition and topical allusions of the various works, and offers detailed evidence of Carew's indebtedness—more extensive than has hitherto been realized—to Marino and other models. There is a catalogue of the early musical settings, and a special note discusses the Vandyck portrait, which is reproduced for the frontispiece.

THE
P O E M S
OF
THOMAS CAREW

THOMAS KILLIGREW AND THOMAS CAREW
Portrait by ANTHONY VAN DYCK, 1638. Royal Collection, Windsor
By gracious permission of His Majesty The King
The identification of Carew (on the right) is traditional though not fully
authenticated. *See pp.* xliv–xlv

THE
POEMS
OF
THOMAS CAREW

WITH HIS

MASQUE
COELUM BRITANNICUM

Edited, with an introduction and notes, by
RHODES DUNLAP

OXFORD
At the CLARENDON PRESS

Oxford University Press, Amen House, London E.C.4

GLASGOW NEW YORK TORONTO MELBOURNE WELLINGTON
BOMBAY CALCUTTA MADRAS KARACHI LAHORE DACCA
CAPE TOWN SALISBURY NAIROBI IBADAN ACCRA
KUALA LUMPUR HONG KONG

FIRST EDITION 1949
REPRINTED LITHOGRAPHICALLY IN GREAT BRITAIN
AT THE UNIVERSITY PRESS, OXFORD
FROM CORRECTED SHEETS OF THE FIRST EDITION
1957, 1964

PREFACE

THIS edition of Carew is intended to present his complete
writings as they appear in the best early copies: the 1634
edition for the masque, the collected *Poems* of 1640 for most
of the pieces in that volume, and for the other works several
printed and manuscript sources. Before selecting these ex-
emplars I made a complete collation of readings from all the
editions and about a hundred early manuscripts; I print as
many of the variants—a very small part of the total number
—as possess external authority or apparent relevance to the
intentions of the poet. It is clear that Carew rewrote some
of his poems, and for these the alternative versions are given
in full.

Carew did not collect his own writings, and there are many
problems of ascription. Lacking evidence to support a more
rigorous method, I have been guided by the traditional
ascriptions, considerations of style and content, and the rela-
tive plausibility of competing claims. Two poems possibly
by Carew (*A Louers passion* and *Of his Mistresse*) are here
edited for apparently the first time; two others (*Vpon the
Royall Ship* and *To a Strumpett*), which were included among
Carew's works by Mr. R. G. Howarth, are shown to be
probably spurious; and *The Carver*, the true provenience of
which has been pointed out by Mr. Alan Herrick, is re-
moved from the canon.

The most important new biographical facts presented in
the Introduction have to do with the date and circumstances
of Carew's death. Concerning the living poet and wit I have
made fewer discoveries, but I attempt to bring together all
the information accessible about the man and his work. The
Commentary, apart from its specifically exegetical tasks, con-
cerns itself principally with the occasions and sources of the
various pieces, and shows that Carew's debt to Marino and
other continental writers is greater than has ordinarily been
recognized.

For very kind personal interest and expert aid I should
like to thank Col. C. H. Wilkinson, under whose guidance

I did my first intensive work on Carew, for a doctoral thesis, while I was at Oxford as a Rhodes Scholar before the war; and Professor D. Nichol Smith, who read and criticized a preliminary version of the present edition. Miss N. D. Church and Mr. P. H. Dobell generously allowed me to use manuscripts and books in their possession; Professor Edward J. Dent and Mr. Percy M. Young answered questions about the musical settings; the Rev. C. A. S. Page, of West Wickham, checked the registers of his parish (though in vain) for records of Carew; the Rev. Frank Hunt, of Toddington, provided information about the monument to Lady Mary Wentworth; and the Rev. D. R. F. M. Creighton, of Iver, helped me to investigate the history of the Salter family. I have received courteous help from officials of the Bodleian Library, the British Museum, the Cambridge University Library, the Library of St. John's College (Cambridge), the Library of the Society of Genealogists, the London Guildhall Library, the Public Record Office, the Search Room at Somerset House, the Dyce Collection at South Kensington, the New York Public Library, the Henry E. Huntington Library, and the libraries of the Universities of Chicago, Illinois, and Iowa. While the text was in proof, Mr. Edwin Wolf, of Philadelphia, very kindly lent me his own notes of variant readings from several manuscript miscellanies which I had not seen. My colleagues at the University of Iowa have shown themselves both learned and long-suffering in assisting me about special problems. And the staff of the Clarendon Press have, in several matters, most generously rendered assistance beyond the call of duty.

R. D.

IOWA CITY
29 November 1948

CONTENTS

CONTENTS

x CONTENTS

CONTENTS

INTRODUCTION

1. *The Life of Thomas Carew*

IN the Oxford University Subscription Register, among
the names of students appearing for matriculation on
10 June 1608, stands the neat italic signature of Thomas
Carew.[1] The University's Matriculation Book records,
under the same date, that his college was Merton, his native
county Kent, his father a knight, and his age thirteen.[2] We
thus know that he was born between June 1594 and June
1595. The exact place of his birth is undetermined. In
1594–5 his parents had lived for a number of years at West
Wickham in Kent, and the names of several infant Carews
occur in the baptismal records there, but there is no entry
for Thomas.[3]

He came of good family. His father, Matthew (later Sir
Matthew) Carew, D.C.L., a Master in Chancery, was de-
scended from landed Cornish stock, and his mother, born
Alice Ryvers, was the daughter and granddaughter of Lord
Mayors of London. According to Richard Carew the anti-
quary, who was Thomas Carew's cousin, the founder of
their family came out of France with the Conqueror, and
the name is derived from 'ancient *Carru* . . . a plowe'.[4]

---

[1] Oxford University, Archive S.P. 38, fol. 143.
[2] Andrew Clark, *Register of the University of Oxford, 1571–1622*, ii. 301.
[3] Information from the Rev. C. A. S. Page, Rector of West Wickham.
[4] *The Survey of Cornwall. Written by Richard Carew of Antonie, Esquire*, 1602,
pp. 64ᵛ, 103ʳ. Part of this detailed account of the Carews is in verse:

> *Carew* of ancient *Carru* was,
> And *Carru* is a plowe,
> Romanes the trade, Frenchmen the word,
> I doe the name auowe. . . .
> The smelling sence wee sundry want,
> But want it without lack:
> For t'is no sense, to wish a weale,
> That brings a greater wrack.
> Through natures marke, we owne our babes,
> By tip of th' upper lip;
> Black-bearded all the race, saue mine,
> Wrong dide by mothership.

'The Armes of our family', adds Richard Carew, 'are *Or*. 3. Lyons passant, sable:
armed and *Langued Gules*.'

But the derivation now accepted connects the name with Carew (Caer Yw) Castle, county Carmarthen.[1] The first recorded Thomas Carew, 'of Carew, county Carmarthen; Mulsford, Berks; and Idrone in Ireland', died in 1431; his daughter-in-law, the wealthy Joan Courtenay, brought lands at East Antony to the Cornish branch of the family. In the following century Sir Wymond Carew of Antony (d. 1549) married Martha, daughter of Sir Antony Denny, and had nineteen children; one of these was Thomas (d. 1564), father of the antiquary Richard Carew of Antony, and another, the tenth child, was Matthew (d. 1618), father of Thomas Carew the poet.

Matthew Carew was an old man when his son Thomas was born. A scholar of Trinity College, Cambridge, Matthew had come up from Westminster School in 1548; he graduated B.A. in 1550–1, in 1551 was made a Fellow of the college, and after twelve years' study of jurisprudence and languages at Louvain, Paris, Padua, Bologna, and Siena returned to England a Doctor of Civil Law. He relinquished an ecclesiastical career to practise law in the Court of Arches, and in 1576 proceeded to a Mastership in Chancery which he was to hold for more than forty years.[2] In 1578 he married Alice, daughter of Sir John Ryvers, Lord Mayor of London in 1573–4, and widow of Richard Ingpen of the Middle Temple;[3] Alice Carew's mother, Lady Ryvers, was Elizabeth, daughter of Sir George Barne, Lord Mayor of London in 1552–3.[4] The Carews lived at West Wickham till about 1598, then moved to London, where they occupied a house in Chancery Lane. In 1603 Matthew Carew was knighted at Whitehall by King James. Only three of his children outlived him—Martha, Matthew the younger, and

---

[1] Genealogies are given in *A Complete Parochial History of the County of Cornwall*, 1867, i. 22–3; Burke, *Landed Gentry of Great Britain*, 1921, p. 289; Burke, *Peerage and Baronetage*, 1925, p. 448. The name was often spelled Cary, Carey, and Carie (though not by the poet or other members of his family), and it is still sometimes so pronounced; but a member of the Carew-Pole family, of Antony, informs me that Carew and not Carey is the preferred pronunciation.

[2] John and J. A. Venn, *Alumni Cantabrigienses*, 1922, I. i. 291; *Dictionary of National Biography*, article 'Matthew Carew'.

[3] Boyd's MS. *Marriage Index*, Society of Genealogists, London; Arthur Robert Ingpen, *The Middle Temple Bench Book*, 1912, pp. 156–7.

[4] J. G. White, *History of the Ward of Walbrook in the City of London*, 1904, p. 209.

INTRODUCTION   xv

Thomas. Martha was twice married: first to James (later
Sir James) Cromer of Tunstall, and secondly to Sir Edward
Hales of Tenterden, knight and baronet, who was a brother
of the 'ever memorable' John Hales of Eton; Sir Edward's
son John, born of a former marriage, himself married
Martha's daughter Christian Cromer.¹ Thomas Carew's
elder brother Matthew was born at West Wickham in 1590.
In 1606 he entered Balliol College, Oxford, but left without
taking a degree, went to Ireland as a soldier, and in 1611
was knighted at Dublin by the Lord Deputy. He married
his sister's stepdaughter Frances Cromer, and he and his
wife lived with his parents in the Chancery Lane house
during the first years of the marriage, as is shown by their
children's baptismal and burial records at the church of St.
Dunstan's-in-the-West between 1615 and 1619.² Later he
retired with his family and widowed mother to the manor
of Middle Littleton in Worcestershire, where Thomas Hab-
ington described him as 'a Knyght practised in wars abroad
and well beloved at home'.³ Wood says that he was 'a
great royalist in the time of the puritanical rebellion'.⁴

Of Thomas Carew's boyhood and early schooling no-
thing is known. When in June 1608 he began study at
Oxford, the choice of Merton as his college may have been
influenced by the fact that its Warden, the learned Henry
Savile, was a kinsman by marriage. The period is said to
have been one when Oxford undergraduates 'were mostly
drawn aside by the vices of these times',⁵ though Arch-
bishop Bancroft, who became Chancellor of the University
in 1608, made efforts at reform. As for Savile, he was re-
membered long afterwards as 'a very severe governour, the
scholars hated him for his austerity. He could not abide
witts: when a young scholar was recommended to him for

¹ Hasted, History of Kent, iii. 88; Harleian Society, The Visitation of Kent, taken in
the Years 1619–21, p. 59.
² In 1618 he got into trouble for the killing of a certain Captain Osborne; his
pardon occurs among the Signet Bills for September of that year (Public Record
Office, Ind. 6805).
³ A Survey of Worcestershire by Thomas Habington, ed. John Amphlett, 1895,
i. 323.
⁴ Anthony à Wood, Athenæ Oxonienses, ed. Philip Bliss, 1815, ii. 657.
⁵ Anthony à Wood, History and Antiquities of the University of Oxford . .
published . . . from the original MS. . . . by John Gutch, 1796, ii. 296.

a good witt, "*Out upon him, I'le have nothing to doe with him*;
*give me the ploding student. If I would look for witts I would
goe to Newgate, there be the witts.*"[1] Sometime tutor in
Greek and politics to Queen Elizabeth, and an admired
translator of Tacitus, Savile was more recently a member of
the Oxford committee engaged in translating the Gospels
for the forthcoming Authorized Version. One of his last and
noblest achievements at Merton, the building of the Fellows'
Quad, occupied the years 1608–10, during Thomas Carew's
residence. It would be interesting to know what impression
Savile formed of his young kinsman, the future author of
A Rapture, but his only recorded comment, in a letter which
he wrote in 1616,[2] leaves the matter in some doubt.

The University Arts Course in Carew's time still followed
the medieval divisions, beginning with Grammar, Logic,
and Rhetoric and progressing to Mathematics (including
Music, Geometry, and Astronomy), Natural Philosophy,
Moral Philosophy, and Metaphysics. The student was re-
quired to attend lectures and take part in frequent 'dispu-
tations'. It is worth mention that John Hales, who was
afterwards Carew's kinsman by marriage and who according
to a plausible story was to deny him absolution on his death-
bed, became a Fellow of Merton in 1606 and could thus
have been his tutor. The college battels books for the period
being lost, no details of Carew's daily life are ascertainable;
but he must have continued residence at Oxford for eleven
consecutive terms until 31 January 1610/11, when he took
his degree.[3] On 14 February he was admitted as a reader
in the Bodleian Library,[4] and during the following Lent he
participated in 'determination', the series of formal disputa-
tions required for completing the degree. He may have
commemorated his departure with a gift to his college: an
inventory of the Merton College plate, taken in 1622, lists,

---

[1] John Aubrey, *Brief Lives*, ed. Andrew Clark, 1898, ii. 214.
[2] See p. xxiii.
[3] Andrew Clark, *Register of the University of Oxford, 1571–1622*, iii. 301. The
course leading to the B.A. extended normally to four years or sixteen terms; but as
the son of an *eques auratus* Carew was privileged to proceed to his degree after twelve
terms, and in addition he must have taken advantage of a decree of 21 Jan. 1610/11
which granted a dispensation of one term to 'generosi'. (*Register*, i. 13–14, 18.)
[4] *Register*, 270.

as in the Warden's House, 'One bowle given by Mr. Carew'.[1] In 1612 he was incorporated a B.A. of Cambridge.[2]

His intended profession was the law. The decision to follow his father's calling was apparently formed late, and may not have been easy: more than a year passed—how employed we do not know—before the admission to the Middle Temple, on 6 August 1612, of 'Mr. Thomas, second son of Matthew Carew, knt., Master in Chancery, specially, by assent of John Lowe, esq., Reader, and other Masters of the Bench; bound with Messrs. Nathaniel Clattworthy and George Carew; fine, 20s.'[3] He set up a chamber and study in the Temple, and for a few months may have seriously believed that he was to be a lawyer. But legal pursuits were not to hold him long. The typical young 'Inns of Court gentleman' was proverbially frivolous, and Thomas Carew, according to a letter which Sir Matthew wrote in February 1613 to Sir Dudley Carleton, studied his law-books 'very little'; moreover, serious financial reverses which now befell the family may have necessitated a change of plans. Carleton, who had married Anne Gerrard, stepdaughter of the Warden of Merton and niece to Sir Matthew Carew, was in Venice in 1613 as English Ambassador, and to him Sir Matthew addressed gloomy news:

My very honorable good Lord.

Ther hathe passed many a drearye and sorowfull daye ouer my head sençe my last writeng vnto your lordship, many griefes, mich sorrow, and great mishaps . . . and yet it pleaseth not God, to ridde me of my wretched life . . . but haue liued to see our hopefull prynce to be taken from us, and my riseng nephewe to falle and dye before me, and my self to be cozened and deceaued, of all my land, whervppon I had levyd my whole estate, and brought my self in debt for it. Where I was in hope to haue left my son a thowsand pound land per annum, I

<hr/>

[1] Brodrick, *Memorials of Merton College*, 1885, p. 350. Thomas was preceded by other Carews at Merton. The bowl has not been preserved.
[2] John and J. A. Venn, *Alumni Cantabrigienses*, i. i. 291.
[3] Hopwood, *Middle Temple Records*, 1904, ii. 552–3. The George Carew with whom Thomas was bound may have been his cousin Sir George Carew, lawyer and diplomatist, second son of Thomas Carew of Antony and younger brother of Richard the antiquary. In June 1612 he proceeded from a Mastership in Chancery to the Mastership of the Court of Wards. He died later in the same year.

am not lyke to leaue him anye, ffor this land which I bought in Worces-tershyre and for the which I haue payd 9000^{li} and now standeth me in tcn thousand, Sir William Bond (whoe sold me the same . . .), hathe made suche former conveiance therof by leases mortgage, and graunting owt of annuityes therof, that I am not lyke to reape any good therof in many ages, and haue lost in one moment all that I had gotten together in many yeres/, *Hec sunt deteriora, meliora tamen spero*, but yet how so euer without great losse, it can not be/, I wold that I had better newes to write but yet I haue none, nor haue bene acquainted with the maske nor mariage triomphes which I haue passed with sorrow in my cabbyn, hauing also my son Crowmer syck in my howse with me, of a lingereng dissease out of the which the phisicions pick twoe of them xx^l a day, and yet know not his disease . . . he desireth me to write his most hartye thankes for the token your lordship sent him . . . my daughter althoughe not in perfect constitution of helth, hathe by her secretary m^r playford written to my ladye, which I send herewith, my twoe sons, the one roneth vp and downe after houndes and hawkes, the other is of the midle temple, where he hath a chamber and studye, but I feare studiethe the lawe very litle, so as I am neither happye in my self nor my children, saue only in my dawghter whom I pray God to blesse and preserue, being the only comfort I haue in this worlde. . . .

Mat Carew

Chancery lane 25 Febr 1612[1]

When Carleton received this letter he had already heard from his friend John Chamberlain 'an vncertain report that Sir Mathew Carie is like to loose and be cousened of eight or nine thousand pound . . . but I hope yt cannot fall out altogether so yll, beeing discouered so soone, and he so well frended in the court of conscience'.[2] It was perhaps in an effort to be of help that Carleton now offered Thomas Carew employment in Italy, presumably as a secretary.

The period of Carew's stay in Italy and the extent of his movements there can only be surmised from what is known of the movements of Carleton and others and from a phrase in a letter which Carew later wrote to Carleton: 'the knowledge which by your Lordships meanes' Lord Arundel 'had of me at Florence'.[3] Thomas Howard, second Earl of Arundel, had come to the Continent in 1613 with other English gentlemen as an escort to the Princess Elizabeth

[1] Public Record Office, S.P. 14/72: 44.
[2] Ibid.: 6, dated 7 Jan. 1612/13.   [3] See p. 203.

after her marriage to the Palsgrave Frederick, and he continued his travels, for health and pleasure, until the end of the following year. One member of the party was Inigo Jones, his reputation as a designer and producer of masques already established, who twenty years later was to join with Carew in the creation of *Coelum Britannicum*. Carleton announced Arundel's imminent arrival to the Venetian Doge and Senate in impressive terms, and the Earl and his party, arriving at Venice on 30 August 1613, were provided with entertainment lasting until 13 September. On 3 October 1613 the party reached Florence; thence they journeyed to Rome and Naples for the winter and spring; and on 19 July 1614 they were again in Florence: 'The English Earl of Arundel is here with his wife, lodged and entertained by His Highness in the Palazzo Vecchio. He was received with a very warm welcome.' It had been proposed to revisit Venice, but the tour was cut short in August 1614 by news of the death of Arundel's uncle the Earl of Northampton, who left him a large inheritance, and by December 1614 Arundel was back in London.[1] This chronology suggests that Thomas Carew did not arrive in Venice before the autumn of 1613, since otherwise he would almost certainly have made the aquaintance of Arundel in Venice instead of having to go to Florence for that purpose. Once in Italy, Carew probably remained there for the final year and a half of Carleton's embassy. Carleton had been summoned home in October 1614, but was stopped at Padua by a messenger from the king; urgent affairs were yet to be settled, the most important being the negotiation of a treaty (that of Asti) between Spain and Savoy. After returning to Venice, Carleton remained there another three months, then on 15 February 1614/15 departed for Turin, where he arrived eleven days later and where Lady Carleton joined him on 3 May. Negotiations for the treaty continued at Turin and Asti until 14 July 1615; and after another short stay in Venice Carleton—with Carew presumably in his train—returned to London, arriving in December.

[1] See *Calendars of State Papers, Venetian*, xiii (1613–15), *passim*; and Mary F. S. Hervey, *The Life, Correspondence, and Collections of Thomas Howard, Earl of Arundel*, 1921, pp. 71–86.

One of Carew's letters, written in 1616, refers to the 'languages' which he has acquired in Carleton's service,[1] and some of his translations and imitations from Italian originals, such as *An Excuse of absence* and *A Ladies prayer to Cupid*, may be prentice-work belonging to this period. In his later writing he was to draw freely on a first-hand knowledge of Italian poetry and philosophy. Moreover the Italian civilization was in itself a school of elegance. In Carew's mind the memorable splendours of Venice and Florence would have been joined with the brilliance of the festivities which the Duke of Savoy provided for his guests at Turin.

His Highness, with the Prince and the others named, performed a magnificent dance in figure of eight, after ordering a dance by twenty pages, lighted by two torches and accompanied by weird music, the whole executed so daintily that the English ambassador was amazed. . . . Thus, though the drums and trumpets are proclaiming war, the nights are passed with music and feasting.[2]

Meanwhile the fortunes of Sir Matthew continued to decline, and he probably set his troubles fully before Carleton when the latter arrived in London. The house in Chancery Lane was mortgaged to a niece, Lady Carew, and the obligation was to fall due the following summer, with no money in sight to meet it. Moreover Sir Matthew was unwell, oppressed with age, and saddened by the recent deaths of his son-in-law and granddaughter.

Carleton offered substantial help. Not only did he re-engage Thomas Carew for his next embassy—to the Netherlands, in March 1615/16[3]—but he left orders with his agent, Edward Sherburne, for a loan to be made to Sir Matthew sufficient to pay off the mortgage. In addition, soon after his arrival at The Hague, he sent Sir Matthew a reassuring letter expressing satisfaction with Thomas's services. Naturally Sir Matthew was grateful, though still beset by troubles. On 20 April 1616 he wrote to his benefactor:

[1] See p. 202.
[2] *Calendars of State Papers, Venetian*, xiii. 365–6.
[3] As chaplain he took John Hales, whom Carew would have remembered from his Merton days and whose brother, Sir Edward Hales, was within a few months to marry Carew's sister Martha.

Right honorable my very good lord   I fynde my self indebted
to your good lordship as for many other honorable fauors, so also
for your letter written to me from the Haghe the viij^th of this instant
moneth, wherby I am put in good hope, of your Lordships good
likeng of my sons service, which I pray God he may trewly performe,
and demean himself duetifullye bothe to your lordship and my ladye
vppon whose fauors his wel doeng, and his fortunes must wholye
depende, myne owne stil decayeng, and one mishap followeng, like
whaues, the one after an other . . . which I paccently must abyde as God
shall geue me his grace, and must frame my self to lyue poorelye
within my compasse, and therfore Thomas must not lauishe, vntil I
can get my self out of debt wherinto I am plonged, . . . the which I
was put in hope that your lordship wold haue disbursed . . . wherin
I beseche yow let me vnderstand your lordships pleasure so soone as
may be. . . .[1]

Negotiations for the loan dragged on into the summer; then
Sherburne discovered that Sir Matthew, having already
given part of his property to the Church, could not furnish
adequate security, and the Chancery Lane house was saved
only when Lady Carew agreed to extend the mortgage. But
this narrowly averted tragedy was far overshadowed by the
disgrace which now befell Thomas Carew.

The exact circumstances must remain a mystery; we know
only that Carew foolishly put to paper certain aspersions on
the character of Sir Dudley and Lady Carleton, and that
when Sir Dudley found the libellous document he resolved
to be rid of his ungrateful protégé. The abortive negotia-
tions with Sir Matthew about the mortgage and loan, in
which he may have suspected some attempt at sharp dealing,
would not have predisposed him to look upon Thomas
Carew's fault with greater charity. Lady Carleton seems to
have been even more deeply offended. She was apparently
an attractive and generous lady, but impulsive and vain; at
the time of the libel she was in delicate health, and thought
to be with child.[2] But neither Sir Dudley nor his lady in-
formed Carew of their discovery, or reproached him for his
ungrateful opinions; Carleton simply sent him back to
England on the pretext that he would have better oppor-
tunity for advancement if he entered the service of Lord

[1] Public Record Office, S.P. 14/86: 141.
[2] Ibid. 14/88: 2 (Elizabeth Williams to Sir Dudley Carleton, 2 July 1616).

Carew, who had been made a member of the Privy Council on 19 July 1616 and who was Thomas Carew's cousin both by marriage and (in more distant degree) by blood. Though reluctant to go, Carew could hardly refuse Carleton's advice. He assumed, moreover, that in the event of failure he might again be received into Carleton's service.

He reached London about the middle of August 1616. There had not been time to inform his father in advance, and Sir Matthew was both annoyed and puzzled. The old man learned, no doubt, that the suggestion to seek out Lord Carew was Carleton's own, but he was inclined to set the blame somehow on Thomas:

It was strange to me [he wrote to Carleton] to see my sonne Thomas appeer before me in my little parlour, whom I looked not for at that tyme, but had destined him *correre la fortuna del suo patrone*, which if he wold haue tarried the tyme, I doubted not, wold vppon his duetyeful servyce and vsage of hym self haue torned hym to more good, then al his precipitate haste can procure hym, none of those whom he seeketh after, being lyke to attayne to that place of employment that must needes be layd vppon hym whom he served, If he had acquainted me, before his commeng, with his purpose, I wold vtterly haue disswaded hym from it, My lord Carewe althoughe he be admitted to the Councel table yet being the last and yongest, is not lykelye to be so greatly employed therin, that he shal haue neede of any more Secretaryes then he hathe, . . . and I am assured that Thomas wold be lothe to supplye the place of an vnder Secretary with hym, If he wold haue abydden owt his fortune, and haue employed him self as he might in the studye of the bookes which he hath gotten, he might bothe haue spent hys tyme wel and thriftylye, and haue made hym self apt for any good fortune that might haue fallen to hym, which if he wil not industriously seeke and follow after, then is he hym self the marrer and destroyer of his own fortunes, *Multi ad scientiam peruenire potuissent, nisi iam se satis doctos credidissent.* And so I think Thomas thinkes to wel of hym self, and wil not tarry his good tyme. He is gon about his dessigne from me to Woodstock where the Court then was, in company with his brother, whoe I fear wil drawe him into suche euel courses as he himself takethe, they haue bene from me these xj dayes, and haue not sence had any theng from them. I humblye beseche your lordship to reteyn stil that mynd yow write your lordship holdeth towardes hym, for I fear that if he be not narrowly looked vnto, and called from his wandereng distractions, he wil soone ouerthrowe hym self, *ipse sibi suæ fortunæ faber est.* . . . I doubt more of his idlenes

and lewd courses here, then I shold doe there, sauing only for the
apprehendeng of that natural vyce of dronkennes, which that Countrye
hathe taught us so wel, that wee far excell them therein. My son
Matthew after many breaches of his promes for the sendeng of
grayhowndes to your lordship hathe now left a bytche here to be
sent to your lordship, which I wishe may be suche as is worthe the
haueng. . . .

Your lordships alwayes most
ready at command

1° Septembr 1616   Mat Carew[1]

Carleton endorsed this letter 'My Vncle Carew' and filed it
away; but he was not to be moved.

With the journey to Woodstock Carew combined a visit
at Oxford to Sir Henry Savile, Warden of his old college
and Lady Carleton's stepfather. 'Your History of the Spaa',
wrote Savile to Carleton on 3 September, 'gives mee good
comfort to stay at home: and so doth the report of my
cosin carew touching the proofe of your Geldinges.'[2] That
Carew, maliciously or not, had made disparaging remarks
about Carleton's horses is repeated in Savile's subsequent
letter to Carleton on 13 October:

your mother and I are very glad of your safe returne from the Spaa . . .
for horses your limitations of sparing them a whole yeare at the
beginning, and travayling them no further then betweene Eaton and
London are not for my purpose, . . . and therefore yf it please you,
that care may bee put over to a further tyme of consultation: the rather
for that Tom Carew at his coming to vs made no great vaunt of the
proofe of yours. but I take him to bee a man of no deepe iudgement
in horses, whatsoever hee is otherwyse. your mothers teeth you haue
sett on edge with your hangings: but the prices of them, by your mans
report had quickly cooled her heate.[3]

As his father had predicted, Carew met with no success
at Woodstock. After being politely refused by Lord Carew,
he addressed himself to the Earl of Arundel, whom he had
met two years before at Florence. The letters which he sent
to Carleton at this time conscientiously recount his efforts
to find a place, and show no apparent suspicion of Carleton's

[1] Public Record Office, S.P. 14/88: 65.
[2] Ibid.: 69.   [3] Ibid.: 126.

real feelings.¹ Meanwhile Carleton had written to Edward
Sherburne a full account of Carew's offence—unfortunately
this is lost, and we have only Sherburne's reply—and had
instructed Sherburne to discuss none of his (Carleton's)
affairs with Carew. But for several weeks nothing was done
which might injure Carew's prospects of another post;
Carleton seems rather to have wished to dispose of his former
secretary with as little unpleasantness as possible. On 21
September 1616 Sherburne reported that

Mr Carewe doth attend my Lord of Arundells answere, who these 10:
dayes yet, is not able to resolue whether to accept or deny his seruice:
I haue had speeche with his Lordship herein; and I find, he is partly
ingaged by promise to receaue another; yet his Lordship told me thus
much, that he so well approues of Mr Carewe, as if he can possibly
be freed from thother, he will most willingly (& that raither for your
Lordship sake) intertayne him into the place desired; whereof when
his Lordship hath resolued, he will acquaint me theirwith.²

Carew had already, on 2 September, written to ask Carleton
for a letter of recommendation which he might present to
Arundel. Two subsequent letters, on 11 and 20 September,
include enough court gossip to show that much of his time
must have been passed at Whitehall, though he spent a few
days with his sister (the widowed Lady Cromer) and his
grandmother Ryvers at Tunstall in Kent. Sherburne has
suggested, he says, that he might attempt the service of
Viscount Villiers (the future Buckingham), but he has 'no
appetite if I fayle in my present proiect, to hazard a third
repulse'.

At this point Carleton, perhaps alarmed lest he might
find Thomas Carew his permanent responsibility, decided to
reveal everything to Sir Matthew. The violence of the old
man's reaction is vividly described by Sherburne, who had
called in person to deliver Carleton's letter.

Right honorable my very good Lord [wrote Sherburne to Carleton]
Amongst the many letters; I receaued in your last pacquet of the 16th
of september, sent by George Martyn; this inclosed returnes your only
answere for the presente; wherein I doubt not, but your Lordship
will perceaue, howe vnpleasing newes, the notice of his sonnes mis-

¹ These letters are printed on pp. 202–6.
² Public Record Office, S.P. 14/88: 89.

demeanour, was, and is vnto that good old gent: At the reading of
your letter I did obserue this passage from him, that when he came to
that part, which did make knowne his sonnes foule offence, he burst
out into these words (Gods boddy) and no sooner had he ended your
Letter, but Mr Carewe came into his studdy, whom presently he
reviled before me, & told him, he had vtterly ouerthrowne his fortune,
who, seeming to make straunge at that speeche of his fathers, (as
being ignorant of the matter), Sr Mathewe gaue him your Lordships
letter to reade, which in a manner he sleighted, as holding the offence
no way worthy of blame, being a thing done by him, not in dishonor
of your Lordship or my Lady nor intended euer to be diuulged, but
only (as his owne words were) for his priuate ends and direction: His
fathers anger I do assure your Lordship, continues extreame against
him, and therefore did inioyne him forthwith to write an humble &
submissiue letter, Acknowledging his fault & desiring your Lordships
pardon, which he promised to do, & to send it vnto me, but as yet I
haue not receaued any such letter from him; & for his hope with my
Lord of Arundell, It is very doubtfull . . .

London the 5th of
October 1616 stil vet: Edw: Sherburne.[1]

On 12 October Sherburne writes: 'For Mr Carewe I
leaue him to himself, not having seene him, since your
Lordships letter deliuered to his father; neither meane I to
solicite further for him, that which I haue done, being
grownded vpon your Lordships to myselfe, who wished me
to give him both aduise, and assistance.'[2] And a few days
afterwards Sherburne, on Carleton's instructions, told the
damaging story to Arundel, thus destroying Carew's already
slim chances of employment with that nobleman.[3] This act
of spite may have resulted from Carleton's resentment upon
hearing of Carew's unrepentant state.

For more than a year Sir Matthew sent pathetic appeals
to his son's offended benefactor. The earliest which has been
preserved reads as follows:

Right honorable my very good lord
    I beseche your lordship to behold, and consyder with me how
afflictions lyke whaues of the sea followe one the other and com
vppon me After the losse of xij thousand poundes (being myche more
then I was able to bear) was imposed vppon me by the treachery of

---

[1] Public Record Office, S.P. 14/88: 117.   [2] Ibid.: 122.   [3] Ibid.: 143.

hym whom I trusted, and was deceaued, . . . now my son Thomas
of whom I had conceaued great hope, whylest he was in your lordships
fauour, being cast of from the same, wandereng idely here without any
imployment, nor knoweng how to bestowe hym, I am at my wittes
end and know not what to doe with hym, but being wearye of my
miserable life, pray God to admit me to the better comfortes of
heauen. . . .

Your lordships poore deiected oncle
Mat: Carew

Chancery lane. 24 Octobr 1616.
 in haste[1]

A fuller and even bitterer missive followed two weeks later:

Right honorable my very good Lord

Acknowledgeng my sonnes fault to be inexcusable, and your Lord-
ships indignation worthelye conceaued aganst him, wherby he hathe
irrecuperablye lost your lordships and my ladyes fauours, in the which
I tooke great comfort and hope of his wel doeng, I am now so far
deiected from any expectance of any goodnes in hym, that he and I be
now irreconciliable, remaineng stupefied what shold moue hym to
commit so great a follye, as to set down with his pen, that which his
hart could neuer conceaue For in my conscience I doe not think that
his hart was any wayes drawen from eyther of you bothe how so euer
he wold set his pen a work in detracteng, which I conceaue to be worse,
if it wer to be published, then that of the tongue, which I neuer hard
vtter any disgraceful or dishonourable speche of eyther of yow, but to
report most honorably of yowr lordship and of my ladye always and by
his letters hathe testified my ladyes goodnes always towardes hym, and
protesteth that he is, was, and alwayes shalbe ready to expose him selfe
to his vttermost in the defense of your honors aganst any so as I am
driuen to my wittes ende, to imagin how he could be induced to lay
suche dishonorable aspersions vppon yowr honors with his pen, wher-
with when I charge hym, he saythe he dothe for his owne instruction
and for the direction of his own actions, set down in notes how he
shold gouern hym which he neuer meant shold be published to any,
but to serue him only for hys owne observation, wherin as I conceaue
smal reason, so I geue as smal credit therto, But I fynd that he
weeneth to wel of hym self, and if he had had more humilitye might
haue don miche better; rather then to shewe him self an Aristarchus,
to fynd faultes in other, not lookeng into his owne, which[2] be great
and hydeous, puffed vp with to miche pryde, wherto I haue bene
brought to geue waye and to furnishe hym, whilest ther was hope of

1 Public Record Office, S.P. 14/88: 135.   2 *Orig.* wch wch.

the Erles servyce, or to haue retorned to your lordships again, of bothe which being now depriued, I geue him ouer for vtterly lost. . . .[1]

On 28 December Sir Matthew informed Carleton that Thomas, 'haueng geuen ouer al studye here eyther of lawe or other lerning, vagrantlye and debauchedlye takethe no maner of good but al lewde courses, with the which he will weary me and al his other friendes, and run hym self into vtter ruyn'. There had been hope of employment with Sir Henry Wotton, but only to be disappointed; and now 'I am infortunate in bothe my sonnes, ther being neyther barrell bef or herryng of any of them bothe, only of my kynd loueng daughter I take great comfort, whom it hathe pleased God to matche to a very worthye knight Baronet'.[2]

Two other letters, sent late in the following year, record that Thomas lay ill—perhaps with the first appearance of the syphilis upon whose later symptoms Suckling was to twit him in the verses 'Upon *T. C.* having the P.':

My honorable very good Lord. . . . I . . . beseche your good lordship to forget al iniuryes done vnto yow by my sonne Thomas . . . I hope that for my ladye and neece, owr kyndred and neerenes of blood, wil sufficiently pleade for reconciliation, and obtein forgeuenes of that my sonnes idle brayn had busyed him self withal, and not to construe it to, any setled fyrm opinion that he had conceaued against her, whom he was bound to honour and loue from his hart which he protestethe to me that he alwayes dyd, and stil doothe, but of his idle writeng he can geue me no other reason, but that he dyd it in an humour, onlye to set his head aworke without any meaneng either to shew it to anye, or to make any other vse therof then to hym selfe but how soeuer, he must needes acknowledge it to be lewdlye and foolishly done of hym, Ever sence his departure from your lordship he hathe lingered heere with me, myspendeng his tyme, and now lieth here syck with me of a new disease com in amongest us, by the which I pray God that he may be chastised to amend his lyfe here or els to take hym awaye to his mercye/ Al the proiectes that haue bene made for hym haue fayled. . . .

Your lordships poore but trew
affected Oncle

4 octobr 1617.   Mat Carew[3]

---

[1] Public Record Office, S.P. 14/89: 10, 7 Nov. 1616.
[2] Ibid.: 96.
[3] Ibid. 14/93: 112. Carleton noted on the back of this: 'From my Vncle Carew ye 4th of 8ber 1617. ansd ye 13.'

My Right honorable and very good lord; . . . your lordships servant my son lyeth styl languisheng here with me, not recouered yet of his sycknes, which is not the least part of my great greefe, he is in hope that vppon his humble submission and speeche with your Lordship, yow wil remit his falt and error . . . I hope God hathe reserved hym onely for your lordship and to none other that as yow haue bene the fyrst beginner of hym; to set hym in the waye of wel doeng, so yow wyl continew your goodnes to reforme hym, . . . And so remembreng al our duetyes and loue to your lordship and my good ladye, whose hart I besech God to moue to forgeuenes and to pytye hym that hathe so greuously offended her. and so I rest

Your lordships most bounden and
serviceable Oncle
Mat Carew[1]

The final letter of the unhappy sheaf was addressed to Lady Carleton at her return to England in March 1618; she omitted her accustomed visit to the Carews' home, and it was only by chance, Sir Matthew complains, that he learned of her presence in the country:

Good madame, by nature my neece, . . . let not the inconsyderate follyes of my son, which I haue as myche blamed and detested as yourself, worke any change of mutual affections, which nature and loue hathe bred in us of long tyme . . . how so euer my son hathe abused hym self to your ladyship . . . I haue so often reproched, and reproved hym therof, that I wold haue vtterly forsaken and haue caste hym of, if I had not found hym sorrowfull and repentant of his foolyshe and inexcusable follye. . . .[2]

A few months later, on 2 August 1618, Sir Matthew Carew died, aged about eighty-five, and was buried in St. Anne's Chapel in the church of St. Dunstan's-in-the-West. He is variously remembered. Arthur Vincent, who made use of the correspondence which is quoted here, said outright that 'the old Master in Chancery was his son's worst enemy'.[3] But his name is also preserved in happier ways. In 1609 he assigned a yearly rent-charge of twenty nobles, from his property in Chancery Lane, to the relief of the poor of the parish of St. Dunstan's, a charity which still

---

[1] Public Record Office, S.P. 14/94: 17, undated. Endorsed on back by Carleton: 'My Vncle Carew red ye 14th of 9ber 1617'.

[2] Ibid. 14/96: 75, 24 March 1617/18.

[3] The Poems of Thomas Carew, ed. Arthur Vincent, Introduction, pp. xviii–xix.

exists. According to Cecil Monro (in the *Acta Cancellariæ*, 1847) his legal opinions were characterized by common sense and an excellent ability to see to the heart of matters. The bitterness of his last years was probably as much senile and temperamental as due to his mounting misfortunes. Several years before his son's disgrace he composed his own melancholy epitaph:

D.O.M.

Memoriæ Posterisque

Felice chi può.   Sacrum

Ne post fata, me defuncto, heredes siue executores, mei immemores, auari, aut ingrati vanitatem ineptam, superflui sumptus, et curiosi sepulchri, contemnentes, mei mortui obliuionem quam memoriam vigilantius colant, Ego adhuc viuus, hoc mihi, posterisque meis posui monumentum . . .

> Annos septuaginta quinque vixi
> & nos bis quinque pater modo puellos
> Et quas hic genuit nouem puellas
> Omnes interijsse morte vidi
> Tantum est mihi soror superstes . . .
> Vrnam ergo mihi posterisque viuus
> Condo, munde vale superna quæro
> In mundo nihil est diu beatum.
> Nos homines morimur, lapides et ligna supersunt
> Heu heu quam fragilis, mollis est omnis homo. . . .[1]

We might expect the years 1616–18 to have been unhappy ones for Thomas Carew. Yet he is mentioned as an especially elegant attendant at the creation of Charles as Prince of Wales on 4 November 1616—at the very time when Sir Matthew, overwhelmed by his son's apparent ruin, took comfort in thoughts of death. 'I have not seen nor heard of Mr. Carew since his coming into England', wrote John Chamberlain to Carleton on 26 October, 'more than Mr. Sherburn told me the other day, that he was to be a squire to one of the Knights of the Bath now at the prince's creation.' Later he reports (9 November) that 'our gallants flaunt it out in their greatest bravery at the prince's creation, which was

---

[1] British Museum, MS. Harl. 1196, fol. 251 et seq., Sir Matthew Carew's hand. The complete inscription on the monument is printed by Nichols, *Collectanea Topographica et Genealogica*, 1838, v. 206, and by J. F. Denham, *Views of St. Dunstan in the West*, [1829], p. 26; this departs considerably from the manuscript version.

performed on Monday at Whitehall, with all solemnity. . . .
Tom Carew and Phil. Lytton, as I hear, were squires of high
degree for cost and bravery, the one to Lord Beauchamp,
the other to his cousin, Rowland St. John. There is little
else to be said touching this troop, but that it was generally
observed that the least behaved themselves best.'[1] It was,
too, at some time during this period that Carew met the
lady who under the name of Celia is celebrated in his poems
—or, alternatively, if she is not to be identified with any
single person, he began to construct her image from frag-
ments of his experience and reading.[2] The poems can be
arranged to form a slender story: the lady had golden hair,
sang divinely, and was at home in noble houses; she returned
the poet's love and wept at his departure, perhaps to France
in 1619; during his absence she underwent a change of
heart and demanded the return of her letters; later she
married another, not happily; and after the marriage she was
again courted by Carew. But there is no external evidence.
Carew never revealed the secret which in one of his poems
he swore to preserve, and Aurelian Townshend, when he
wrote in 1632 that

> I loue thy Celia if shee did infuse
> That fire into thee which begott thy Muse,

sounds as though he knew no more about the matter than
we. Another type of writing which Carew may have under-
taken at this time, perhaps during his long illness under the
gloomy eye of Sir Matthew, was the versification of the
Psalms, of which nine examples, one of them incomplete,
survive. There are transcripts of two of these (Psalms 91
and 104) dating from the early 1620s.[3]

1 *The Court and Times of James the First*, 1848, i. 433–4. The Knight of the Bath
whom Carew attended as Esquire was Edward Seymour, Lord Beauchamp (1587–
1618), grandson of the Earl of Hertford.

2 William Percy's *Sonnets to the Fairest Cœlia* had appeared in 1594; for the
Renaissance vogue of the name Sir Sidney Lee cites the Latin lyrics of Angerianus
(1512) and the sonnets printed by Sir David Murray of Gorthy with *The Tragicall
Death of Sophonisba* (1611). Cf. also Celia in *As You Like It* and Celia in *Volpone*;
the latter contains the fine song 'Come, my Celia', and Jonson also addresses *To Celia*
his lyrics 'Kiss me, sweet. The wary lover' and 'Drink to me only with thine eyes'.
In an obviously different category is Spenser's Dame Cœlia (*Faerie Queene*, I. x),
the mother of Faith, Hope, and Charity.

3 See pp. lxx–lxxi.

Soon after his father's death Carew resumed his broken career. The Chancery Lane house was sold to Sir Robert Rich, Sir Matthew's successor in Chancery;[1] Sir Matthew the younger moved to the estate at Middle Littleton, Worcestershire, which his father had purchased and where Dame Alice Carew, his mother, came to live with him; and Thomas Carew was among the train of 'an hundred and odd persons' who on the day of Anne of Denmark's funeral—13 May 1619—departed with Sir Edward Herbert (later Lord Herbert of Cherbury), philosopher and poet, on his embassy to Paris. Herbert's *Autobiography* records that the entire group, after journeying to Paris by way of Dover and Calais, were lodged in a richly furnished house 'in Fauburg St. Germain, Rue Tournon'. With characteristic pride Herbert recalls that

my chief secretary was William Boswell, now the King's agent in the Low Countries; my secretary for the French tongue was one Monsieur Ozier, who afterwards was the King's agent in France. . . . Mr. Crofts was one of my principal gentlemen, and afterwards made the King's Cup-bearer; and Thomas Carew, that excellent wit, the King's Carver; Edmund Taverner, whom I made my under secretary, was afterwards chief secretary to the Lord Chamberlain; and one Mr. Smith, secretary to the Earl of Northumberland.[2]

Carew may have accompanied Herbert to Tours and other cities in France, but his name does not recur in Herbert's narrative. We can be certain only that while in France he composed two poems. One is the complaint *Vpon some alterations in my Mistresse, after my departure into France*; the other is the *Elegie* on Lady Peniston, who died in January 1619/20. But *My mistris commanding me to returne her letters* may also be assigned plausibly to this period, as may the lines *To my Mistresse in absence*, those *To her in absence*. *A Ship*, and perhaps the fine poems *Parting, Celia weepes*, and *To Celia, upon Love's Vbiquity*. The widely circulated verses

---

[1] London Guildhall, MS. 2968/2, fol. 159ᵛ.

[2] *The Autobiography of Edward, Lord Herbert of Cherbury*, ed. Sir Sidney Lee, second edition, pp. 103–6. Herbert had been hospitably received at Venice by Sir Dudley and Lady Carleton in 1614, and probably first met Carew at that time. Several interesting parallels between his poems and Carew's are noted in the Commentary below.

on *A flye that flew into my Mistris her eye*, which are also early,[1] were more likely written before he left England.

John Crofts, Carew's companion in Herbert's service, was three or four years younger than Carew. He was the author of three 'Hymnes to God the Father, God the Son, God the Holy Ghost' which are set by Henry Lawes in *The Second Book of Ayres, and Dialogues*, 1655, and probably of the song 'Go little winged Archer', assigned to 'Mr. *I. C.*' in the same volume. Herrick and Davenant addressed poems to him. On 5 February 1619/20 Herbert sent him to England with a letter and a book for King James;[2] it is possible that Carew accompanied him and that Carew's lines which John Crofts recited *To the King* (p. 30) were written for the royal visit of February 1619/20 to the Crofts' family home at Little Saxham, Suffolk. Carew could, of course, have furnished the lines without himself going to Saxham on this occasion; but we know that he was soon on terms of cordial friendship with all the Crofts family, who occupy an important place in his poems.

At Paris Carew should have followed with interest the conversation of the numerous literary circles, though his only reference to current French writing is an attack in *Coelum Britannicum* (lines 165–73) apparently on the stylistic and moralistic pretensions of Guez de Balzac. He had read the poetry of the Pléiade and their successors, and echoes them in his own verses. It is of more special significance that while in Paris he may have known personally Giambattista Marino, in whose fantastic Italian lyrics he found an evidently congenial source and model. Marino, who resided in Paris from 1615 to 1623, was regularly to be seen at the Hôtel de Rambouillet and at court.

Herbert was recalled from his embassy temporarily in 1621 and permanently in 1624. There is nothing to indicate whether Carew remained in France for the entire period. In the winter of 1624–5 there was a rumour that he planned to marry the rich widow of Sir George Smith.[3] Meanwhile his first printed verses appeared in 1622—a commendatory

[1] See Commentary, p. 231.
[2] *Old Herbert Papers at Powis Castle and in the British Museum*, 1886, pp. 274–5.
[3] *The Letters of John Chamberlain*, ed. N. E. McClure, 1939, ii. 594.

piece prefixed to Thomas May's comedy *The Heir*, which
had been produced in 1620. May was one of a large and
brilliant circle of friends. Clarendon, in his *Life*, gives brief
portraits of several leading members of the group, including
Carew; the period referred to is approximately that between
1625 and 1632.

Whilst He [Clarendon] was only a Student of the Law, and stood
at Gaze, and irresolute what Course of Life to take, his chief Acquain-
tance were *Ben. Johnson*, *John Selden*, *Charles Cotton*, *John Vaughan*,
Sir *Kenelm Digby*, *Thomas May*, and *Thomas Carew*, and some others
of eminent Faculties in their several Ways. . . .

Thomas Carew was a younger Brother of a good Family, and of
excellent Parts, and had spent many Years of his Youth in *France*
and *Italy*; and returning from Travel, followed the Court; which the
Modesty of that Time disposed Men to do some Time, before They
pretended to be of it; and He was very much esteemed by the most
eminent Persons in the Court, and well looked upon by the King
himself, some Years before He could obtain to be Sewer to the King;
and when the King conferred that Place upon him, it was not without
the Regret even of the whole *Scotch* Nation, which united themselves
in recommending another Gentleman to it; of so great Value were
those Relations held in that Age, when Majesty was beheld with the
Reverence it ought to be. He was a Person of a pleasant and facetious
Wit, and made many Poems (especially in the amorous Way) which
for the Sharpness of the Fancy, and the Elegancy of the Language,
in which that Fancy was spread, were at least equal, if not superior to
any of that Time. . . .

Among these Persons Mr. *Hyde's* [Clarendon's] usual Time of
Conversation was spent, till He grew more retired to his more serious
Studies, and never discontinued his Acquaintance with any of them,
though He spent less Time in their Company.[1]

At the head of the poems 'in the amorous Way' which
brought Carew a reputation in the early 1620s we may place,
with some confidence, his bold fantasy *A Rapture*. Though
it circulated only in manuscript until its appearance in the
posthumous *Poems* of 1640, what seem to be direct echoes
from it are recognizable in the anonymous tragedy of *Nero*,
which was printed in 1624.[2]

Besides the brilliant group mentioned by Clarendon,

---

[1] *The Life of Edward Earl of Clarendon . . . Written by Himself*, 1759, i. 30, 36.
[2] See Commentary, pp. 236-7.

Carew's circle of friends during this period included William
Davenant, to whom he addressed commendatory verses in
1630, and the poet Aurelian Townshend, with whom he ex-
changed verse letters in 1632. His enthusiasm for Donne,
worthily expressed in the *Elegie* printed with Donne's *Poems*
in 1633, need not have been based on close acquaintance,
though Carew's own poems show with what care he had read
Donne's and the *Elegie* implies that he had heard Donne
preach. More surprising is the apparent lack of cordiality
between Carew and Thomas Randolph, whom Ben Jonson
adopted as a son; but Randolph's only reference to Carew
sounds rather patronizing:

> A third speaks raptures, and hath gaind a wit
> By praising *Cœlia;* else had mis't of it.[1]

A friend of a different order, and more useful for advancing
Carew's career at court, was Christopher Villiers, the Duke
of Buckingham's younger brother. This 'unattractive and
unintelligent' youth, fortunate in his kinship with the famous
favourite, was in February 1616/17 appointed a Gentleman
of the Bedchamber to James I, became Master of the Robes
not long afterwards, and in March 1623/4 was created Baron
Villiers of Daventry and Earl of Anglesey. The efforts of
'Kit Villers', somewhat ineptly assisted by King James, to
find a suitable wife were long unsuccessful, but a match
was finally negotiated with Elizabeth, daughter of Thomas
Sheldon of Hoby, Leicestershire. And it was Thomas
Carew, doubtless eager and grateful for advantageous em-
ployment, who acted as intermediary in this courtship. His
lines *To the Countesse of Anglesie* recall his services:

[1] Thomas Randolph, *Poems*, 1638, p. 16 (in 'A complaint against Cupid that
he never made him in Love'). What may be a really hostile glance at Carew appears
in the memorial verses contributed by Randolph's brother-in-law Richard West,
Student of Christ Church, who praises Randolph's un-'metaphysical' clarity:

> There's none needs feare to surfet with his phrase,
> He has no *Gyant* raptures to amaze
> And torture weake capacities with wonder:
> He (by his Laurell guarded) nere did Thunder
> As those strong bumbast Wits, whose Poetrie
> Sounds like a Charme, or *Spanish* Pedigree.
> Who with their Phancy towring 'bove the Sun,
> Have in their stile *Babells* confusion.

The '*Gyant* raptures' sounds specific, though the criticism as a whole is not very
justly applicable to Carew.

I could remember how his noble heart
First kindled at your beauties, with what Art
He chas'd his game through all opposing feares,
When I his sighes to you, and back your teares
Convay'd to him.

It is perhaps to Elizabeth Sheldon that Carew refers in his poem *Vpon the sicknesse of (E. S.)*; and besides composing an elegy on her husband's death he wrote three poems on the death of an infant who may have been their daughter, the Lady Mary Villiers.

Despite important friends, Carew seems to have gained no official position at court until 6 April 1630, when 'My L^d' (Pembroke, the Lord Chamberlain) approved 'A warr^t to sweare Mr Thomas Carew A gent of ye priuy Chamber extraordinary'.[1] It was probably about the same time that he was given the active post of Sewer in Ordinary to the King—a post gained (as Clarendon recalls) in competition with a strongly supported Scottish rival. From an anecdote related by 'old G. Clarke, Esq., formerly Lord of the Admiralty and Secretary to Prince George of Denmark', we catch a possible glimpse of the poet as courtier: 'Queen Henrietta Maria.—Thomas Carew, Gentleman of the Privy Chamber, going to light King Charles into her chamber, saw Jermyn Lord St. Albans with his arm round her neck;—he stumbled and put out the light;—Jermyn escaped; Carew never told the King, and the King never knew it. The Queen heaped favours on Carew.'[2] The anecdote must be taken with some caution; it is preceded in the single manuscript where it occurs by the statement that 'Milton, the poet, died a Papist'. Yet it represents the sort of quick-witted serviceability that might well have assisted Carew in his rise. Jermyn was appointed Vice-Chamberlain to the Queen on 2 July 1628; as for the old George Clarke who told the tale, he (if the identification holds) had been sworn 'A Page of his Ma^tes remooueing Wardrobe in ordinary' on 20 March 1627/8,[3] and should consequently have been well abreast of court gossip.

[1] Public Record Office, L.C. 5/132, p. 181.
[2] *Historical Manuscripts Commission, Seventh Report*, 1879, p. 244.
[3] Public Record Office, L.C. 5/132, p. 3.

To judge from the slight evidence, Carew's existence as a courtier, once he had climbed to that official rank, was an enviably serene one. His name never appears among the petitions for debt which pursued many of his fellows such as Jonson, Crofts, and Suckling, and his sole reproach ('a great libertine in his life and talke', says Walton)[1] implies at least a carefree state. His masque *Coelum Britannicum*, based on dialogues by Bruno which he had read with obvious relish, was performed by the King and his gentlemen on 18 February 1633/4 in a setting devised by Inigo Jones; the Queen praised the production, and the King wished to repeat it. Carew wrote no other known masque, but his poems include prologue and epilogue for a Whitehall 'Entertainment' otherwise not recorded, and there are songs for an unidentified play. With the currently vexing issues of politics and religion he refused to be troubled: he had had enough of adversity. In his *Obsequies to the Lady Anne Hay* he described himself, with something like pride, as

> I that ne're more of private sorrow knew
> Then from my Pen some froward Mistresse drew,
> And for the publike woe, had my dull sense
> So sear'd with ever adverse influence,
> As the invaders sword might have, unfelt,
> Pierc'd my dead bosome,

and when Aurelian Townshend asked him to join with the other poets who commemorated the death of Gustavus Adolphus in 1632, he replied that

> Tourneyes, Masques, Theaters, better become
> Our *Halcyon* dayes; what though the German Drum
> Bellow for freedome and revenge, the noyse
> Concernes not us, nor should divert our joyes.

An occasional passage[2] reveals, to be sure, political prejudices of a conventional sort; but the poet applied his mind more

---

[1] See below, p. xli.
[2] As in the verses *Vpon the Kings sicknesse*, which echo James I's *Trew Law of free Monarchies*; or lines 34–6 of the commendatory poem on Davenant's *Just Italian*:
> perhaps the State
> Hath felt this rancour, where men great and good,
> Have by the Rabble beene misunderstood.

Cf. also a reference to the 'virulent humors' expelled to New England, in *Coelum Britannicum*, lines 387–90.

congenially to such a topic as the nature of Jealousy—a
question debated with his friends Cecilia Crofts and Thomas
Killigrew and afterwards turned into a poetic dialogue—or
to the composition of commendatory or familiar verses to
such other friends as Walter Montagu, Henry Lord Cary of
Leppington, George Sandys, the Countess of Carlisle, and
the notorious Chief Justice Finch. Specific mention of his
activities during the 1630s is rare, but 'T. Ca.' is named
by James Howell in a letter dated from Westminster on 5
April 1636 (undependably, as with all of Howell's dates) as
being present at a dinner given by Ben Jonson and 'buzzing'
in Howell's ear a reproof of the bad taste of the host, who
'began to vapour extremely of himself'.[1] Towards Jonson
personally his attitude seems never to have been quite that
of a loyal 'son', and the criticism which he whispered to
Howell was only a repetition of what he had already said
openly in the lines *To Ben. Iohnson. Vpon occasion of his Ode of
defiance annext to his Play of the new Inne.* Moreover, though
Carew expressed admiration for Jonson's work and drew
upon it for his own poems, he was not represented by any
composition to Jonson's memory in *Ionsonus Virbius* (1638),
though Viscount Falkland mentions him in that volume in a
way that shows something was expected of him:

> Let *Digby*, *Carew*, *Killigrew*, and *Maine*,
> *Godolphin*, *Waller*, that inspired *Traine*,
> Or whose rare *Pen* beside deserves the *grace*,
> Or of an *equall*, or a neighbouring *Place*,
> Answer thy *wish*, for none so fit appeares
> To raise his *Tombe*, as who are left his *Heires*.[2]

Thomas Carew could hardly have been, as Vincent assumed,[3]
the 'noble Carew' mentioned by Jonson in the *Execration
upon Vulcan* as having assisted him in research for the history
of Henry V; this was evidently George Carew, Baron Carew
of Clopton and Earl of Totnes (1555–1629), whose service
Thomas Carew unsuccessfully tried to enter in 1616 and
who, according to Wood, 'made several collections, notes,
and extracts for the writing of the *History of the Reign of K.*

[1] *Epistolæ Ho-Elianæ*, ed. Joseph Jacobs, 1890, pp. 403–4; Bk. II, Letter xiii.
[2] *Ionsonus Virbius*, 1638, p. 8.
[3] *The Poems of Thomas Carew*, ed. Arthur Vincent, Introduction, p. xxv.

Hen. 5. which were remitted into the *History of Great Britain*, &c. published by *Joh. Speed*'.[1]

With Sir John Suckling, who joined him as a Gentleman of the Privy Chamber Extraordinary on 20 November 1638,[2] Carew stood in a less reserved relationship. The two poets, who are mentioned together on 21 January 1638/9 as 'the best wittes of the time',[3] are united in a poetic dialogue praising the fair Lucy, Countess of Carlisle;[4] and Suckling's letters contain a long composition 'to a Friend to diswade him from marrying a Widow which he formerly had been in Love with, and quitted', apparently addressed to Carew, together with 'Tom's' madcap answer. Another letter of Suckling's, which calls Carew by name, is addressed to him at West Horsley, the home of his friend and distant cousin Carew Ralegh, and is full of gay topical allusions whose point is now lost.[5] Carew was seemingly in ill health when it was written, and one of Suckling's short poems refers jocularly, as was the fashion of the time, to the 'pox' which may have afflicted him ever since the illness of 1617–18. Carew figures also in Suckling's *A Sessions of the Poets*, written about 1638; here we catch a glimpse of the witty courtier as a slow and careful artist:

> *Tom Carew* was next, but he had a fault
> That would not well stand with a Laureat;
> His Muse was hard bound, and th' issue of 's brain
> Was seldom brought forth but with trouble and pain.
> > And
>
> All that were present there did agree,
> A Laureat Muse should be easie and free,
> Yet sure 'twas not that, but 'twas thought that his Grace
> Consider'd he was well he had a Cup-bearers place.[6]

His actual movements during this period must have followed those of the court. He also visited Horsley and Wrest, and

---

[1] Wood, *Athenæ Oxonienses*, 1691, i. 452. Lord Carew is likewise thanked by Camden in the *Britannia* (ed. Gibson, 1772, ii. 338) for aid given in Irish matters.

[2] Public Record Office, L.C. 5/134, p. 286.

[3] Ibid., S.P. 16/409: 167; 'Madam Mericke to Mrs Lydall' from Wrest—apparently a literary exercise.

[4] See Commentary, pp. 227–8.

[5] These letters are given at pp. 211–13.

[6] Suckling, *Fragmenta Aurea*, 1646, p. 8.

probably stayed frequently with the Crofts family at Little
Saxham. Saxham and Wrest he commemorated in verse. It
was at Saxham ('apud J. C.'—i.e. John Crofts) that Clement
Barksdale, author of *Nympha Libethris*, sent him a copy of
Davenant's poems—if a printed book, this must have been
Madagascar, 1638—together with a friendly Latin epigram
expressing gratitude for some kindness. At Wrest, the seat
of the De Greys, Earls of Kent, he probably received a
special welcome as a friend of the grave and learned John
Selden, who for many years made that house a second home.

'But his Glory was', writes Clarendon, 'that after fifty
Years of his Life, spent with less Severity or Exactness than
it ought to have been, He died with the greatest Remorse
for that Licence, and with the greatest Manifestation of
Christianity, that his best Friends could desire.'[1] A more
circumstantial account of the remorseful end is preserved by
Izaak Walton in manuscript notes which are quoted on p. xli.
Carew's final 'Manifestation of Christianity' need not sur-
prise us, for conventional religious sentiment appears in the
various elegies which he wrote throughout his life; but in
1638 a more personal strain, touched with an unfamiliar
poignancy, sounds in his verses on Sandys's translation of
the Psalms:

> Perhaps my restlesse soule, tyr'de with persuit
> Of mortall beauty, seeking without fruit
> Contentment there, which hath not, when enjoy'd,
> Quencht all her thirst, nor satisfi'd, though cloy'd;
> Weary of her vaine search below, Above
> In the first Faire may find th'immortall Love. . . .
> Then, I no more shall court the verdant Bay,
> But the dry leavelesse Trunke on *Golgotha*;
> And rather strive to gaine from thence one Thorne,
> Then all the flourishing wreathes by Laureats worne.

The idea of Carew as a repentant sinner has its picturesque
aspects, and somewhat of a legend has been built up around
it. The boldest assumptions were made in the anonymous
Memoir prefixed to the edition of 1845:

It is to be regretted that the excitements and dissipations of the court
of Charles banished from the mind of Carew those solemn and en-

---

[1] Clarendon, *Life*, 1759, i. 36.

nobling reflections, that in a retired life are more apt to force their way
upon our attention. . . . It was soon after *Cœlum Britannicum* made
its appearance that ill-health first assailed Carew; the temptations by
which he had been assailed had led him too far from the paths of
virtue; and when failing health bid him prepare to die, he awoke from
a long dream of security, to find himself upon the brink of another
world,—upon the verge of eternity, into which he gazed with feelings
of unmingled awe.

> One step to the white death-bed and one to the bier,
> And one to the Charnel, and one—oh, where?

From this time to his decease, love-songs were exchanged for peni-
tential psalms; his muse abandoned the service of Venus, and was
employed in pouring forth passionate strains of sorrow and prayer.

More recently a similar conception of Carew's final period,
though without the gratuitous edification, has been presented
by Mr. R. G. Howarth in the course of an otherwise
admirable essay;[1] he thinks it not improbable that the trans-
lated Psalms belong to this time of 'moral revolution', and
even finds in one of them a reference to the stricken poet's
state of mind. But such accounts probably exaggerate both
the nature and the extent of Carew's spiritual regeneration.
It has already been mentioned that two of his Psalms (91 and
104) belong to a period not later than the early 1620s, so
that we must reject the assumption that the project of trans-
lation was initiated in the late 1630s as penance for a sinful
life.[2] As for Carew's other poetry, the only verses which
may be dependably dated with or after the pious composition
to Sandys are the song on the wedding of Lord Lovelace
(1638), the verses on Davenant's *Madagascar* (1638), those
on Lord Cary's *Romulus and Tarquin* (1638), and the verse-
letter to G. N. from Wrest (1639–40); and though these
do not offend by licentiousness, they are as mundane poems as
Carew ever wrote. There is no reason to believe that Carew's
career as a poet included any specifically 'religious' period at
all. How, then, are we to interpret the remorse and the signal
manifestation of Christianity recorded by Clarendon? What
seems to be the only tenable answer to this question is pre-

[1] *Minor Poets of the Seventeenth Century*, ed. R. G. Howarth (Everyman's
Library), Introduction, p. xiii.
[2] See pp. lxx–lxxi. There is no evidence by which to date the seven other versified
Psalms, but these are at least as likely to be early work as late.

served in the notes which Izaak Walton collected for a life of John Hales:

Ther was told this by m^r Antony ffaringdon, and haue heard it discourst by others: that m^r Thomas cary a poet of note and a great libertine in his life and talke and one that had in his youth beine aquainted with m^r Ha: sent for m^r Hales to come to him in a dangerose fit of sicknes and desyrd his aduise and absolution w^{c}h m^r Ha vppon a promise of amendment gaue him (this was I think in the country.) but m^r cary came to london fell to his old company and into a more visable Scandalus life and espetialy in his discourse and be[ing] taken very sick that which prou'd his last and being much trobled in minde procur'd m^r Ha to come to him in this his sicknes and agony of minde desyring earnestly after a confession of many of his sins to haue his prayers and his absolution. m^r Ha, told him he shood haue his prayers, but wood by noe meanes giue him then ether the sacrament or absolution.[1]

John Hales was not only Carew's relative by marriage; he had been, it will be remembered, a Fellow of Merton College (1606 to 1613) when Carew was an undergraduate there, and in 1616 he had gone as chaplain with Sir Dudley Carleton to The Hague, on the embassy from which Carew was soon sent home in disgrace. According to Joseph Hunter (in the *Chorus Vatum Anglicanorum*) the story of Carew's double repentance is one which 'Lady Salter used to relate as a certain fact'.[2] Hunter does not cite his source for this statement, but Lady Salter, second wife of the Sir William Salter whose first wife Carew commemorated in a poem dated 1631, is known to have been a good friend of Hales's; and the anecdote thus seems reasonably well authenticated. The important point is that Carew did not feel any permanent change of heart, such as might have manifested itself in his way of life or his writing, but rather two separate and apparently sudden moods of spiritual uneasiness, once while seriously ill and again while fatally so.

If Carew's health failed in later life, his death may have been hastened by the hardships of the expedition which Charles led against Scotland in 1639 in the first Bishops' War, a prelude to the more sanguinary civil strife which Carew did not live to see. It is from the verses to his friend

[1] Transcribed from Corpus Christi College, Oxford, Fulman MS., vol. 10, fol. 80r–v, by John Butt, *Modern Language Review*, xxix (1934), 273.
[2] British Museum, MS. Add. 24489, p. 254.

G. N. (possibly Gilbert North) from Wrest that we learn of the poet's recent presence with the royal forces:

> I breathe (sweet *Ghib*:) the temperate ayre of *Wrest*
> Where I no more with raging stormes opprest,
> Weare the cold nights out by the bankes of Tweed,
> On the bleake Mountains, where fierce tempests breed,
> And everlasting Winter dwells;

—and the poem concludes with a reference to 'the memory of our Armes'. Other contemporary writers corroborate this account of the discomforts of the north. The spring of 1639 was abnormally cold, and supplies were inadequate. Even Secretary Coke had no tent. When Berwick was reached, famine threatened; the soldiers 'called and complained for want of bread and drink' and became 'so disorderly that they shoot bullets through our own tents'; even the King's tent was fired into. But on 18 June 1639, Articles of Pacification brought hostilities to an end without a battle.

The lines from Wrest, in Bedfordshire, were perhaps his last. They are not entirely clear in their indication of the season, and indeed they may have been composed over a considerable period of time. But a passage towards the close:

> Our Vintage here in *March* doth nothing owe
> To theirs in Autumne,

affords apparent evidence that they were completed not many days before his death, which occurred on or about 21 March 1639/40. Wood says that Carew died 'about 1639', and 1639 is accordingly the year given in most handbooks and histories. But this date, which is correct only by Old Style reckoning, may be rendered more precise by a group of hitherto unnoticed documents. The first of these is an entry in the Lord Chamberlain's records:[1]

Champneys W^m / A warr^t to sweare Mr William Champneys a Sewer to attend his Ma^tes Person in Ordinary in place of Mr Thomas Carew deceased. March 22. 1639[/40].

The post which Carew had won against strong competition was thus re-awarded before he was yet in his grave, for his interment did not take place until the next day. The registers

---

[1] Public Record Office, L.C. 5/134, p. 382.

of the church of St. Dunstan's-in-the-West for March 1639/40 contain the entry:

23. Thomas Carewe Esq[r] was buried,

and additional information concerning the funeral occurs in the 'Receipts of Burialls' among the Churchwardens' Accounts of St. Dunstan's:[1]

March 1639[/40]

Item 23° for the ground for M[r]. Thomas Carew in S[t].

Annes Chapell	xxvj[s]. viij[d]
Item for the knell	xj[s]. iiij[d]
Item for the Peales	viij[s]
Item ~~for~~ toward the Cloth	ij[s].

The total fees of 48s. are larger than usual, and it may be assumed that the funeral was a fine one. Fees for the burial of Sir Matthew Carew, also in St. Anne's Chapel, in 1618 had been only 24s. It would be interesting to know whether it was by his own desire that Thomas Carew was buried beside his father. At the reconstruction of the church, in the years 1829–33, the marble memorial of Sir Matthew Carew was relegated to the crypt. No trace of the tomb of Thomas Carew survives.

The place of Carew's death is doubtful. Not everyone buried at St. Dunstan's was an inhabitant of the parish or had died there, and sufficient reason for Carew's burial at St. Dunstan's can be found in his family's connexion with that church. Davenant, in a poem published in 1638, places his lodging in King Street, Westminster;[2] it was an important thoroughfare, now swept away, leading from Charing Cross to Westminster.

King Charles, says Wood, 'always esteemed him to the last one of the most celebrated wits in his court, and therefore by him as highly valued, so afterwards grieved at his untimely death'—which came 'to the reluctancy of many of his poetical acquaintance'.[3] But it is not probable that any

---

[1] London Guildhall, MS. 2968/3, fol. 578[r].

[2] Davenant's poem to Carew appears at p. 209.

[3] Wood, *Athenæ Oxonienses*, ed. Philip Bliss, 1815, ii. 658. Wood's sources of information about Carew are not known. On 15 Sept. 1688 he wrote to Sir Edward Sherburne for information 'about Thomas Carew the poet' (Andrew Clark, *Life*

immediate relatives participated in the funeral. So complete
was the breach between Carew and his family that when his
mother, Dame Alice Carew, drew up her will on 10 December
1637, a year before her death,[1] she made bequests to
her son Sir Matthew and his wife Frances; to her grandsons
John, Matthew, Henry, George, Thomas, James, and William
Carew; to her granddaughters Martha, Christian, and Alice
Carew (her granddaughter Elizabeth Carew being already
provided for); to her granddaughter Alice Williams; to Jone
Smith, perhaps a servant; and to Jeremy Wright and his wife,
tenants of a house 'near Lincoln's Inn Fields'—probably a
remnant of old Sir Matthew's property; but of her son
Thomas she made no mention.

The Van Dyck Portrait (Frontispiece)

The painting of Thomas Carew and Thomas Killigrew in
the Royal Collection, Windsor Castle, is signed 'A. Van
Dÿck 1638'. Killigrew, at the left, is dressed in black silk,
the sleeves slashed in white; upon the paper which he holds
in his right hand are drawn two female figures on pedestals.
Carew is similarly dressed, and holds a paper (of verses?).

There are other pictures of Killigrew, but this is the only
purported likeness of Carew.[2] His appearance agrees with
Aurelian Townshend's description:

I loue thy personn which being large and tall,
Containes a speritt that full mans it all;

and Times of Anthony Wood, 1894, iii. 252); on 22 Sept. Sherburne replied: 'I am
sorry I cannot make you an answerable return to yor Quere about Mr. Tho. Cary,
for tho I was well acquainted with him, yet in those Juvenile Times I concerned
my selfe in nothing more then the Pleasure of his Conversation, so that I neither
thought of informing my selfe of his Birth Education, Place of Study or any thing
of the like Nature. I had likewise the familiar Acquaintance of Tho. May, Tho.
Randol, James Shirley, Ro. Herrick and some other Contemporary Witts. . . .'
(G. Thorn-Drury, Poems of Thomas Randolph, 1929, pp. viii–ix, from 'Original
letter in the editor's collection'.)

[1] She was buried at Middle Littleton on 7 Dec. 1638, according to British Museum
MS. Lansdowne 1233, fol. 30^r. Her will is preserved at Somerset House (Prerogative Court of Canterbury, 45 Harvey).

[2] George Vertue noted, in 1721: 'M^r. Thomas May. Poet. ⟨died 1652⟩ his
picture & Mr Thomas Carew Poet both painted in Ovals by S^r. Peter Lilly.
at the Lord Bristols in St. James Square.' (Vertue Note Books, i. 88: Walpole
Society, 1929–30.) Lely did not come to England till after Carew's death, but
might have copied from Van Dyck.

and the dark colouring bears out Richard Carew's 'black-bearded all the race' (see p. xiii).

Walpole's anecdote (from Vertue) about the occasion of this painting is probably spurious.[1] A more probable occasion is suggested by Ernest Law, who thinks that the two female figures, intended perhaps for a sepulchral monument, may have reference to the deaths on 1 January 1637/8 of Thomas Killigrew's wife Cecilia (Carew had written a song upon the wedding in 1636) and the Countess of Cleveland; they were sisters of Carew's friend John Crofts. At the same time Law questions the traditional identification of the right-hand figure as Carew, but his only strong argument is based on the incorrect assumption, derived from Ebsworth, that Carew died early in 1638.[2]

The picture 'was brought from Spain by Sr Dan Arthurs. Widow' and 'sold by Mr Bagnal her second husband to Frederick Prince of Wales 1748'.[3] George III had it moved from Leicester House to Windsor. There is apparently no replica. 'A sketch for it, however, purporting to be Vandyck's original one, was sold at Christie's in 1782 for £4 18s.'[4] The figure of Carew, engraved separately and published by Walker in 1824, appears as frontispiece in Ebsworth's edition.

A medal by Jean Warin of Thomas Carey (1597–1634), son of the Earl of Monmouth and Gentleman of the Bed-chamber, has often been taken for a portrait of Thomas Carew. It reads: THO · CARV · R · CAROL · CVBICVLAR · ÆTATIS SVÆ · 75 · 1633. A head of Carey's wife Margaret appears sometimes on the reverse, sometimes as a separate medal. An engraving of the medal was made by Thomas Snelling the numismatist,[5] and a drawing appears, with altered inscription, as frontispiece to W. C. Hazlitt's edition of Carew, 1870. The similarity of names, and the '75' of Warin's inscription (a mistake for '35') misled Edmond Malone into the belief that Carew died at seventy-five and that 'many of his Love verses were written after he was 60'.[6]

[1] See Commentary, p. 244.
[2] Ernest Law, *Vandyck's Pictures at Windsor Castle*, 1899, pp. 77–8, 80.
[3] *Vertue Note Books*, v. 79: Walpole Society, 1937–8.   [4] Law, op. cit., p. 80.
[5] *Thirty Three Plates of English Medals*, 1776, plate 13.
[6] Malone's manuscript note in Langbaine's *Account of the English Dramatick Poets*, 1691: Malone 129, Bodleian Library.

II. *Carew's Early Reputation*

'His Sonnets', noted William Oldys, 'were more in re-
quest than any poet's of his time, that is between 1630 &
1640.'[1] This vogue is confirmed not only by the large num-
ber of manuscript copies of Carew's poems but also by the
tributes of his fellow poets, to whom he was a supremely
'witty' amorist, the author of *A Rapture*. 'I loue thy witt',
wrote Aurelian Townshend—

> thy witt, that chooses to be sweete
> Rather then sharpe, therefore in Lirique feete
> Steales to thy mistris; letting others write
> Rough footed Satires that in kissing bite.
>   I loue thy Celia if shee did infuse
> That fire into thee which begott thy Muse,
> And all thy louers that with listening eares
> Sipp in and relish thy Ambrosian teares.[2]

To Thomas Randolph, whatever his personal feeling, Carew
is still the poet of 'wit' who 'speaks raptures'.[3] Lord Herbert
of Cherbury twice refers to Carew, first (*c.* 1632) as 'my
witty Carew' and again, in his *Autobiography*, as 'Thomas
Carew, that excellent wit, the King's Carver'.[4] Davenant
makes a flattering show of indignation in expressing the
grievances of lovers against Carew's 'witty' Muse.[5] James
Shirley, in complimenting 'his honoured friend Tho. Stanley
Esquire' upon his 'learned loves', takes Carew's love-poems
as a point of reference for Stanley's further achievement:

> *Carew*, whose numerous language did before
> Steer every genial soul, must be no more
> The Oracle of Love, and might he come
> But from his own to thy Elizium,
> He would repent his immortality
> Given by loose Idolaters, and die
> A Tenant to these shades, and by thy ray
> He need not blush to court his *Celia*.[6]

[1] Manuscript note, Malone 129, Bodleian Library.
[2] The poem is given complete on pp. 207–8.
[3] Randolph, *Poems*, 1638, p. 16.
[4] Lord Herbert, *Elegy for Doctor Dunn*, line 50; *Autobiography*, ed. Sir Sidney Lee,
second edition, p. 106.
[5] Davenant's poem is printed on pp. 209–10.   [6] Shirley, *Poems*, 1646, p. 31.

Shirley's lines are echoed in 1650 by Robert Baron when in
Pocula Castalia he addresses the 'excellent Carevv' as 'dearest
Tom, Love's Oracle'; Baron couples him with Suckling ('the
glory of the Bower') as a master of love and lovers.[1] The
publisher Humphrey Moseley is praised by Jo. Leigh in
1651 for his editions of Suckling and Carew:

> *Thou rais'd brave* SUCKLING, *gav'st him all his own,*
> Aglaura *else had not been waited on:*
> *Then gav'st us melting* CAREVV, *who so long*
> *Maintain'd the* Court *with many a charming Song.*[2]

Similarly Carew and Waller appear together in the verses
prefixed by 'John Pinchebacke *Col.*' to Lovelace's *Lucasta*
(1649):

> *Well might that charmer his faire* Cælia *crowne,*
> *And that more polish't* Tyterus *renowne*
> *His* Sacarissa, *when in groves and bowres*
> *They could repose their limbs on beds of flowrs:*
> *When wit had prayse, and merit had reward,*
> *And every noble spirit did accord*
> *To love the Muses, and their Priests to raise,*
> *And interpale their browes with flourishing bayes.*

Such comments establish the esteem generally accorded to
Carew's poetry. The rest is suggested by Izaak Walton's
'm^r Thomas cary a poet of note and a great libertine
in his life and talke', which with Clarendon's similar remark
('fifty Years of his Life, spent with less Severity or Exactness
than it ought to have been') suggests that Carew's fame was
partly a matter of notoriety. And that *A Rapture*, in parti-
cular, not only delighted but shocked is proved by the fullest
of all the early criticisms—that in *The Great Assises Holden
in Parnassus by Apollo and his assessours*, 1645. The anony-
mous author of this satire (apparently George Wither)
presents Carew and other poets as prospective jurymen at the
'Assises', where certain scandalous news-sheets were to be
brought to justice. The action of the poem begins with the
choosing of the jury.

[1] Baron, *Pocula Castalia*, 1650, p. 102.
[2] Cartwright, *Comedies, Tragi-Comedies, With other Poems*, 1651, p. (*)^r.

> Hee, who was called first in all the List,
> *George Withers* hight, entitled Satyrist;
> Then *Cary*, *May*, and *Davenant* were call'd forth;
> Renowned Poets all, and men of worth,
> If wit may passe for worth. Then *Sylvester*,
> *Sands*, *Drayton*, *Beaumont*, *Fletcher*, *Massinger*,
> *Shakespeare*, and *Heywood*, Poets good and free.

To Carew, however, the prisoner offered an objection.

> He gentle Mr. *Cary* did refuse,
> Who pleas'd faire Ladies with his courtly muse:
> He said, that he by his luxurious penne,
> Deserv'd had better the *Trophonian Denne*,
> Then many now which stood to be arraign'd,
> For he the *Thespian Fountaine* had distain'd,
> With foule conceits, and made their waters bright,
> Impure, like those of the *Hermophrodite*,
> He said, that he in verse, more loose had bin,
> Then old *Chærephanes*, or *Aretine*,
> In obscæne portraitures: and that this fellow
> In *Helicon* had reard the first *Burdello*,
> That he had chang'd the chast *Castalian spring*,
> Into a *Carian Well*, whose waters bring
> Effeminate desires, and thoughts uncleane,
> To minds that earst were pure, and most serene,

—but a 'furious glance' from Apollo interrupted this tirade, and 'learn'd *Scaliger*' was called to speak in Carew's defence. Scaliger explains that

> I have try'd my industry and wit,
> Both Arts, and Authours to refine, and mend,
> As well as times, yet can I not defend,
> But some luxuriant witt, will often vent
> Lascivious Poëms, against my consent:
> Of which offence, if *Cary* guilty be,
> Yet may some chaster Songs him render free
> From censure sharp, and expiate those crimes
> Which are not fully his, but rather Times:
> But let your Grace vouchsafe, that he may try
> How he can make his own Apology:
> *Apollo* then gave *Cary* leave to speake,
> Who thus in modest sort, did silence breake.

In wisdomes nonage, and unriper yeares,
Some lines slipt from my penne, which since with teares
I labour'd to expunge: This Song of mine
Was not infused by the Virgins nine,
Nor through my dreames divine upon this Hill,
Did this vain *Rapture* issue from my quill,
No Thespian waters, but a Paphian fire,
Did me with this foule extasie inspire:
I oft have wish'd, that I (like *Saturne*) might
This Infant of my folly smother quite,
Or that I could retract, what I had done,
Into the bosome of Oblivion.
Thus *Cary* did conclude: for prest by griefe,
He was compell'd to be concise, and briefe:
Phœbus at his contrition did relent,
And Edicts soon through all *Parnassus* sent,
That none should dare to attribute the shame
Of that fond *rapture*, unto *Caryes* name,
But Order'd that the infamy should light
On those, who did the same read, or recite.[1]

The recantation here reported need not be taken more seriously than the satirist probably intended it, though it forms an interesting appendage to the legend of Carew's reformation. That *A Rapture* was indeed a work of 'wisdomes nonage, and unriper yeares' is, however, indicated by other evidence, and it is thus probably the principal composition by which, for better or worse, Carew's reputation first grew.

His changing status in the century after his death is suggested by the dates of the first five editions: 1640, 1642, 1651, 1670, 1772. In his declining popularity he shared the fate of all Donne's Caroline successors,[2] though he is the smoothest of them and might have been expected to appeal, at least more strongly than he did, to Augustan taste. Not that his verses went entirely out of fashion in his own century. His lyrics appear frequently in the song-books;[3] he continues

[1] *The Great Assises*, 1645, pp. 19, 24–7.
[2] See three articles by Arthur H. Nethercot: 'The Reputation of the "Metaphysical Poets" during the Seventeenth Century'; 'during the Age of Pope'; and 'during the Age of Johnson and the "Romantic Revival" ', in *J. of Eng. and Germ. Phil.*, xxiii (1924), 173; *Philological Quarterly*, iv (1925), 161; and *Studies in Philology*, xxii (1925), 81.
[3] A check-list of musical settings is given on pp. 289–93.

to be imitated and plagiarized; and verses of his are to be found in the following collections: *Poems: by Wil. Shakespeare*, 1640; *Wits Recreations*, 1640 and 1641; *The Academy of Complements*, 1650; *The Marrow of Complements*, 1655; *Musarum Deliciæ*, 1655; *Wits Interpreter*, 1655, 1662, and 1671; Joshua Poole's *English Parnassus*, 1657; *Wit Restored*, 1658; Phillips's *Mysteries of Love and Eloquence*, 1658 and 1685; Pembroke and Rudyerd's *Poems*, 1660; *Recreation, for Ingenious Headpieces*, 1663 and 1667; *Oxford Drollery*, 1671; *Westminster-Drollery*, 1671; *The New Academy of Compliments*, 1671 and 1713; *Windsor-Drollery*, 1672; *Holborn-Drollery*, 1673; and *Wit and Drollery*, 1682. But as his wit and ease became more nearly common property he naturally began to be outmoded by the newer elegances of such men as Cowley and Waller. In 1668 David Lloyd, briefly mentioning the main writers of the previous generation, recalls that Carew 'was reckoned . . . Elaborate and Accurate'.[1] Clarendon's account, produced at about the same time, also hints at obsolescence: 'He was a Person of a pleasant and facetious Wit, and made many Poems (especially in the amorous Way) which for the Sharpness of the Fancy, and the Elegancy of the Language, in which that Fancy was spread, were at least equal, if not superior to any of that Time.' Edward Phillips's account in 1675 concurs—'he was reckon'd among the Chiefest of his time for delicacy of wit and Poetic Fancy, by the strength of which his extant Poems still maintain their fame amidst the Curious of the present Age'.[2] Winstanley, in 1687, echoes Phillips's account;[3] Langbaine, in 1691, mentions *Coelum Britannicum* and adds: 'He writ besides, several Poems, Songs, and Sonnets which are received with good Esteem by the Wits of this Age',[4] and he quotes Suckling's good-natured cavil and Davenant's tribute. Wood likewise gives a favourable account in general terms derived in part from the earlier critics: 'Thomas Carew, one of the famed poets of his time for the charming

---

1 David Lloyd, *Memoires of the Lives . . . of those . . . Personages that suffered . . . for the Protestant Religion*, 1668, p. 159.

2 Edward Phillips, *Theatrum Poetarum*, 1675, p. 174 of second pagination.

3 William Winstanley, *The Lives of the Most Famous English Poets*, 1687, pp. 169, 170.

4 Gerard Langbaine, *An Account of the English Dramatick Poets*, 1691, pp. 43–5.

sweetness of his lyric odes and amorous sonnets . . . became reckon'd among the chiefest of his time for delicacy of wit and poetic fancy'; his 'most admirable ingenuity' made him 'one of the most celebrated wits'; he was 'respected, if not ador'd by the poets of his time' and 'by the strength of his curious fancy hath written many things which still maintain their fame amidst the curious of the present age'.[1] Such a reputation was fragile. As between Waller and Carew, Phillips had called Waller 'not inferior to *Carew* himself'; Waller's publisher in 1690 admitted that Carew (and Suckling) 'wrote some things smoothly enough: but . . . all they did in this kind was not very considerable'; from this depreciation there is no great leap to Pope's terse 'Carew (a bad Waller)'.[2]

Yet Pope's criticism was not so absolute as this phrase, and his famous lumping of Carew with 'The mob of gentlemen who wrote with ease',[3] might seem to imply. Joseph Warton records that 'from the dregs of Crashaw, of Carew, of Herbert, and others, (for it is well known he was a great reader of all those poets) POPE has very judiciously collected gold';[4] and in an outline for a history of poetry, first published in Ruffhead's *Life*, Pope credits Carew and his homonymous contemporary T. Carey with being Waller's models 'in matter', though not in versification. Even at its nadir of estimation Carew's work never disappeared entirely from the miscellanies, and Mrs. Elizabeth Cooper's *The Muses' Library*, 1737, is adulatory. In 1772 a complete edition with sympathetic notes by Thomas Davies 'deservedly revived' the poetry of 'this elegant, and almost-forgotten writer'—to quote Bishop Percy, who printed the first two stanzas of 'Hee that loves a Rosie cheeke', in a text taken directly from the 1640 *Poems*, in his *Reliques*: and in collections issued during the following half-century Carew's writings again became generally accessible and their modern fame was established, though with an occasional protest at their 'extravagance' or immorality.

[1] Wood, *Athenæ Oxonienses*, ed. Philip Bliss, 1815, ii. 657–8; first included in the edition of 1721, from a collection made by Wood of writers overlooked in the edition of 1691.

[2] Joseph Spence, *Anecdotes*, ed. Singer, 1820, p. 21.

[3] Pope, *The First Epistle of the Second Book of Horace*, lines 107–10.

[4] J. Warton, *An Essay on the Writings and Genius of Pope*, 1756, pp. 87–8.

III. *Carew's Achievement*

The moral issue need not detain us. Where the writings most offend against present standards they offend in a manner that no expurgation could fully remedy: in spite of all that is graceful, witty, intelligent, and moving in these poems admiration is still cooled, not so much by their sensuality and libertinism (the obvious but magnificent licentiousness of *A Rapture*) as by the sharp disproportion which exists between Carew's sure lyrical genius and an ethos circumscribed and corrupted by a hundred random influences of literary and social fashion. Much of his work is occasional; nearly all of it is directed to a narrow and specific audience. Yet these very limitations help to give Carew's poetry its distinctive tone. 'In Carew's poems and Vandyke's pictures', as Sir Herbert Grierson has remarked, 'the artistic taste of Charles's court is vividly reflected, a dignified voluptuousness, an exquisite elegance, if in some of the higher qualities of man and artist Carew is as inferior to Wyatt or Spenser as Vandyke is to Holbein.'[1] And even these limitations ought not to be laid down too rigidly. In *Coelum Britannicum*, for instance, which was composed by royal command for a Shrove Tuesday festivity, not only is the pageantry varied and the wit nimble, as might have been expected, but the philosophic speeches, based on Giordano Bruno, achieve a graver beauty that foreshadows *Comus*. The uncourtly Thoreau was to quote from them in *Walden*.

His most obvious debts are to Donne, Jonson, and Marino, though he never became whole-heartedly a disciple to any master. From Donne he borrows phrases and conceits; Donne's passionate rhetoric would have been beyond him, and in fact he makes little apparent effort to match some of the other achievements which in the *Elegie* on Donne he most praises. Thus

> the goodly exil'd traine
> Of gods and goddesses, which in thy just raigne
> Were banish'd nobler Poems,

---

[1] *Metaphysical Lyrics and Poems of the Seventeenth Century*, ed. Herbert J. C. Grierson, 1921, Introduction, p. xxxvi.

are present throughout his verse; the *Elegie* itself is not free
of classical paraphernalia. He praises Donne for having
thrown away

> The lazie seeds
> Of servile imitation . . .
> And fresh invention planted,

but his own writings show little concern for such a principle.
A third and mightier element in Donne's work—that subtle
fusion of thought and emotion and image which could

> the deepe knowledge of darke truths so teach,
> As sense might judge, what phansie could not reach—

does sometimes touch Carew's verse with a 'metaphysical'
splendour, though probably by no mere artifice of the poet;
so that, as Ernest Rhys declares, 'when you have decided
that his lute is but a toy, two lines start to life which speak of
the fading rose and save the reproach—

> "For in your beauty's orient deep
> These flowers, as in their causes, sleep." '[1]

But Carew has too sportive a humour, too much elegance, to
be the complete 'metaphysical'. He is almost completely
lacking in Donne's sardonic quality, even in such a poem as
The second Rapture, where the impudent mock-moral—

> No worldling, no, tis not thy gold . . .

might have been expected to introduce a subtle and disturb-
ing complication of ideas such as Donne loved. Carew's
tone here is rather one of good-natured frivolity, of wit drawn
not too fine, of exquisite feeling that can rejoice in its own
inconsequence. Or consider the contrasting treatments of an
identical conceit. Donne's *The Dampe* begins:

> When I am dead, and Doctors know not why,
>   And my friends curiositie
> Will have me cut up to survay each part,
> When they shall finde your Picture in my heart . . ..

Carew concludes *Secresie protested* with:

> If when I dye, Physicians doubt
> What caus'd my death, and there to view

[1] Ernest Rhys, *Lyric Poetry*, 1913, p. 210.

Of all their judgements which was true,
Rip up my heart, Oh then I feare
The world will see thy picture there.

Here most of the elements that give Donne's lines vividness
and strength are discarded. The glum certainty of death
for the unhappy lover, the malicious assurance that doctors
will be ignorant and friends unfeelingly curious—these
Carew replaces with a hypothetical situation stated in general
terms. This is not to say that Carew has tried to imitate
Donne and failed, for there is a clear difference of intention:
Donne constructs a strong dramatic beginning for a cynical
challenge to his mistress, the uneven lines of his stanzas
pulsating with violent feeling; whereas Carew preserves a
gentler mood in his own carefully proportioned couplets,
with only a momentary quickening of emotion in his cry at
the end. But the contrast helps to measure the distance
separating the two men. Though Carew is highly sensitive,
his curiosity is strictly channelled. His admirable poise saves
him from the worst 'metaphysical' eccentricities, but it also
limits him. Significantly, the few poems which seem to be
immediately personal in content, such as the lines beginning
'Grieve not my *Celia*' and the introspective address to
George Sandys, are generally quiet in tone and sober in
expression.

But as we have seen, it is not an occasional deepening of
sincerity that caught the Caroline reader, but 'wit'; and
conversely it is Carew's witty conceits that have been most
often turned to reproach by his later critics. 'Extravagancy',
wrote Giles Jacob in *The Poetical Register*, 1719; 'glittering
icicles', added a writer in the *Retrospective Review*, 1822;
and W. J. Courthope's *History of English Poetry*, 1903, takes
Carew's ingenious figures as veritable symptoms of a deca-
dent society and a corrupt morality. Similar charges, to be
sure, have been levelled at most of Carew's contemporaries,
including Donne. But to attack Carew, or to defend him, on
precisely the same grounds as Donne and Donne's closer
imitators is to fall into a confusion. For unlike Donne's,
Carew's wit does not usually spring from the establishment
or discovery of new and pregnant relationships within the
world of experience; it relies instead on skilful hyperbole

and logically extended metaphor. To the extent that Carew's wit is derivative, it derives less from John Donne than from Giambattista Marino. In responding to Marino's baroque showiness Carew was anticipated among British poets by both Samuel Daniel and William Drummond of Hawthornden; indeed, more than twenty of Drummond's lyrics are translations from Marino. But Carew's success, though his actual translations are few, is more impressive. As an adaptor from foreign sources his only peers within his century are probably Thomas Stanley and Richard Crashaw, men who like Carew could render the substance of their 'witty' model with the freedom and verve of original work. And Carew excels both of them in the sure musical sense which everywhere joins with his quick mind to control and direct the development of his themes. A good example of this lyrical genius is provided by what he does with the last stanza of Marino's canzone *Belleza caduca*, translated by Daniel about 1600 and independently utilized by Carew for the larger portion of his poem *To A. L. Perswasions to love*. Thus Marino:

> Che prò dunque ti fia
> O giouentù mal saggia,
> In grembo a leggiadria
> Qual serpe in lieta piaggia
> Nodrir voglia seluaggia;
> Cogli cogli il tuo fiore,
> Che quasi in vn sol punto, e nasce, e more.

Daniel's *A Description of Beauty, translated out of Marino* phrases this as follows:

> What then wilt it auaile
> O youth aduised ill,
> In lap of beauty fraile
> To nurse a way-ward will,
> Like snake in sunne-warme hill?
> Plucke, plucke, betime thy flower,
> That springs, and parcheth in one short howre.

Carew's poem, less faithful to its original, concludes:

> Oh, then be wise, and whilst your season
> Affords you dayes for sport, doe reason;
> Spend not in vaine your lives short houre,

But crop in time your beauties flower:
Which will away, and doth together
Both bud, and fade, both blow and wither.

The contrast does not flatter Daniel; his lines appear awkward
and frigid when set beside Carew's. And this disparity of
effect does not result primarily from Daniel's weakening of
the final conceit, though he extends *vn sol punto* to an hour's
time whereas Carew at the other extreme ignores Marino's
prudential *quasi*; the essential difference lies in the sound
of the verses. 'Plucke, plucke, betime thy flower' is so
cacophonous as to impede any emotion consistent with the
argument of the poem; Daniel's other lines are not much
more fortunate, and his ragged, short-winded stanza, too
faithfully copied from the original, accentuates the harsh-
ness. Carew, on the other hand, creates and sustains his
mood by a masterly control of pace and tone. The power of
his final couplet derives only in part from Marino's meta-
phor, which was already hackneyed when Marino used it;
Carew's total effect is, rather, a matter of sound and sugges-
tion, and proceeds from his simple but strongly connotative
diction, his subtle employment of assonance, the soft plain-
tiveness of 'will away', the gusty *th*-sounds, the artfully
retarded rhythm, and the hollow reverberation of labial
consonants.

The great Elizabethan lyrics, sometimes brilliant in
orchestral effect, anticipate but rarely this thinner but sensi-
tively modulated verbal melody. It is an art of which the
touchstones first appear in the early song-books, especially in
the works of Thomas Campion. And just as the song-books
foreshadow a lyricism that Carew brings to perfection, so
Carew's songs—which are genuine songs, meant for singing
—appear with deeper expressiveness and clearer proportion
when set by Henry Lawes and other composers of the
period.[1] In the song 'If the quick spirits', for instance, the
final stanza overflows in an extra couplet, summarizing and
pointing what has gone before; in Henry Lawes's setting

[1] This is true in general, even though Henry Lawes appears sometimes to have
read his texts very carelessly. The setting of Carew's *Parting, Celia weepes*, for
instance, destroys grammar and sense by dividing the poem into three four-line
stanzas and a couplet.

this couplet provides the opportunity for an effective coda,
in which the rhythm is delicately syncopated and the tune
given a fresh twist to round off and bring to a climax the
strophic melody.

The final important element in shaping Carew's art was
probably the influence of Ben Jonson. There are points of
kinship both in temperament and in artistic creed. Jonson's
was the ampler mind, but it was characteristic of Carew as
of Jonson that without being creative in any philosophic
sense he could play brilliantly with certain congenial ideas;
and in logical texture—the smoothly inferential development
of the theme in each poem as a whole[1]—Carew's poems
closely resemble some of Jonson's: parts of *The Celebration
of Charis*, for instance, or *The Dreame*, with its opening 'Or
Scorne, or pittie on me take', which Carew made his own
text, or *The Musicall strife; In a Pastorall Dialogue*, with
which all of Carew's dialogues show kinship, or the song
'Come my Celia', from *Volpone*, which W. C. Hazlitt,
finding it in an anonymous manuscript, thought Carew's
own. Moreover, Carew's artistic punctilio represents an
instinct reinforced by Jonson's example:

> Repine not at the Tapers thriftie waste,
> That sleekes thy terser Poems,

though written by Carew to Jonson, no more than echoes
Jonson's own Horatian faith that 'things, wrote with labour,
deserve to be so read, and will last their Age'. In this
perfectionism Carew stands closest, after Jonson, to Herrick;
the surviving versions of Herrick's poems show how care-
fully the pieces must have been revised which finally appeared
in *Hesperides*. With Carew, who did not trouble to send his
work to the printer, the processes of composition are harder
to read, since with some poems it is by no means evident
which of several versions is the one finally approved by the
author, nor can the existence of a definitely 'final' version
always be assumed. Yet, after due allowance has been made
for legitimately alternative readings, and for corruptions in

---

[1] This characteristic is discussed in detail by C. J. Sembower, 'A Note on the
Verse Structure of Carew', in *Studies in Language and Literature in Celebration of
the Seventieth Birthday of James Morgan Hart*, New York, 1910, p. 456.

manuscript and posthumously printed copies, certain read-
ings—usually those of the 1640 *Poems*—are plainly superior
to others, and may be taken to represent Carew's later
versions. The poem *To A. L. Perswasions to love*, for in-
stance, begins, in the printed version:

> Thinke not cause men flatt'ring say,
> Y' are fresh as Aprill, sweet as May,
> Bright as is the morning starre,
> That you are so, or though you are
> Be not therefore proud. . . .

All the manuscript versions examined for the present edition
read at line 2:

> You'r faire as Hellen, fresh as May,

which is probably the earlier reading. The revision is towards
intensity and economy; the merely ornamental comparison
to Helen is discarded, and April, May, and the morning
star—all symbols of fleeting youth and transitory beauty—
immediately set the tone and foreshadow the argument of
the poem. Another change for the better has taken place in
the concluding couplet of *The Comparison*, where most manu-
scripts read:

> For formes sake only, thats exposed to view,
> Bee Goddesse like dispos'd Bee good Bee true

—a gaucherie replaced in the 1640 *Poems* by the easy sim-
plicity of

> But as you are divine in outward view
> So be within as faire, as good, as true.

Some other poems, such as 'Aske me no more' and *A prayer
to the Wind*, have undergone extensive reworkings.[1] There
are two separate versions of *A Looking-Glasse*, one printed in
the 1640 *Poems* and the other preserved in early manuscripts;
these two pieces develop quite differently a common theme
set in the first six lines (which are nearly identical in both),
and show Carew's mind examining his subject from different
angles, experimenting with a specification and expansion of
idea.[2] Such detailed revisions further illuminate Carew's

---

[1] The most important of these are indicated in the Commentary.

[2] Cf. similar pairings in Campion's songs (*A Booke of Ayres*, xvii, and *Fourth
Booke of Ayres*, xxiii) and in the alternative texts (printed as x and xi in *More Poems*)
of A. E. Housman's posthumous rendering from Sappho, 'The rainy Pleiads wester'.

gifts and limitations as already suggested on other grounds:
his 'hard-bound' muse; his passion not powerful enough to
make choice of expression secondary; his lively critical sense;
and his sensitivity, poetic erudition, and craftsmanship which
despite all limitations found fulfilment in some of the most
nearly perfect lyrics of a great age of song. More than that
need not be claimed for Carew.

IV. *Text and Canon*

i. PRINTED SOURCES

Ten of Carew's poems appeared in print during his life-
time, three of them without his name and at least one of
these without his authorization. His single masque *Coelum
Britannicum* (1634) was also anonymous. The volumes in
which he is represented before 1640 are as follows:

1. THE HEIRE AN EXCELLENT COMEDIE. As
   it was lately Acted by the Company of the Reuels.
   Written by *T. M.* Gent. . . . 1622 (and 1633). (Com-
   mendatory verses: *'The Heire being borne, was in his
   tender age'*, signed *Thomas Carew*.)

2. THE IVST ITALIAN. Lately presented in the priuate
   house at Blacke Friers, *By his Maiesties Seruants* . . .
   1630. (Commendatory verses: *'Ile not misspend in
   prayse, the narrow roome'*, signed Tho. Carew.)

3. MADRIGALES AND *AYRES* . . . By WALTER
   PORTER, one of the Gentlemen of his MAIESTIES ROYALL
   Chappell . . . 1632. (Songs: 'In *Celias* face a question
   did a rise' and 'He that loues a Rosie Cheeke', both un-
   signed.)

4. POEMS, *By* J. D. WITH ELEGIES ON THE
   AUTHORS DEATH . . . 1633 (1635, 1639). (In
   Elegies upon the Author: 'Can we not force from wid-
   dowed Poetry', signed *M*ᵣ. *Tho: Carie*.)

5. *Cœlum Britanicum*. | A | MASQUE | *AT* | WHITE-
   HALL | IN THE BANQVET- | TING-HOVSE, ON
   SHROVE- | TVESDAY-NIGHT, THE | 18. of
   February, 1633. | [*line*] | *Non habeo ingenium*; Cæsar

sed jussit: habebo. | *Cur me posse negem, posse quod ille putat?* | [*line*] | [*double line*] | *LONDON:* | Printed for *Thomas VValkley,* and are to be sold | at his Shop neare *White-Hall,* | 1634.

Collation: 4°: Sigg. [A], B–E⁴, F²; Pp. [2] + 35 + [1]. The text exists in several states: see below.

Contents: P. [1], title; 1–35, text of masque; 35, The Names of the Masquers, and The names of the young Lords and Noblemens Sonnes.

Of twelve copies examined, only three are identical. The copies collated are as follows:

In the British Museum—

a. Shelfmark C.34.c.8. Pagination regular.
b. Shelfmark 161.a.14. Identical with *a.* Not cited separately.
c. Shelfmark 1103.e.70. Pages 33–5 misnumbered 30, 28, 29.
m. Shelfmark G. 18790. Pages misnumbered 20 for 22, 21 for 23, 30 for 33, 28 for 34, 29 for 35.

In the Dyce Collection, South Kensington—

p. Shelfmark Dyce 1827 [25.A.55]. Pages misnumbered as in *m.* Text not quite identical.
t. Shelfmark Dyce 1827 [25.A.56]. Pages misnumbered 19 for 9, 20 for 10, 17 for 11, 18 for 12, 23 for 13, 24 for 14, 21 for 15, 22 for 16, 30 for 32, 29 for 33, 28 for 34, 29 for 35.

In the Bodleian Library—

d. Shelfmark Mal. 159 (4). Pages misnumbered 19 for 9, 20 for 10, 17 for 11, 18 for 12, 23 for 13, 24 for 14, 21 for 15, 22 for 16, 20 for 22, 21 for 23, 29 for 33, 28 for 34, 29 for 35.

In the Cambridge University Library—

f. Shelfmark Syn. 7.64.61⁷. Pages misnumbered 19 for 9, 20 for 10, 17 for 11, 18 for 12, 23 for 13, 24 for 14, 21 for 15, 22 for 16, 30 for 32, 29 for 33, 28 for 34, 29 for 35.
g. Shelfmark Syn. 7.63.21. Identical with *a.* Not cited separately.
h. Shelfmark Syn. 6.63.20. Pages misnumbered 20 for 10, 17 for 11, 24 for 14, 21 for 15.

In the Henry E. Huntington Library—

w. Shelfmark HEH 97458. Pages misnumbered as in *m* and *p.* Text not quite identical.
x. Shelfmark HEH 97457. Pages misnumbered as in *h.* Text not quite identical.

In all twelve copies the title-page is identical. Signature B shows two settings of type, one represented in copies *adfhtx* and the other in copies *cmpw*. For signature C the outer forme was set three times (copies *ahx*, *dft*, and *cmpw*) and the inner forme twice (copies *adfhtx* and *cmpw*). Signature D shows three settings of type, represented in *ahx*, *ft*, and *cdmpw*. Signatures E and F were apparently set once only. It is evident that corrections were made piecemeal as the printing progressed, but new faults were introduced with the new settings of type. The present text reproduces copy *c*, necessary corrections being derived in part from the other copies.

6. THE VVITTS. A Comedie, PRESENTED AT THE Private House in Blacke Fryers, by his Majesties Servants. *The Authour* VVILLIAM D'AVENANT, *Servant to Her Majestie* . . . 1636. (Commendatory verses: 'It hath been said of old, that Playes are Feasts', signed T. CAREVV.)

7. A PARAPHRASE VPON THE DIVINE POEMS. BY *GEORGE SANDYS* . . . M.DC.XXXVIII. (Commendatory verses: 'I presse not to the Quire, nor dare I greet', signed *Tho: Carew*. The second edition; not in the first edition, 1636.)

8. ROMVLVS AND TARQVIN *First Written in Italian* By the *Marquis Virgilio Malvezzi*: And now *taught English;* by *H: L*ᵈ*. Cary of Lepingtō the second Edition* . . . 1638. (Commendatory verses: 'My Lord, *In every triviall worke 'tis knowne*', signed THO. CAREW. The first edition of *Romulus and Tarquin*, 1637, contains no commendatory verses.)

9. Madagascar; WITH OTHER Poems. By W. DAVENANT . . . 1638. (Commendatory verses: 'When I behold, by warrant from thy Pen', signed *Thomas Carew*.)

10. *Festum Voluptatis*, Or the BANQUET OF PLEASURE; . . . By *S. P.* Gent. . . . 1639. (An eight-line SONET: 'Young men flie, when beauty darts', plagiarized from Carew's '*SONG*. Conquest by flight',

lines 9–16. The dedication of *Festum Voluptatis* is
signed SAMUEL PICK. Several authors besides
Carew are similarly plundered.)

The rest of Carew's poems circulated only in numerous
manuscript copies. But on the day of his funeral (23 March
1639/40) 'a booke called *The Workes* of Thomas Carew
Esquire. late Sewer to his Maiesty being *Poems and Masques*'
was licensed to Thomas Walkley,[1] who had published
Coelum Britannicum in 1634. Matthew Clay's imprimatur
is dated 29 April, and that the work had left the press before
26 June 1640 is shown by an entry for that date in the diary
of Sir Humphrey Mildmay: 'for Tho: Carewe his Poem——
00:02:03:'[2] The volume carries no prefatory matter, and
probably received only such hasty editing as Walkley him-
self could give it.[3] Some of the poems are not by Carew, and
not all of Carew's poems are included. The text appears to
have been put together in at least two stages. Walkley's
original collection, itself perhaps derived from several
sources, fills pages 1–167; for nearly all of these poems
Carew's authorship is unquestioned, and there seems to have
been some effort at arrangement. Pages 1–89 contain a
group of songs and lyrics, ending with *A Rapture*; 90–9, a
group of epitaphs; 100–7, six songs for a play; 108–55,
various poems, mostly occasional; 156–67, commendatory
verses. The faultiest texts occur in the commendatory
verses—a curious fact, seeing that these pieces were already
available in print. For the poem contributed to *Madagascar*
(which Walkley had published two years before) the 1640
volume prints a nonsensical hybrid, fourteen lines by Hab-
ington and six by Carew; and the *Elegie* on Donne appears
in a version generally considered inferior to that published
with Donne's *Poems* in 1633. But pages 1–167 provide a
much more trustworthy source for the Carew canon than do
pages 168–206, which contain the remaining poems; these,

1 Arber, *Transcript of the Registers of the Company of Stationers, 1554–1640*, iv. 478.
2 MS. Harl. 454, fol. 160ᵛ, British Museum. In the British Museum copy of the
Poems, 1640 (shelfmark C.71.a.9), a seventeenth-century hand has written: 'pre:
2ˢ—6ᵈ.'
3 There is nothing to support J. B. Ebsworth's suggestion (*Works of Carew*,
p. 260) that the volume was edited by Aurelian Townshend.

beginning with *The Comparison*, were probably added singly
or in small groups as Walkley succeeded in obtaining copies
of them, and include the following false or seriously disputed
attributions (the page-numbers are those of 1640):[1]

p. 170. The Enquiry. (By Herrick; printed in *Hesperides*,
1648.)

p. 172. The Sparke. (Authorship doubtful; manuscript
attribution to Walton Poole; printed in Suckling's *Last
Remains*, 1659.)

p. 181. Song. 'Would you know what's soft?' (Claimed
by Shirley in his *Poems*, 1646.)

p. 184. The Hue and Cry. (By Shirley; printed in *The
Wittie Faire One*, 1633, and in Shirley's *Poems*, 1646.)

p. 186. To his Mistris confined. (Claimed by Shirley in
his *Poems*, 1646. Previously printed by the plagiarist
Samuel Pick in *Festum Voluptatis*, 1639—see p. lxi.)

p. 188. The Primrose. (By Herrick; printed in *Hesperides*,
1648.)

p. 192. The Carver. *To his Mistris*. (Probably by Henry
Constable; printed in *Diana*, 1594.)

p. 204. The Dart. (Manuscript attribution to William
Strode.)

p. 205. The Mistake. (Manuscript attribution to Henry
Blount.)

Walkley's volume concludes with a reprint of *Coelum
Britannicum* from the 1634 edition. Because this masque
was later included in the posthumous *Works of Sr William
D'avenant K^t*, 1673, Carew's authorship has sometimes been
questioned; and Davenant's most recent biographer finds it
'not impossible that D'avenant may at least have aided his
friend in this spectacular *divertissement*'.[2] But as the same
writer points out, *Coelum Britannicum* was more probably
included in the 1673 volume by mistake for Davenant's own
Britannia Triumphans, which was omitted; and surely
Walkley, as publisher of the anonymous *Coelum Britannicum*
of 1634, is our best guide as to its authorship.

[1] All of these misattributions and disputed authorships are noted by Arthur
Vincent except that of *The Carver*, which was first pointed out by Mr. Alan
Herrick in *The Times Literary Supplement* for 12 April 1947.
[2] Arthur H. Nethercot, *Sir William D'avenant*, 1938, p. 117.

Despite many defects, the 1640 *Poems* must provide the most important single source for any edition of Carew. A detailed description is as follows:

Title: POEMS. | *By* | THOMAS CAREVV | Esquire. | One of the Gentlemen of the | Privie-Chamber, and Sewer in| Ordinary to His Majesty. | [*two lines*] | LONDON, | Printed by *I. D.* for *Thomas Walkley,* | and are to be sold at the signe of the | flying Horse, between Brittains | Burse, and York-House. | 1640.¹

Collation: 8°: Sigg. [A]², B–R⁸, S⁴; Pp. [4]+262+ [2]. Fol. B4 is marked A4, fol. E4 is marked F4, and fol. S3 is marked S5. Pages 207 (second title-page) and 208 (blank) are not numbered, and page 259 is misnumbered 159. Leaf G7 is a cancel. A copy containing the un-cancelled leaf is in the Huntington Library, shelfmark HEH 80753; see also *The Library*, 3rd series, vii (April 1916), 158, for the description of another.

Contents: P. [1], title; [3], Errata, as follows:

ERRATA.

*P*Age 5. *Line* 4. for their, *reade* your. *p.* 15. *l.* 3. for sent, *r.* lent. *p.* 43. *l* 11. *for* it, *reade* not. *p.* 77. *l.* 3. *for* danke, *r.* dampe. *p.* 85. *l.* 7. *for* Souldiers, *r.* Lovers. *p.* 11. *l.* 15. *r.* I straight might feele. *p.* 113. *l.* 17. for the, *r.* that. *p.* 122. *l.* 2. for where, *r.* what. *p.* 138. *l.* 3. *for* pastime, *r.* passion. *p.* 148. *for* circle, *r.* sickle. *p.* 168. *l.* 18. *for* frisketh in, *r.* Iris-struts in.

[4], Imprimatur, | MATTHEVV CLAY. | *Aprill.* 29. 1640.; 1–206, text of Poems; [207], second title-page, as follows: *Cœlum Brittanicum.* | A | MASQVE AT | WHITE-HALL IN | the Banquetting house, | on *Shrove-Tuesday-night,* | the 18. of *February,* | 1633. | [*line*] | The Inventors. | *Tho: Carew. Jnigo Iones.* | [*line*] | *Non habet ingenium*; Cæsar *sed jussit: habebo.* | *Cur me posse negem, posse quod ille putat.* | [*line*] | *LONDON,* | Printed for *Thomas Walkley.* | 1640.

209–62, text of masque; [1], The Names of the

¹ Professor David Nichol Smith informs me that in his own copy the word POEMS is followed by a comma. The printer *I. D.* was presumably John Dawson. See Plomer, *Dictionary of Booksellers and Printers, 1641–67,* p. 63.

Masquers, and The names of the young Lords and Noble-
mens Sonnes; [2], The Songs and Dialogues of this Booke
were set with apt Tunes to them, by M^r. *Henry Lawes*,
one of His Majesties Musitians.

Another issue of the same year—apparently representing
the earlier form of the text—exhibits minor differences. The
Errata (there headed 'Errates') lack the correction for page
168; 'M^r. *Henry Lawes*' on p. [2] is given without the 'M^r.';
and there are a few variants in the text—e.g. 'wrat' for 'wrath'
on page 11, line 8, and the correct 'cull' instead of 'call' in
line 54 of the *Elegie* on Donne.

There must have been a good demand for the volume,
since Walkley produced a second edition in 1642. This is
a close reprint of the first, except for the addition of eight
new poems and the correction of the old ones (not quite
accurately) by the Errata of 1640.

Title: POEMS. | *By* | THOMAS CAREVV | Esquire. | One of
the Gentlemen of the | Privie-Chamber, and Sewer | in
Ordinary to His Majesty. | [*line*] | *The second Edition
revised and enlarged.* | [*line*] | LONDON, | Printed by *I. D.*
for *Thomas Walkley*, | and are to be sold at the signe of the |
flying Horse, betweene *Brittains* | *Burse*, and York-House. |
1642.

Collation: 8°: Sigg. A–R⁸, S⁶; Pp. [2]+279+[1]. A1
(presumably blank) is missing. A3 is marked B3, B4 is
marked C4, F4 is marked G4, and N3 is marked N5. Page
16 is misnumbered 15, 171 is misnumbered 173, 237–
66 are misnumbered 247–76, 268 is misnumbered 278,
and 269–79 are misnumbered 209–19. Pages 223
(second title-page) and 224 (blank) are not numbered.
Page 222 (containing *A Fancy*) exists in two states.

Contents: P. [1], title; 1–222, Poems; [223], second
title-page, as follows:

Cælum Brittanicum. | A | MASKE AT | WHITE-
HALL IN | the Banquetting House, | on *Shrove-
Tuesday-night*, | the 18. of *February*, | 1633. | [*line*] |
The Inventors. | *Tho. Carew. Inigo Iones.* | [*line*] |
Non habit ingenium; Cæsar *sed jussit: habebo.* | *Cur me*

posse negem, posse quod ille putat. | *[line]* | *LONDON,* |
Printed for *Thomas Walkley.* | 1642.

225–218 [278], text of Masque; 219 [279], The Names of
the Masquers, and The names of the young Lords and
Noblemens Sonnes; [1], The Songs and Dialogues of this
Booke were set with apt Tunes to them, by Mr. *Henry
Lawes,* one of his Majesties Musicians.

Of the new poems, which occupy pp. 207–22, the first,
To my Lord Admirall on his late sicknesse, and recovery, is
certainly not by Carew, but by Waller; it appears in both
of the 1645 editions of Waller's poems and in the authorized
edition of 1668. Carew's claim to *A divine Love,* which
was also first printed in the 1642 volume, has likewise been
questioned, but on purely stylistic grounds. Thomas Carey,
Gentleman of the Bedchamber, has been suggested as a
possible author: 'The metaphysical vein and the sustained
argument are both somewhat uncommon in Thomas Carew,
but were probably not so in the author of *Methodus Amandi.*'[1]
The poem has also been claimed tentatively for Lord Herbert
of Cherbury and printed by G. C. Moore Smith in his
edition of that writer. Whatever the correct ascription, most
readers will probably agree that *A divine Love* does not
sound much like Carew, being pompous, long-winded, and
without a trace of his usual gusto.

On 8 June 1650 the publisher Humphrey Moseley had
'Assigned over unto him by vertue of a note under the hand
& seale of Tho: Walkeley & subscribed by Master
Flesher warden, all the estate, right, title & interest wch the
said Thomas Walkeley hath in this booke or copie called
Poems, by Thomas Carew Esqr',[2] and a third edition of the
Poems appeared, with Moseley's imprint, in the following
year.

Title: POEMS. | With a | MASKE, | BY | *THOMAS
CAREW* Esq; | One of the Gent. of the privie- | Chamber,
and Sewer in Ordina- | ry to His late Majesty. | The *Songs*

---

[1] Arthur Vincent, *Poems of Thomas Carew,* p. 257. Vincent prints two of Carey's
poems (*On His Mistress Going to Sea* and *Methodus Amandi*) in an appendix.
[2] Arber, *Transcript, 1640–1708,* i. 344.

were set in *Musick* by | Mr. Henry Lawes Gent: of the |
Kings Chappell, and one of his late | Majesties Private
Musick. | [*line*] | *The third Edition revised and enlarged.* |
[*line*] | LONDON, | Printed for Humphrey Moseley | and
are to be sold at his Shop at the | signe of the Princes Armes
in St. | *Pauls*-Church-yard. 1651.

   Collation: 8°: Sigg. A–O⁸; Pp. [2]+221+[1]. Page
32 is misnumbered 35; 47, 61; 50, 64; 51, 65; 54, 68;
55, 69; 58, 72; 59, 73; 62, 76; 76, 78; 108, 109; 109,
108; 126, 125; 148, 149; 149, 148; 152, 1h5; 153, 159;
157, 163; 160, 150; 161, 151; 164, 154; 165, 155; 168,
158; 169, 159; 173, 163; 180, 181; 185, 186; 186, 187;
187, 186; 190, 186; 217, 216. Pages 171 (second title-
page) and 172 and 216 (both blank) are not numbered.

   Contents: P. [1], title; 1–170, Poems; [171], second
title-page, as follows:

Coelum Britannicum. | A | MASKE | AT | WHITE-
HALL IN | the Banqueting House, | on *Shrove-
Tuesday-night*, | the 18. of *February*, | 1633. | [*line*] |
The Inventors. | *Tho. Carew. Inigo Iones.* | [*line*] | *Non
habet ingenium*; Cæsar *sed jussit: habebo.* | *Cur me posse
negem, posse quod ille putat.* | [*line*] | LONDON, |
Printed for Hum. Moseley | and are to be sold at his
Shop at the | signe of the Princes Armes in St. | *Pauls*-
Church-yard. 1651.

163 [173]–215, text of masque; 215, The Names of the
Masquers, and The names of the young Lords and Noble-
mens Sonnes; 216 [217]–21, three additional poems;
[1], The Songs and Dialogues of this Booke were set
with apt Tunes to them, by Mr. *Henry Lawes*, one of His
Majesties Musicians.

A second issue in the same year has the following cancel
title-page:

POEMS, | With a | MASKE, | BY | *THOMAS
CAREW* Esq; | One of the Gent. of the Privy- | Cham-
ber, and Sewer in Ordi- | nary to his late Majestie. |
The *Songs* were set in *Musick* by | Mr. Henry Lawes
Gent. of the | Kings Chappell, and one of his late |
Majesties Private Musick. | [*line*] | *The third Edition*

revised and enlarged. | [*line*] | LONDON | Printed for
H. M. and are to be sold | by *J: Martin*, at the signe of
the | Bell in St. *Pauls*-Church- | Yard. 1651.

Moseley's text, with the exception of his three new poems
('Grieve not my *Celia*', 'You, that will a wonder know', and
To Celia, upon Love's Vbiquity), was set up from a copy of the
1642 edition. He corrected, however, a few obvious errors
and improved the punctuation, which was sometimes careless
in both the 1640 and 1642 texts. He advertised his volume
at the end of Brome's *Five new Playes*, 1653, in Sir Aston
Cokaines's *Dianea*, 1654, and in some copies of *The Last
Remains of S' John Suckling*, 1659. The fact that copies
remained for several years unsold may be taken to indicate
a waning interest in Carew's work, and Moseley died in
1661 without bringing out any other edition. His volume
completes the early printed sources for Carew's writings;
there were later reprints, but not until W. C. Hazlitt's
edition of 1870 was a systematic effort made to supplement
from manuscripts the canon of the 1651 edition.

ii. MANUSCRIPT SOURCES

Only a youthful signature, three letters, and one poem are
known to survive in Carew's own hand. The signature is
that in the Oxford University Subscription Register for
June 1608.[1] The letters were written to Sir Dudley Carleton,
after Carew's dismissal from Carleton's service, in the autumn
of 1616.[2] The poem is a copy, unsigned, of Carew's verses
headed 'To Ben Johnson Vppon occasion of his Ode to
Himself', and is to be dated about 1631.[3] One revision has
been made in this copy—'world' changed to 'age' in line
2—and there are a few other verbal discrepancies from the
printed text of 1640. There is a sixth document possibly in
Carew's hand, though the identification must be uncertain;
this is a copy of the lines 'To my Frend m' Georg Sandys',
signed Tho: Carew. It is pasted in a copy of Fry's *Selections*,
1810, owned by Mr. P. J. Dobell; its earlier history is un-
known. Many of the letters are formed in a manner charac-

1 Arch. S.P. 38, fol. 143.
2 Public Record Office, S.P. 14/88: 67, 14/88: 77, and 14/88: 87.
3 Ibid. S.P. 16/155: 79. See pp. 64–5 and p. 246.

---

teristic of Carew's hand, but if Carew's the writing has been somewhat modified by illness or fatigue. Textually the manuscript agrees with the lines prefixed to Sandys's *Paraphrase upon the Divine Poems*, 1638, rather than with the less perfect version in the *Poems* of 1640.

If Carew's own hand has left little, the hands of his contemporaries were obviously busy in multiplying copies of his poems—none of the copies, unfortunately, really authoritative. In the manuscript anthologies of his period Carew is easily one of the most popular poets. There seems to be, however, only one collection devoted almost exclusively to his work, or what was taken for his work: this is the first half of the 'Wyburd' MS. (now MS. Don.b.9, Bodleian Library), which was first described and used by W. C. Hazlitt for his edition of Carew in 1870. Its earlier history is not known. Half of the volume is devoted mostly to Carew; the rest, on paper of a different size but in the same hand, contains principally prose by Donne. Carew's pieces, intermingled with a few compositions in verse and in prose obviously not of his authorship, are forty-two in number, including seven of the nine versified Psalms; for four of these pieces (the Prologue and Epilogue to a play, the doubtfully canonical lines beginning 'Bright Albion, where the Queene of love', and Psalm 119) the manuscript is unique. A break in the text shows that some of its pages have been lost.

Another collection, containing sixty-five of the poems, is represented only by a list of titles at the end (fol. 89) of MS. S.23 (James 416), St. John's College, Cambridge. After each title appears the number of lines in the poem named. The list has no reference to the manuscript in which it occurs, though the latter, an anthology dating from about 1640, contains several of Carew's poems. It is also independent of the printed *Poems* of 1640, since it contains the following items not represented in that edition:

Dialogue song   35
(None of Carew's known songs or dialogues is 35 lines long. The poem may be one now lost.)
To the greene sicknes   18
(Probably the 18 lines beginning 'White Innocence', first included among Carew's poems by W. C. Hazlitt in 1870. The

poem *On Mistris N. to the greene sicknesse*, published in the
Poems of 1642, and 'Bright Albion', in the Wyburd MS., total
16 lines each.)

commanded to trauill,   26
(This poem is apparently lost.)

psalme. 119   353
(The only surviving version of this psalm, in the Wyburd MS.,
breaks off imperfectly at line 128. The total 353 is questionable,
since the psalm is rendered in couplets and an even number of
lines would be expected.)

psalme 1   30
psalme 2   30
(As preserved in MSS. Wyburd and Ashmole 38 this psalm con-
tains only 25 lines; the rendering omits nothing of the original.
It seems more likely that the present figure is erroneous, perhaps
miscopied from the line above it, than that Carew should have
made two versions of the psalm.)

psalme 51   44
psalme 113   15
psalme 114   20
psalme 137   45
psalme 91   30
psalme 14   72
(The 14 is clearly an error for 104; Carew's Psalm CIV is 72
lines long, and completes the list of nine psalms which he is
known to have translated.)

Of the remaining fifty-three titles, 'Song ——— 18' is too
vague for identification; but the rest of the poems appear in
the first 145 pages of the 1640 edition, combined with some
others (notably *A Rapture*) not contained in the list.

Carew's nine versified psalms occur in two principal collec-
tions: 2, 51, 91, 104, 113, 114, and 119 in the Wyburd
MS., and 1, 2, 51, 91, 104, 113, 114, and 137 in MS.
Ashmole 38, the latter a miscellany compiled by Nicholas
Burghe, who headed the renderings 'Eight Psalmes Trans-
lated by Mr Thomas Carew'. Some such collection must
have become known to Walkley, for on 27 June 1640—
soon, that is, after his publication of Carew's *Poems*—he
'Entred for his Copy . . . *Certaine Psalmes* of David trans-
lated into English verse by Thomas Carew Esquire'.[1] The

---

[1] Arber, *Transcript, 1554–1640*, iv. 488.

volume was never published, doubtless because the available
psalms were too few; there is no reason for supposing that
Carew translated more than the nine psalms known to-day.
The publication of one of these had been projected some
fifteen years earlier; this is shown by the inclusion of his
version of the 91st Psalm in MS. Rawl. poet. 61, which
contains *Certaine selected Psalmes of Dauid. (in Verse) differ-
ent from Those usually sung in the Church. Composed by Francis
Dauison esq*. deceased: and other Gentlemen. Manuscribed by
R. Crane.* The forty-five versions of thirty-five psalms are
signed Fr. Da., Jos. Br., Rich. Gipps., Chr. Da:, Th. Carey.
From a second title-page it appears that these renderings
were intended to be published with the *Meditations* of W.
Austen, which finally reached print in 1635; but that the
manuscript is nine or ten years earlier than this is suggested
by the date 1626 which Crane gives to a final collection in
his volume.[1] Psalm 104, which occurs in seven manuscripts,
may be assigned to an even earlier date from its inclusion in
MS. Egerton 2877, a compilation completed about 1622.
The only one of Carew's psalms to be printed before the
nineteenth century is 137, which was used as the first of
Henry Lawes's *Select Psalmes of a New Translation*, 1655.

Carew wrote or may have written fourteen other poems
which are preserved in manuscript. The *Prologue* and *Epi-
logue* from the Wyburd MS., though unsigned like the other
pieces in that collection, accompany his known poems there
and reveal a manner distinctively his. 'Bright Albion', in
the same manuscript, follows the two other poems which he
wrote on the Green Sickness ('Stay coward blood' and 'White
innocence'), but the strained and artificial style does not much
suggest his hand. 'White innocence' itself, *To his mistresse
retiring in affection*, *An Excuse of absence*, *A Ladies prayer to
Cupid*, and *On his Mistres lookeinge in a glasse*—this being
a variant of *A Looking-Glasse*—show close kinship with
Carew's known work and are ascribed to him in various
manuscripts. All of these pieces, including the nine psalms,
were first printed among Carew's poems by W. C. Hazlitt

[1] Crane was already an old man in the 1620s, and his career cannot be traced
later than 1632. See F. P. Wilson, 'Ralph Crane, Scrivener to the King's Players',
The Library, 4th series, vii (1927), 194–215.

in 1870. The poem *To a Friend*, assigned to Carew in MS. Ashmole 38, was published as Carew's by Philip Bliss in his edition of Wood's *Athenæ Oxonienses* (1815), and has been accepted as canonical by Hazlitt and succeeding editors. Bertram Dobell, to be sure, included it in his edition of William Strode, but cited no evidence in support of this attribution, and the lines themselves contain nothing to make us reject Carew's authorship. For *A Louers passion* there are manuscript attributions to both Carew and 'W. S.'—i.e. Strode.[1] It is printed anonymously in *Wits Interpreter*, 1655. Despite its mediocrity there are a few cadences suggestive of Carew—e.g.

> And 'tis heavens pleasure sure, shee should be sent
> As pure from earth to heaven, as shee was lent
> To vs.

But on the available evidence no assurance as to the authorship seems possible. The lines *To a Strumpett*, ascribed to 'TC' in MS. Add. 25303, were first published among Carew's poems by R. G. Howarth in 1931. They had previously been printed, in a version differing from that of the manuscripts, in Henry Bold's *Latin Songs, With their English: and Poems*, 1685, a volume collected and edited by Captain William Bold. The probability that Henry Bold is the author is strongly supported by comparison with other examples of his work in *Poems Lyrique Macaronique Heroique, &c.*, 1664 (some of the individual poems being dated from the 1640s), where he reveals a marked fondness for the Thersites strain. On the other hand, *To a Strumpett* is, within its genre, a great deal better than any of these pieces, and Bold's claim is further compromised by the fact that in a still earlier volume he plagiarizes copiously from Herrick and others. *A Health to a Mistris*, first included in Hazlitt's edition, is ascribed to Carew in MS. Harl. 6057, but in MS. Add. 15229 it is signed 'R: Clerke', and MS. Add. 21433 assigns it to 'R: C:' likewise. In *The Academy of Complements*, 1650, the lines are printed anonymously. Richard Clerke

---

[1] A third possible attribution is suggested by the fact that in MS. HM116 (Huntington Library) this poem immediately follows a transcription of 'Farewell, fair Saint', by Thomas Carey, Gentleman of the Bedchamber.

INTRODUCTION lxxiii

of Lincoln's Inn, Cowley's talented 'Friend and Cousen' upon whose death he published an Elegy in the *Poetical Blossomes*, 1633, should certainly have been capable of producing this little poem. A few others of his verses still exist in manuscript. The poem *Of his Mistresse* from MS. Add. 22602 might be a counter-piece to the authentic *A divine Mistris*. Thomas Jordan, in *Claraphil and Clarinda*, [1650?], prints a variant ('I will not *Saint* my fair *Clarinda*, SHE') with the unlikely reading 'for' for 'that' in the penultimate line. *The Departure*, included in Jordan's volume with the initials 'T. C.', was reprinted as possibly Carew's by Howarth in *Notes and Queries*, cxcvii (1952), 518, along with an answer presumably by Jordan himself. There remains, finally, a poem published as Carew's by Howarth in 1931; this is the set of verses *Vpon ye Royall Ship called ye Soueraign of ye Seas . . . 1637*, contained in a fair though slightly imperfect copy in MS. Add. 34217 with the signature 'Tho: Carew' and a Latin rendering signed 'Hen: Jacob'. We need not, however, depend upon a manuscript source for these verses, since they are reproduced by John Payne in the two upper corners of his engraving *The True Portraicture of his Maties Royall Ship the Soveraigne of the Seas built in the yeare 1637*; they are there signed 'Henr. Iacob' and 'Tho: Cary'. Jacob is readily identifiable as 'Henry Jacob of Merton coll. the greatest prodigy of criticism in his time',[1] who, shortly after being elected to a Merton fellowship in 1629, 'retired to London on private law-business'.[2] He turned into Latin verse Carew's *Ingratefull beauty threatned*, and the two men may have known each other. But the author of the English verses on *The Soveraigne of the Seas* seems likely to have been not Thomas Carew but his namesake Thomas Cary of Tower-Hill, a dogged but uninspired versifier to whose translation of Puget de la Serre's *The Mirrour which Flatters Not*, 1639, Henry Jacob contributed a series of verses in English, Latin, and Greek, headed '*To my endeared Friend, the Translatour*, Mr Thomas Cary'.[3]

---

[1] Wood, *Athenæ Oxonienses*, ed. Bliss, 1815, ii. 658.
[2] Brodrick, *Memorials of Merton College*, 1885, pp. 285–6.
[3] For further details concerning Cary and the poem see a discussion by the present editor in *Modern Language Notes* for April 1941.

Besides preserving these poems the manuscripts supply a few corrections for the early printed texts; their attributions help to check Walkley's and Moseley's canon; they supply a few dates and names not fully indicated in the early editions; and they often furnish alternative titles or readings which, even if there is no guarantee of authenticity, are of sufficient interest to be recorded, especially since they may afford cumulative evidence as to the nature and scope of Carew's revisions. A manuscript of particular interest and value for this latter purpose is Henry Lawes's autograph collection of his own songs, including thirty-eight with lyrics by Carew; here Carew's *A divine Mistris* appears with opening lines entirely different from those of the standard text, and some of the other lyrics show smaller variants. The best and most important of the non-musical miscellanies is MS. Harl. 6917, which contains thirty-five of Carew's poems in two groups, the order in each being nearly the same as that of the 1640 edition. Its variant readings are for the most part plausible, and probably authentic; the total impression is that of versions preliminary to those printed in 1640.[1] Another miscellany of some importance is MS. Harl. 3511, which contains twenty-seven of the poems; this is sometimes extremely close to the printed text of 1640, even as regards punctuation, though here also some of the poems appear in variant forms, some obviously corrupt and others apparently unrevised.[2]

A fuller adoption of manuscript readings than is resorted to for the present text is urged by C. L. Powell in an article which has apparently provoked no dissent since its publication more than thirty years ago.[3] The 1640 edition, he argues, was

compiled from a very faulty manuscript, as is shown by the fact that it includes several poems by other writers, omits several which are undoubtedly Carew's, and exhibits a text which in many cases certainly does not give us the actual words of the poet. . . . Since, as I have

[1] At a few points (e.g. p. 34, line 4; p. 47, line 5; p. 57, line 7) it preserves an apparently sound reading where the 1640 text is faulty.

[2] This manuscript is described fully by Geoffrey Tillotson, 'The Commonplace Book of Arthur Capell', *Modern Language Review*, xxvii (1932), pp. 381 ff.

[3] C. L. Powell, 'New Material on Thomas Carew', *Modern Language Review*, xi (1916), pp. 285 ff.

shown, the early printed copies were based on some manuscript similar to these, and a very faulty one at that, it must be clear that evidence drawn from any contemporary manuscript should have certainly equal weight with that of the first or succeeding early editions, as the latter failed to correct the mistakes already made. . . . In small matters there are differences of reading in almost every poem, and the editor here can do no more than take that reading which seems to him the best; in larger things a change of reading may legitimately be made where a passage is at present nonsense and a single new version is intelligible, or where the change is supported by the agreement of several manuscripts.

But to the principles thus enunciated there are three serious objections. First, it is a mistake to think that the manuscript source or sources of the 1640 *Poems* must have been 'very faulty' as a whole. It has been shown that the 'bad' section of the volume occupies only pages 168–206, which contain poems apparently added by Walkley to a more trustworthy though incomplete collection. Secondly, even for the poems on pages 168–206 the text shows no marked decline in quality; the particular faults of this section lie not in its readings but in its inclusion of poems not by Carew. Finally, some of Mr. Powell's suggested emendations, from MS. Harl. 6917 and other manuscripts, exemplify the dangers which are likely to attend the sort of eclecticism he proposes: in the second *Epitaph on the Lady Mary Villers*, for instance, he prefers an alternative text which, though possibly Carew's own preliminary version, halts both metrically and in sense, and in the *Epitaph on the Lady S.*, line 15, he would read 'whiter' for the demonstrably correct 'witty' of the 1640 *Poems*. The fact is that where divergencies exist between manuscript and printed versions the printed text of 1640 (or 1642 or 1651 in the case of poems then first printed) is almost always the clearer, the exacter, the smoother, and thus presumably the later and nearer to the poet's final intention. Accordingly the present text, except for correction of obvious errors, departs from these early printed versions only rarely and for specifically indicated reasons. A complete collation of the manuscript variants would necessitate an unreasonably bulky apparatus, but the most important of them have been reported in the Commentary.

iii. LATER EDITIONS

Collations of the first three editions of Carew's poems are given under 'Printed Sources' (pp. lxiv–lxviii); the subsequent editions and reprints are as follows:

4. Poems, Songs and Sonnets, Together with a Masque. By Thomas Carew, Esq; One of the Gentlemen of the Privy-Chamber, and Sewer in Ordinary to His late Majesty. The Songs set in Musick by Mr Henry Lawes, Gentleman of the Kings Chappel, and one of His late Majesties Private Musick. The Fourth Edition revised and enlarged. London, Printed for Henry Herringman at the Sign of the Blew Anchor in the New-Exchange. 1670. [8°: two issues, the second bearing a title-page which reads: Printed for H. Herringman at the Blew Anchor in the Lower Walk of the New Exchange, and are to be sold by Hobart Kemp at the Sign of the Ship in the Vpper Walk of the New Exchange, 1671. In both issues the separate title-page of *Coelum Britannicum* is dated 1670. The 'revised and enlarged' on the general title-page is incorrect; the volume is based entirely upon Humphrey Moseley's edition of 1651. The assignment to Herringman by Moseley's widow of her title to '*Poems with a maske* by Thomas Carewe Esqr', along with works by Cowley, Donne, Davenant, Crashaw, Jonson, Fanshawe, Suckling, and Denham, is dated 19 August 1667. (Arber, *Transcript, 1640–1708*, ii. 380.) Herringman licensed the volume on 22 November 1670 for publication in Michaelmas Term. (Arber, *The Term Catalogues, 1668–1709*, i. 62.)]

5. Poems, Songs, and Sonnets: Together with a Masque. By Thomas Carew, Esq; . . . A new Edition . . . Printed for T. Davies, . . . M DCC LXXII. [12°. Davies, who according to Doctor Johnson had 'learning enough to give credit to a clergyman', introduces the volume with a seven-page 'Life of Thomas Carew', and furnishes occasional notes. He prints from the text of 1670–1.]

6. A reprint of Davies's text, with a short 'Life', in Anderson, *A Complete Edition of the Poets of Great Britain*, 1793.

7. Another reprint from Davies, with a short 'Life', in Chalmers, *The Works of the English Poets . . . in twenty-one volumes*, 1810.

8. A Selection from the Poetical Works of Thomas Carew . . . 1810. [Edited by John Fry, who printed from the edition of 1642 and supplied a Preface, a brief Biographical Notice, and a few notes. Fry's announced project of a complete edition did not reach fulfilment. A copy of the 1810 volume in the Dyce Collec-

tion, South Kensington, contains manuscript notes which he collected for this purpose.]

9. A selection in *The Works of the British Poets. With Lives of the Authors*, by Ezekiel Sanford ... Philadelphia, 1819.

10. The Works of Thomas Carew ... Reprinted from the Original Edition of M.DC.XL. Edinburgh: Printed for W. and C. Tait. M.DCCC.XXIV. [8°. The text, which is preceded by a biographical and critical Notice, is a reprint of the *Poems*, 1640, with original spelling but modernized punctuation. An Appendix contains the poems added in 1642 and 1651; the text of these is very carelessly reproduced, and the spelling modernized. In the prefatory Notice is a reprint of Carew's version of Psalm 137 as published from manuscript by Philip Bliss in his edition of Wood's *Athenæ Oxonienses*, 1815. Hazlitt states that the volume was edited by Thomas Maitland (Lord Dundrennan) and only 125 copies printed.]

11. A selection in Southey's *Select Works of the British Poets, from Chaucer to Jonson*, 1831.

12. The Poetical Works of Thomas Carew ... London: H. G. Clarke and Co., 1845. [The text, reprinted apparently from 1824 though with modernized spelling, is preceded by an anonymous Memoir, biographical and critical.]

13. The Poems of Thomas Carew ... Now first collected and edited with notes from the former editions and new notes and a memoir by W. Carew Hazlitt. The text formed from a collation of all the old printed copies and many early MSS. Printed for the Roxburghe Library [London] M DCCC LXX. [The first scholarly edition. For his text Hazlitt collated seventeen manuscripts with the early editions, and his footnotes reproduce the commentary of Davies and subsequent editors. He prints a number of new poems from manuscript, some of them unfortunately the well-attested work of Ben Jonson, Michael Drayton, Dr. Henry King, Thomas Carey (Gentleman of the Bedchamber), and others; and in his prefatory 'Some Account of Thomas Carew' he confuses the poet with another Thomas Carew who was rector of Sunninghill. His text is highly eclectic.]

14. The Poems and Masque of Thomas Carew ... with an Introductory Memoir, an Appendix of Unauthenticated Poems from MSS., Notes, and a Table of First Lines. Edited by Joseph Woodfall Ebsworth, M.A., F.S.A., Etc. London: Reeves and Turner, ... 1893. [The text, in modernized spelling, seems to derive from a copy of Hazlitt's edition, imperfectly corrected. In

addition, Ebsworth rewrites a number of lines (such as the final couplet of *A Rapture*) which he finds morally or artistically unsatisfactory. His commentary contains many unsupported statements, some of them demonstrably wrong.]

15. The Poems of Thomas Carew edited by Arthur Vincent. London: Lawrence & Bullen, Ltd. . . . New York: Charles Scribner's Sons . . . 1899. (The Muses Library; later issues carry the imprint of Routledge, n.d.) [A modernized text, with good introduction and notes. Vincent corrects nearly all of Hazlitt's mistakes in biography and canon, but with perhaps excessive caution rejects all but three of the poems from manuscript.]

16. A selection in *Orinda Booklets* no. 2, 1903, with an appreciative Preface by H. A. S[purr].

17. *A Rapture* . . . with engravings by J. E. Laboureur. Waltham Saint Lawrence, 1927. Golden Cockerel Press. [Text from *Poems*, 1640.]

18. Minor Poets of the Seventeenth Century edited with an Introduction by R. G. Howarth. Dent (Everyman's Library), 1931. [A sound modernized text of Carew, complete except for *Coelum Britannicum* and a few verses of doubtful authenticity. The volume also contains the poems of Suckling, Lovelace, and Lord Herbert of Cherbury. The introduction is a critical essay on the four poets.]

NOTE

In the footnotes and commentary reference is made to manuscript and printed sources as follows:

	MSS.		Sigla
British Museum	Additional	11811	A118
	"	14047	A14
	"	15227	A15
	"	18220	A18
	"	19268	A19
	"	21433	A21
	"	22118	A221
	"	22602	A226
	"	23229	A23
	"	25303	A303
	"	25707	A7
	"	30982	A30
	"	31434	A4
	Egerton	2013	E20
	"	2421	E24
	"	2877	E28
	Harley	3511	H35
	"	4955	H4
	"	6057	H6
	"	6917	H17
	"	6918	H18
	"	6931	H31
	Lansdowne	777	L
	Sloane	1446	S14
	"	1792	S17
Bodleian Library	Rawl. poet.	61	R6
	"	84	R84
	"	199	R1
	"	209	R2
	Eng. poet.	E.37	C
	Don.b.9		W
	Ashmole	36–37	Ash 36
	"	38	Ash 38
	"	47	Ash 47
	Malone	13	M13
St. John's College, Cambridge	S.23 (James 416)		S.23
	S.32 (James 423)		S.32

	MSS.	*Sigla*
Public Record Office	S.P. 16/155:79	PRO
New York Public Library	Drexel 4257	Dx
Henry E. Huntington	HM116	HM116
Library	HM172	HM172
	HM198	HM198
Miss Naomi D. Church,	A volume of songs with	
Beaconsfield	music, in the auto-	
	graph of Henry Lawes	HL

(There is an account of this manuscript in Todd's *Poetical Works of John Milton*, 1801, v. 213–14. Several pages are reproduced in facsimile in *The Poems of Richard Lovelace*, ed. C. H. Wilkinson, 2 vols., 1925.)

P. J. Dobell, Esq.,	Three manuscript	D2, D4,
Tunbridge Wells	miscellanies	and D8

(*D2* is a folio containing poems, mostly unsigned, by several authors; six are Carew's. Inscribed: 'Miscentur seria iocis. | 1647. | Elegies, Exequies, Epitaphes, Epigrams, Songs | Satires and other Poems.' *D4* is a quarto marked: Phillipps MS 9510. Strode is strongly represented, and there are elegies on the death of Gustavus Adolphus; four poems are by Carew. *D8* is an octavo devoted principally to Strode and Donne; Carew's name does not appear, but eleven of the poems are his, one being misattributed to Donne and three to Strode.)

The 1634 edition of *Coelum Britannicum* is indicated by *34*. The letters *a, c, d, f, h, m, p, t, w*, and *x* refer to different copies of that edition (see pp. lx–lxi). The printed *Poems* of 1640, 1642, 1651, and 1670–1 are indicated by *40, 42, 51*, and *70*. Later editions are indicated by either the year in full or the name of the editor.

POEMS.

By
THOMAS CAREVV
Efquire.

One of the Gentlemen of the
Privie-Chamber, and Sewer in
Ordinary to His Majesty.

───────────────

───────────────

LONDON,

Printed by *I. D.* for *Thomas Walkley,*
and are to be fold at the figne of the
flying Horfe, between Brittains
Burfe, and York-Houfe.
1640

Title-page, first edition (British Museum, shelfmark C.71.a.9)

POEMS.

The Spring.

NOW that the winter's gone, the earth hath lost
   Her snow-white robes, and now no more the frost
Candies the grasse, or castes an ycie creame
Vpon the silver Lake, or Chrystall streame:
But the warme Sunne thawes the benummed Earth,   5
And makes it tender, gives a sacred birth
To the dead Swallow; wakes in hollow tree
The drowzie Cuckow, and the Humble-Bee.
Now doe a quire of chirping Minstrels bring
In tryumph to the world, the youthfull Spring.   10
The Vallies, hills, and woods, in rich araye,
Welcome the comming of the long'd for May.
Now all things smile; onely my *Love* doth lowre:
Nor hath the scalding Noon-day-Sunne the power,
To melt that marble yce, which still doth hold   15
Her heart congeald, and makes her pittie cold.
The Oxe which lately did for shelter flie
Into the stall, doth now securely lie
Jn open fields; and love no more is made
By the fire side; but in the cooler shade   20
Amyntas now doth with his *Cloris* sleepe
Vnder a Sycamoure, and all things keepe
Time with the season, only shee doth carry
Iune in her eyes, in her heart *Ianuary*.

Except where otherwise indicated, the text is that of Carew's *Poems*, 1640. For
explanation of symbols see pp. lxxix–lxxx.
  The Spring. 6 sacred] second *A118, A23, H6, HM198. See Commentary*
8 Humble-Bee. *51*: Humble-Bee, *40*   20 shade *51*: shade. *40*: shade, *42*

To

To *A. L.*

Perswasions to love.

THinke not cause men flatt'ring say,
Y' are fresh as Aprill, sweet as May,
Bright as is the morning starre,
That you are so, or though you are
Be not therefore proud, and deeme   5
All men unworthy your esteeme.
For being so, you loose the pleasure
Of being faire, since that rich treasure
Of rare beauty, and sweet feature
Was bestow'd on you by nature   10
To be enjoy'd, and 'twere a sinne,
There to be scarce, where shee hath bin
So prodigall of her best graces;
Thus common beauties, and meane faces
Shall have more pastime, and enjoy   15
The sport you loose by being coy.
Did the thing for which I sue
Onely concerne my selfe not you,
Were men so fram'd as they alone
Reap'd all the pleasure, women none,   20
Then had you reason to be scant;
But 'twere a madnesse not to grant
That which affords (if you consent)
To you the giver, more content
Then me the beggar; Oh then bee   25
Kinde to your selfe if not to mee;
Starue not your selfe, because you may
Thereby make me pine away;
Nor let brittle beautie make
You your wiser thoughts forsake: 30
For that lovely face will faile,
Beautie's sweet, but beautie's fraile;
'Tis sooner past, 'tis sooner done
Then Summers raine, or winters Sun:

To A. L. 2 Aprill, *42*: April *40*

Most

Most fleeting when it is most deare,   35
'Tis gone while wee but say 'tis here.
These curious locks so aptly twind,
Whose every haire 'a soule doth bind,
Will change their abroun hue, and grow
White, and cold as winters snow.   40
That eye which now is *Cupids* nest
Will proue his grave, and all the rest
Will follow; in the cheeke, chin, nose
Nor lilly shall be found nor rose.
And what will then become of all   45
Those, whom now you servants call?
Like swallowes when your summers done,
They'le flye and seeke some warmer Sun.
Then wisely chuse one to your friend,
Whose love may, when your beauties end,   50
Remaine still firme: be provident
And thinke before the summers spent
Of following winter; like the Ant
In plenty hoord for time of scant.
Cull out amongst the multitude   55
Of lovers, that seeke to intrude
Into your favour, one that may
Love for an age, not for a day;
One that will quench your youthfull fires,
And feed in age your hot desires.   60
For when the stormes of time have mou'd
Waves on that cheeke which was belou'd,
When a faire Ladies face is pin'd
And yellow spred, where red once shin'd,
When beauty, youth, and all sweets leave her,   65
Love may returne, but lover never:
And old folkes say there are no paynes
Like itch of love in aged vaines.
Oh love me then, and now begin it,
Let us not loose this present minute: 70
For time and age will worke that wrack

47 your *40* (*Errata*): their *40* (*Text*): the *most MSS.*   58 day; *51*: day. *40*
61 mou'd] mou'd, *40*: mov'd *42, 51*   65 beauty, *51*: beauty *40*   66
never: *51*: never. *40*

Which

Which time or age shall ne're call backe.
The snake each yeare fresh skin resumes,
And Eagles change their aged plumes;
The faded Rose each spring, receives   75
A fresh red tincture on her leaves:
But if your beauties once decay,
You never know a second *May*.
Oh, then be wise, and whilst your season
Affords you dayes for sport, doe reason;   80
Spend not in vaine your lives short houre,
But crop in time your beauties flower:
Which will away, and doth together
Both bud, and fade, both blow and wither.

Lips and Eyes.

IN *Celia's* face a question did arise
    Which were more beautifull, her lips or eyes:
We (said the eyes,) send forth those poynted darts
Which pierce the hardest adamantine hearts.
From us (replyd the lips,) proceed those blisses   5
Which louers reape by kind words and sweet kisses.
Then wept the eyes, and from their springs did powre
Of liquid orientall pearle a shower.
Whereat the lips, mou'd with delight and pleasure,
Through a sweete smile vnlockt their pearlie treasure; 10
And bad Love judge, whether did adde more grace:
Weeping or smiling pearles to *Celia's* face.

A divine Mistris.

IN natures peeces still I see
    Some errour, that might mended bee;
Something my wish could still remove,
Alter or adde; but my faire love

80 sport, *51*: sport *40*
Lips and Eyes. 4 hearts.] hearts *40 (some copies)*   9 lips,] lips *40*   10
treasure; *51*: treasure. *40*   11 Love *51*: love *40*   grace:] graee. *40 (some*
copies)

Was

Was fram'd by hands farre more divine;   5
For she hath every beauteous line:
Yet I had beene farre happier,
Had Nature that made me, made her;
Then likenes, might (that love creates)
Have made her love what now she hates: 10
Yet I confesse I cannot spare
From her iust shape the smallest haire;
Nor need I beg from all the store
Of heaven, for her one beautie more:
Shee hath too much divinity for mee,   15
You Gods teach her some more humanitie.

SONG.

A beautifull Mistris.

IF when the Sun at noone displayes
   His brighter rayes,
   Thou but appeare,
He then all pale with shame and feare,
   Quencheth his light,   5
Hides his darke brow, flyes from thy sight,
  And growes more dimme
Compar'd to thee, then starres to him.
If thou but show thy face againe,
When darkenesse doth at midnight raigne,   10
The darkenesse flyes, and light is hurl'd
Round about the silent world:
So as alike thou driu'st away
Both light and darkenesse, night and day.

A divine Mistris. 11 spare] spare, *40*
Song. 11 hurl'd] hurl'd, *40*   13 away] away, *40*

A

A cruell Mistris.

WEE read of Kings and Gods that kindly tooke
    A pitcher fil'd with water from the brooke;
But I have dayly tendred without thankes
Rivers of teares that overflow their bankes.
A slaughter'd bull will appease angry *Iove*,   5
A horse the Sun, a Lambe the God of love,
But shee disdaines the spotlesse sacrifice
Of a pure heart that at her altar lyes.
Vesta is not displeas'd if her chast vrne
Doe with repayred fuell ever burne;   10
But my Saint frownes though to her honour'd name
I consecrate a never dying flame.
Th' Assyrian King did none i'th' furnace throw,
But those that to his Image did not bow;
With bended knees J daily worship her,   15
Yet she consumes her owne Idolater.
Of such a Goddesse no times leave record,
That burnt the temple where she was ador'd.

SONG.

Murdring beautie.

ILe gaze no more on her bewitching face,
   Since ruine harbours there in every place:
For my enchanted soule alike shee drownes
With calmes and tempests of her smiles and frownes.
I'le love no more those cruell eyes of hers,   5
Which pleas'd or anger'd still are murderers:
For if she dart (like lightning) through the ayre
Her beames of wrath, she kils me with despaire.
Jf shee behold me with a pleasing eye,
I surfet with excesse of joy, and dye.   10

A cruell Mistris. 1 tooke] tooke, 40: took 51   5 *Iove,* 42: *Iove* 40   11
name 42: name, 40 (*some copies*): name: 40 (*other copies*)
    Song. 4 *frownes.*] *frownes,* 40 (*some copies*)   8 *wrath,*] *wrat,* 40 (*some copies*)

My

My mistris commanding me
to returne her letters.

SO grieves th' adventrous Merchant, when he throwes
All the long toyld for treasure his ship stowes,
Into the angry maine, to save from wrack
Himselfe and men, as I grieve to give backe
These letters, yet so powerfull is your sway,   5
As if you bid me die I must obey.
Goe then blest papers, you shall kisse those hands
That gave you freedome, but hold me in bands,
Which with a touch did give you life, but I
Because I may not touch those hands, must die.   10
Me thinkes, as if they knew they should be sent
Home to their native soile from banishment,
I see them smile, like dying Saints, that know
They are to leave the earth, and tow'rd heaven goe.
When you returne, pray tell your Soveraigne   15
And mine, I gave you courteous entertaine;
Each line receiv'd a teare, and then a kisse,
First bath'd in that, it scap'd vnscorcht from this:
I kist it because your hand had been there
But 'cause it was not now, I shed a teare.   20
Tell her no length of time, nor change of ayre,
No crueltie, disdaine, absence, dispaire;
No nor her stedfast constancie can deterre,
My vassall heart from ever hon'ring her.
Though these be powerfull arguments to prove   25
I love in vaine; yet I must ever love.
Say, if she frowne when you that word rehearse,
Service in prose, is oft call'd love in verse:
Then pray her, since I send back on my part
Her papers, she will send me back my heart.   30
If she refuse, warne her to come before
The God of Love, whom thus I will implore.
Trav'ling thy Countries road (*great God*) I spide
By chance this Lady, and walkt by her side
From place, to place, fearing no violence,   35

My mistris, &c. 26 love. 51: love; 40

For

For I was well arm'd, and had made defence
In former fights, 'gainst fiercer foes, then shee
Did at our first incounter seeme to bee.
But going farther, every step reveal'd
Some hidden weapon, till that time conceal'd.   40
Seeing those outward armes, I did begin
To feare, some greater strength was lodg'd within.
Looking into her mind, I might survay
An hoast of beauties that in ambush lay;
And won the day before they fought the field;   45
For I unable to resist, did yeild.
But the insulting tyrant so destroyes
My conquer'd mind, my ease, my peace, my joyes,
Breaks my sweete sleepes, invades my harmelesse rest,
Robs me of all the treasure of my brest,   50
Spares not my heart, nor yet a greater wrong;
For having stolne my heart, she binds my tongue.
But at the last her melting eyes vnseal'd,
My lips, enlarg'd, my tongue, then I reveal'd
To her owne eares the story of my harmes   55
Wrought by her vertues, and her beauties charmes.
Now heare (*Iust judge*) an act of savagenesse,
When I complaine in hope to find redresse,
Shee bends her angry brow, and from her eye,
Shootes thousand darts, I then well hop'd to die,   60
But in such soveraigne balme, love dips his shot
That though they wound a heart, they kill it not;
Shee saw the bloud gush forth from many a wound,
Yet fled, and left me bleeding on the ground,
Nor sought my cure, nor saw me since: 'tis true   65
Absence, and time, (two cunning Leaches) drew
The flesh together, yet sure though the skin
Be clos'd without, the wound festers within.
Thus hath this cruell Lady, vs'd a true
Servant, and subject to her selfe, and you,   70
Nor know I (great Love,) if my life be lent
To shew thy mercy or my punishment;
Since by the onely Magick of thy Art

42 within. *51*: within, *40*   56 charmes.] charmes; *40*: charms. *51*
wound] wouud *40*   71 lent *40* (*Errata*), MSS.: sent *40* (*Text*)

A lover still may live that wants his heart.
If this enditement fright her, so as shee   75
Seeme willing to returne my heart to mee,
But cannot find it, (for perhaps it may
Mong'st other trifeling hearts be out oth' way,)
If she repent and would make me amends
Bid her but send me hers, and we are friends.   80

Secresie protested.

FEare not (deare Love) that I'le reveale
Those houres of pleasure we two steale;
No eye shall see, nor yet the Sun
Descry, what thou and I have done;
No eare shall heare our love, but wee   5
Silent as the night will bee.
The God of love himselfe (whose dart
Did first wound mine, and then thy heart)
Shall never know, that we can tell
What sweets in stolne embraces dwell.   10
This only meanes may find it out,
If when I dye, Physicians doubt
What caus'd my death, and there to view
Of all their judgements which was true,
Rip up my heart, Oh then I feare   15
The world will see thy picture there.

A prayer to the Wind.

GOe thou gentle whispering wind,
Beare this sigh; and if thou find
Where my cruell faire doth rest,
Cast it in her snowie brest,
So, enflamed by my desire,   5
It may set her heart a-fire.

77 may] may; 40: may, 42, 51   78 way,)] way.) 40: way) 42, 51
A prayer, &c. *Several versions exist; see Commentary.*

Those

Those sweet kisses thou shalt gaine,
Will reward thee for thy paine:
Boldly light upon her lip,
There suck odours, and thence skip   10
To her bosome; lastly fall
Downe, and wander over all:
Range about those Ivorie hills,
From whose every part distills
Amber deaw; there spices grow,   15
There pure streames of Nectar flow;
There perfume thy selfe, and bring
All those sweets upon thy wing:
As thou return'st, change by thy power,
Every weed into a flower;   20
Turne each Thistle to a Vine,
Make the Bramble Eglantine.
For so rich a bootie made,
Doe but this, and I am payd.
Thou canst with thy powerfull blast,   25
Heat apace, and coole as fast:
Thou canst kindle hidden flame,
And ag'en destroy the same;
Then for pittie, either stir
Vp the fire of love in her,   30
That alike both flames may shine,
Or else quite extinguish mine.

Mediocritie in love rejected.

SONG.

GIve me more love, or more disdaine;
    The Torrid, or the frozen Zone,
Bring equall ease unto my paine;
    The temperate affords me none:
Either extreame, of love, or hate,   5
Is sweeter than a calme estate.

Give

Give me a storme; if it be love,
   Like Danae *in that golden showre*
I swimme in pleasure; if it prove
   Disdaine, that torrent will devoure   10
My Vulture-hopes; and he's possest
Of Heaven, that's but from Hell releast:
   Then crowne my joyes, or cure my paine;
   Give me more love, or more disdaine.

Good counsel to a young Maid.
SONG.

G<small>*Aze not on thy beauties pride,*</small>
   Tender Maid, in the false tide,
That from Lovers eyes doth slide.

Let thy faithfull Crystall show,
How thy colours come, and goe: 5
Beautie takes a foyle from woe.

Love, that in those smooth streames lyes,
Vnder pitties faire disguise,
Will thy melting heart surprize.

Netts, of passions finest thred,   10
Snaring Poems, will be spred,
All, to catch thy maiden-head.

Then beware, for those that cure
Loves disease, themselves endure
For reward, a Calenture.   15

Rather let the Lover pine,
Then his pale cheeke, should assigne
A perpetuall blush to thine.

Mediocritie, &c. 12 *release:* 51: *release;* 40
Good counsel, &c. 5 *goe:*] *goe,* 40   10 *passions* 51: *passion* 40

To

To my Mistris sitting by
a Rivers side.
AN EDDY.

MArke how yond Eddy steales away,
 From the rude streame into the Bay,
There lockt up safe, she doth divorce
Her waters from the chanels course,
And scornes the Torrent, that did bring   5
Her headlong from her native spring.
Now doth she with her new love play,
Whilst he runs murmuring away.
Marke how she courts the bankes, whilst they
As amorously their armes display,   10
T'embrace, and clip her silver waves:
See how she strokes their sides, and craves
An entrance there, which they deny;
Whereat she frownes, threatning to flye
Home to her streame, and 'gins to swim   15
Backward, but from the chanels brim,
Smiling, returnes into the creeke,
With thousand dimples on her cheeke.
 Be thou this Eddy, and I'le make
My breast thy shore, where thou shalt take   20
Secure repose, and never dreame
Of the quite forsaken streame:
Let him to the wide Ocean hast,
There lose his colour, name, and tast;
Thou shalt save all, and safe from him,   25
Within these armes for ever swim.

SONG. Conquest

SONG.
Conquest by flight.

*L*Adyes, *flye from Love's smooth tale,*
  Oathes steep'd in teares doe oft prevaile;
Griefe is infectious, and the ayre
Enflam'd with sighes, will blast the fayre:
Then stop your eares, when lovers cry,   5
Lest your selfe weepe, when no soft eye
Shall with a sorrowing teare repay
That pittie which you cast away.
  Young men fly, when beautie darts
Amorous glances at your hearts: 10
The fixt marke gives the shooter ayme;
And Ladyes lookes have power to mayme;
Now 'twixt their lips, now in their eyes,
Wrapt in a smile, or kisse, Love lyes;
Then flye betimes, for only they   15
Conquer love that run away.

SONG.
To my inconstant Mistris.

*W*Hen thou, *poore excommunicate*
  From all the joyes of love, shalt see
The full reward, and glorious fate,
  Which my strong faith shall purchase me,
Then curse thine owne inconstancie.   5

A fayrer hand then thine, shall cure
  That heart, which thy false oathes did wound;
And to my soule, a soule more pure
  Than thine, shall by Loves hand be bound,
  And both with equall glory crown'd.   10

Song. Conquest, &c. 6 *eye 51: eye, 40*   9 *darts 51: darts, 40*

Then

Then shalt thou weepe, entreat, complaine
To Love, as I did once to thee;
When all thy teares shall be as vaine
As mine were then, for thou shalt bee
Damn'd for thy false Apostasie.   15

SONG.

Perswasions to enjoy.

IF the quick spirits in your eye
   Now languish, and anon must dye;
If every sweet, and every grace,
Must fly from that forsaken face:
      Then (Celia) let us reape our joyes,   5
      E're time such goodly fruit destroyes.

Or, if that golden fleece must grow
For ever, free from aged snow;
If those bright Suns must know no shade,
Nor your fresh beauties ever fade: 10
Then feare not (Celia) to bestow,
What still being gather'd, still must grow.
   Thus, either Time *his Sickle brings*
   In vaine, or else in vaine his wings.

A deposition from Love.

I Was foretold, your rebell sex,
   Nor love, nor pitty knew;
And with what scorne, you use to vex
   Poore hearts, that humbly sue;
Yet I believ'd, to crowne our paine,   5
   Could we the fortresse win,
The happy lover sure should gaine
   A Paradise within:
I thought loves plagues, like Dragons sate,
Only to fright us at the gate.   10

Song. 8 *snow*;] *snow*: 40   10 *fade*:] *fade*; 40
A deposition, &c.   7 *gaine*] gaine, 40: gain 51

But

But I did enter, and enjoy,
   What happy lovers prove;
For I could kisse, and sport, and toy,
   And tast those sweets of love;
Which had they but a lasting state,   15
   Or if in *Celia's* brest,
The force of love might not abate,
   Jove were too meane a guest.
But now her breach of faith, far more
Afflicts, then did her scorne before.   20

Hard fate! to have been once possest
   As victor, of a heart,
Atchiev'd with labour, and unrest,
   And then forc'd to depart.
If the stout Foe will not resigne,   25
   When I besiege a Towne,
I lose, but what was never mine;
   But he that is cast downe
From enjoy'd beautie, feeles a woe,
Onely deposed Kings can know.   30

Ingratefull beauty threatned.

KNow *Celia*, (since thou art so proud,)
   'Twas I that gave thee thy renowne:
Thou hadst, in the forgotten crowd
   Of common beauties, liv'd unknowne,
Had not my verse exhal'd thy name,   5
And with it, ympt the wings of fame.

That killing power is none of thine,
   I gave it to thy voyce, and eyes:
Thy sweets, thy graces, all are mine;
   Thou art my starre, shin'st in my skies;   10
Then dart not from thy borrowed sphere
Lightning on him, that fixt thee there.

17 not *42*: nor *40*   abate, *51*: abate; *40*

Tempt me with such affrights no more,
    Lest what I made, I uncreate;
Let fooles thy mystique formes adore,   15
    I'le know thee in thy mortall state:
Wise Poets that wrap't Truth in tales,
Knew her themselves, through all her vailes.

Disdaine returned.

HEE that loves a Rosie cheeke,
    Or a corall lip admires,
Or from star-like eyes doth seeke
    Fuell to maintaine his fires;
As old *Time* makes these decay,   5
So his flames must waste away.

But a smooth, and stedfast mind,
    Gentle thoughts, and calme desires,
Hearts, with equall love combind,
    Kindle never dying fires.   10
Where these are not, I despise
Lovely cheekes, or lips, or eyes.

No teares, *Celia*, now shall win,
    My resolv'd heart, to returne;
I have searcht thy soule within,   15
    And find nought, but pride, and scorne;
I have learn'd thy arts, and now
    Can disdaine as much as thou.
Some power, in my revenge convay
That love to her, I cast away.   20

Disdaine returned. 3 seeke] seeke, *40*: seek *51*   19 convay] convay, *40*: convey *51*

A Loo-

A Looking-Glasse.

THat flattring Glasse, whose smooth face weares
   Your shadow, which a Sunne appeares,
Was once a river of my teares.

About your cold heart, they did make
A circle, where the brinie lake   5
Congeal'd, into a crystall cake.

Gaze no more on that killing eye,
For feare the native crueltie
Doome you, as it doth all, to dye.

For feare lest the faire object move   10
Your froward heart to fall in love,
Then you your selfe my rivall prove.

Looke rather on my pale cheekes pin'de,
There view your beauties, there you'le finde
A faire face, but a cruell minde.   15

Be not for ever frozen, coy;
One beame of love, will soone destroy,
And melt that yce, to flouds of joy.

An Elegie on the La : PEN : sent to my Mistresse out of France.

LEt him, who from his tyrant Mistresse, did
   This day receive his cruell doome, forbid
His eyes to weepe that losse, and let him here
Open those floud-gates, to bedeaw this beere;
So shall those drops, which else would be but brine,   5
Be turn'd to Manna, falling on her shrine.

A Looking-Glasse. *An alternative version is included under the Poems from Manuscript, p. 132.*   10 move 51: move, 40

Let

Let him, who banisht farre from her deere sight
Whom his soule loves, doth in that absence write
Or lines of passion, or some powerfull charmes,
To vent his owne griefe, or unlock her armes;   10
Take off his pen, and in sad verse bemone
This generall sorrow, and forget his owne;
So may those Verses live, which else must dye;
For though the Muses give eternitie
When they embalme with verse, yet she could give   15
Life unto that Muse, by which others live.
Oh pardon me (faire soule) that boldly have
Dropt, though but one teare, on thy silent grave,
And writ on that earth, which such honour had,
To cloath that flesh, wherein thy selfe was clad.   20
And pardon me (sweet Saint) whom I adore,
That I this tribute pay, out of the store
Of lines, and teares, that's only due to thee;
Oh, doe not thinke it new Idolatrie;
Though you are only soveraigne of this Land,   25
Yet universall losses may command
A subsidie from every private eye,
And presse each pen to write; so to supply,
And feed the common griefe; if this excuse
Prevaile not, take these teares to your owne use,   30
As shed for you; for when I saw her dye,
I then did thinke on your mortalitie;
For since nor vertue, witt, nor beautie, could
Preserve from Death's hand, this their heavenly mould,
Where they were framed all, and where they dwelt,   35
I then knew you must dye too, and did melt
Into these teares, but thinking on that day:
And when the gods resolv'd to take away
A Saint from us, I that did know what dearth
There was of such good soules upon the earth,   40
Began to feare lest Death, their Officer,
Might have mistooke, and taken thee for her;

An Elegie, &c. 8 write] write, 40   18 grave,] grave. 40: grave; 51   33
witt, 51, all MSS.: will, 40   34 mould, 51: mould. 40   37 teares,]
teares: 40   day:] day, 40   39 us, 51: us; 40   41 Officer, 42:
Officer 40

So

So had'st thou rob'd us of that happinesse
Which she in heaven, and I in thee possesse.
But what can heaven to her glory adde?   45
The prayses she hath dead, living she had,
To say she's now an Angell, is no more
Praise then she had, for she was one before;
Which of the Saints can shew more votaries
Then she had here? even those that did despise   50
The Angels, and may her now she is one,
Did whilst she liv'd with pure devotion
Adore, and worship her; her vertues had
All honour here, for this world was too bad
To hate, or envy her; these cannot rise   55
So high, as to repine at Deities:
But now she's 'mongst her fellow Saints, they may
Be good enough to envy her; this way
There's losse i'th' change 'twixt heav'n and earth, if she
Should leave her servants here below, to be   60
Hated of her competitors above;
But sure her matchlesse goodnesse needs must move
Those blest soules to admire her excellence;
By this meanes only can her journey hence
To heaven prove gaine, if as she was but here   65
Worshipt by men, she be by Angels there.
But I must weepe no more over this urne,
My teares to their owne chanell must returne;
And having ended these sad obsequies,
My Muse must back to her old exercise,   70
To tell the story of my martyrdome:
But, oh thou Idoll of my soule, become
Once pittifull, that she may change her stile,
Drie up her blubbred eyes, and learne to smile.
Rest then blest soule; for as ghosts flye away,   75
When the shrill Cock proclaimes the infant-day,
So must I hence, for loe I see from farre,
The minions of the Muses comming are,
Each of them bringing to thy sacred Herse,
In either eye a teare, each hand a Verse.   80

55 her; 42: her, 40   58 her;] her, 40   way] way. Hazlitt, Ebsworth
66 there.] there 40 (some copies)   75 soule; 42: soule, 40 (some copies)

To

To my Mistresse in absence.

THough I must live here, and by force
   Of your command suffer divorce;
Though I am parted, yet my mind,
(That's more my selfe) still stayes behind;
I breath in you, you keepe my heart;   5
'Twas but a carkasse that did part.
Then though our bodyes are dis-joynd,
As things that are to place confin'd;
Yet let our boundlesse spirits meet,
And in loves spheare each other greet;   10
There let us worke a mystique wreath,
Vnknowne unto the world beneath;
There let our claspt loves sweetly twin;
There let our secret thoughts unseen,
Like nets be weav'd, and inter-twin'd,   15
Wherewith wee'le catch each others mind:
There whilst our soules doe sit and kisse,
Tasting a sweet, and subtle blisse,
(Such as grosse lovers cannot know,
Whose hands, and lips, meet here below;)   20
Let us looke downe, and marke what paine
Our absent bodyes here sustaine,
And smile to see how farre away
The one, doth from the other stray;
Yet burne, and languish with desire   25
To joyne, and quench their mutuall fire.
There let us joy to see from farre,
Our emulous flames at loving warre,
Whilst both with equall luster shine,
Mine bright as yours, yours bright as mine.   30
There seated in those heavenly bowers,
Wee'le cheat the lag, and lingring houres,
Making our bitter absence sweet,
Till soules, and bodyes both, may meet.

To her in absence.

A SHIP.

TOst in a troubled sea of griefes, I floate
Farre from the shore, in a storme-beaten boat,
Where my sad thoughts doe (like the compasse) show
The severall points from which crosse winds doe blow.
My heart doth like the needle toucht with love   5
Still fixt on you, point which way I would move.
You are the bright Pole-starre, which in the darke
Of this long absence, guides my wandring barke.
Love is the Pilot, but o're-come with feare
Of your displeasure, dares not homewards steare;   10
My fearefull hope hangs on my trembling sayle;
Nothing is wanting but a gentle gale,
Which pleasant breath must blow from your sweet lip:
Bid it but move, and quick as thought this Ship
Into your armes, which are my port, will flye   15
Where it for ever shall at Anchor lye.

SONG.

Eternitie of love protested.

HOw ill doth he deserve a lovers name,
Whose pale weake flame,
Cannot retaine
His heate in spight of absence or disdaine;
But doth at once, like paper set on fire,   5
Burne, and expire!
True love can never change his seat,
Nor did he ever love, that could retreat.

To her in absence. 13 lip:] lip, 40: lip. 51
Song. 6 *expire!*] *expire?* 40: *expire;* 42

That

That noble flame, which my brest keepes alive,
            Shall still survive,   10
            When my soule's fled;
Nor shall my love dye, when my bodye's dead,
That shall waite on me to the lower shade,
            And never fade:
My very ashes in their urne,   15
Shall like a hallowed Lamp, for ever burne.

Vpon some alterations in my Mistresse, after my departure into France.

OH gentle Love, doe not forsake the guide
    Of my fraile Barke, on which the swelling tide
            Of ruthlesse pride
Doth beat, and threaten wrack from every side.
Gulfes of disdaine, do gape to overwhelme   5
This boat, nigh sunke with griefe, whilst at the helme
            Dispaire commands;
            And round about, the shifting sands
Of faithlesse love, and false inconstancie,
            With rocks of crueltie,   10
Stop up my passage to the neighbour Lands.

My sighs have rays'd those winds, whose fury beares
My sayles or'e-boord, and in their place spreads teares,
            And from my teares
This sea is sprung, where naught but Death appeares; 15

---

10 *Shall*] shall 40
Vpon some alterations, &c. *Title*: France.] France, 40   13 or'e-boord,]
or'e boord, 40 (*some copies*)   15 appeares;] appeares, 40: appears; 51

                                                      A

A mystie cloud of anger, hides the light
Of my faire starre, and every where black night
      Vsurpes the place
   Of those bright rayes, which once did grace
My forth-bound Ship: but when it could no more   20
      Behold the vanisht shore,
In the deep flood she drown'd her beamie face.

Good counsell to a young Maid.

WHen you the Sun-burnt Pilgrim see
    Fainting with thirst, hast to the springs,
Marke how at first with bended knee
   He courts the crystall Nimphe, and flings
   His body to the earth, where He   5
Prostrate adores the flowing Deitie.

But when his sweaty face is drencht
   In her coole waves, when from her sweet
Bosome, his burning thirst is quencht;
   Then marke how with disdainfull feet   10
   He kicks her banks, and from the place
That thus refresht him, moves with sullen pace.

So shalt thou be despis'd, faire Maid,
   When by the sated lover tasted;
What first he did with teares invade,   15
   Shall afterwards with scorne be wasted;
   When all thy Virgin-springs grow dry,
When no streames shall be left, but in thine eye.

20 Ship:] Ship, *40*
  Good counsell, &c. 2 Fainting] fainting *40*   springs,] springs; *40*   4
Nimphe, *all MSS.*: Nimphs, *40*

Celia

Celia *bleeding, to the Surgeon.*

FOnd man, that canst beleeve her blood
   Will from those purple chanels flow;
Or that the pure untainted flood
   Can any foule distemper know;
Or that thy weake steele can incize   5
The Crystall case, wherein it lyes.

Know; her quick blood, proud of his seat,
   Runs dauncing through her azure veines;
Whose harmony no cold, nor heat
   Disturbs, whose hue no tincture staines;   10
And the hard rock wherein it dwells,
The keenest darts of Love repels.

But thou reply'st, behold she bleeds;
   Foole, thou'rt deceivd; and dost not know
The mystique knot whence this proceeds,   15
   How Lovers in each other grow;
Thou struckst her arme, but 'twas my heart
Shed all the blood, felt all the smart.

To T. H. *a Lady resembling my Mistresse.*

FAyre copie of my *Celia's* face,
   Twin of my soule, thy perfect grace
Claymes in my love an equall place.

Disdaine not a divided heart,
Though all be hers, you shall have part;   5
Love is not tyde to rules of art.

For as my soule first to her flew,
Yet stay'd with me; so now 'tis true
It dwells with her, though fled to you.

Celia bleeding, &c. 3 flood] flood, 40

Then

Then entertaine this wandring guest,   10
And if not love, allow it rest;
It left not, but mistooke the nest.

Nor thinke my love, or your faire eyes
Cheaper, 'cause from the sympathise
You hold with her, these flames arise.   15

To Lead, or Brasse, or some such bad
Mettall, a Princes stamp may adde
That valew, which it never had.

But to the pure refined Ore,
The stamp of Kings imparts no more   20
Worth, then the mettall held before.

Only the Image gives the rate
To Subjects; in a forraine State
'Tis priz'd as much for its owne waight.

So though all other hearts resigne   25
To your pure worth, yet you have mine
Only because you are her coyne.

To Saxham.

THough frost, and snow, lockt from mine eyes
      That beautie which without dore lyes;
Thy gardens, orchards, walkes, that so
I might not all thy pleasures know;
Yet (*Saxham*) thou within thy gate,   5
Art of thy selfe so delicate;
So full of native sweets, that blesse
Thy roofe with inward happinesse;
As neither from, nor to thy store
Winter takes ought, or Spring addes more.   10

To T. H., &c. 11 not 40 (*Errata*): it 40 (*Text*)   19 Ore, 51: Ore; 40
21 before. 42: before, 40   23 Subjects;] Subjects, 40, 51: Subjects 42
To Saxham. 1 eyes 51: eyes, 40

The cold and frozen ayre had sterv'd
Much poore, if not by thee preserv'd;
Whose prayers have made thy Table blest
With plenty, far above the rest.
The season hardly did afford   15
Course cates unto thy neighbours board,
Yet thou hadst daintyes, as the skie
Had only been thy Volarie;
Or else the birds, fearing the snow
Might to another deluge grow: 20
The Pheasant, Partiridge, and the Larke,
Flew to thy house, as to the Arke.
The willing Oxe, of himselfe came
Home to the slaughter, with the Lambe,
And every beast did thither bring   25
Himselfe, to be an offering.
The scalie herd, more pleasure tooke,
Bath'd in thy dish, then in the brooke:
Water, Earth, Ayre, did all conspire,
To pay their tributes to thy fire,   30
Whose cherishing flames themselves divide
Through every roome, where they deride
The night, and cold abroad; whilst they
Like suns within, keepe endlesse day.
Those chearfull beames send forth their light,   35
To all that wander in the night,
And seeme to becken from aloofe,
The weary Pilgrim to thy roofe;
Where if refresh't, he will away,
Hee's fairly welcome, or if stay   40
Farre more, which he shall hearty find,
Both from the Master, and the Hinde.
The strangers welcome, each man there
Stamp'd on his chearfull brow, doth weare;
Nor doth this welcome, or his cheere   45
Grow lesse, 'cause he staies longer here.
There's none observes (much lesse repines)
How often this man sups or dines.
Thou hast no Porter at the doore
T'examine, or keep back the poore;   50

Nor

Nor locks, nor bolts; thy gates have bin
Made onely to let strangers in;
Vntaught to shut, they doe not feare
To stand wide open all the yeare;
Carelesse who enters, for they know,   55
Thou never didst deserve a foe;
And as for theeves, thy bountie's such,
They cannot steale, thou giv'st so much.

Vpon a Ribband.

THis silken wreath, which circles in mine arme,
   Is but an Emblem of that mystique charme,
Wherewith the magique of your beauties binds
My captive soule, and round about it winds
Fetters of lasting love; This hath entwind   5
My flesh alone, That hath empalde my mind:
Time may weare out These soft weak bands; but Those
Strong chaines of brasse, Fate shall not discompose.
This holy relique may preserve my wrist,
But my whole frame doth by That power subsist: 10
To That my prayers and sacrifice, to This
I onely pay a superstitious kisse:
This but the Idoll, That's the Deitie,
Religion There is due; Here ceremonie.
That I receive by faith, This but in trust;   15
Here I may tender dutie, There I must.
This order as a Layman I may beare,
But I become Loves Priest when That I weare.
This moves like ayre; That as the Center stands:
That knot your vertue tide; This but your hands: 20
That Nature fram'd, but This was made by Art;
This makes my arme your prisoner, That my heart.

57 such, *42*: such; *40*
Vpon a Ribband. 14 There *51*: there *40*

To the King at his entrance
into Saxham, by Master
Io. Crofts.

SIR,
Ere you passe this threshold, stay,
And give your creature leave to pay
Those pious rites, which unto you,
As to our houshold Gods, are due.
  In stead of sacrifice, each brest   5
Is like a flaming Altar, drest
With zealous fires, which from pure hearts
Love mixt with loyaltie imparts.
  Incense, nor gold have we, yet bring
As rich, and sweet an offering;   10
And such as doth both these expresse,
Which is our humble thankfulnesse,
By which is payd the All we owe
To gods above, or men below.
The slaughter'd beast, whose flesh should feed   15
The hungrie flames, we, for pure need
Dresse for your supper, and the gore
Which should be dasht on every dore,
We change into the lustie blood
Of youthfull Vines, of which a flood   20
Shall sprightly run through all your veines,
First to your health, then your faire traines.
  We shall want nothing but good fare,
To shew your welcome, and our care;
Such rarities that come from farre,   25
From poore mens houses banisht are;
Yet wee'le expresse in homely cheare,
How glad we are to see you here.
Wee'le have what e're the season yeelds,
Out of the neighbouring woods, and fields;   30
For all the dainties of your board,
Will only be what those afford;
And having supt, we may perchance
Present you with a countrie dance.

12 thankfulnesse,] thankfulnesse. 40

Thus

Thus much your servants, that beare sway   35
Here in your absence, bade me say,
And beg besides, you'ld hither bring,
Only the mercy of a King;
And not the greatnesse, since they have
A thousand faults must pardon crave;   40
But nothing that is fit to waite
Vpon the glory of your state.
Yet your gracious favour will,
They hope, as heretofore, shine still
On their endeavours, for they swore   45
Should *Jove* descend, they could no more.

Vpon the sicknesse of (E. S.)

MVst she then languish, and we sorrow thus,
And no kind god helpe her, nor pitty us?
Is justice fled from heaven? can that permit
A foule deformed ravisher to sit
Vpon her Virgin cheek, and pull from thence   5
The Rose-buds in their maiden excellence?
To spread cold palenesse on her lips, and chase
The frighted Rubies from their native place?
To lick up with his searching flames, a flood
Of dissolv'd Corall, flowing in her blood;   10
And with the dampes of his infectious breath,
Print on her brow moyst characters of death?
Must the cleare light, 'gainst course of nature cease
In her faire eyes, and yet the flames encrease?
Must feavers shake this goodly tree, and all   15
That ripened fruit from the faire branches fall,
Which Princes have desir'd to taste? must she
Who hath preserv'd her spotlesse chastitie
From all solicitation, now at last
By Agues, and diseases be embrast?   20
Forbid it holy *Dian*; else who shall
Pay vowes, or let one graine of Incense fall
On thy neglected Altars, if thou blesse
No better this thy zealous Votaresse?

                                        Haste

Haste then, O maiden Goddesse, to her ayde,   25
Let on thy quiver her pale cheeke be layd;
And rock her fainting body in thinc armes;
Then let the God of Musick, with still charmes,
Her restlesse eyes in peacefull slumbers close,
And with soft straines sweeten her calme repose.   30
Cupid descend; and whilst *Apollo* sings,
Fanning the coole ayre with thy panting wings,
Ever supply her with refreshing wind;
Let thy faire mother, with her tresses bind
Her labouring temples, with whose balmie sweat,   35
She shall perfume her hairie Coronet,
Whose precious drops, shall upon every fold
Hang, like rich Pearles about a wreath of gold:
Her looser locks, as they unbraded lye,
Shall spread themselves into a Canopie: 40
Vnder whose shadow let her rest secure
From chilling cold, or burning Calenture;
Vnlesse she freeze with yce of chast desires,
Or holy Hymen kindle nuptiall fires.
And when at last Death comes to pierce her heart, 45
Convey into his hand thy golden dart.

A New-yeares Sacrifice.

To Lucinda.

THose that can give, open their hands this day,
   Those that cannot, yet hold them up to pray;
That health may crowne the seasons of this yeare,
And mirth daunce round the circle, that no teare
(Vnlesse of joy) may with its brinie dew,   5
Discolour on your cheeke the rosie hue;
That no accesse of yeares presume to abate
Your beauties ever-flourishing estate:
Such cheape, and vulgar wishes, I could lay
As triviall offrings at your feet this day;   10

A New-yeares Sacrifice. 7 abate] abate, 40

                                                But

But that it were Apostasie in me,
To send a prayer to any Deitie
But your divine selfe, who have power to give
Those blessings unto others, such as live
Like me, by the sole influence of your eyes,   15
Whose faire aspects governe our destinies.
    Such Incense, vowes, and holy rites, as were
To the involved Serpent of the yeare,
Payd by Egyptian Priests, lay I before
Lucinda's sacred shrine, whilst I adore   20
Her beauteous eyes, and her pure Altars dresse
With gums and spice of humble Thankfulnesse;
    So may my Goddesse from her heaven, inspire
My frozen bosome with a Delphique fire,
And then the world shall by that glorious flame,   25
Behold the blaze of thy immortall name.

SONG.

To one who when I prais'd
my Mistris beautie, said I
was blind.

*W*Onder *not though I am blind,*
            For you must bee
Darke in your eyes, or in your mind,
            If when you see
Her face, you prove not blind like me.   5
If the powerfull beames that flye
            From her eye,
And those amorous sweets that lye
Scatter'd, in each neighbouring part,
Find a passage to your heart,   10
Then you'le confesse your mortall sight
Too weake, for such a glorious light;
For if her graces you discover,
You grow like me a dazel'd lover;
But if those beauties you not spy,   15
Then are you blinder farre then I.

Song. 10 *heart,* 51: *heart;* 40

SONG.
To my Mistris, I burning
in love.

I Burne, and cruell you, in vaine
  Hope to quench me with disdaine;
If from your eyes, those sparkles came,
That have kindled all this flame,
What bootes it me, though now you shrowde   5
Those fierce Comets in a cloude?
Since all the flames that I have felt,
Could your snow yet never melt,
Nor, can your snow (though you should take
Alpes into your bosome) slake   10
The heate of my enamour'd heart;
But with wonder learne Loves art!
No seaes of yce can coole desire,
Equall flames must quench Loves fire:
Then thinke not that my heat can dye,   15
Till you burne aswell as I.

SONG.
To her againe, she burning
in a Feaver.

N Ow she burnes as well as I,
  Yet my heat can never dye;
She burnes that never knew desire,
She that was yce, she now is fire.
Shee whose cold heart, chaste thoughts did arme   5
So, as Loves flames could never warme
The frozen bosome where it dwelt,
She burnes, and all her beauties melt;
She burnes, and cryes, Loves fires are milde;
Feavers are Gods, and He's a childe.   10

Song. To her againe, &c. 4 *now is fire*. H17: *that was fire*. 40, W, HL   10
Feavers are Gods, and He's all MSS.: *Peavers are Gods, He's* 40

                                                   Love

Love; let her know the difference
Twixt the heat of soule, and sence.
Touch her with thy flames divine,
So shalt thou quench her fire, and mine.

Vpon the Kings sicknesse.

SIcknesse, the minister of death, doth lay
  So strong a seige against our brittle clay,
As whilst it doth our weake forts singly win,
It hopes at length to take all man-kind in:
First, it begins upon the wombe to waite,   5
And doth the unborne child there uncreate;
Then rocks the cradle where the infant lyes,
Where, e're it fully be alive, it dyes.
It never leaves fond youth, untill it have
Found, or an early, or a later grave.   10
By thousand subtle sleights from heedlesse man,
It cuts the short allowance of a span;
And where both sober life, and Art combine
To keepe it out, Age makes them both resigne.
Thus by degrees it onely gain'd of late,   15
The weake, the aged, or intemperate;
But now the Tyrant hath found out a way
By which the sober, strong, and young, decay:
Entring his royall limbes that is our head,
Through us his mystique limbs the paine is spread, 20
That man that doth not feele his part, hath none
In any part of his dominion;
If he hold land, that earth is forfeited,
And he unfit on any ground to tread.
This griefe is felt at Court, where it doth move   25
Through every joynt, like the true soule of love.
All those faire starres that doe attend on Him,
Whence they deriv'd their light, wax pale and dim.
That ruddie morning beame of Majestie,
Which should the Suns ecclipsed light supply,   30

Vpon the Kings sicknesse. 12 span; *51*: span. *or* span *40*

Is

Is overcast with mists, and in the liew
Of cherefull rayes, sends us downe drops of dew:
That curious forme made of an earth refin'd,
At whose blest birth, the gentle Planets shin'd
With faire aspects, and sent a glorious flame   35
To animate so beautifull a frame;
That Darling of the Gods and men, doth weare
A cloude on's brow, and in his eye a teare:
And all the rest, (save when his dread command
Doth bid them move,) like livelesse statues stand;   40
So full a griefe, so generally worne
Shewes a good King is sick, and good men mourne.

SONG.

To a Lady not yet enjoy'd
by her Husband.

COme Celia, *fixe thine eyes on mine,*
  And through those Crystalls our soules flitting,
Shall a pure wreathe of eye-beames twine,
  Our loving hearts together knitting;
Let Eaglets the bright Sun survey,   5
Though the blind Mole discerne not day.

When cleere Aurora *leaves her mate,*
  The light of her gray eyes dispising,
Yet all the world doth celebrate
  With sacrifice, her faire up-rising: 10
Let Eaglets, &c.

A Dragon kept the golden fruit,
  Yet he those dainties never tasted;
As others pin'd in the pursuit,
  So he himselfe with plentie wasted: 15
Let Eaglets, &c.

Song. 6 *day.* 51: *day:* 40

SONG.

SONG.
The willing Prisoner to his
Mistris.

*L*Et fooles great Cupids yoake disdaine,
 　Loving their owne wild freedome better;
Whilst proud of my triumphant chaine
 　I sit, and court my beauteous fetter.

Her murdring glances, snaring haires,　　　　　　5
 　And her bewitching smiles, so please me,
As he brings ruine, that repaires
 　The sweet afflictions that disease me.

Hide not those panting balls of snow,
 　With envious vayles, from my beholding;　　10
Vnlock those lips, their pearly row,
 　In a sweet smile of love unfolding.

And let those eyes, whose motion wheeles
 　The restlesse Fate of every lover,
Survey the paines, my sicke heart feeles,　　　　15
 　And wounds themselves have made, discover.

A flye that flew into my Mistris
her eye.

WHen this Flye liv'd, she us'd to play
 　In the Sun-shine all the day;
Till comming neere my *Celia's* sight,
She found a new, and unknowne light
So full of glory, as it made
The noone-day Sun a gloomy shade;
Then this amorous Flye became
My rivall, and did court my flame.

Song. The willing Prisoner, &c. 16 *themselves 51: themselves, 40*　　*made,*
51: made 40

She

She did from hand to bosome skip,
And from her breath, her cheeke, and lip,   10
Suckt all the incense, and the spice,
And grew a bird of Paradise:
At last into her eye she flew,
There scorcht in flames, and drown'd in dew,
Like *Phaeton* from the Suns spheare   15
She fell, and with her dropt a teare:
Of which a pearle was straight compos'd,
Wherein her ashes lye enclos'd.
Thus she receiv'd from *Celia*'s eye,
Funerall flame, tombe, Obsequie.   20

SONG.

Celia singing.

HArke how my Celia, *with the choyce*
Musique of her hand and voyce
Stills the loude wind; and makes the wilde
Incensed Bore, and Panther milde!
Marke how those statues like men move,   5
Whilst men with wonder statues prove!
This stiffe rock bends to worship her,
That Idoll turnes Idolater.
Now see how all the new inspir'd
Images, with love are fir'd!   10
Harke how the tender Marble grones,
And all the late transformed stones,
Court the faire Nymph with many a teare,
Which she (more stony then they were)
Beholds with unrelenting mind;   15
Whilst they amaz'd to see combin'd
Such matchlesse beautie, with disdaine,
Are all turn'd into stones againe.

A flye that flew, &c. 14 dew, 51: dew: 40   20 tombe,] tombe 40
Song.   14 *stony*] flyntie *all MSS.*

SONG.

SONG.
Celia singing.

*Y*Ou that thinke Love can convey,
　　　No other way,
But through the eyes, into the heart,
　　　His fatall Dart:
Close up those casements, and but heare　　　5
　　　This Syren sing;
　　　And on the wing
Of her sweet voyce, it shall appeare
That Love can enter at the eare:
　　　Then unvaile your eyes, behold　　　10
　　　The curious mould
Where that voyce dwels, and as we know,
　　　When the Cocks crow,
　　　We freely may
　　　Gaze on the day;　　　15
So may you, when the Musique's done
Awake and see the rising Sun.

SONG.
To one that desired to know
my Mistris.

*S*Eeke not to know my love, for shee
　Hath vow'd her constant faith to me;
Her milde aspects are mine, and thou
Shalt only find a stormy brow:
For if her beautie stirre desire　　　5
In me, her kisses quench the fire.
Or, I can to Love's fountaine goe,
Or dwell upon her hills of snow;
But when thou burn'st, she shall not spare
One gentle breath to coole the ayre;　　　10

Song. To one, &c. 8 *snow;* 5*1*: *snow.* 40　　　10 *ayre;*] *ayre.* 40: *ayr;* 5*1*
　　　　　　　　　　　　　　　　　　　　　Thou

Thou shalt not climbe those Alpes, *nor spye*
Where the sweet springs of Venus *lye.*
Search hidden Nature, and there find
A treasure to inrich thy mind;
Discover Arts not yet reveal'd,   15
But let my Mistris live conceal'd;
Though men by knowledge wiser grow,
Yet here 'tis wisdome not to know.

In the person of a Lady to her inconstant servant.

WHen on the Altar of my hand,
　　(Bedeaw'd with many a kisse, and teare;)
Thy now revolted heart, did stand
　　An humble Martyr, thou didst sweare
　　Thus; (and the God of love did heare,)   5
By those bright glances of thine eye,
Vnlesse thou pitty me, I dye.

When first those perjurd lips of thine,
　　Bepal'd with blasting sighes, did seale
Their violated faith on mine,   10
　　From the soft bosome that did heale
　　Thee, thou my melting heart didst steale;
My soule enflam'd with thy false breath,
Poyson'd with kisses, suckt in death.

Yet I nor hand, nor lip will move,   15
　　Revenge, or mercy, to procure
From the offended God of love;
　　My curse is fatall, and my pure
　　Love, shall beyond thy scorne endure:
If I implore the Gods, they'le find   20
Thee too ingratefull, me too kind.

Song. To one, &c.   12 *lye.* 51: *lye;* 40

Truce

Truce in Love entreated.

NO more, blind God, for see my heart
   Is made thy Quiver, where remaines
No voyd place for another Dart;
And alas! that conquest gaines
Small praise, that only brings away   5
A tame and unresisting prey.

Behold a nobler foe, all arm'd,
Defies thy weake Artillerie,
That hath thy Bow and Quiver charm'd;
A rebell beautie, conquering Thee!   10
If thou dar'st equall combat try,
Wound her, for 'tis for her I dye.

To my Rivall.

HEnce vaine intruder, hast away,
   Wash not with thy unhallowed brine
The foot-steps of my *Celia's* shrine;
Nor on her purer Altars lay
Thy empty words, accents that may   5
   Some looser Dame to love encline;
   She must have offerings more divine;
Such pearlie drops, as youthfull *May*
Scatters before the rising day;
   Such smooth soft language, as each line   10
Might stroake an angry God, or stay
   Joves thunder, make the hearers pine
With envie; doe this, thou shalt be
Servant to her, Rivall with me.

To my Rivall. 8 *May* 51: May, 40

Boldnesse

Boldnesse in love.

MArke how the bashfull morne, in vaine
   Courts the amorous Marigold,
With sighing blasts, and weeping raine;
Yet she refuses to unfold.
But when the Planet of the day,   5
Approacheth with his powerfull ray,
Then she spreads, then she receives
His warmer beames into her virgin leaves.
So shalt thou thrive in love, fond Boy;
If thy teares, and sighes discover   10
Thy griefe, thou never shalt enjoy
The just reward of a bold lover:
But when with moving accents, thou
Shalt constant faith, and service vow,
Thy *Celia* shall receive those charmes   15
With open eares, and with unfolded armes.

A Pastorall Dialogue.

Celia.   *Cleon.*

AS *Celia* rested in the shade
   With *Cleon* by her side,
The swaine thus courted the young Maid,
And thus the Nymph replide.

CL.

Sweet! let thy captive, fetters weare   5
   Made of thine armes, and hands;
Till such as thraldome scorne, or feare,
   Envie those happy bands.

A Pastorall Dialogue. In Henry Lawes's *Ayres and Dialogues, The First Booke,*
1653, the first stanza is marked: Cho. *Cælia. Cleon.*
  2 side, *51:* side; *40*   8 Envie] envie *40*

CE.

CE.

Then thus my willing armes I winde
    About thee, and am so   10
Thy pris'ner; for my selfe I bind,
    Vntill I let thee goe.

CL.

Happy that slave, whom the faire foe
    Tyes in so soft a chaine.
CE.   Farre happier I, but that I know   15
    Thou wilt breake loose againe.

CL.

    By thy immortall beauties never.
CE. Fraile as thy love's thine oath.
CL. Though beautie fade, my faith lasts ever.
CE. Time will destroy them both.   20

CL.

    I dote not on thy snow-white skin.
CE. What then? *CL.* Thy purer mind.
CE. It lov'd too soone. *CL.* Thou hadst not bin
    So faire, if not so kind.

CE.

    Oh strange vaine fancie! *CL.* But yet true. 25
CE. Prove it. *CL.* Then make a brade
Of those loose flames, that circle you,
    My sunnes, and yet your shade.

CE.

'Tis done. *CL.* Now give it me. *CE.* Thus thou
    Shalt thine owne errour find,   30
If these were beauties, I am now
    Lesse faire, because more kind.

CL.

You shall confesse you erre; that haire
    Shall it not change the hue,
Or leave the golden mountaine bare?   35
CE. Aye me! it is too true.

34 Shall] shall *40*

CL.

CL.

But this small wreathe, shall ever stay
    In its first native prime,
And smiling when the rest decay,
    The triumphs sing of time.   40

CE.

Then let me cut from thy faire grove,
    One branch, and let that be
An embleme of eternall love,
    For such is mine to thee.

CL.

Thus are we both redeem'd from time,   45
    I by thy grace. *CE.* And I
Shall live in thy immortall rime,
    Vntill the Muses dye.

CL.

By heaven! *CE.* Sweare not; if I must weepe,
    Jove shall not smile at me;   50
This kisse, my heart, and thy faith keepe.
CL. This breathes my soule to thee.

Then forth the thicket *Thirsis* rusht,
    Where he saw all their play:
The swaine stood still, and smil'd, and blusht,   55
    The Nymph fled fast away.

Griefe ingrost.

WHerefore doe thy sad numbers flow
          So full of woe?
Why dost thou melt in such soft straines,
          Whilst she disdaines?
    If she must still denie,   5
    Weepe not, but dye:

A Pastorall Dialogue.   45 *CL.*] *Both together. Lawes*   46 I by] *Cle.* I,
by *Lawes*   *CE.*] *CL.* 40: *Cæl. Lawes*   53 Then] Cho. Then *Lawes*
                                         And

And in thy Funerall fire,
Shall all her fame expire.
Thus both shall perish, and as thou on thy Hearse
Shall want her teares, so she shall want thy Verse;   10
Repine not then at thy blest state:
Thou art above thy fate;
But my faire *Celia* will nor give
Love enough to make me live,
Nor yet dart from her eye   15
Scorne enough to make me dye.
Then let me weepe alone, till her kind breath,
Or blow my teares away, or speake my death.

A Pastorall Dialogue.

Shepherd.   Nymph.   Chorus.

Hep.   This mossie bank they prest.   *Ny.* That aged
      Oak
Did canopie the happy payre
All night from the dampe ayre.
Cho. Here let us sit and sing the words they spoke,
Till the day breaking, their embraces broke.   5

Shep.

See love, the blushes of the morne appeare,
And now she hangs her pearlie store
(Rob'd from the Easterne shore)
I'th' Couslips bell, and Roses eare:
Sweet, I must stay no longer here.   10

Nymph.

Those streakes of doubtfull light, usher not day,
But shew my sunne must set; no Morne
Shall shine till thou returne,
The yellow Planets, and the gray
Dawne, shall attend thee on thy way.   15

Griefe ingrost.   13 nor] not *42 and all later edd*.   14 live,] live; *40*
A Pastorall Dialogue. 1 prest.] prest *40* (*some copies*)   3 dampe *40* (*Errata*):
danke *40* (*Text*), MSS.   9 eare: *70, MSS.*: rare: *40*   15 way. *42*: way: *40*
                                                                        Shep.

Shep.

If thine eyes guild my pathes, they may forbeare
  Their uselesse shine. *Nymph.* My teares will quite
   Extinguish their faint light.
She. Those drops will make their beames more cleare,
  Loves flames will shine in every teare.   20

Cho.

They kist, and wept, and from their lips, and eyes,
  In a mixt dew, of brinie sweet,
   Their joyes, and sorrowes meet,
But she cryes out. *Nymp.* Shepherd arise,
The Sun betrayes us else to spies.   25

Shep.

The winged houres flye fast, whilst we embrace,
  But when we want their help to meet,
   They move with leaden feet.
Nym. Then let us pinion *Time*, and chase
The day for ever from this place.   30

Shep.

Harke! *Ny.* Aye me stay! *She.* For ever.
  Ny. No, arise,
Wee must be gone. *Shep.* My nest of spice.
  Nymph. My soule. *Shep.* My Paradise.
Cho. Neither could say farewell, but through their eyes
  Griefe, interrupted speach with teares supplyes.   35

Red, and white Roses.

REade in these Roses, the sad story
  Of my hard fate, and your owne glory:
In the White you may discover
  The palenesse of a fainting lover:
In the Red, the flames still feeding   5
  On my heart with fresh wounds bleeding.

A Pastorall Dialogue.   31 *Ny.* No, *42*: *Ny*, No, *40*   33 My Paradise.] my
Paradise. *40*

The

The White will tell you how I languish,
And the Red expresse my anguish.
The White my innocence displaying,
The Red my martyrdome betraying.   10
The frownes that on your brow resided,
Have those Roses thus divided.
Oh let your smiles but cleare the weather,
And then they both shall grow together.

To my Cousin (C. R.) marry-
ing my Lady (A.)

HAppy Youth, that shalt possesse
    Such a spring-tyde of delight,
        As the sated Appetite
Shall enjoying such excesse,
Wish the flood of pleasure lesse: 5
        When the Hymeneall Rite
Is perform'd, invoke the night,
That it may in shadowes dresse
Thy too reall happinesse;
        Else (as *Semele*) the bright   10
Deitie in her full might,
May thy feeble soule oppresse.
        Strong perfumes, and glaring light,
        Oft destroy both smell, and sight.

Red, and white Roses. 9 White *51*: white *40*
To my Cousin, &c. 5 Wish *H17*, *HL*: With *40*   lesse:] lesse. *40* (*some copies*)

A Lover upon an Accident ne-
cessitating his departure,
consults with Reason.

LOVER.

WEepe not, nor backward turne your beames
  Fond eyes, sad sighes locke in your breath,
Lest on this wind, or in those streames
 My griev'd soule flye, or sayle to death.
Fortune destroys me if I stay,   5
Love kills me if I goe away:
Since *Love*, and *Fortune*, both are blind,
Come *Reason*, and resolve my doubtfull mind.

REASON.

Flye, and blind *Fortune* be thy guide,
  And 'gainst the blinder God rebell,   10
Thy love-sick heart shall not reside
 Where scorne, and selfe-will'd error dwell;
Where entrance, vnto *Truth* is bar'd;
Where *Love* and *Faith* find no reward;
For, my just hand may sometime move   15
The wheele of *Fortune*, not the spheare of *Love*.

Parting, Celia *weepes.*

WEepe not (my deare) for I shall goe
  Loaden enough with mine owne woe;
Adde not thy heavinesse to mine:
 Since Fate our pleasures must dis-joyne,
Why should our sorrowes meet? if I   5
Must goe, and lose thy company,
I wish not theirs; it shall relieve
 My griefe, to thinke thou dost not grieve.

A Lover, &c. *5 Fortune*] Fortune *40*   12 dwell; *51*: dwell. *40*
Parting, Celia weepes. 3 mine: *51*: mine, *40*

                Yet

Yet grieve, and weepe, that I may beare
Every sigh, and every teare   10
Away with me, so shall thy brest
And eyes discharg'd, enjoy their rest.
And it will glad my heart to see,
Thou wer't thus loath to part with mee.

A Rapture.

I Will enjoy thee now my *Celia*, come
  And flye with me to Loves Elizium:
The Gyant, Honour, that keepes cowards out,
Is but a Masquer, and the servile rout
Of baser subjects onely, bend in vaine   5
To the vast Idoll, whilst the nobler traine
Of valiant Lovers, daily sayle betweene
The huge Collosses legs, and passe unseene
Vnto the blissfull shore; be bold, and wise,
And we shall enter, the grim Swisse denies   10
Only tame fooles a passage, that not know
He is but forme, and onely frights in show
The duller eyes that looke from farre; draw neere,
And thou shalt scorne, what we were wont to feare.
We shall see how the stalking Pageant goes   15
With borrowed legs, a heavie load to those
That made, and beare him; not as we once thought
The seed of Gods, but a weake modell wrought
By greedy men, that seeke to enclose the common,
And within private armes empale free woman.   20
    Come then, and mounted on the wings of love
Wee'le cut the flitting ayre, and sore above
The Monsters head, and in the noblest seates
Of those blest shades, quench, and renew our heates.
There, shall the Queene of Love, and Innocence,   25
Beautie and Nature, banish all offence

A Rapture. 7 Lovers, *40* (*Errata*): souldiers, *40* (*Text*)   11 Only tame
all MSS.: Only to tame *40*   fooles a passage,] fools passage, *70*   25 Queene
42, most MSS.: Queens *40*

From

From our close Ivy twines, there I'le behold
Thy bared snow, and thy unbraded gold.
There, my enfranchiz'd hand, on every side
Shall o're thy naked polish'd Ivory slide.   30
No curtaine there, though of transparant lawne,
Shall be before thy virgin-treasure drawne;
But the rich Mine, to the enquiring eye
Expos'd, shall ready still for mintage lye,
And we will coyne young *Cupids*. There, a bed   35
Of Roses, and fresh Myrtles, shall be spread
Vnder the cooler shade of Cypresse groves:
Our pillowes, of the downe of *Venus* Doves,
Whereon our panting lims wee'le gently lay
In the faint respites of our active play;   40
That so our slumbers, may in dreames have leisure,
To tell the nimble fancie our past pleasure;
And so our soules that cannot be embrac'd,
Shall the embraces of our bodyes taste.
Meane while the bubbling streame shall court the shore, 45
Th'enamoured chirping Wood-quire shall adore
In varied tunes the Deitie of Love;
The gentle blasts of Westerne winds, shall move
The trembling leaves, & through their close bows breath
Still Musick, whilst we rest our selves beneath   50
Their dancing shade; till a soft murmure, sent
From soules entranc'd in amorous languishment
Rowze us, and shoot into our veines fresh fire,
Till we, in their sweet extasie expire.
    Then, as the empty Bee, that lately bore,   55
Into the common treasure, all her store,
Flyes 'bout the painted field with nimble wing,
Deflowring the fresh virgins of the Spring;
So will I rifle all the sweets, that dwell
In my delicious Paradise, and swell   60
My bagge with honey, drawne forth by the power
Of fervent kisses, from each spicie flower.
I'le seize the Rose-buds in their perfum'd bed,
The Violet knots, like curious Mazes spread
O're all the Garden, taste the ripned Cherry,   65

58 Spring; *51*: Spring. *40*   65 Cherry,] cherries, *most MSS*.

The

The warme, firme Apple, tipt with corall berry:
Then will I visit, with a wandring kisse,
The vale of Lillies, and the Bower of blisse:
And where the beauteous Region doth divide
Into two milkie wayes, my lips shall slide   70
Downe those smooth Allies, wearing as I goe
A tract for lovers on the printed snow;
Thence climbing o're the swelling *Appenine*,
Retire into thy grove of Eglantine;
Where I will all those ravisht sweets distill   75
Through Loves Alimbique, and with Chimmique skill
From the mixt masse, one soveraigne Balme derive,
Then bring that great *Elixar* to thy hive.
    Now in more subtile wreathes I will entwine
My sinowie thighes, my legs and armes with thine;   80
Thou like a sea of milke shalt lye display'd,
Whilst I the smooth, calme Ocean, invade
With such a tempest, as when *Jove* of old
Fell downe on *Danae* in a storme of gold:
Yet my tall Pine, shall in the *Cyprian* straight   85
Ride safe at Anchor, and unlade her fraight:
My Rudder, with thy bold hand, like a tryde,
And skilfull Pilot, thou shalt steere, and guide
My Bark into Loves channell, where it shall
Dance, as the bounding waves doe rise or fall: 90
Then shall thy circling armes, embrace and clip
My willing bodie, and thy balmie lip
Bathe me in juyce of kisses, whose perfume
Like a religious incense shall consume,
And send up holy vapours, to those powres   95
That blesse our loves, and crowne our sportfull houres,
That with such Halcion calmenesse, fix our soules
In steadfast peace, as no affright controules.
There, no rude sounds shake us with sudden starts,
No jealous eares, when we unrip our hearts   100
Sucke our discourse in, no observing spies
This blush, that glance traduce; no envious eyes

    66 Apple, . . . corall berry:] Apples, . . . crimson berries *most MSS.*   91
Then] They 40 (*some copies*)   92 willing] naked *most MSS.*   101-2 spies . . .
envious eyes] eyes . . . politique spies *some MSS.*

                                        Watch

Watch our close meetings, nor are we betrayd
To Rivals, by the bribed chamber-maid.
No wedlock bonds unwreathe our twisted loves;   105
We seeke no midnight Arbor, no darke groves
To hide our kisses, there, the hated name
Of husband, wife, lust, modest, chaste, or shame,
Are vaine and empty words, whose very sound
Was never heard in the Elizian ground.   110
All things are lawfull there, that may delight
Nature, or unrestrained Appetite;
Like, and enjoy, to will, and act, is one,
We only sinne when Loves rites are not done.
     The Roman *Lucrece* there, reades the divine   115
Lectures of Loves great master, *Aretine*,
And knowes as well as *Lais*, how to move
Her plyant body in the act of love.
To quench the burning Ravisher, she hurles
Her limbs into a thousand winding curles,   120
And studies artfull postures, such as be
Caru'd on the barke of every neighbouring tree
By learned hands, that so adorn'd the rinde
Of those faire Plants, which as they lay entwinde,
Have fann'd their glowing fires. The Grecian Dame,   125
That in her endlesse webb, toyl'd for a name
As fruitlesse as her worke, doth there display
Her selfe before the Youth of *Ithaca*,
And th'amorous sport of gamesome nights prefer,
Before dull dreames of the lost Traveller.   130
Daphne hath broke her barke, and that swift foot,
Which th'angry Gods had fastned with a root
To the fixt earth, doth now unfetter'd run,
To meet th'embraces of the youthfull Sun:
She hangs upon him, like his Delphique Lyre,   135
Her kisses blow the old, and breath new fire:
Full of her God, she sings inspired Layes,
Sweet Odes of love, such as deserve the Bayes,
Which she her selfe was. Next her, *Laura* lyes
In *Petrarchs* learned armes, drying those eyes   140
That did in such sweet smooth-pac'd numbers flow,

123 rinde] rinde, 40

As

As made the world enamour'd of his woe.
These, and ten thousand Beauties more, that dy'de
Slave to the Tyrant, now enlarg'd, deride
His cancell'd lawes, and for their time mispent,   145
Pay into Loves Exchequer double rent.
   Come then my *Celia*, wee'le no more forbeare
To taste our joyes, struck with a Pannique feare,
But will depose from his imperious sway
This proud *Vsurper* and walke free, as they   150
With necks unyoak'd; nor is it just that Hee
Should fetter your soft sex with Chastitie,
Which Nature made unapt for abstinence;
When yet this false Impostor can dispence
With humane Justice, and with sacred right,   155
And maugre both their lawes command me fight
With Rivals, or with emulous Loves, that dare
Equall with thine, their Mistresse eyes, or haire:
If thou complaine of wrong, and call my sword
To carve out thy revenge, upon that word   160
He bids me fight and kill, or else he brands
With markes of infamie my coward hands,
And yet religion bids from blood-shed flye,
And damns me for that Act. Then tell me why
This Goblin Honour which the world adores,   165
Should make men Atheists, and not women Whores.

Epitaph on the Lady
Mary Villers.

THE Lady *Mary Villers* lyes
   Vnder this stone; with weeping eyes
The Parents that first gave her birth,
And their sad Friends, lay'd her in earth:
If any of them (Reader) were   5
Knowne unto thee, shed a teare,
Or if thyselfe possesse a gemme,
As deare to thee, as this to them,

Epitaph, &c. 8 them, *51*: them; *40*

Though

Though a stranger to this place,
Bewayle in theirs, thine owne hard case;   10
For thou perhaps at thy returne
Mayest find thy Darling in an Vrne.

An other.

THe purest Soule that e're was sent
    Into a clayie tenement
Inform'd this dust, but the weake mold
Could the great guest no longer hold,
The substance was too pure, the flame   5
Too glorious that thither came:
Ten thousand *Cupids* brought along
A Grace on each wing, that did throng
For place there, till they all opprest
The seat in which they sought to rest;   10
So the faire Modell broke, for want
Of roome to lodge th'Inhabitant.

An other.

THis little Vault, this narrow roome,
    Of Love, and Beautie is the tombe;
The dawning beame that 'gan to cleare
Our clouded skie, lyes darkned here,
For ever set to us, by death   5
Sent to enflame the world beneath;
'Twas but a bud, yet did containe
More sweetnesse then shall spring againe,
A budding starre that might have growne
Into a Sun, when it had blowne.   10
This hopefull beautie, did create
New life in Loves declining state;
But now his Empire ends, and we
From fire, and wounding darts are free:
His brand, his bow, let no man feare,   15
The flames, the arrowes, all lye here.

An other. 5-10 *See Commentary*   6 came: *51*: came, *40*
An other. 2 tombe; *51*: tombe, *40*   10 blowne.] blowne: *40 (some copies)*
                                                            Epitaph

Epitaph on the Lady S.
Wife to Sir W. S.

THe harmony of colours, features, grace,
  Resulting Ayres (the magicke of a face)
Of musicall sweet tunes, all which combind,
To crown one Soveraigne beauty, lies confind
To this darke Vault. Shee was a Cabinet   5
Where all the choysest stones of price were set;
Whose native colours, and purest lustre, lent
Her eye, cheek, lip, a dazling ornament:
Whose rare and hidden vertues, did expresse
Her inward beauties, and minds fairer dresse;   10
The constant Diamond, the wise Chrysolite,
The devout Saphyre, Emrauld apt to write
Records of Memory, cheerefull Agat, grave
And serious Onyx, Tophaze, that doth save
The braines calme temper, witty Amathist.   15
This precious Quarrie, or what else the list
On *Aarons* Ephod planted, had, shee wore:
One only Pearle was wanting to her store,
Which in her Saviours booke she found exprest,
To purchase that, she sold Death all the rest.   20

Epitaph, &c. The leaf on which this and part of the next poem appear is a cancel
in most copies of *40*. The uncancelled leaf, preserved in a Huntington Library copy,
shelfmark HEH 80753, omits line 4 of the present poem, the omission doubtless
necessitating the cancel; otherwise it differs from the cancel only in a few details of
punctuation and spelling, not recorded here except where followed in the text.

  7 lustre, *Huntington*: lustre *40* (*cancel*)   16 Quarrie, *42*: Quartie, *40* (*all
copies*)   17 planted, *Huntington*: planted *40* (*cancel*)   18 store,] store; *40*
(*all copies*)   20 Death *Huntington*: death *40* (*cancel*)

Maria

Maria Wentworth, Thomæ Comitis Cleveland, filia præmortua prima Virgineam animam exhalauit
An. Dom. 1632   Æt. suæ 18.

ANd here the precious dust is layd;
  Whose purely-tempered Clay was made
So fine, that it the guest betray'd.

Else the soule grew so fast within,
It broke the outward shell of sinne,   5
And so was hatch'd a Cherubin.

In heigth, it soar'd to God above;
In depth, it did to knowledge move,
And spread in breadth to generall love.

Before, a pious duty shind   10
To Parents, courtesie behind,
On either side an equall mind,

Good to the Poore, to kindred deare,
To servants kind, to friendship cleare,
To nothing but her selfe, severe.   15

So though a Virgin, yet a Bride
To every Grace, she justifi'd
A chaste Poligamie, and dy'd.

Learne from hence (Reader) what small trust
We owe this world, where vertue must   20
Fraile as our flesh, crumble to dust.

Maria Wentworth, &c. *Title:* In 40 printed *Maria Wentworth. Thomæ Comitis
Cleveland, filia præmortuæ prima Virginiam animam exhaluit. An, Dom. Æt. suæ,*
(The uncancelled leaf in HEH 80753, Huntington Library, has periods instead of
commas after *An* and *suæ*.)

On

On the Duke of *Buckingham.*
Beatissimis Manibus charissimi viri Illma Conjunx sic Parentavit.

WHen in the brazen leaves of Fame,
The life, the death, of *Buckingham*
Shall be recorded, if Truth's hand
Incize the story of our Land,
Posteritie shall see a faire   5
Structure, by the studious care
Of two Kings rays'd, that did no lesse
Their wisdome, than their Power expresse;
By blinded zeale (whose doubtfull light
Made murders scarlet robe seeme white,   10
Whose vain-deluding phantosmes charm'd
A clouded sullen soule, and arm'd
A desperate hand, thirstie of blood)
Torne from the faire earth where it stood;
So the majestique fabrique fell.   15
His Actions let our Annals tell:
Wee write no Chronicle; This Pile
Weares onely sorrowes face and stile,
Which, even the envie that did waite
Vpon his flourishing estate,   20
Turn'd to soft pitty of his death,
Now payes his Hearse; but that cheape breath
Shall not blow here, nor th'unpure brine
Puddle those streames that bathe this shrine.
These are the pious Obsequies,   25
Drop'd from his chast Wifes pregnant eyes
In frequent showres, and were alone
By her congealing sighes made stone,
On which the Carver did bestow
These formes and Characters of woe;   30
So he the fashion onely lent,
Whilst she wept all this Monument.

On the Duke of Buckingham. 7 that did no *H17*: that no *40*   11 phan-
tosmes] phantasmes *51*: phantomes *H17*

An

An other.

Siste Hospes sive Indigena sive
Advena vicissitudinis rerum
memor pauca pellege.

REader, when these dumbe stones have told
    In borrowed speach, what Guest they hold,
Thou shalt confesse, the vaine pursuit
Of humane Glory yeelds no fruit,
But an untimely Grave. If Fate   5
Could constant happinesse create,
Her Ministers, Fortune and Worth,
Had here that myracle brought forth;
They fix'd this childe of Honour, where
No roome was left for Hope, or Feare,   10
Of more, or lesse: so high, so great
His growth was, yet so safe his seate.
Safe in the circle of his Friends:
Safe in his Loyall heart, and ends:
Safe in his native valiant spirit: 15
By favour safe, and safe by merit;
Safe by the stampe of Nature, which
Did strength, with shape and Grace enrich:
Safe in the cheerefull Curtesies
Of flowing gestures, speach, and eyes: 20
Safe in his Bounties, which were more
Proportion'd to his mind then store;
Yet, though for vertue he becomes
Involv'd Himselfe in borrowed summes,
Safe in his care, he leaves betray'd   25
No friend engag'd, no debt unpay'd.
    But though the starres conspire to shower
Vpon one Head th'united power
Of all their Graces, if their dire
Aspects, must other brests inspire   30

An other. *Title: pellege.*] *perlege. 51*   2 hold,] hold; *40*   24 summes,
51: summes; *40*   26 friend engag'd,] friend, engag'd *1772*

With

With vicious thoughts, a Murderers knife
May cut (as here) their Darlings life.
Who can be happy then, if Nature must
To make one Happy man, make all men just?

Foure Songs by way of *Cho-rus* to a play, at an entertainment of the King and Queene, by my Lord Chamberlaine;

The first of *Iealousie*. Dialogue.

Question.

FRom whence was first this furie hurld,
 This Jealousie into the world?
Came she from Hell?   Ans. *No there doth raigne*
Eternall hatred, with disdaine,
But she the Daughter is of Love,   5
Sister of Beauty.   Reply.   *Then above*
She must derive from the third Spheare
Her heavenly Off-spring.   Ans.   *Neither there*
From those immortall flames, could shee
Draw her cold frozen Pedigree.   10
  Quest.   *If nor from heaven nor hell, where then*
Had she her birth?   An.   *I'th'hearts of men,*
Beauty, and Feare did her create,
Younger then Love, Elder then Hate,
Sister to both, by Beauties side   15
To Love, by Feare to Hate ally'de:
Despayre her issue is, whose race
Of fruitfull mischiefes drownes the space
Of the wide earth in a swolne flood
Of wrath, revenge, spight, rage, and blood.   20
  Quest.   *Oh how can such a spurious line*
Proceed from Parents so divine?

Foure Songs, &c. 1 Question.] Question *40*   16 *Love, 51: love, 40*
17 *Despayre*] *Despoyre 40*: Chorus Despayre *M13*

              Ans.

Ans.   *As streames, which from their Crystall spring*
Doe sweet and cleare their waters bring,
Yet mingling with the brackish maine,   25
Nor taste, nor colour they retaine.
    Qu.   *Yet Rivers 'twixt their owne bankes flow*
Still fresh, can jealousie doe so?
    An.   *Yes, whilst shee keepes the stedfast ground*
Of Hope, and Feare, her equall bound;   30
Hope sprung from favour, worth, or chance,
Towar'ds the faire object doth advance;
Whil'st Feare, as watchfull Sentinell
Doth the invading Foe repell;
And Jealousie thus mixt, doth prove   35
The season, and the salt of love:
But when Feare takes a larger scope,
Stifling the child of Reason, Hope,
Then sitting on th'usurped throne,
She like a Tyrant rules alone,   40
As the wilde Ocean unconfin'de,
And raging as the Northern-winde.

2.

Feminine Honour.

*I*N *what esteeme did the Gods hold*
    Faire Innocence, and the chaste bed,
When scandall'd vertue might be bold
    Bare-foot, upon sharpe Cultures, spread
O're burning coles to march, yet feele   5
Nor scorching fire, nor piercing steele?

Why, when the hard edg'd Iron did turne
    Soft as a bed of Roses blowne,
When cruell flames forgot to burne
    Their chaste pure limbes, should man alone   10
'Gainst female Innocence conspire,
Harder then steele, fiercer then fire?

Foure Songs, &c.   37 *But*] Chorus. But Mr3

                                                            Oh

Oh haplesse sex! Vnequall sway
Of partiall Honour! Who may know
Rebels from subjects that obey,   15
When malice can on vestals throw
Disgrace, and Fame fixe high repute
On the close shamelesse Prostitute?

Vaine Honour! thou art but disguise,
A cheating voyce, a jugling art,   20
No judge of vertue, whose pure eyes
Court her owne Image in the heart,
More pleas'd with her true figure there,
Then her false Eccho in the eare.

3.
Separation of Lovers.

STop the chafed Bore, or play
With the Lyons paw, yet feare
From the Lovers side to teare
Th'Idoll of his soule away.

Though Love enter by the sight   5
To the heart, it doth not flye
From the mind, when from the eye
The faire objects take their flight.

But since want provokes desire,
When we lose what wee before   10
Have enjoy'd, as we want more,
So is Love more set on fire.

Love doth with an hungrie eye
Glut on Beautie, and you may
Safer snatch the Tygers prey   15
Then his vitall food deny.

Feminine Honour. 19 *disguise,* 51: *disguise* 40

Yet

Yet though absence for a space,
Sharpen the keene Appetite,
Long continuance, doth quite
All Loves characters efface.   20

For the sense not fed, denies
Nourishment unto the minde,
Which with expectation pinde,
Love of a consumption dyes.

4.

Incommunicabilitie of Love.

Q Vest.   *By what power was Love confinde*
       To one object? who can binde,
Or fixe a limit to the free-borne minde?

An.   *Nature; for as bodyes may*
      Move at once but in one way,   5
So nor can mindes to more then one love stray.

Reply.   *Yet I feele a double smart,*
       Loves twinn'd-flame, his forked dart.
An.   *Then hath wilde lust, not love possest thy heart.*

Qu.   *Whence springs love?*   An.   *From beauty.*   10
    Qu.   *Why*
   Should th'effect not multiply
As fast i'th'heart, as doth the cause i'th'eye?

An.   *When two Beauties equall are,*
      Sense preferring neither fayre,
Desire stands still, distracted 'twixt the paire.   15

    So in equall distance lay
    Two fayre Lambes in the Wolfe's way;
The hungry beast will sterve e're chuse his prey.

    But where one is chiefe, the rest
    Cease, and that's alone possest   20
Without a Rivall, Monarch of the breast.

Incommunicabilitie of Love. 7 *smart,*] smart 40   21 *Rivall,*] Rivall 40
                                                              Songs

Songs in the Play.

A Lover in the disguise of
an Amazon, is dearly beloved
of his Mistresse.

CEase thou afflicted soule to mourne,
Whose love and faith are paid with scorne;
For I am starv'd that feele the blisses
Of deare embraces, smiles, and kisses
From my soules Idoll, yet complaine   5
Of equall love more then disdaine.

Cease, Beauties exile to lament
The frozen shades of banishment,
For I in that faire bosome dwell
That is my Paradise, and Hell;   10
Banisht at home, at once at ease
In the safe Port, and tost on Seas.

Cease in cold jealous feares to pine
Sad wretch, whom Rivals undermine;
For though I hold lockt in mine armes   15
My lifes sole joy, a Traytors charmes
Prevaile, whilst I may onely blame
My selfe, that myne owne Rivall am.

Another.

A Lady rescued from death by a
Knight, who in the instant leaves her,
complaines thus.

OH whither is my fayre Sun fled,
Bearing his light, not heat away?
If thou repose in the moyst bed
Of the Sea-Queene, bring backe the day
To our darke clime, and thou shalt lye   5
Bath'd in the sea flowes from mine eye.

Vpon

Vpon what whirlewind didst thou ride
Hence, yet remaine fixt in my heart,
From me, and to me; fled, and ty'de?
    Darke riddles of the amorous art;   10
Love lent thee wings to flye, so Hee
Vnfeather'd, now must rest with mee.

Helpe, helpe, brave Youth, I burne, I bleed,
    The cruell God with Bow and Brand
Pursues the life thy valour freed,   15
    Disarme him with thy conquering hand;
And that thou mayest the wilde boy tame
Give me his dart, keepe Thou his flame.

To Ben. Iohnson.
Vpon occasion of his Ode of defiance annext to his Play of the new Inne.

'Tis true (deare *Ben*:) thy just chastizing hand
  Hath fixt upon the sotted Age a brand
To their swolne pride, and empty scribbling due,
It can nor judge, nor write, and yet 'tis true
Thy commique Muse from the exalted line   5
Toucht by thy *Alchymist*, doth since decline
From that her Zenith, and foretells a red
And blushing evening, when she goes to bed,
Yet such, as shall out-shine the glimmering light
With which all stars shall guild the following night.   10
Nor thinke it much (since all thy Eaglets may
Endure the Sunnie tryall) if we say
This hath the stronger wing, or that doth shine
Trickt up in fairer plumes, since all are thine;
Who hath his flock of cackling Geese compar'd   15
With thy tun'd quire of Swans? or else who dar'd

To Ben. Iohnson. The fair copy in Carew's autograph, in the State Papers (*PRO*), agrees with the printed text verbatim except as shown.   2 Age] age, *PRO* (*corrected from* world,)   13 or] & *PRO*   16 With] To *PRO* or else who dar'd] or whoe hath dar'd *PRO, most other MSS.*

To

To call thy births deformed? but if thou bind
By Citie-custome, or by *Gavell-kind*,
In equall shares thy love on all thy race,
We may distinguish of their sexe, and place;   20
Though one hand form them, & though one brain strike
Soules into all, they are not all alike.
Why should the follies then of this dull age
Draw from thy Pen such an immodest rage
As seemes to blast thy (else-immortall) Bayes,   25
When thine owne tongue proclaimes thy ytch of praise?
Such thirst will argue drouth. No, let be hurld
Vpon thy workes, by the detracting world,
What malice can suggest; let the Rowte say,
The running sands, that (ere thou make a play)   30
Count the slow minutes, might a *Goodwin* frame
To swallow when th'hast done thy ship-wrackt name.
Let them the deare expence of oyle upbraid
Suckt by thy watchfull Lampe, that hath betray'd
To theft the blood of martyr'd Authors, spilt   35
Into thy inke, whilst thou growest pale with guilt.
Repine not at the Tapers thriftie waste,
That sleekes thy terser Poems, nor is haste
Prayse, but excuse; and if thou overcome
A knottie writer, bring the bootie home;   40
Nor thinke it theft, if the rich spoyles so torne
From conquered Authors, be as Trophies worne.
Let others glut on the extorted praise
Of vulgar breath, trust thou to after dayes:
Thy labour'd workes shall live, when Time devoures   45
Th'abortive off-spring of their hastie houres.
Thou art not of their ranke, the quarrell lyes
Within thine owne Virge, then let this suffice,
The wiser world doth greater Thee confesse
Then all men else, then Thy selfe onely lesse.   50

19 on] to *PRO, most other MSS.*   21 form] shape *PRO*: shape *or* shap't
most other MSS.   34 that] wᶜʰ *PRO*   37 the] thy *PRO*

An Hymeneall Dialogue.

Bride and Groome.

GRoome.   Tell me (my love) since Hymen ty'de
    The holy knot, hast thou not felt
A new infused spirit slide
   Into thy brest, whilst thine did melt?

Bride.   First tell me (sweet) whose words were those?   5
   For though your voyce the ayre did breake,
Yet did my soule the sence compose,
   And through your lips my heart did speake.

Groo.   Then I perceive, when from the flame
   Of love, my scorch'd soule did retire,   10
Your frozen heart in her place came,
   And sweetly melted in that fire.

Bride.   'Tis true, for when that mutuall change
   Of soules, was made with equall gaine,
I straight might feele diffus'd a strange,   15
   But gentle heat through every veine.

Chorus.   Oh blest dis-union, that doth so
   Our bodyes from our soules divide,
As two doe one, and one foure grow,
   Each by contraction multiply'de.   20

Bride.   Thy bosome then I'le make my nest,
   Since there my willing soule doth pearch.
Groom.   And for my heart in thy chast brest,
   I'le make an everlasting search.

Chorus.   Oh blest disunion, &c.   25

An Hymeneall Dialogue. 6 your voyce the ayre *all MSS.*] the voyce your ayre
40   9 Groo.] *Groo, 40*   10 retire, *51*: retire; *40*   12 fire. *42*:
fire, *40*   14 gaine,] gaine; *40*: gain, *51*   15 I straight might feele *40*
(*Errata*): I straight feele *40* (*Text*)

Obsequies

Obsequies to the Lady
ANNE HAY.

I Heard the Virgins sigh, I saw the sleeke
And polisht Courtier, channell his fresh cheeke
With reall teares; the new-betrothed Maid
Smild not that day; the graver Senate layd
Their businesse by; of all the Courtly throng,   5
Griefe seald the heart, and silence bound the tongue.
I that ne're more of private sorrow knew
Then from my Pen some froward Mistresse drew,
And for the publike woe, had my dull sense
So sear'd with ever adverse influence,   10
As the invaders sword might have, unfelt,
Pierc'd my dead bosome, yet began to melt:
Griefe's strong instinct, did to my blood suggest
In the unknowne losse peculiar interest.
But when I heard, the noble *Carlil's* Gemme,   15
The fayrest branch of *Dennye's* ancient stemme,
Was from that Casket stolne, from this Trunke torne,
I found just cause, why they, why I should mourne.
   But who shall guide my artlesse Pen, to draw
Those blooming beauties, which I never saw?   20
How shall posteritie beleeve my story,
If I, her crowded graces, and the glory
Due to her riper vertues, shall relate
Without the knowledge of her mortall state?
Shall I, as once *Apelles*, here a feature,   25
There steale a Grace, and rifling so.whole Nature
Of all the sweets a learned eye can see,
Figure one *Venus*, and say, such was shee?
Shall I her legend fill, with what of old
Hath of the Worthies of her sex beene told,   30
And what all pens, and times to all dispence,
Restraine to her, by a prophetique sence?
Or shall I, to the Morall, and Divine
Exactest lawes, shape by an even line,
A life so straight, as it should shame the square   35

Obsequies, &c. 17 that 40 (*Errata*): the 40 (*Text*)

Left

Left in the rules of *Katherine*, or *Clare*,
And call it hers, say, so did she begin,
And had she liv'd, such had her progresse been?
These are dull wayes, by which base pens, for hire,
Dawbe glorious vice, and from *Apollo's* quire   40
Steale holy Dittyes, which prophanely they
Vpon the herse of every strumpet lay,
   We will not bathe thy corps with a forc'd teare,
Nor shall thy traine borrow the blacks they weare:
Such vulgar spice, and gums, embalme not thee,   45
Thou art the Theame of Truth, not Poetrie.
Thou shalt endure a tryall by thy Peeres,
Virgins of equall birth, of equall yeares,
Whose vertues held with thine an emulous strife,
Shall draw thy picture, and record thy life.   50
One shall enspheare thine eyes, another shall
Impearle thy teeth; a third, thy white and small
Hand, shall besnow; a fourth, incarnadine
Thy rosie cheeke, untill each beauteous line,
Drawne by her hand, in whom that part excells,   55
Meet in one Center, where all beautie dwells.
Others, in taske shall thy choyce vertues share,
Some shall their birth, some their ripe growth declare;
Though niggard *Time* left much unhach'd by deeds,
They shall relate how thou hadst all the seeds   60
Of every Vertue, which in the pursuit
Of time, must have brought forth admired fruit.
Thus shalt thou, from the mouth of envy, raise
A glorious journall of thy thrifty dayes,
Like a bright starre, shot from his spheare, whose race   65
In a continued line of flames, we trace.
This, if survay'd, shall to thy view impart
How little more then late, thou wer't, thou art,
This shall gaine credit with succeeding times,
When nor by bribed pens, nor partiall rimes   70
Of engag'd kindred, but the sacred truth
Is storied by the partners of thy youth;
Their breath shall Saint thee, and be this thy pride,
Thus even by Rivals to be Deifide.

     49 vertues 51: vertues, 40   58 declare;] declare, 40

To

To the Countesse of Anglesie *upon the immoderatly-by-her-lamented death of her Husband.*

Madam, men say you keepe with dropping eyes
  Your sorrowes fresh, wat'ring the Rose that lyes
Fall'n from your cheeks upon your deare Lords Hearse.
Alas! those odors now no more can pierce
His cold pale nosthrill, nor the crymson dye   5
Present a gracefull blush to his darke eye.
Thinke you that flood of pearly moysture hath
The vertue fabled of old *Æsons* bath?
You may your beauties, and your youth consume
Over his Vrne, and with your sighes perfume   10
The solitarie Vault, which as you grone
In hollow Ecchoes shall repeate your moane;
There you may wither, and an Autumne bring
Vpon your selfe, but not call back his spring.
Forbeare your fruitlesse griefe then, and let those   15
Whose love was doubted, gaine beliefe with showes
To their suspected faith; you, whose whole life
In every act crown'd you a constant Wife,
May spare the practise of that vulgar trade,
Which superstitious custome onely made;   20
Rather a Widow now of wisedome prove
The patterne, as a Wife you were of love:
Yet since you surfet on your griefe, 'tis fit
I tell the world, upon what cates you sit
Glutting your sorrowes; and at once include   25
His story, your excuse, my gratitude.
You, that behold how yond' sad Lady blends
Those ashes with her teares, lest, as she spends
Her tributarie sighes, the frequent gust
Might scatter up and downe the noble dust,   30
Know when that heape of Atomes, was with bloud

To the Countesse of Anglesie, &c. 8 bath? *51*: bath. *40*   12 moane;]
moane. *40*: moan; *51*

Kneaded

Kneaded to solid flesh, and firmely stood
On stately Pillars, the rare forme might move
The froward *Juno's*, or chast *Cinthia's* love.
In motion, active grace, in rest, a calme   35
Attractive sweetnesse, brought both wound and balme
To every heart. He was compos'd of all
The wishes of ripe Virgins, when they call
For Hymens rites, and in their fancies wed
A shape of studied beauties to their bed.   40
Within this curious Palace dwelt a soule
Gave lustre to each part, and to the whole.
This drest his face in curteous smiles; and so
From comely gestures, sweeter manners flow.
This courage joyn'd to strength, so the hand, bent,   45
Was valours, open'd, Bounties instrument
Which did the scale, and sword, of Justice hold,
Knew how to brandish steele, and scatter gold.
This taught him, not to engage his modest tongue
In suites of private gaine, though publike wrong;   50
Nor mis-employ (*As is the Great-mans use,*)
His credit with his Master, to traduce,
Deprave, maligne, and ruine Innocence
In proud revenge of some mis-judg'd offence.
But all his actions had the noble end   55
T'advance desert, or grace some worthy friend.
He chose not in the active streame to swim,
Nor hunted Honour; which, yet hunted him.
But like a quiet Eddie, that hath found
Some hollow creeke, there turnes his waters round,   60
And in continuall circles, dances free
From the impetuous Torrent; so did hee
Give others leave to turne the wheele of State,
(*Whose restlesse motion spins the subjects fate*)
Whilst he retir'd from the tumultuous noyse   65
Of Court, and suitors presse; apart, enjoyes
Freedome, and mirth, himselfe, his time, and friends,
And with sweet rellish tastes each houre he spends.
I could remember how his noble heart

First kindled at your beauties, with what Art   70
He chas'd his game through all opposing feares,
When I his sighes to you, and back your teares
Convay'd to him, how loyall then, and how
Constant he prov'd since to his mariage vow,
So as his wandring eyes never drew in   75
One lustfull thought to tempt his soule to sinne,
But that I feare such mention rather may
Kindle new griefe, than blow the old away.
   Then let him rest joyn'd to great *Buckingham*,
And with his brothers, mingle his bright flame: 80
Looke up, and meet their beames, and you from thence
May chance derive a chearfull influence.
Seeke him no more in dust, but call agen
Your scatterd beauties home, and so the pen
Which now I take from this sad Elegie   85
Shall sing the Trophies of your conquering eye.

An Elegie upon the death of the
Deane of Pauls, D^r. Iohn Donne.

CAn we not force from widdowed Poetry,
  Now thou art dead (Great DONNE) one Elegie
To crowne thy Hearse? Why yet dare we not trust
Though with unkneaded dowe-bak't prose thy dust,
Such as the uncisor'd Churchman from the flower   5
Of fading Rhetorique, short liv'd as his houre,
Dry as the sand that measures it, should lay
Upon thy Ashes, on the funerall day?
Have we no voice, no tune? Did'st thou dispense
Through all our language, both the words and sense? 10

To the Countesse of Anglesie, &c.   74 vow, *51:* vow. *40*   80 flame:]
flame, *40*   82 influence. *42:* influence, *40*
  An Elegie, &c.   Text from *Poems, By J. D. with elegies on the authors death*
1633 (1635, 1639), collated with *40*. See Commentary. Verse paragraphs as in *40*.
  Title: An Elegie upon the death of the Deane of Pauls, D^r. Iohn Donne: By
M^r. Tho: Carie. 1633. An Elegie upon the death of Doctor Donne, *Deane* of Pauls. *40*.
1 not] nor *40 (some copies)*   3 dare] did *40*   5 Churchman] Lect'rer *40*
7 should] might *40*   8 thy] the *40*   9 no voice, no tune ?] nor tune,
nor voyce ? *40*

                                                      'Tis

'Tis a sad truth; The Pulpit may her plaine,
And sober Christian precepts still retaine,
Doctrines it may, and wholesome Uses frame,
Grave Homilies, and Lectures, But the flame
Of thy brave Soule, (that shot such heat and light,   15
As burnt our earth, and made our darknesse bright,
Committed holy Rapes upon our Will,
Did through the eye the melting heart distill;
And the deepe knowledge of darke truths so teach,
As sense might judge, what phansie could not reach;) 20
Must be desir'd for ever. So the fire,
That fills with spirit and heat the Delphique quire,
Which kindled first by thy Promethean breath,
Glow'd here a while, lies quench't now in thy death;
The Muses garden with Pedantique weedes   25
O'rspred, was purg'd by thee; The lazie seeds
Of servile imitation throwne away;
And fresh invention planted, Thou didst pay
The debts of our penurious bankrupt age;
Licentious thefts, that make poëtique rage   30
A Mimique fury, when our soules must bee
Possest, or with Anacreons Extasie,
Or Pindars, not their owne; The subtle cheat
Of slie Exchanges, and the jugling feat
Of two-edg'd words, or whatsoever wrong   35
By ours was done the Greeke, or Latine tongue,
Thou hast redeem'd, and open'd Us a Mine
Of rich and pregnant phansie, drawne a line
Of masculine expression, which had good ˙
Old Orpheus seene, Or all the ancient Brood   40
Our superstitious fooles admire, and hold
Their lead more precious, then thy burnish't Gold,
Thou hadst beene their Exchequer, and no more
They each in others dust, had rak'd for Ore.
Thou shalt yield no precedence, but of time,   45
And the blinde fate of language, whose tun'd chime

15–20 (that . . . reach;)] that . . . reach; *1633*: that . . . reach, *1635, 1639, 40*
17 our Will,] the will, *40*   20 what] where *40 (Text)*: what *40 (Errata)*
29 bankrupt] banquerout *40*   44 dust, had rak'd] dung had search'd *40*

More

More charmes the outward sense; Yet thou maist claime
From so great disadvantage greater fame,
Since to the awe of thy imperious wit
Our stubborne language bends, made only fit   50
With her tough-thick-rib'd hoopes to gird about
Thy Giant phansie, which had prov'd too stout
For their soft melting Phrases. As in time
They had the start, so did they cull the prime
Buds of invention many a hundred yeare,   55
And left the rifled fields, besides the feare
To touch their Harvest, yet from those bare lands
Of what is purely thine, thy only hands
(And that thy smallest worke) have gleaned more
Then all those times, and tongues could reape before; 60
    But thou art gone, and thy strict lawes will be
Too hard for Libertines in Poetrie.
They will repeale the goodly exil'd traine
Of gods and goddesses, which in thy just raigne
Were banish'd nobler Poems, now, with these   65
The silenc'd tales o'th' Metamorphoses
Shall stuffe their lines, and swell the windy Page,
Till Verse refin'd by thee, in this last Age
Turne ballad rime, Or those old Idolls bee
Ador'd againe, with new apostasie;   70
    Oh, pardon mee, that breake with untun'd verse
The reverend silence that attends thy herse,
Whose awfull solemne murmures were to thee
More then these faint lines, A loud Elegie,
That did proclaime in a dumbe eloquence   75
The death of all the Arts, whose influence
Growne feeble, in these panting numbers lies
Gasping short winded Accents, and so dies:
So doth the swiftly turning wheele not stand
In th'instant we withdraw the moving hand,   80
But some small time maintaine a faint weake course
By vertue of the first impulsive force:

50 stubborne] troublesome *40*   51 tough-thick-rib'd] tough thick-rib'd *40*
54 cull] call *40 (some copies)*   58 is purely] was onely *40*   59 thy] their
40   63 repeale] recall *40*   65 Were] Was *40*   66 o' th'] i' th' *40*
73 awfull solemne] solemne, awfull *40*   74 faint] rude *40*   81 small]
short *40*   maintaine] maintaines *1635, 1639:* retaine *40*

                                        And

And so whil'st I cast on thy funerall pile
Thy crowne of Bayes, Oh, let it crack a while,
And spit disdaine, till the devouring flashes   85
Suck all the moysture up, then turne to ashes.
 I will not draw the envy to engrosse
All thy perfections, or weepe all our losse;
Those are too numerous for an Elegie,
And this too great, to be express'd by mee.   90
Though every pen should share a distinct part,
Yet art thou Theme enough to tyre all Art;
Let others carve the rest, it shall suffice
I on thy Tombe this Epitaph incise.

Here lies a King, that rul'd as hee thought fit   95
The universall Monarchy of wit;
Here lie two Flamens, and both those, the best,
Apollo's first, at last, the true Gods Priest.

In answer of an Elegiacall Letter upon the death of the King of Sweden *from* Aurelian Townsend, *inviting me to write on that subject.*

WHy dost thou sound, my deare *Aurelian*,
  In so shrill accents, from thy *Barbican*,
A loude allarum to my drowsie eyes,
Bidding them wake in teares and Elegies
For mightie *Swedens* fall? Alas! how may   5
My Lyrique feet, that of the smooth soft way
Of Love, and Beautie, onely know the tread,
In dancing paces celebrate the dead
Victorious King, or his Majesticke Hearse
Prophane with th'humble touch of their low verse?   10
Virgil, nor *Lucan,* no, nor *Tasso* more
Then both, not *Donne,* worth all that went before,

An Elegie, &c. 88 our] the 40   89 an] one 40   91-2 *Omitted in* 40
94 Tombe] Grave 40   95-8 *No italics or indentation in* 40   97 *lie*] lyes 40
                                                            With

With the united labour of their wit
Could a just Poem to this subject fit,
His actions were too mighty to be rais'd   15
Higher by Verse, let him in prose be prays'd,
In modest faithfull story, which his deedes
Shall turne to Poems: when the next Age reades
Of *Frankfort*, *Leipsigh*, *Worsburgh*, of the *Rhyne*;
The *Leck*, the *Danube*, *Tilly*, *Wallestein*,   20
Bavaria, *Papenheim*, *Lutzenfield*, where Hee
Gain'd after death a posthume Victorie,
They'le thinke his Acts things rather feign'd then done
Like our Romances of the Knight o'th' Sun.
Leave we him then to the grave Chronicler,   25
Who though to Annals he can not refer
His too-briefe storie, yet his Journals may
Stand by the *Cæsars* yeares, and every day
Cut into minutes, each, shall more containe
Of great designement then an Emperours raigne;   30
And (since 'twas but his Church-yard) let him have
For his owne ashes now no narrower Grave
Then the whole *German* Continents vast wombe,
Whilst all her Cities doe but make his Tombe.
Let us to supreame providence commit   35
The fate of Monarchs, which first thought it fit
To rend the Empire from the *Austrian* graspe,
And next from *Swedens*, even when he did claspe
Within his dying armes the Soveraigntie
Of all those Provinces, that men might see   40
The Divine wisedome would not leave that Land
Subject to any one Kings sole command.
Then let the Germans feare if *Cæsar* shall,
Or the Vnited Princes, rise, and fall,
But let us that in myrtle bowers sit   45
Vnder secure shades, use the benefit
Of peace and plenty, which the blessed hand
Of our good King gives this obdurate Land,
Let us of Revels sing, and let thy breath
(Which fill'd Fames trumpet with *Gustavus* death,   50

In answer of an Elegiacall Letter, &c.   34 Tombe.] Tombe: *40 (some copies)*

Blowing

Blowing his name to heaven) gently inspire
Thy past'rall pipe, till all our swaines admire
Thy song and subject, whilst they both comprise
The beauties of the *SHEPHERDS PARADISE;*
For who like thee (whose loose discourse is farre   55
More neate and polisht then our Poems are,
Whose very gate's more gracefull then our dance)
In sweetly-flowing numbers may advance
The glorious night? When, not to act foule rapes,
Like birds, or beasts, but in their Angel-shapes   60
A troope of Deities came downe to guide
Our steerelesse barkes in passions swelling tide
By vertues Carde, and brought us from above
A patterne of their owne celestiall love.
Nor lay it in darke sullen precepts drown'd   65
But with rich fancie, and cleare Action crown'd
Through a misterious fable (that was drawne
Like a transparant veyle of purest Lawne
Before their dazelling beauties) the divine
Venus, did with her heavenly *Cupid* shine.   70
The stories curious web, the Masculine stile,
The subtile sence, did Time and sleepe beguile,
Pinnion'd and charm'd they stood to gaze upon
Th'Angellike formes, gestures, and motion,
To heare those ravishing sounds that did dispence   75
Knowledge and pleasure, to the soule, and sense.
It fill'd us with amazement to behold
Love made all spirit, his corporeall mold
Dissected into Atomes melt away
To empty ayre, and from the grosse allay   80
Of mixtures, and compounding Accidents
Refin'd to immateriall Elements.
But when the Queene of Beautie did inspire
The ayre with perfumes, and our hearts with fire,
Breathing from her celestiall Organ sweet   85
Harmonious notes, our soules fell at her feet,
And did with humble reverend dutie, more
Her rare perfections, then high state adore.

71 stile, *51*: stile; *40*   74 motion,] motion. *40*   88 adore. *51*: adore, *40*

These

These harmelesse pastimes let my *Townsend* sing
To rurall tunes; not that thy Muse wants wing   90
To soare a loftier pitch, for she hath made
A noble flight, and plac'd th'Heroique shade
Above the reach of our faint flagging ryme;
But these are subjects proper to our clyme.
Tourneyes, Masques, Theaters, better become   95
Our *Halcyon* dayes; what though the German Drum
Bellow for freedome and revenge, the noyse
Concernes not us, nor should divert our joyes;
Nor ought the thunder of their Carabins
Drowne the sweet Ayres of our tun'd Violins;   100
Beleeve me friend, if their prevailing powers
Gaine them a calme securitie like ours,
They'le hang their Armes up on the Olive bough,
And dance, and revell then, as we doe now.

Vpon Master W. Mounta-gue *his returne from travell.*

L Eade the black Bull to slaughter, with the Bore
    And Lambe, then purple with their mingled gore
The Oceans curled brow, that so we may
The Sea-Gods for their carefull waftage pay:
Send gratefull Incense up in pious smoake   5
To those mild spirits, that cast a curbing yoake
Vpon the stubborne winds, that calmely blew
To the wisht shore, our long'd for *Mountague.*
Then whilst the Aromatique odours burne,
In honour of their Darling's safe returne;   10
The Muses Quire shall thus with voyce and hand,
Blesse the fayre Gale that drove his ship to land.

        Sweetly breathing Vernall Ayre,
        That with kind warmth doest repayre
        Winters ruines, from whose brest   15
        All the gums, and spice of th'East

                                    Borrow

Borrow their perfumes, whose eye
Guilds the morne, and cleares the skie,
Whose disheveld tresses shed
Pearles upon the Violet bed,   20
On whose brow with calme smiles drest
The Halcion sits and builds her nest:
Beautie, Youth, and endlesse spring,
Dwell upon thy rosie wing.
Thou, if stormie Boreas *throwes*   25
Downe whole Forrests when he blowes,
With a pregnant flowery birth
Canst refresh the teeming Earth;
If he nip the early bud,
If he blast what's faire or good;   30
If he scatter our choyce flowers,
If he shake our hills or bowers,
If his rude breath threaten us,
Thou canst stroake great Æolus,
And from him the grace obtaine   35
To binde him in an Iron chaine.

Thus, whilst you deale your body 'mongst your friends,
And fill their circling armes, my glad soule sends
This her embrace: Thus we of *Delphos* greet,
As Lay-men claspe their hands, we joyne our feet.   40

To *Master* W. Moun-
tague.

SIR, I arest you at your Countreyes suit,
Who as a debt to her, requires the fruit
Of that rich stock; which she by Natures hand
Gave you in trust, to th'use of this whole Land.
Next, she endites you of a Felonie,   5
For stealing, what was her Proprietie:

Vpon Master W. Mountague, &c. 22 *Halcion* 42: *Halcions* 40   nest:] nest. 40:
nest, 51   26 *Forrests* 51: *Forrest* 40   32 *he* 1772, H35: *she* 40   39
greet, 51: greet 40
    To Master W. Mountague. 6 Proprietie:] Proprietie. 40: Propriety: 51
                                                        Your

Your selfe from hence, so seeking to convey
The publike treasure of the state away.
More, y'are accus'd of Ostracisme, the Fate
Impos'd of old by the Athenian state   10
On eminent vertue, but that curse which they
Cast on their men, You on your Countrey lay:
For, thus divided from your noble parts
This Kingdome lives in exile, and all hearts
That rellish worth, or honour, being rent   15
From your perfections, suffer banishment.
These are your publike injuries; but I
Have a just private quarrell to defie
And call you Coward, thus to run away
When you had pierc'd my heart, not daring stay   20
Till I redeem'd my honour; but I sweare
By *Celia's* eyes, by the same force to teare
Your heart from you, or not to end this strife
Till I or find revenge, or lose my life.
But as in single fights it oft hath beene   25
In that unequall equall tryall seene,
That he who had receiv'd the wrong at first,
Came from the Combat oft too with the worst;
So if you foyle me when we meet, I'le then
Give you fayre leave to wound me so agen.   30

On the Mariage of T. K. and C. C. the morning stormie.

SVch should this day be, so the Sun should hide
His bashfull face, and let the conquering Bride
Without a Rivall shine, whilst He forbeares
To mingle his unequall beames with hers;
Or if sometimes he glance his squinting eye·   5
Betweene the parting cloudes, 'tis but to spye,

To Master W. Mountague.   12 lay: *51*: lay. *40*   15 honour,] honout,
40   16 banishment. *51*: banishment: *40*

Not

Not emulate her glories, so comes drest
In vayles, but as a Masquer to the feast.
Thus heaven should lower, such stormy gusts should blow
Not to denounce ungentle Fates, but show   10
The cheerefull Bridegroome to the clouds and wind
Hath all his teares, and all his sighes assign'd.
Let Tempests struggle in the Ayre, but rest
Eternall calmes within thy peacefull brest,
Thrice happy Youth; but ever sacrifice   15
To that fayre hand that dry'de thy blubbred eyes,
That cround thy head with Roses, and turn'd all
The plagues of love into a cordiall,
When first it joyn'd her Virgin snow to thine,
Which when to day the Priest shall recombine,   20
From the misterious holy touch such charmes
Will flow, as shall unlock her wreathed armes,
And open a free passage to that fruit
Which thou hast toyl'd for with a long pursuit.
But ere thou feed, that thou may'st better taste   25
Thy present joyes, thinke on thy torments past.
Thinke on the mercy freed thee, thinke upon
Her vertues, graces, beauties, one by one,
So shalt thou relish all, enjoy the whole
Delights of her faire body, and pure soule.   30
Then boldly to the fight of Love proceed,
'Tis mercy not to pitty though she bleed,
Wee'le strew no nuts, but change that ancient forme,
For till to morrow wee'le prorogue this storme,
Which shall confound with its loude whistling noyse   35
Her pleasing shreekes, and fan thy panting joyes.

On the Mariage, &c.   14 brest,] brest. *40*   34 storme,] storme. *40*

For

For a Picture where a Queen Laments over the Tombe of a slaine Knight.

B Rave Youth; to whom Fate in one hower
Gave death, and Conquest, by whose power
Those chaines about my heart are wound,
With which the Foe my Kingdome bound,
Freed, and captiv'd by thee, I bring   5
For either Act an offering;
For victory, this wreathe of Bay:
In signe of Thraldome, downe I lay
Scepter and Crowne: Take from my sight
Those Royall Robes; since fortunes spight   10
Forbids me live thy Vertues prize,
I'le dye thy Valours sacrifice.

To a Lady that desired I would love her.

1.

N Ow you have freely given me leave to love,
What will you doe?
Shall I your mirth, or passion move
When I begin to wooe;
Will you torment, or scorne, or love me too?   5

2.

Each pettie beautie can disdaine, and I
Spight of your hate
Without your leave can see, and dye;
Dispence a nobler Fate,
'Tis easie to destroy, you may create.   10

For a Picture, &c. 2 Gave 51: Grave 40
To a Lady, &c. 3 passion 40 (*Errata*): pastime 40 (*Text*)   6 2.] 2: 40

3.

Then give me leave to love, and love me too,
        Not with designe
    To rayse, as Loves curst Rebells doe,
        When puling Poets whine,
Fame to their beautie, from their blubbr'd eyne.   15

4.

Griefe is a puddle, and reflects not cleare
        Your beauties rayes,
    Joyes are pure streames, your eyes appeare
        Sullen in sadder layes,
In chearfull numbers they shine bright with prayse; 20

5.

Which shall not mention to expresse you fayre
        Wounds, flames, and darts,
    Stormes in your brow, nets in your haire,
        Suborning all your parts,
Or to betray, or torture captive hearts.   25

6.

I'le make your eyes like morning Suns appeare,
        As milde, and faire;
    Your brow as Crystall smooth, and cleare,
        And your dishevell'd hayre
Shall flow like a calme Region of the Ayre.   30

7.

Rich Natures store, (which is the Poets Treasure)
        I'le spend, to dresse
    Your beauties, if your mine of Pleasure
        In equall thankfulnesse
You but unlocke, so we each other blesse.   35

11 too,] too *40*   13 doe, *51*: doe; *40*   20 prayse;] prayse. *40* 27
faire;] faire *40*: fair; *51*

Vpon

Vpon my Lord Chiefe Iustice his election of my Lady A. W. for his Mistresse.

1.

HEare this, and tremble all
 Vsurping Beauties, that create
A government Tyrannicall
       In Loves free state,
Justice, hath to the sword of your edg'd eyes   5
His equall ballance joyn'd, his sage head lyes
In Loves soft lap, which must be just and wise.

2.

      Harke how the sterne Law breathes
Forth amorous sighs, and now prepares
No fetters, but of silken wreathes,   10
      And, braded hayres;
His dreadfull Rods and Axes are exil'd
Whilst he sits crown'd with Roses: Love hath fil'de
His native roughnesse, Justice is growne milde.

3.

      The golden Age returnes,   15
Loves bowe, and quiver, uselesse lye,
His shaft, his brand, nor wounds, nor burnes,
      And crueltie
Is sunke to Hell, the fayre shall all be kind,
Who loves, shall be belov'd, the froward mind   20
To a deformed shape shall be confin'd.

Vpon my Lord Chiefe Iustice, &c.   13 Roses:] Roses, 40

Astræa

4.

Astræa hath possest
An earthly seate, and now remaines
In *Finches* heart, but *Wentworths* brest
    That Guest containes;   25
With her she dwells, yet hath not left the skies,
Nor lost her Spheare, for, new-enthron'd she cryes
I know no Heaven but fayre *Wentworths* eyes.

To A. D. unreasonable distrust-
full of her owne beauty.

FAyre *Doris* breake thy Glasse, it hath perplext
  With a darke Comment, beauties clearest Text;
It hath not told thy faces story true,
But brought false Copies to thy jealous view.
No colour, feature, lovely ayre, or grace,   5
That ever yet adorn'd a beauteous face,
But thou maist reade in thine, or justly doubt
Thy Glasse hath beene suborn'd to leave it out,
But if it offer to thy nice survey
A spot, a staine, a blemish, or decay,   10
It not belongs to thee, the treacherous light
Or faithlesse stone abuse thy credulous sight.
Perhaps the magique of thy face, hath wrought
Vpon th'enchanted Crystall, and so brought
Fantasticke shadowes to delude thine eyes   15
With ayrie repercussive sorceries.
Or else th'enamoured Image pines away
For love of the fayre Object, and so may
Waxe pale and wan, and though the substance grow
Lively and fresh, that may consume with woe;   20
Give then no faith to the false specular stone,
But let thy beauties by th'effects be knowne:
Looke (sweetest *Doris*) on my love-sick heart,
In that true mirrour see how fayre thou art.
There, by Loves never-erring Pensill drawne   25
Shalt thou behold thy face, like th'early dawne

                                              Shoot

Shoot through the shadie covert of thy hayre,
Enameling, and perfuming the calme Ayre
With Pearles, and Roses, till thy Suns display
Their lids, and let out the imprison'd day;   30
Whilst Delfique Priests, (enlightned by their Theame)
In amorous numbers court thy golden beame,
And from Loves Altars cloudes of sighes arise
In smoaking Incence to adore thine eyes.
If then Love flow from Beautie as th'effect   35
How canst thou the resistlesse cause suspect?
Who would not brand that Foole, that should contend
There were no fire, where smoke and flames ascend?
Distrust is worse then scorne, not to beleeve
My harmes, is greater wrong then not to grieve;   40
What cure can for my festring sore be found,
Whilst thou beleev'st thy beautie cannot wound?
Such humble thoughts more cruell Tyrants prove
Then all the pride that e're usurp'd in Love,
For Beauties Herald, here denounceth war,   45
There her false spies betray me to a snare.
If fire disguis'd in balls of snow were hurl'd
It unsuspected might consume the world;
Where our prevention ends, danger begins,
So Wolves in Sheepes, Lyons in Asses skins,   50
Might farre more mischiefe worke, because lesse fear'd,
Those, the whole flock, these, might kill all the herd.
Appeare then as thou art, break through this cloude,
Confesse thy beauty, though thou thence grow proud,
Be faire though scornfull, rather let me find   55
Thee cruell, then thus mild, and more unkind;
Thy crueltie doth only me defie,
But these dull thoughts thee to thy selfe denie.
Whether thou meane to bartar, or bestow
Thy selfe, 'tis fit thou thine owne valew know.   60
I will not cheate thee of thy selfe, nor pay
Lesse for thee then th'art worth, thou shalt not say
That is but brittle glasse, which I have found
By strict enquirie a firme Diamond.

To A.D., &c. 30 day;] day. 40   32 court MSS.: count 40   52 herd.]
herd, 40   53 cloude,] cloude 40: cloud, 51   60 selfe,] selfe; 40: self, 51
                                                              I'le

I'le trade with no such Indian foole as sells   65
Gold, Pearles, and pretious stones, for Beads and Bells;
Nor will I take a present from your hand,
Which you or prize not, or not understand;
It not endeares your bountie that I doe
Esteeme your gift, unlesse you doe so too;   70
You undervalew me, when you bestow
On me, what you nor care for, nor yet know.
No (Lovely *Doris*) change thy thoughts, and be
In love first with thy selfe, and then with me.
You are afflicted that you are not faire,   75
And I as much tormented that you are,
What I admire, you scorne; what I love, hate,
Through different faiths, both share an equall Fate,
Fast to the truth, which you renounce, I stick,
I dye a Martyr, you an Heretique.   80

To my friend G. N. from Wrest.

I Breathe (sweet *Ghib:*) the temperate ayre of *Wrest*
  Where I no more with raging stormes opprest,
Weare the cold nights out by the bankes of Tweed,
On the bleake Mountains, where fierce tempests breed,
And everlasting Winter dwells; where milde   5
Favonius, and the Vernall windes exilde,
Did never spread their wings: but the wilde North
Brings sterill Fearne, Thistles, and Brambles forth.
Here steep'd in balmie dew, the pregnant Earth
Sends from her teeming wombe a flowrie birth,   10
And cherisht with the warme Suns quickning heate,
Her porous bosome doth rich odours sweate;
Whose perfumes through the Ambient ayre diffuse
Such native Aromatiques, as we use
No forraigne Gums, nor essence fetcht from farre,   15
No Volatile spirits, nor compounds that are

To my friend, &c. 9 Earth] Earth, *40*   16 No] Vo *40*
                                        Adulterate,

Adulterate, but at Natures cheape expence
With farre more genuine sweetes refresh the sense.
Such pure and uncompounded beauties, blesse
This Mansion with an usefull comelinesse,   20
Devoide of Art, for here the Architect
Did not with curious skill a Pile erect
Of carved Marble, Touch, or Porpherie,
But built a house for hospitalitie;
No sumptuous Chimney-peece of shining stone   25
Invites the strangers eye to gaze upon,
And coldly entertaines his sight, but cleare
And cheerefull flames, cherish and warme him here:
No Dorique, nor Corinthian Pillars grace
With Imagery this structures naked face,   30
The Lord and Lady of this place delight
Rather to be in act, then seeme in sight;
In stead of Statues to adorne their wall
They throng with living men, their merry Hall,
Where at large Tables fill'd with wholsome meates   35
The servant, Tennant, and kind neighbour eates.
Some of that ranke, spun of a finer thred
Are with the Women, Steward, and Chaplaine fed
With daintier cates; Others of better note
Whom wealth, parts, office, or the Heralds coate   40
Have sever'd from the common, freely sit
At the Lords Table, whose spread sides admit
A large accesse of friends to fill those seates
Of his capacious circle, fill'd with meates
Of choycest rellish, till his Oaken back   45
Vnder the load of pil'd-up dishes crack.
Nor thinke, because our Piramids, and high
Exalted Turrets threaten not the skie,
That therefore *Wrest* of narrownesse complaines
Or streightned Walls, for she more numerous traines 50
Of Noble guests daily receives, and those
Can with farre more conveniencie dispose
Then prouder Piles, where the vaine builder spent
More cost in outward gay Embellishment
Then reall use: which was the sole designe   55

20 comelinesse,] comelinesse. *40:* comeliness' *51*   30 face,] face *40 (some copies)*
Of

Of our contriver, who made things not fine,
But fit for service. *Amalthea's* Horne
Of plentie is not in Effigie worne
Without the gate, but she within the dore
Empties her free and unexhausted store.   60
Nor, croun'd with wheaten wreathes, doth *Ceres* stand
In stone, with a crook'd sickle in her hand:
Nor, on a Marble Tunne, his face besmear'd
With grapes, is curl'd uncizard *Bacchus* rear'd.
We offer not in Emblemes to the eyes,   65
But to the taste those usefull Deities.
Wee presse the juycie God, and quaffe his blood,
And grinde the Yeallow Goddesse into food.
Yet we decline not, all the worke of Art,
But where more bounteous Nature beares a part   70
And guides her Hand-maid, if she but dispence
Fit matter, she with care and diligence
Employes her skill, for where the neighbour sourse
Powers forth her waters she directs their course,
And entertaines the flowing streames in deepe   75
And spacious channells, where they slowly creepe
In snakie windings, as the shelving ground
Leades them in circles, till they twice surround
This Island Mansion, which i' th' center plac'd,
Is with a double Crystall heaven embrac'd,   80
In which our watery constellations floate,
Our Fishes, Swans, our Water-man and Boate,
Envy'd by those above, which wish to slake
Their starre-burnt limbes, in our refreshing lake,
But they stick fast nayl'd to the barren Spheare,   85
Whilst our encrease in fertile watèrs here
Disport, and wander freely where they please
Within the circuit of our narrow Seas.
   With various Trees we fringe the waters brinke,
Whose thirstie rootes the soaking moysture drinke,   90
And whose extended boughes in equall rankes
Yeeld fruit, and shade, and beautie to the bankes.
On this side young *Vertumnus* sits, and courts

57 service.] service *40 (some copies)*   62 sickle *40 (Errata)*: circle *40 (Text)*
90 drinke,] drinke. *40*

His

His ruddie-cheek'd *Pomona, Zephyre* sports
On th'other, with lov'd *Flora,* yeelding there   95
Sweetes for the smell, sweetes for the palate here.
But did you taste the high & mighty drinke
Which from that Fountaine flowes, you'ld cleerly think
The God of Wine did his plumpe clusters bring,
And crush the Falerne grape into our spring;   100
Or else disguis'd in watery Robes did swim
To *Ceres* bed, and make her big of Him,
Begetting so himselfe on Her: for know
Our Vintage here in *March* doth nothing owe
To theirs in Autumne, but our fire boyles here   105
As lustie liquour as the Sun makes there.
　　Thus I enjoy my selfe, and taste the fruit
Of this blest Peace, whilst toyl'd in the pursuit
Of Bucks, and Stags, th'embleme of warre, you strive
To keepe the memory of our Armes alive.   110

A New-yeares gift.
To the King.

LOoke back old *Janus,* and survey
　　From *Times* birth, till this new-borne day,
All the successfull season bound
With Lawrell wreathes, and Trophies crown'd;
Turne o're the Annals past, and where   5
Happie auspitious dayes appeare,
Mark'd with the whiter stone, that cast
On the darke brow of th'Ages past
A dazeling luster, let them shine
In this succeeding circles twine,   10
Till it be round with glories spread,
Then with it crowne our *Charles* his head,
That we th'ensuing yeare may call
One great continued festivall.
Fresh joyes in varied formes apply,   15
To each distinct captivitie.

To my friend, &c.　　94 *Pomona,* 51: *Pomona.* 40　　95 there] thete 40　　109
warre,] warre 40

Season

Season his cares by day with nights
Crown'd with all conjugall delights,
May the choyce beauties that enflame
His Royall brest be still the same,   20
And he still thinke them such, since more
Thou canst not give from Natures store.
Then as a Father let him be
With numerous issue blest, and see
The faire and God-like off-spring growne   25
From budding starres to Suns full blowne.
Circle with peacefull Olive bowes,
And conquering Bayes, his Regall browes.
Let his strong vertues overcome,
And bring him bloodlesse Trophies home: 30
Strew all the pavements, where he treads
With loyall hearts, or Rebels heads;
But *Byfront*, open thou no more,
In his blest raigne the Temple dore.

To the Queene.

THou great Commandresse, that doest move
  Thy Scepter o're the Crowne of Love,
And through his Empire with the Awe
Of Thy chaste beames, doest give the Law,
From his prophaner Altars, we   5
Turne to adore Thy Deitie:
He, only can wilde lust provoke,
Thou, those impurer flames canst choke;
And where he scatters looser fires,
Thou turn'st them into chast desires: 10
His Kingdome knowes no rule but this,
What ever pleaseth lawfull is;
Thy sacred Lore shewes us the path
Of Modestie, and constant faith,
Which makes the rude Male satisfied   15
With one faire Female by his side;

To the Queene. 4 Law, *51*: Law. 40

Doth

Doth either sex to each unite,
And forme loves pure Hermophradite.
To this Thy faith behold the wilde
Satyr already reconciled,   20
Who from the influence of Thine eye
Hath suckt the deepe Divinitie;
O free them then, that they may teach
The Centaur, and the Horsman preach
To Beasts and Birds, sweetly to rest   25
Each in his proper Lare and nest:
They shall convey it to the floud,
Till there Thy law be understood.
    So shalt thou with thy pregnant fire,
    The water, earth, and ayre, inspire.   30

To the New-yeare, for the Countesse of Carlile.

GIve *Lucinda* Pearle, nor Stone,
    Lend them light who else have none,
Let Her beautie shine alone.

Gums nor spice bring from the East,
For the Phenix in Her brest   5
Builds his funerall pile, and nest.

No attire thou canst invent,
Shall to grace her forme be sent,
She adornes all ornament.

Give Her nothing, but restore   10
Those sweet smiles which heretofore,
In Her chearfull eyes she wore.

Drive those envious cloudes away,
Vailes that have o're-cast my day,
And ecclips'd Her brighter ray.   15

To the Queene.   20 reconciled,] reconciled. *40*: reconcil'd, *51*   23 teach *70*,
H4: teach, *40*
To the New-yeare, &c. *Title: New-yeare, H4: New-yeare 40*   3 beautie]
beautis *40*: beauty *42*: beauties *H4*   7 attire *H4*: tyre *40*: rich tyre *70*
                                                                                        Let

Let the royall Goth mowe downe
This yeares harvest with his owne
Sword, and spare *Lucinda's* frowne.

Janus, if when next I trace
Those sweet lines, I in her face   20
Reade the Charter of my grace,

Then from bright *Apollo's* tree,
Such a Garland wreath'd shall be,
As shall Crowne both Her and thee.

To my Honoured friend, Master Thomas May, *upon his* Comedie, *The Heire.*

THe *Heire* being borne, was in his tender age
Rockt in the Cradle of a private Stage,
Where lifted up by many a willing hand,
The child did from the first day fairely stand.
Since having gather'd strength, he dares preferre   5
His steps into the publike Theater
The World: where he dispaires not but to find
A doome from men more able, not lesse kind;
I but his Vsher am, yet if my word
May passe, I dare be bound he will afford   10
Things must deserve a welcome, if well knowne,
Such as best writers would have wisht their owne.
You shall observe his words in order meet,
And softly stealing on with equall feet
Slide into even numbers, with such grace   15
As each word had beene moulded for that place.

To the New-yeare, &c.   17 owne] owne, *40 (some copies)*
To my Honoured friend, &c.   First printed with *The Heire*, *1622* and *1633*;
present text from *40*.   4 did] doth *1622, 1633*   8 not *1633, 40*: but *1622*
11 if *1633, 40*: it *1622*   knowne,] knowne *1622, 1633, 40*: known, *51*   14
softly *1633, 40*: often *1622*

You

You shall perceive an amorous passion, spunne
Into so smooth a web, as had the Sunne
When he pursu'd the swiftly flying Maid,
Courted her in such language, she had staid,   20
A love so well exprest, must be the same
The Authour felt himselfe from his faire flame.
The whole plot doth alike it selfe disclose
Through the five Acts, as doth the Locke that goes
With letters, for till every one be knowne,   25
The Lock's as fast, as if you had found none.
And where his sportive Muse doth draw a thread
Of mirth, chast Matrons may not blush to reade.
Thus have I thought it fitter to reveale
My want of art (deare friend) then to conceale   30
My love. It did appeare I did not meane
So to commend thy well-wrought Comick-scene,
As men might judge my aime rather to be,
To gaine praise to my selfe, then give it thee;
Though I can give thee none, but what thou hast   35
Deserv'd, and what must my faint breath out-last.
Yet was this garment (though I skillesse be
To take thy measure) onely made for thee,
And if it prove to scant, 'tis cause the stuffe
Nature allow'd me was not large enough.   40

To my worthy friend Master Geo. Sands, on his translation of the Psalmes.

I Presse not to the Quire, nor dare I greet
The holy place with my unhallowed feet;
My unwasht Muse, polutes not things Divine,
Nor mingles her prophaner notes with thine;

To my Honoured friend, &c. 22 flame. *1622*, *1633*: flame: *40*   23 alike
1633, *40*: like *1622*   24 the Locke] a Lock *1622*, *1633*   39 to scant,
1622, *40*: too scant, *1633*, *42*

To my worthy friend, &c. First printed in *A Paraphrase upon the Divine Poems.*
by George Sandys, 1638 (colophon 1637; the second edition, the first having appeared,
without Carew's verses, in 1636). Present text from *40.*   *Title:* To my worthy
friend M^r. *George Sandys.* 1638

Here,

Here, humbly at the porch she listning stayes,   5
And with glad eares sucks in thy sacred layes.
So, devout penitents of Old werc wont,
Some without dore, and some beneath the Font,
To stand and heare the Churches Liturgies,
Yet not assist the solemne exercise: 10
Sufficeth her, that she a lay-place gaine,
To trim thy Vestments, or but beare thy traine;
Though nor in tune, nor wing, she reach thy Larke,
Her Lyrick feet may dance before the Arke.
Who knowes, but that her wandring eyes that run,   15
Now hunting Glow-wormes, may adore the Sun,
A pure flame may, shot by Almighty power
Into her brest, the earthy flame devoure.
My eyes, in penitentiall dew may steepe
That brine, which they for sensuall love did weepe.   20
So (though 'gainst Natures course) fire may be quencht
With fire, and water be with water drencht.
Perhaps my restlesse soule, tyr'de with persuit
Of mortall beauty, seeking without fruit
Contentment there, which hath not, when enjoy'd,   25
Quencht all her thirst, nor satisfi'd, though cloy'd;
Weary of her vaine search below, Above
In the first Faire may find th'immortall Love.
Prompted by thy example then, no more
In moulds of clay will I my God adore;   30
But teare those Idols from my heart, and write
What his blest Sprit, not fond Love shall indite;
Then, I no more shall court the verdant Bay,
But the dry leavelesse Trunke on *Golgotha*;
And rather strive to gaine from thence one Thorne,   35
Then all the flourishing wreathes by Laureats worne.

5 she listning stayes, *1638*: she stayes, *40*   22 drencht. *1638*: drencht; *40*
28 Faire *1638*: faire *40*   32 Sprit,] Sp'rit, *1638*

To

To my much honoured friend, HENRY *Lord* CARY *of* Lepington, *upon his translation of* MALVEZZI.

My Lord,

IN every triviall worke 'tis knowne
Translators must be masters of their owne,
And of their Authors language, but your taske
A greater latitude of skill did aske.
For your *Malvezzi* first requir'd a man   5
To teach him speake vulgar Italian:
His matter's so sublime, so new his phrase,
So farre above the stile of *Bemboe's* dayes,
Old *Varchies* rules, or what the *Crusca* yet
For currant *Tuscan* mintage will admit,   10
As I beleeve your Marquesse, by a good
Part of his Natives hardly understood.
You must expect no happier fate, 'tis true
He is of noble birth, of nobler you:
So nor your thoughts, nor words fit common eares, 15
He writes, and you translate, both to your Peeres.

To my worthy Friend, M. D'AVENANT, *Vpon his Excellent Play,* The Iust Italian.

I'Le not mispend in praise, the narrow roome
I borrow in this leafe; the Garlands bloome
From thine owne seedes, that crowne each glorious page
Of thy triumphant worke; the sullen Age

To my much honoured friend, &c. First printed with *Romulus and Tarquin,* 1638; present text from *40.*   7 new *1638:* now *40*   8 dayes,] dayes *1638:* dayes; *40*

To my worthy Friend, &c. First printed with *The Iust Italian,* 1630; present text from *40.*

Requires

Requires a Satyre. What starre guides the soule   5
Of these our froward times, that dare controule,
Yet dare not learne to judge? When didst thou flie
From hence, cleare, candid Ingenuitie?
I have beheld, when pearch'd on the smooth brow
Of a faire modest troope, thou didst allow   10
Applause to slighter workes; but then the weake
Spectator, gave the knowing leave to speake.
Now noyse prevailes, and he is tax'd for drowth
Of wit, that with the crie, spends not his mouth.
Yet aske him, reason why he did not like;   15
Him, why he did; their ignorance will strike
Thy soule with scorne, and Pity: marke the places
Provoke their smiles, frownes, or distorted faces,
When, they admire, nod, shake the head: they'le be
A scene of myrth, a double Comedie.   20
But thy strong fancies (raptures of the braine,
Drest in Poetique flames) they entertaine
As a bold, impious reach; for they'le still slight
All that exceeds Red Bull, and Cockpit flight.
These are the men in crowded heapes that throng   25
To that adulterate stage, where not a tong
Of th'untun'd Kennell, can a line repeat
Of serious sence: but like lips, meet like meat;
Whilst the true brood of Actors, that alone
Keepe naturall unstrain'd Action in her throne   30
Behold their Benches bare, though they rehearse
The terser *Beaumonts* or great *Johnsons* verse.
Repine not Thou then, since this churlish fate
Rules not the stage alone; perhaps the State
Hath felt this rancour, where men great and good,   35
Have by the Rabble beene misunderstood.
So was thy Play; whose cleere, yet loftie straine,
Wisemen, that governe Fate, shall entertaine.

25 heapes *1630, 51*: heape *40*

To

To the Reader of Master
William Davenant's
Play.

IT hath beene said of old, that Playes are Feasts,
Poets the Cookes, and the Spectators Guests,
The Actors Waitors: From this Similie,
Some have deriv'd an unsafe libertie
To use their Judgements as their Tastes, which chuse   5
Without controule, this Dish, and that refuse:
But Wit allowes not this large Priviledge,
Either you must confesse, or feele it's edge;
Nor shall you make a currant inference
If you trans-fer your reason to your sense: 10
Things are distinct, and must the same appeare
To every piercing Eye, or well-tun'd Eare.
Though sweets with yours, sharps best with my tast meet
Both must agree, this meat's, or sharpe or sweet:
But if I scent a stench, or a perfume,   15
Whilst you smell nought at all, I may presume
You have that sense imperfect: So you may
Affect a sad, merry, or humerous Play,
If, though the kind distaste or please, the Good
And Bad, be by your Judgement understood;   20
But if, as in this Play, where with delight
I feast my Epicurean appetite
With rellishes so curious, as dispence
The utmost pleasure to the ravisht sense,
You should professe that you can nothing meet   25
That hits your taste, either with sharpe or sweet,
But cry out, 'tis insipid; your bold Tongue
May doe it's Master, not the Author wrong;
For Men of better Pallat will by it
Take the just elevation of your Wit.   30

To the Reader, &c. First printed with *The Witts,* 1636; present text from *40.*
15 scent] sent *1636, 40*

To *Will. Davenant* my Friend.

WHen I behold, by warrant from thy Pen,
    A Prince rigging our Fleets, arming our Men,
Conducting to remotest shores our force
(Without a *Dido* to retard his course)
And thence repelling in successe-full fight,   5
Th'usurping Foe (whose strength was all his Right)
By two brave *Heroes*, (whom wee justly may
By *Homer's Ajax* or *Achilles* lay,)
I doubt the Author of the Tale of Troy,
With him, that makes his Fugitive enjoy   10
The Carthage Queene, and thinke thy Poem may
Impose upon Posteritie, as they
Have done on us: What though Romances lye
Thus blended with more faithfull Historie?
Wee, of th'adult'rate mixture not complaine,   15
But thence more Characters of Vertue gaine;
More pregnant Patterns, of transcendent Worth,
Than barren and insipid Truth brings forth:
So, oft the Bastard nobler fortune meets,
Than the dull Issue of the lawfull sheets.   20

The Comparison.

DEarest thy tresses are not threads of gold,
    Thy eyes of Diamonds, nor doe I hold
Thy lips for Rubies: Thy faire cheekes to be
Fresh Roses; or thy teeth of Ivorie:
Thy skin that doth thy daintie bodie sheath   5
Not Alablaster is, nor dost thou breath

To Will. Davenant my Friend. Text from *Madagascar*, 1638 (1648). In *40* the poem *TO MY FRIEND*, WILL. D'AVENANT. consists of the first fourteen lines of a poem contributed to *Madagascar* by William Habington, joined to the final six lines of Carew's poem.   1 behold, *1638*: beheld, *1648*   2 our Men,] our, Men, *1638, 1648*.   17 transcendent *40, 1648*: transcedent *1638*

Arabian

Arabian odours, those the earth brings forth
Compar'd with which would but impaire thy worth.
Such may be others Mistresses, but mine
Holds nothing earthly, but is all divine.   10
Thy tresses are those rayes that doe arise
Not from one Sunne, but two; Such are thy eyes:
Thy lips congealed Nectar are, and such
As but a Deitie, there's none dare touch.
The perfect crimson that thy cheeke doth cloath   15
(But onely that it farre exceeds them both)
Aurora's blush resembles, or that redd
That *Iris* struts in when her mantl's spred.
Thy teeth in white doe *Leda's* Swan exceede,
Thy skin's a heavenly and immortall weede,   20
And when thou breath'st, the winds are readie strait
To filch it from thee, and doe therefore wait
Close at thy lips, and snatching it from thence
Beare it to Heaven, where 'tis *Joves* frankincense.
Faire Goddesse, since thy feature makes thee one,   25
Yet be not such for these respects alone;
But as you are divine in outward view
So be within as faire, as good, as true.

The Complement.

O My deerest I shall grieve thee
　　When I sweare, yet sweete beleeve me,
By thine eyes the tempting booke
On which even crabbed old men looke
I sweare to thee, (though none abhorre them)   5
Yet I doe not love thee for them.

I doe not love thee for that faire,
Rich fanne of thy most curious haire;

The Comparison. 18 *Iris* struts in *51, most MSS.*: Iris-struts in *40 (Errata)*:
frisketh in *40 (Text)*: Iris walks in *D8*   20 weede,] weede *40*: weed, *51*
21 when thou *42, most MSS.*: thou when *40*: as thou *some MSS.*   25 God-
desse, *42*: Goddesse *40*   one, *42*: one *40*   26 alone; *42*: alone. *40*.
Though

Though the wires thereof be drawne
Finer then the threeds of lawne,   10
And are softer then the leaves
On which the subtle spinner weaues.

I doe not love thee for those flowers,
Growing on thy cheeks (loves bowers)
Though such cunning them hath spread   15
None can parte their whit and red:
Loves golden arrowes thence are shot,
Yet for them I loue thee not.

I doe not love thee for those soft,
Red corrall lips I've kist so oft;   20
Nor teeth of pearle, the double guard
To speech, whence musicke still is heard:
Though from those lips a kisse being taken,
Might tyrants melt and death awaken.

I doe not love thee (O my fairest)   25
For that richest, for that rarest
Silver pillar which stands vnder
Thy round head, that globe of wonder;
Though that necke be whiter farre,
Then towers of pollisht Ivory are.   30

I doe not love thee for those mountaines
Hill'd with snow, whence milkey fountaines,
(Suger'd sweete, as sirropt berries)
Must one day run through pipes of cherries;
O how much those breasts doe move me,   35
Yet for them I doe not love thee:

I doe not love thee for that belly,
Sleeke as satten, soft as jelly,
Though within that Christall round
Heapes of treasure might be found,   40

The Complement. 12 weaues.] weaues 40: weaues: 42: weaues. 51   16
parte their *most MSS.*: paint them 40: paint their 51: part the *Ash 38*   18
not.] not 40   25 O] ô 40   28 round *all MSS.*] sound 40   29 necke]
neeke 40   33 sweete, *all MSS.*: sweets, 40   35 O] ô 40

So

So rich that for the least of them,
A King might leave his Diadem.

I doe not love thee for those thighes,
Whose Alablaster rocks doe rise
So high and even that they stand   45
Like Sea-markes to some happy land.
Happy are those eyes have seene them,
More happy they that saile betweene them.

I love thee not for thy moist palme,
Though the dew thereof be balme: 50
Nor for thy pretty legge and foote,
Although it be the precious roote,
On which this goodly cedar growes,
(Sweete) I love thee not for those:

Nor for thy wit though pure and quicke,   55
Whose substance no arithmeticke
Can number downe: nor for those charmes
Mask't in thy embracing armes;
Though in them one night to lie,
Dearest I would gladly die.   60

I love not for those eyes, nor haire,
Nor cheekes, nor lips, nor teeth so rare;
Nor for thy speech, thy necke, nor breast,
Nor for thy belly, nor the rest:
Nor for thy hand, nor foote so small,   65
But wouldst thou know (deere sweet) for all.

41 least *all MSS.*: best *40*   44 rise *51, all MSS.*: use *40*   54 those:] those. *40*
58 armes;] armes. *40*   62 rare; *51*: rare. *40*

On

On sight of a Gentlewomans face in the water.

STand still you floods, doe not deface
   That Image which you beare:
So Votaries from every place,
   To you shall Alters reare.

No winds but Lovers sighs blow here,   5
   To trouble these glad streames,
On which no starre from any Spheare,
   Did ever dart such beames.

To Christall then in hast congeale,
   Least you should loose your blisse: 10
And to my cruell faire reveale,
   How cold, how hard she is.

But if the envious *Nymphes* shall feare,
   Their beauties will be scorn'd,
And hire the ruder winds to teare   15
   That face which you adorn'd,

Then rage and foame amaine that we
   Their malice may despise:
When from your froath we soone shall see,
   A second *Venus* rise.   20

A Song.

ASke me no more where Iove *bestowes,*
   When Iune *is past, the fading rose:*
For in your beauties orient deepe,
These flowers as in their causes, sleepe.

On sight, &c. 1 floods, 51: floods 40   deface 51: deface, 40   5–8 *See Commentary*   15 teare] teare, 40: tear 51   16 adorn'd, 42: adorn'd. 40
17 we 51: we, 40
A Song. For the manuscript variants, see Commentary.   2 *past,* 51: *past* 40
Aske

Aske me no more whether doth stray,   5
The golden Atomes of the day:
For in pure love heaven did prepare
Those powders to inrich your haire.

Aske me no more whether doth hast,
The Nightingale when May is past: 10
For in your sweet dividing throat,
She winters and keepes warme her note.

Aske me no more where those starres light,
That downewards fall in dead of night:
For in your eyes they sit, and there,   15
Fixed become as in their sphere.

Aske me no more if East or West,
The Phenix builds her spicy nest:
For vnto you at last shee flies,
And in your fragrant bosome dyes.   20

The second Rapture.

NO worldling, no, tis not thy gold,
Which thou dost use but to behold;
Nor fortune, honour, nor long life,
Children, or friends, nor a good wife,
That makes thee happy; these things be   5
But shaddowes of felicitie.
Give me a wench about thirteene,
Already voted to the Queene
Of lust and lovers, whose soft haire,
Fann'd with the breath of gentle aire   10
O're spreads her shoulders like a tent,
And is her vaile and ornament:
Whose tender touch, will make the blood
Wild in the aged, and the good;

A Song.   7 *prepare* 51: *prepare,* 40   15 *sit,* 42: *sit* 40
The second Rapture. 5 happy;] haypy; 40   14 good; 51: good. 40
                                                      Whose

Whose kisses fastned to the mouth 15
Of threescore yeares and longer slouth,
Renew the age, and whose bright eye
Obscures those lesser lights of skie:
Whose snowy breasts (if we may call
That snow, that never melts at all) 20
Makes *Jove* invent a new disguise,
In spite of *Iunoes* jealousies:
Whose every part doth re-invite
The old decayed appetite:
And in whose sweet imbraces I, 25
May melt myselfe to lust, and die.
    This is true blisse, and I confesse,
    There is no other happinesse.

The tinder.

OF what mould did nature frame me?
    Or was it her intent to shame me,
That no woman can come neere me
Faire, but her I court to heare me?
Sure that mistris to whose beauty 5
First I paid a lovers duty,
Burnt in rage my heart to tinder,
That nor prayers, nor teares can hinder,
But where ever I doe turne me,
Every sparke let fall doth burne me. 10
Women since you thus inflame me,
Flint and steele Il'e ever name yee.

---

15 mouth *51*: mouth, *40*   16 slouth, *51*: slouth. *40*: slouth *42*   17 eye]
eye, *40*: ey *51*   18 Obscures *51*: Obscure *40*   skie:] skie. *40* (*some copies*)
20 all)] all.) *40* (*some copies*)   23 re-invite *51*: re-invite, *40*   28 happi-
nesse.] happinesse, *40* (*some copies*)
    The tinder. 5 beauty *42*: beauty. *40*   6 duty, *42*: duty. *40*   7 tinder,]
tinder. *40*   8 hinder, *42*: hinder. *40*

A

A Song.

IN her faire cheekes two pits doe lye,
  To bury those slaine by her eye,
So spight of death this comforts me,
That fairely buried I shall be.
My grave with rose and lilly spread,   5
O 'tis a life to be so dead.
  Come then and kill me with thy eye,
  For if thou let me live, I die.

When I behold those lips againe,
Reviving what those eyes have slaine,   10
With kisses sweet, whose balsome pure,
Loves wounds as soone as made, can cure,
Me thinkes 'tis sickenes to be sound,
And there's no health to such a wound.
  Come then &c.   15

When in her chaste breast I behold,
Those downy mounts of snow ne're cold,
And those blest hearts her beauty kills,
Reviv'd by climing those faire hills,   20
Mee thinkes there's life in such a death,
And so t' expire, inspires new breath.
  Come then, &c.

Nymphe since no death is deadly where   25
Such choice of Antidotes are neere,
And your keene eyes but kill in vaine,
Those that are sound, as soone as slaine,
That I no longer dead survive,
Your way's to bury me alive   30
Jn Cupids cave, where happy J,
May dying live, and living die.
  Come then and kill me with thy eye,
  For if thou let me live, I die.

A Song. 12 cure,] cure. 40   20 hills,] hills. 40   25 where 42:
where. 40

To

To the Painter.

FOnd man that hop'st to catch that face,
   With those false colours, whose short grace
Serves but to shew the lookers on,
The faults of thy presumption;
Or at the least to let us see,   5
That is divine, but yet not shee:
Say you could imitate the rayes,
Of those eyes that out-shine the dayes,
Or counterfeite in red and white,
That most vncounterfeited light   10
Of her complexion; yet canst thou,
(Great Master though thou be) tell how
To paint a vertue? Then desist,
This faire, your Artifice hath mist:
You should have markt how shee begins,   15
To grow in vertue, not in sinnes:
In stead of that same rosie die,
You should have drawne out modestie,
Whose beauty sits enthroned there,
And learne to looke and blush at her.   20
Or can you colour just the same,
When vertue blushes or when shame:
When sicknes, and when innocence,
Shewes pale or white unto the sence?
Can such course varnish ere be sed,   25
To imitate her white and red?
This may doe well else-where in *Spaine*,
Among those faces died in graine,
So you may thrive and what you doe,
Prove the best picture of the two.   30
Besides (if all I heare be true,)
'Tis taken ill by some that you
Should be so insolently vaine,
As to contrive all that rich gaine
Into one tablet, which alone   35
May teach us superstition;

To the Painter. 4 presumption; *51*: presumption. *40*   18 modestie,]
modestie. *40*: modesty, *42*

Instructing

Instructing our amazed eyes,
To admire and worship Imag'ries,
Such as quickly might out shine
Some new Saint, wer't allow'd a shrine,   40
And turne each wandring looker on,
Into a new *Pigmaleon*.
Yet your Art cannot equalize
This *Picture* in her lovers eyes,
His eyes the pencills are which limbe   45
Her truly, as her's coppy him,
His heart the Tablet which alone,
Is for that porctraite the tru'st stone.
If you would a truer see,
Marke it in their posteritie: 50
And you shall read it truly there,
When the glad world shall see their Heire.

Loves Courtship.

KIsse lovely *Celia* and be kind,
  Let my desires freedome find,
      Sit thee downe,
And we will make the Gods confesse,
Mortals enjoy some happines.   5

Mars would disdaine his Mistris charmes,
If he beheld thee in my armes,
      And descend:
Thee his immortall Queene to make,
Or live as mortall for thy sake.   10

Venus must loose her title now,
And leave to brag of *Cupid's* bow,
      Silly Queene.
Shee hath but one, but I can spie,
Ten thousand *Cupids* in thy eye.   15

43 equalize 51: equalize, 40   45 limbe] limbe, 40
Loves Courtship. 9 immortall] mortall 40, MSS. See Commentary

Nor

Nor may the sunne behold our blisse,
For sure thy eyes doe dazle his;
   If thou fcare
That he'll betray thee with his light,
Let me ecclipse thee from his sight.   20

And while I shade thee from his eye,
Oh let me heare thee gently cry,
   Celia yeelds.
Maids often loose their Maidenhead,
Ere they set foote in Nuptiall bed.   25

On a Damaske rose sticking
vpon a Ladies breast.

LEt pride grow big my rose, and let the cleare
 And damaske colour of thy leaves appeare.
Let scent and lookes be sweete and blesse that hand,
That did transplant thee to that sacred land.
O happy thou that in that garden rest's,   5
That Paradice betweene that Ladies breasts.
There's an eternall spring; there shalt thou lie,
Betwixt two lilly mounts, and never die.
There shalt thou spring amongst the fertile valleyes,
By budds like thee that grow in midst of Allyes.   10
There none dare plucke thee, for that place is such
That but a god devine, there's none dare touch,
If any but approach, straite doth arise
A blushing lightning flash, and blasts his eyes.
There stead of raine shall living fountaines flow,   15
For wind her fragrant breath for ever blow.
Nor now, as earst, one Sun shall on thee shine,
But those two glorious suns, her eyes devine.
O then what Monarch would not think't a grace,
To leave his Regall throne to have thy place.   20
My selfe to gaine thy blessed seat do vow,
Would be transformd into a rose as thou.

Loves Courtship. 17 his;] his *40* 18 feare] feare. *40*
 On a Damaske rose, &c: 12 god devine, *70*: good devine, *40, MSS. See Com-*
mentary

               The

The protestation, a Sonnet.

NO more shall meads be deckt with flowers,
    Nor sweetnesse dwell in rosie bowers:
Nor greenest buds on branches spring,
Nor warbling birds delight to sing,
Nor Aprill violets paint the grove,   5
If I forsake my *Celias* love.

The fish shall in the Ocean burne,
And fountaines sweet shall bitter turne,
The humble oake no flood shall know,
When floods shall highest hills ore-flow;   10
Blacke *Læthe* shall oblivion leave,
If ere my *Celia* I deceive.

Love shall his bow and shaft lay by,
And *Venus* doves want wings to flie:
The Sun refuse to shew his light,   15
And day shall then be turn'd to night,
And in that night no starre appeare,
If once I leave my *Celia* deere.

Love shall no more inhabite earth,
Nor lovers more shall love for worth,   20
Nor joy above in heaven dwell,
Nor paine torment poore soules in hell;
Grim death no more shall horrid prove,
If ere I leave bright *Celias* love.

The tooth-ach cured by a kisse.

FAte's now growne mercifull to men,
    Turning disease to blisse:
For had not kind Rheume vext me then,
    I might not *Celia* kisse.

The protestation, &c. *Title: protestation,*] *protestation* 40: Protestation, *51*   10
ore-flow; *51*: ore-flow. *40*   22 hell; *51*: hell. *40*

Phisitians

Phisitians you are now my scorne: 5
  For I have found a way
To cure diseases (when forlorne
  By your dull art) which may
Patch vp a body for a time,
  But can restore to health,   10
No more then Chimists can sublime
  True Gold, the Indies wealth.
That Angell sure that us'd to move
  The poole, men so admir'd,
Hath to her lip the seat of love,   15
  As to his heaven retir'd.

To his jealous Mistris.

ADmit (thou darling of mine eyes)
    I have some Idoll lately fram'd:
That under such a false disguise,
  Our true loves might the lesse be fam'd.
    Canst thou that knowest my heart suppose,   5
    I'le fall from thee, and worship those?

Remember (deare) how loath and slow,
  I was to cast a looke or smile,
Or one love-line to mis-bestow,
  Till thou hadst chang'd both face and stile,   10
    And art thou growne afraid to see,
    That maske put on thou mad'st for me?

I dare not call those childish feares,
  Comming from love, much lesse from thee,
But wash away with frequent teares,   15
  This counterfeit Idolatrie,
    And henceforth kneele at ne're a shrine,
    To blind the world, but only thine.

The tooth-ach, &c. 6 way 51: way: 40
  To his jealous Mistris. 6 I'le] 'Ile 40   those?] those. 40   10 stile,]
stile. 40 (some copies)   12 me? 51: me. 40   16 Idolatrie, 42: Idolatrie. 40

POEMS.

POEMS.

By

THOMAS CAREVV

Esquire.

One of the Gentlemen of the
Privie-Chamber, and Sewer
in Ordinary to His Majesty.

The second Edition revised and enlarged.

LONDON,

Printed by *I. D.* for *Thomas Walkley*,
and are to be fold at the figne of the
flying Horfe, betweene *Brittains
Burfe*, and Yorke-Houfe.
1642.

On Mistris N. to the greene sicknesse.

STay coward blood, and doe not yield
To thy pale sister, beauties field,
Who there displaying round her white
Ensignes, hath usurp'd thy right;
Invading thy peculiar throne,   5
The lip, where thou shouldst rule alone;
And on the cheeke, where natures care
Allotted each an equall share,
Her spreading Lilly only growes,
Whose milky deluge drownes thy Rose.   10
  Quit not the field faint blood, nor rush
In the short salley of a blush,
Vpon thy sister foe, but strive
To keepe an endlesse warre alive;
Though peace doe petty States maintaine,   15
Here warre alone makes beauty raigne.

Vpon a Mole in Celias bosome.

THat lovely spot which thou dost see
In Celias bosome was a Bee,
Who built her amorous spicy nest
I'th Hyblas of her either breast,
But from close Ivery Hyves, she flew   5
To suck the Arromattick dew,
Which from the neighbour vale distils,
Which parts those two twin-sister hils.
There feasting on Ambrosiall meat,
A rowling file of Balmy sweat,   10
(As in soft murmurs before death,

On Mistris N., &c. Text from *42*; not included in *40*   4 right; *1772*,
all MSS.: night; *42*
Vpon a Mole, &c. Text from *42*; not included in *40*   5 close *42*, *H35*:
those *W*   8 hils.] hils, *42* (*some copies*)

Swan-like

Swan-like she sung) chokt up her breath,
So she in water did expire,
More precious then the Phænix fire;
   Yet still her shaddow there remaines   15
Confind to those Elizian plaines;
With this strict Law, that who shall lay
His bold lips on that milky way,
The sweet, and smart, from thence shall bring
Of the Bees Honey, and her sting.   20

An Hymeneall Song on the Nuptials of the Lady *Ann Wentworth,* and the Lord *Louelace.*

*B*Reake not the slumbers of the Bride,
  But let the Sunne in Triumph ride,
    Scattering his beamy light,

When she awakes, he shall resigne
  His rayes: And she alone shall shine   5
    In glory all the night.

For she till day returne must keepe
  An Amarous Vigill, and not steepe
    Her fayre eyes in the dew of sleepe.

Yet gently whisper as she lies,   10
  And say her Lord waits her uprise,
    The Priests at the Altar stay,

With Flowry wreathes the Virgin crew
  Attend while some with roses strew,
    And Mirtles trim the way.   15

18 way, 51: way; 42
An Hymeneall Song, &c. Text from 42; not included in 40   6 In] in 42
               Now

Now to the Temple, and the Priest,
See her convaid, thence to the Feast;
Then back to bed, though not to rest:

For now to crowne his faith and truth,
Wee must admit the noble youth,   20
*   To revell in Loves spheare;*

To rule as chiefe Intelligence
That Orbe, and happy time dispence
*   To wretched Lovers here.*

For the're exalted farre above   25
All hope, feare, change, or they do move
The wheele that spins the fates of Love.

They know no night, nor glaring noone,
Measure no houres of Sunne or Moone,
*   Nor mark times restlesse Glasse:*   30

Their kisses measure as they flow,
Minutes, and their embraces show
*   The howers as they passe.*

Their Motions, the yeares Circle make,
And we from their conjunctions take   35
Rules to make Love an Almanack.

A married Woman.

WHen I shall marry, if I doe not find
A wife thus moulded, I'le create this mind:
Nor from her noble birth, nor ample dower,
Beauty, or wit, shall she derive a power
To prejudice my Right; but if she be   5
A subject borne, she shall be so to me:

17 *Feast;* 51: *Fast;* 42   21 *spheare.*] *spheare.* 42   22 *Intelligence* 51:
Intelligence, 42   23 *Orbe,*] *Orbe* 42: *Orb,* 51   *dispence* 51: *dispence,*
42   25 *above*] *above,* 42   26 *do*] *to* 42   28 *noone,*] *noone* 42
30 *Glasse:*] *Glasse.* 42   32 *Minutes,* 51: *Minutes* 42   *their*] *there* 42   *show*
51: *show,* 42   35 *take* 70: *take,* 42
    A married Woman. Text from 42; not included in 40   *Title: Woman.*] *Woman* 40
                                                                        As

As to the soule the flesh, as Appetite
To reason is, which shall our wils unite;
In habits so confirm'd, as no rough sway
Shall once appeare, if she but learne t'obay.   10
For in habituall vertues, sense is wrought
To that calme temper, as the bodie's thought
To have nor blood, nor gall, if wild and rude
Passions of Lust, and Anger, are subdu'd;
When 'tis the faire obedience to the soule,   15
Doth in the birth those swelling Acts controule.
If I in murder steepe my furious rage,
Or with Adult'ry my hot lust asswage,
Will it suffice to say my sense, the Beast
Provokt me to't? could I my soule devest,   20
My plea were good, Lyons, and Buls commit
Both freely, but man must in judgement sit,
And tame this Beast, for Adam was not free,
When in excuse he said, Eve gave it me:
Had he not eaten, she perhaps had beene   25
Vnpunisht, his consent made hers a sinne.

Loves Force.

IN the first ruder Age, when Love was wild,
   Not yet by Lawes reclaim'd, not reconcil'd
To order, nor by Reason mann'd, but flew
Full-summ'd by Nature, on the instant view
Vpon the wings of Appetite, at all   5
The eye could faire, or sense delightfull call:
Election was not yet, but as their cheape
Food from the Oake, or the next Acorne-heape,
As water from the nearest spring or brooke,
So men their undistinguisht females tooke   10
By chance, not choyce; but soone the heavenly sparke
That in mans bosome lurkt, broke through this darke
Confusion, then the noblest breast first felt
It selfe, for its owne proper object melt.

A married Woman. 7 Appetite 51: Appetitite 42   20 to 't? 51: to 't, 42
Loves Force. Text from 42; not included in 40.

A

A Fancy.

MArke how this polisht Easterne sheet
   Doth with our Northerne tincture meet,
For though the paper seeme to sinke,
Yet it receives, and bears the Inke;
And on her smooth soft brow these spots   5
Seeme rather ornaments then blots;
Like those you Ladies use to place
Mysteriously about your face:
Not only to set off and breake
Shaddowes and Eye beames, but to speake   10
To the skild Lover, and relate
Vnheard, his sad or happy Fate:
Nor doe their Characters delight,
As carelesse workes of black and white:
But 'cause you underneath may find   15
A sence that can enforme the mind;
Divine, or moral rules impart
Or Raptures of Poetick Art:
So what at first was only fit
To fold up silkes, may wrap up wit.   20

A Fancy. Text from *42*; two states of the text exist, distinguished in the collation as (*a*) and (*b*). Not in *40*   1 polisht *42* (*b*): peevish *42* (*a*)   sheet *51*: sheeet *42*   5 spots *70*: spots, *42*: spots. *51*   19 fit *51*: fit. *42*   20 silkes, *42* (*b*): silkes *42* (*a*)

POEMS.

POEMS.

With a
MASKE,

BY

THOMAS CAREW Esq;

One of the Gent. of the privie-
Chamber, and Sewer in Ordina-
ry to His late Majesty.

The *Songs* were set in *Musick* by
Mr. HENRY LAWES Gent: of the
Kings Chappell, and one of his late
Majesties Private Musick.

The third Edition revised and enlarged.

LONDON,
Printed for HUMPHREY MOSELEY
and are to be sold at his Shop at the
signe of the Princes Armes in St.
Pauls-Church-yard, 1651.

POEMS,

With a

MASKE,

BY

THOMAS CAREW Esq;

One of the Gent. of the Privy-
Chamber, and Sewer in Ordi-
nary to his late Majestie.

The *Songs* were set in *Musick* by
Mr. HENRY LAWES Gent. of the
Kings Chappell, and one of his late
Majesties Private Musick.

The third Edition revised and enlarged.

LONDON

Printed for *H. M.* and are to be sold
by *J : Martin,* at the signe of the
Bell in St. *Pauls*-Church-
Yard. 1651.

To his mistris.

1.   GRieve not my *Celia*, but with hast
      Obey the fury of thy fate,
'Tis some perfection to waste
  Discreetly out our wretched state,
To be obedient in this sence,   5
Will prove thy vertue, though offence:

2.   Who knowes but destiny may relent,
  For many miracles have bin,
Thou proving thus obedient
  To all the griefs she plundgd thee in?   10
And then the certainty she meant
Reverted is by accident.

3.   But yet I must confesse tis much
  When we remember what hath bin,
Thus parting never more to touch   15
  To let eternall absence in,
Though never was our pleasure yet
So pure, but chance distracted it.

4.   What, shall we then submit to fate,
  And dye to one anothers love?   20
No, *Celia*, no, my soul doth hate
  Those Lovers that inconstant prove,
Fate may be cruell, but if you decline,
The cryme is yours, and all the glory mine.

Fate and the Planets sometymes bodies part,   25
But Cankerd nature onely alters th'heart.

To his mistris. Text from *51*; not included in *40* or *42*   26 th' heart.] th' heart *51*

In praise of his
Mistris.

1.   YOu, that will a wonder know,
                Goe with me,
Two suns in a heaven of snow
                Both burning bee,
All they fire, that but eye them,   5
Yet the snow's unmelted by them.

2.   Leaves of Crimson Tulips met
                Guide the way
Where two pearly rowes be set
                As white as day: 10
When they part themselves asunder
She breathes Oracles of wonder.

3.   Hills of Milk with Azure mixd
                Swell beneath,
Waving sweetly, yet still fixd,   15
                While she doth breath.
From those hils descends a valley
Where all fall, that dare to dally.

4.   As fair Pillars under-stand
                Statues two,   20
Whiter than the Silver swan
                That swims in *Poe;*
If at any tyme they move her
Every step begets a Lover.

5.   All this but the Casket is   25
                Which conteynes
Such a Iewell, as the misse
                Breeds endlesse paynes;
That's her mind, and they that know it
May admire, but cannot show it.   30

In praise of his Mistris. Text from *51;* not included in *40* or *42*   *Title:*
Mistris.] Mistris *51*   10 day:] day *51*   21 Whiter *70:* Whither *51*
25 5. All] All *51*   30 it.] it *51*.

                                                        To

To *Celia,* upon Love's Vbiquity.

AS one that strives, being sick, and sick to death
By changing places, to preserve a breath,
A tedious restlesse breath, removes and tryes
A thousand roomes, a thousand policyes,
To cozen payne, when he thinks to find ease,   5
At last he finds all change, but his disease,
So (like a Ball with fire and powder fild)
I restles am, yet live, each minute kild,
And with that moving torture must retain
(With change of all things else) a constant payn.   10
Say I stay with you, presence is to me
Nought but a light, to shew my miserie,
And partings are as Rackes, to plague love on,
The further stretchd, the more affliction.
Goe I to *Holland, France,* or furthest *Inde,*   15
I change but onely Countreys not my mind;
And though I passe through ayr and water free,
Despair and hopelesse fate still follow me.
Whilest in the bosome of the waves I reel
My heart I'le liken to the tottering keel,   20
The sea to my own troubled fate, the wind
To your disdayn, sent from a soul vnkind:
But when I lift my sad lookes to the skyes,
Then shall I think I see my *Celia's* eyes,
And when a Cloud or storm appeares between,   25
I shall remember what her frownes have been.
Thus, whatsoever course my fates allow,
All things but make me mind my busines, you.
The good things that I meet I think streames be
From you the fountain, but when bad I see,   30
How vile and cursed is that thing thinke I,
That to such goodnes is so contrary?
My whole life is bout you, the Center starre,

To Celia, &c. Text from *51*; not included in *40* or *42*   13 partings
HM*172*: parting *51*   16 mind;] mind. *51*   18 me.] me, *51*   30 see,]
see *51*

But

But a perpetuall Motion Circular:
I am the dyalls hand, still walking round,   35
You are the Compasse, and I never sound
Beyond your Circle, neyther can I shew
Ought, but what first expressed is in you:
That wheresoever my teares doe cause me move
My fate still keepes me bounded with your love;   40
Which ere it dye, or be extinct in me,
Time shall stand still, and moist waves flaming be.
Yet, being gon, think not on me, I am
A thing too wretched for thy thoughts to name;
But when I dye, and wish all comforts given,   45
Ile think on you, and by you think on heaven.

38 you:] you. *51*   39 wheresoever] whereso'er *HM172*

POEMS

POEMS
FROM
MANUSCRIPT

The prologue to a Play presented before the King and Queene, att an Entertanement of them by the Lord Chamberlaine in Whitehall hall.

Sir,
   Since you haue beene pleas'd this night to vnbend
Your serious thoughts, and with your Person lend
Your Pallace out, and soe are hither come
A stranger in your owne howse, not att home,
Diuesting State, as if you meant alone   5
To make your Servants Loyall heart your Throne,
Oh see how wide those Values themselues display
To entertaine his royall Guests, survey
What Arques Trivmphall, Statues, Alters, Shrines,
Inscribd to your great names, hee there assignes;   10
Soe from that stock of Zeale, his Course Cates may
Borrow some rellish though but thinly they
Coverd his narrow Table, soe may theis
Succeeding trifles by that title pleas:
Els gratious Maddam, must the influence   15
Of your faire Eyes propitious beames dispence
To Crowne such pastimes as hee could prouide
To oyle the lazie Minutes as they slide,
For well hee knowes vpon your smiles depends
This night Success since that alone Commends   20
All his endeauors, gives the Musick praise
Painters and vs, and guilds your Poetts baise.

The Epilogue to the same Play.

HUnger is sharp, the Sated Stomack dull,
  Feeding delights, t'wixt Emptiness and full:
The pleasure lyes, not in the end, but streames
That flowe betwixt two opposite Extreames.

The prologue, &c. Text from *W*. Punctuation partly the editor's.
The Epilogue, &c. Text from *W*. Punctuation partly the editor's.

Soe

Soe doth the flux from hott to cold Combine   5
An equall temper, such is noble wine
Twixt fullsome Must and Vinegar too tart:
Pleasures the scratching betwixt Itch and smart,
It is a shifting Tartar, that still flyes
From place to place, if it stand still it dyes;   10
After much rest labour delights, when paine
Succeeds long trauaile rest growes sweete againe;
Paine is the base, on which his nimble feete
Move in contynuall chaunge from sower to sweete.
    This the contriuer of your sports to night   15
Hath well obserued, and soe to fix delight
In a perpetuall circle hath applyed
The choysest obiects, that care could provide
To euery sence. Onely himself hath felt
The load of this greate honour, and doth melt   20
All into humble thancks, and at your feete
Of both your Maiestyes prostrates the sweete
Perfume, of gratefull service, which hee sweares
Hee will extend to such a length of yeares
As fitts not vs to tell, but doth belong   25
To a farre abler pen, and nobler tongue.
Our task ends heere, if wee haue hitt the lawes
Of true delight his gladd heart Ioyes, yet cause
You cannot to succeeding pleasures climbe
Till you growe weary of the instant tyme   30
Hee was Content this last peece should grow sower
Onely to sweeten the Insueing hower.
But if the Cook, Musitian, Player, Poett,
Painter and all haue fail'd, hee'le make them know itt
That haue abusd him, yett must greiue att this,   35
Hee should doe Pennance, when the Sin was his.

15 to night] two night *W*

To

To M^ris Katherine Nevill on her greene sicknesse.

WHite innocence that now lies spread
    Forsaken on thy widdowed bed
Could; and alone; if feare, loue, hate,
Or shame recall thy crimson mate,
From his darke mazes, to reside   5
With thee his chast, and mayden bride,
Least that he backward thence should flow
Congeale him with thy virgin snow:
But if his·owne heate with thy payre
Of neghb'ring sunnes, and flaming haire,   10
Thaw him vnto a new devorce,
Least that from thee he take his course
O lodge me there, where Ile defeate
All future hope of his retreate,
And force the fugitiue to seeke   15
A constant station in thy cheeke.
Soe each shall haue his proper place,
I in your heart, he in your face.

To his mistresse retiring in affection.

FLy not from him whose silent miserie
    Breath's many an vnwitnes'd sigh to thee:
Who having felt thy scorne, yet constant is,
And whom, thy self, thou has cal'd, onely his.
When first mine eyes threw flames, whose spirit moov'd 5
    thee

To M^ris Katherine Nevill, &c. Text from *A118*, collated with *A221*, *H18*, and *W*   *Title:* To Mistrisse Katharine Neuill on her greene sicknesse. *A221:* Vpon one hauing the Greene Sicknesse: *H18:* An other of the same (following 'Vppon the Greene Sicknesse of Mrs. K. N. Song') *W*   1 lies] lyest *W*   7 Least that] and least *H18: W* reads: That hee may never backward flowe   8 with thy virgin *A221:* with virgin *A118:* in thy virgin *H18, W*   9 his owne heate *A221, H18, W:* his heate *A118*   11 vnto *A118, A221:* into *H18, W*   12 that from thee] to the heart *H18:* to thy heart *W*   14 hope] hopes *W*   17 haue] keepe *W*

To his mistresse, &c. Text from *A118*, collated with *A221*   5 spirit] spirits *A221*

Had'st not thou look't againe I had not lov'd thee.
Nature did neare two different thinges vnite
With peace, which are by nature opposite.
If thou force nature, and be backward gone,
O blame not me that striue to draw thee on: 10
But if my constant loue shall faile to moue thee,
Then know my reason hates thee, though I loue thee.

To a Friend.

Like as the hand that hath beene used to play
  One lesson long, still runns the usuall way;
And waits not what the hearer bids it strike,
But doth presume by custome this will like;
So runne my thoughts, which are so perfect growne, 5
So well acquainted with my passion,
That now they dare prevent mee with their haste,
And ere I thinke to sighe, my sighe is past;
Tis past, and flowne to you, for you alone
Are all the obiect that I thinke upon;   10
And did not you supply my soule with thought
For want of action it to none were brought;
What though our absent armes may not infolde
Reall embraces, yet we firmely hold
Each other in possession; thus we see   15
The Lord enioyes his land where ere he bee;
If Kings possest noe more then where they sate
What were they better then a meane estate?
This makes me firmely yours, you firmely mine,
That something, more then bodies, us combine. 20

To his mistresse, &c. 6 not thou look't] not look't *A221* 12 thee.] thee: *A118*
To a Friend. Text from *H17*, collated with *A221, A30* (where the poem is copied twice), *S17*, and *Ash 38*. *Title:* To a Friend. *A221, A30 (both copies), S17*: Mr Carew to his frind *Ash 38*: To his mistrisse: *H17* 1 as] to *A221, A30 (twice), S17, Ash 38* that] wch *A30 (twice)* 2 usuall] selfe same *Ash 38* 3 waits *A221, A30 (twice), S17, Ash 38*: cares *H17* hearer bids] hearers bid *A221, A30 (twice), S17, Ash 38* 4 this *A221, A30 (twice), S17, Ash 38*: it *H17* 8 And *S17, Ash 38, A30 (twice)*: For *H17, A221* 9 Tis] I'ts *Ash 38* 11 And did not you *S17, A30 (twice), Ash 38*: If you did not *H17*: And did you not *A221* 16 enioyes] enioy *A30 (1), S17* land] lands *A30 (twice), Ash 38* 17 possest] posses *Ash 38* 18 better] greater *Ash 38, A30 (twice)* meane estate?] meaner state *A221*

A

A Ladies prayer to Cupid.

SInce I must needes into thy schoole returne
Be pittifull (O Loue) and doe not burne
Mee with desier of cold, and frozen age,
Nor let me follow a fond boy or page:
But gentle Cupid giue mee if you can,   5
One to my loue, whom I may call a man,
Of person comely, and of face as sweete,
Let him be sober, secret, and discreete,
Well practis'd in loue's schoole, let him within
Weare all his beard, and none vppon his chinn.   10

An Excuse of absence.

YOu'le aske perhaps wherefore I stay,
Loving so much, so long away,
O doe not thinke t'was I did part,
It was my body, not my hearte,
For like a Compasse in your loue,   5
One foote is fix'd and cannot mooue,
The other may follow her blinde guide
Of giddy fortune, but not slide
Beyound your service, nor dares venture
To wander farre from you the Center.   10

A Ladies prayer to Cupid. Text from *C,* collated with *R2* and with printed
version in *The Academy of Complements,* 1650   3 desier] desires *Academy of
Complements*   4 Nor] or *R2*   10 and none vppon] none on *R2*: and not
upon *Academy of Complements*
    An Excuse of absence. Text from *A15,* collated with *A30, L, E24, C, D2, R2,*
and *Ash 47*   1 You'le] yould *A30*: You wil *R2, Ash 47*   5 in] on *C*
6 fix'd] fast, *Ash 47*   and] itt *D2*   7 her] the *L, E24, A30, R2*   9 dares
venture] dares venter *E24, D2*: dare venter *L, C, R2, Ash 47*

On

On his Mistres lookeinge in a glasse.

THis flatteringe glasse whose smooth face weares
   Your shaddow, which a sunne appeares
Was once a Riuer of my teares.

About your cold heart they did make
A circle, where the brinie lake   5
Congeal'd into a Christall cake.

This glasse and shaddow seeme to say,
Like vs the beauties you suruay
Will quickly breake or fly away.

Since then my teares can onely show   10
You your owne face, you cannot know
How faire you are, but by my woe.

Nor had the world else knowne your name
But that my sad verse spread the fame
Of thee most faire and cruell dame.   15

Forsake but your disdainefull minde
And in my songe the world shall finde
That you are not more faire then kinde.

Change but your scorne, my verse shall chase
Decay far from you, and your face   20
Shall shine with an immortall grace.

On his Mistres, &c. (An alternative version of 'A Looking-Glasse', p. 19.)
Text *C*, collated with *A21, A303, S14, H6*   2 which] where *H6*   4 they]
that *H6*   5 brinie] burninge *S14*   7 seeme] seemd *A21*   say,] say *C*
9 or] and *H6*   12 woe.] woo. *C*   15 thee] yᵉ *C*   and] most *S14*
18 are not more] are more *A21, A303, H6*

A

A
TRANSLATION
OF
CERTAIN
PSALMES

Psalme the first.

1 Happie the man that dothe not walke
    In wicked Counsells, nor hath lent
His glad Eare to the rayling talke
    Of Skorners, nor his prompt steeps bent
    To wicked pathes, whear sinners went;   5

2 But to those saffer tractes Confinde
    Which Godes Law giueing finger made,
Neuer withdrawes his Weried mynde
    From practize of that holye trade,
    By noone dayes sunn, or midnightes shade.   10

3 Like the Fayre plante whome Neighbouring flouds
    Refresh, whose leafe feeles no decayes,
That not alone with flattering buds
    But Earely fruittes his Lords hope payes,
    So shall hee thriue In all his wayes.   15

4 Butt the loose sinner shall not share
    Soe fixt a state; like the light dust
That vpp and downe the Emptie Ayre
    The wilde wynd driues, with various Gust
    Soe shall Crosse fortunes toss the vnJust.   20

5 Therfore att the last Judgement day
    The trembling sinnefull Soule shall hyde
His Confused face, nor shall hee stay
    Whear the Elected Troopes abyde,
    But shall be Chased farr from theire side.   25

6 For the Clere pathes of Righteous men
    To the all seeing Lord are knowne,
But the darke maze and dismall den
    Whear sinners wander vpp and downe
    Shall by his hand be ouer throwne.   30

Psalme the first. Text from *Ash 38*. Punctuation partly the editor's.   *Title:*
Psalme the first, verse the i *Ash 38*

Psalme

Psalme 2.

1.2.   Why rage the heathen, wherefore swell
3.   The People with vaine thoughts, why meete
Theire kings in Counsell to rebell
    Gainst God and Christ, trampling their sweete
    But broaken bonds vnder their feete?   5

4.5.   Alass the glorious God, that hath
6.   His throne in heauen, derides th'vnsound
Plotts of weak Mortalls; in his wrath
    Thus shall hee speak, my self haue crownd
    The Monarch of my holy ground.   10

7.8.   I will declare what God hath told:
    Thou art my sonne, this happie day
Did thie incarnate birth vnfould;
    Ask, and the heathen shall obey:
    With the remotest Earth thy sway.   15

9.10.   Thy rodd of Iron shall if kings rise
11.   Against thee, bruise them into dust
Like potts of Clay, therefore bee wise
    Yee Princes, and learne Iudgments iust,
    Serve God with feare, Tremble, yet trust,   20

12.   Kisse and doe hommage to the Sunn,
    Least his displeasure ruyne bring:
For if that fire bee but begunn,
    Then happie those, that themselues fling
    Vnder the Shelter of his wing.   25

Psalme 2. Text from *W*, collated with *Ash 38*. Punctuation partly the editor's.
1 heathen,] Heathens *Ash 38*   4–5 *Ash 38 reads:*
        Gainst god and Christ trampling his sweete,
        but broken bones vnder their feete
9 haue] hath *Ash 38*

Psalme

Psalme 51.

1. Good god vnlock thy Magazines
   Of Mercie, and forgive my Sinns.

2. Oh wash and purifie the foule
   .Pollution of my Sin-staynd Soule.

3. For I confess my faults that lye   5
   In horrid shapes before myne Eye.

4. Against thee onely, and alone
   In thie sight was this evill donne,
   That all Men might thy Iustice see
   When thou art Iudg'd for Iudging mee.   10

5. Euen from my birth I did begin
   With mothers milk to Suck in Sinn.

6. But thou lov'st truth, and shalt impart
   Thy secrett wisdome to my heart.

7. Thou shalt with ysopp purge me; soe   15
   Shall I seeme white as Mountaine snowe.

8. Thou shalt send ioyfull newes, and then
   My broaken bones growe strong againe.

9. Lett not thine Eyes my Sins survey,
   But cast those Cancelld debts away.   20

10. Oh make my Cleansd heart, a pure Cell
    Where a renewed Spiritt may dwell.

11. Cast mee not from thy sight, nor chase
    Away from mee thy Spiritt of grace.

Psalme 51. Text from *W*, collated with *Ash 38*. Punctuation partly the editor's.
Title: Psalme. 51ᵗʰ. *W*   1 thy *Ash 38*] the *W*   4 Pollution] Polutions
Ash 38   16 Mountaine] Alpine *Ash 38*   18 strong] firme *Ash 38*

12. Send

12. Send mee thy Saueing health againe,   25
And with thy Spirritt those Ioyes mainetaine.

13. Then will I preach thy wayes, and drawe
Converted Sinners to thy lawe.

14.15. Oh God my God of health, vnseale
My blood-shutt lipps, and Ile reveale   30
What mercyes in thy Iustice dwell,
And with Lowd voyce thy Praises tell.

16.17. Could Sacrifice haue purgd my vice
Lord I had brought thee Sacrifice:
But though burnt offerings are refus'd   35
Thou shalt accept the heart that's bruis'd;
The humbled Soule, the Spiritt opprest,
Lord such oblations please thee best.

18. Bless Syon lord, repaire with pittie
The ruynes of thy holy Cittie.   40

19. Then will wee holy vowes present thee,
And peace offerings that Content thee,
And then thyne Alters shall be prest
With many a Sacrificed beast.

Psalme 91.

1.2. Make the greate God thy Fort, and dwell
3.   In him by Faith, and doe not Care
(Soe shaded) for the power of hell
Or for the Cunning Fowlers snare
Or poyson of th'infected Ayre.   5

4.5. His plumes shall make a downy bedd
Where thou shalt rest, hee shall display
His wings of truth over thy head,
Which like a shield shall drive away
The feares of night, the darts of day.   10

27 preach] teach *Ash 38*   37 humbled] humblest *Ash 38*   38 thee]
the *W*   40 thy] the *Ash 38*
  Psalme 91. Text from *W*, collated with *Ash 38* and *R6*. Punctuation partly the
editor's.   3 power] Fires *R6*   10 darts] darkes *Ash 38*

6.7. The

6.7. The winged plague that flyes by night,
    The murdering sword that kills by day,
Shall not thy peacefull sleepes affright
    Though on thy right and left hand they
    A thousand and ten thousand slay.   15

8.9. Yet shall thine Eyes behould the fall
10.   Of Sinners, but because thy heart
Dwells with the Lord, not one of all
    Those ills, nor yett the plaguie dart
    Shall dare approach neere where thou art.   20

11.12. His angells shall direct thie leggs
13.   And guard them in the Stony streete;
On Lyons whelps, and Addars Eggs
    Thy Stepps shall March, and if thou meete
    With Draggons, they shall kiss thy feete.   25

14.15. When thou art troubled, hee shall heare
16.   And help thee, for thy Loue embrast
And knewe his name, Therefore hee'l reare
    Thy honours high, and when thou hast
    Enioyd them long, Saue thee att last.   30

Psalme 104.

1. My soule the great Gods prayses sings,
   Encircled round with gloryes wings,

2. Clothed with light, o're whome the Skie
   Hangs like a Starry Cannopie:

13 peacefull sleepes] quiet Peace *R6*   14 thy] the *R6*   16 *R6 reads*:
Only thine Eies shall see the Fall   19 Those] theis *R6*   nor *Ash 38, R6*:
not *W*   22 streete;] streets *W*: strette *Ash 38*: Streete: *R6*   24 thou]
they *R6*   26 shall] will *R6*   28 knewe] know *Ash 38*   30 thee] the *W*
   Psalme 104. Text from *W*, collated with *Ash 38, A21, A221, A303, A4, E28*.
Punctuation partly the editor's.   *Title:* Psalme. 104th. *W*   2 Encircled
A221, A21: Circled *W, A303, A4, E28, Ash 38*   gloryes] glorious *Ash 38*
3 Clothed *A221, A4, E28, Ash 38*: Cloathd *W, A21, A303*

3. Whoe

3. Whoe dwells vppon the glideing streames,   5
   Enameld with his golden beames;
   Enthron'd in Clouds as in a Chayre,
   Hee rydes in tryvmph through the ayre:

4. The winds and flameing Element
   Are on his greate Ambassage sent.   10

5. The Fabrick of the Earth shall stand
   For aye, built by his powerfull hand.

6.7. The floods that with theire watry roabe
8.9. Once coverd all this Earthlie Globe,
     (Soone as thie thundering Voyce was heard,)   15
     Fledd fast, and straight the hills appeard.
     The humble Vallies sawe the Sunn,
     Whilst the affrighted waters runn
     Into theire Channells, and noe more
     Shall drowne the Earth, or passe the Shoare.   20

10. Along those vailes the Coole Springs flowe
    And wash the Mountaines feete belowe.

11. Thither for Drinck, the whole heard strayes,
    There the wild Asse, his Thirst allayes;

12. And on the Bowghes that shade the spring   25
    The featherd quire shall sitt and sing.

13.14. When on her wombe thy dewe is shedd
   15. The pregnant Earth is brought to bedd,
       And with a fruitfull birth encreast
       Yeilds hearbes and grass for Man and beast,   30
       Heart-strengthening breade, Care-drowneing wyne,
       And oyle, that makes the sleeke face shine.

6 *E28 reads*: enameled wth golden beames,   14 this Earthlie] ye earthy *A221*:
this Earthy *Ash 38*   16 Fledd] flie *E28*   20 passe the] passe theyre, *A21, A303,*
A4   21 Along] Amonge *A221*: Amongst *Ash 38*   Coole] Coulde *Ash 38*
23 whole] hote *Ash 38*   26 shall] doth *A21, A221, A303, E28*   27 thy]
y^e *A221, E28, Ash 38*   shedd] spredd *E28*   28 pregnant] fertile *E28*   32
the sleeke face] ye sad face *E28*: ye face to *A221*

16. On

16. On Libanon his Cedars stand,
Trees full of Sapp, works of his hand;

17. In them the Birds their Cabines dight,   35
The Firr tree is the Storks delight,

18. The wild Goat on the hills, in Cells
Of Rock, the hermitt, Conye, dwells.

19. The Moone obserues her Course, the Sunn
Knowes when his weary race is donne: 40

20. And when the night her dark vaile spredds
The wilder beasts forsake their shedds;

21. The hungrie Lions hunt for blood,
And roareing begg from God their food.

22.23. The Sunn returnes, theis beasts of pray   45
Flye to their Denns, and from the day;
And whilst they in dark Cavernes lurk
Mann till the evening goes to work.

24. How full of Creatures is the Earth,
To which thy wisdome gaue their birth!   50

25. And those that in the wide Sea breed
The bounds of number farre exceed:

26. There the huge whales with finy feete
Dance vnderneath the Saileing fleete.

27.28. All theis expect theire nourishment   55
29.30. From thee, and gather what is Sent.

35–6 *E28 reads*:
In them yᵉ birdes their Cabyns buildes
to'th storke yᵉ firr tree harbour yeildes
41 her] his *A21, A221, A303, A4*   44 from God their food.] their food from
God. *A21, A303*   45 theis] those *Ash 38*   47 in dark Cavernes lurk] all in
darke Caues lurke *A21, A303*   48 *E28 reads*: man till th' even goes fourth to
worke   51 wide Sea breed] broad Seas breedes *E28*   52 exceed:]
exceedes, *E28*

Bee

Bee thy hand open, they are fedd:
Bee thie face hidd, astonished.
If thou withdrawe their Soule, they must
Returne into theire former dust.   60
If thou send back thy breath the face
Of the Earth, is spread with a new race.

31. Gods glorie shall for ever stay,
     Hee shall with ioy his works survey.

32.33. The stedfast Earth shall shake, if hee   65
        Look downe, & if the Mountaines bee
        Toucht, they shall smoak. Yet still my verse
        Shall whilst I liue his praise reherse;

34. In him with ioy my thoughts shall meete,
     Hee makes my Meditations sweete.   70

35. The Sinner shall appeare noe more.
     Then oh my Soule, thy Lord adore.

Psalme 113.

1.2. Yee Children of the Lord, that waite
  3.   Vppon his will, sing Hymnes divine
       From henceforth, to tymes endless date
         To his name prais'd, from the first shine
         Of th'Early Sunn, till it decline.   5

4.5. The hoasts of Heauen, or Earth have none
  6.   May to his height of glory rise:
       For whoe like him hath fix'd his Throne
       Soe high, yet bends downe to the skyes
       And lower Earth his humble Eyes?   10

57 hand] face E28   59–60 Omitted in Ash 38   59 withdrawe] wth hold A221   61 thy] their A221   62 the Earth] th' Earth A21, A221, E28: Earth Ash 38   66 Look] Lookes A221   72 thy] the A21, A221, E28: Ash 38

Psalme 113. Text from W, collated with Ash 38. Punctuation partly the editor's. Title: Psalme: 113th. W   5 th' Early] the Eartes Ash 38

7.8. The

7.8. The poore from loathed Dust hee drawes,
9.   And makes them regall state invest
Mongst kings, that gives his People Lawes:
Hee makes the barren Mother rest
Vnder her roofe with Children blest.   15

Psalme 114.

1.2. When the seed of Jacob fledd
From the cruell Pharaohs land,
Iuda was in Safety ledd
By the Lord, whose powerfull hand
Guided all the Hebrew band.   5

3.4. This the Sea saw, and dismayde
Flyes, swift Iourdane backward makes,
Mountaines skipt like Ramms affraid,
And the lower hillocks shakes
Like a tender Lambe that quakes.   10

5.6. What oh Sea, hath thee dismaide?
Why did Iourdane backwards make?
Mountaines, why like Ramms affraide
Skipt yee, wherefore did yee shake
Hillocks, like the Lambes that quake?   15

7.8. Tremble oh thou stedfast Earth
Att the presence of the Lord
That makes rocks give Rivers birth,
And by virtue of whose word
Flints shall floweing springs afford.   20

Psalme 114. Text from *W*, collated with *Ash 38*. Punctuation partly the editor's.
12 backwards] backward *Ash 38*   19 whose] his *Ash 38*

Psalme

Psalme 119.

Beati Immaculati. 1st.

Aleph:

1. Blest is hee that Spottless stands
   In the way of Gods Commaunds:

2. Blessed hee that keepes his word,
   Whose intire heart seekes the Lord:

3. For the Man that walketh in
   His iust paths, Committs noe Sinn.

4. By thie strickt Comaunds wee are
   Bound to keepe thy Lawes with care,

5. Oh that my stepps might not slide
   From thy Statutes perfect guide.

6. Soe shall I decline thy wrath
   Treading thy Comaunded path;

7. Haueing learn'd thy righteous wayes
   With true heart I'le sing thy praise;

8. In thy Statutes I'le persevere,
   Then forsake mee not for ever.

In quo Corriget. 2.

Beth:

9. How shall youth but by the leuell
   Of thy word bee kept from euill?

10. Lett my soule that seekes the way
    Of thy truth not goe astraye;

11. Where least my fraile Feete might slide
    In my heart thy words I hide.

12. Blest bee thou oh lord, oh showe
    How I may thy statutes knowe.

Psalme 119. Text from *W.* Punctuation partly the editor's.
Psalme. 119th. *W*

Title:

13. I

13. I haue publisht the divine   25
    Iudgments of thy Mouth with myne,

14. Which haue filld my Soule with pleasure
    More then all the heaps of treasure.

15. They shall all the Subiect prove
    Of my talk, and of my love;   30

16. Those my darlings noe tyme shall
    From my Memory lett fall.

            Retribue Servo tuo. 3.
Gimel:
17. Lett thie grace o Lord preserve mee
    That I may but live to serve thee;

18. Open my dark Eyes that I   35
    May thy wonderous lawes descry;

19. Lett thy glorious light appeare:
    I am but a pilgrime heere,

20. Yet the zeale of theire desyre
    Hath euen sett my heart on fire.   40

21. Thy fearce rodd, and curse o're taketh
    Him that proudly thee forsaketh:

22. I haue kept thy Lawes oh God,
    Turne from mee thy Curse and rodd.

23. Though combined Princes raild,   45
    Yet thy Servant hath not faild

24. In theire Studdie to abide,
    For they are my Ioy, my guide.

            Adhæsit pavimento. 4.
Daleth:
25. For thy words sake, give new birth
    To my soule that Cleaues to Earth.   50

917.25   L   26. Thou

26. Thou hast heard my Tongue vntwine
   All my waies, Lord teach mee thyne.

27. Make mee knowe them that I may
   All thie wonderous workes display.

28. Thou hast said the word, then bring .   55
   Ease to my Soule languishing.

29. Plant in mee, thy Lawes true Love
   And the vaile of Lyes remove.

30. I have choosen truth to Lye
   The fixt obiect of myne Eye.   60

31. On thy word my faith I grounded,
   Lett me not then bee confounded.

32. When my Soule from bonds is freed
   I shall runne thy wayes with speed.

Legem pone. 5.

He:

33. Teach mee Lord, thy waies, and I   65
   From that roade will never fly.

34. Give mee knowledge that I may
   With my heart, thy Lawes obey.

35. Vnto that Path, my stepps move,
   For I there haue fixt my Love.   70

36. Fill my heart with those pure fires,
   Not with Covetous desyres.

37. To vaine sights Lord lett mee bee
   Blinde, but thy waies lett mee see.

38. Make thy promise firme to mee   75
   That with feare have served thee.

39. Cause

39. Cause thy Iudgements ever were
    Sweete divert the shame I feare.

40. Lett not him in Iustice perish
    That desyres, thy Lawes to cherish.   80

                Et veniat Super me. 6.
Vau:

41. Lett thy Loveing Mercies cure mee,
    As thy promisses assure mee,

42. Soe shall the Blasphemer see
    I not vainely trust in thee;

43. Take not quite the words away   85
    Of thy truth, that are my stay,

44. Then I'le keepe thy lawes, even till
    Winged tyme it self stand still;

45. And whilst I pursue thy search
    With secure stepps will I march.   90

46. Vnashamed Ile record
    Euen before great kings thy word.

47. That shall be my ioy, for there
    My thoughts ever fixed were.

48. With bent mynd and stretch'd-out hands   95
    I will seek thie lov'd Commaunds.

                Memor esto verbi tui. 7.
Zaine:

49. Thinck vppon thy promiss made,
    For in that my trust is layd,

50. That my Comfort in distress,
    That hath brought my life redresse.   100
                        51. Though

51. Though the proud hath scorn'd mee, they
    Made mee not forsake thy waie;

52. Thy eternall Iudgements brought
    Ioy, to my remembring thought.

53. With greate Sorrowe I am taken   105
    When I see thy lawes forsaken,

54. Which haue made me songs of myrth
    In this pilgrimage of Earth;

55. Which I myndefull was to keepe
    When I had forgott to sleepe.   110

56. Thy Comaundes I did embrace,
    Therefore I obtain'd thy grace.

Portio mea Domine. 8.

Heth:

57. Thou o lord, art my reward,
    To thie lawes my thoughts are squard.

58. With an humble heart I craue   115
    Thou wilt promis'd mercy haue.

59. I have mark'd my stepps, and now
    To thie waies my feete I bowe;

60. Nor haue I the tyme delaid,
    But with hast this Iourney made,   120

61. Where though bands of sinners lay
    Snareing netts, I keepe my waie.

62. I my self att Midnight raise,
    Singing thy iust Iudgements praise.

63. I converse with those that beare   125
    To thie lawes obedyent feare.

                                      64. Teach

64. Teach mee them Lord, by that grace
Which hath fild the worlds wide space.

(*Here the manuscript ends imperfectly.*)

Psalme 137.

1. Sitting by the streames that Glide
Downe by Babells Towring wall,
With our tears wee filde the tyde
Whilst our Myndfull thoughtes recall
Thee Oh Sion, and thy fall.   5

2. Our neglected harps vnstrunge,
Not acquainted with the hand
Of the skillfull Tuner, hunge
On the willow trees that stand
Planted in the Neighbour land.   10

3. Yett the spightfull foe Commands
Songes of Mirthe, and bids vs lay
To dumbe harps, our Captiue hands,
And, (to scoffe our sorrowes) say
Sing vs som sweet hebrewe lay.   15

4. But say wee, our holye strayn
Is too pure for heathen land,
Nor may wee godes Himnes prophane,
Or moue eyther voyce or hand
To delight a sauage band.   20

5. Holye Salem yf thy loue
Fall from my forgettfull harte,
May the skill by which I moue
Stringes of Musicke tund with art,
From my withered hand departe!   25

Psalme 137. Text from *Ash 38*, collated with *A18, A4*, and Henry Lawes's printed
Select Psalmes of a New Translation, 1655. Punctuation partly the editor's.   *Title:*
Psalme the 137 *Ash 38*   1 1.] ve: i *Ash 38*   5 Thee] The *Ash 38*
17 too] to *Ash 38*   18 godes] our *A18, Select Psalmes*   19 moue] tune *A18,
Select Psalmes, A4*   24 with] by *Select Psalmes*

6. May

6. May my speachles tongue giue sound
   To noe accentes, but remayne
   To my prisen Roofe fast bound,
   Iff my sad soule Entertayne
   Mirth, till thou reioyce agayne!   30

7. In that day remember, Lord
   Edoms brood, that in our groanes
   They Triumph; with fier and sword
   Burne their Cittie, hew their bones
   And make all One heape of stones.   35

8. Cruell Babell, thou shalt feele
   The Reuenger of our groanes,
   When the happie Victors steele
   As thine, ours, shall hew thy bones,
   And make thee one heape of stones.   40

9. Men shall bless the hand that teares
   From the Mothers softe embraces
   Sucking Infants, and besmeares
   With their braynes, the Rugged faces
   Of the Rockes and stony places.   45

26 speachles *A18, Select Psalmes*: speaches *Ash 38*   27 accentes,] accent *A18,*
Select Psalmes   32 that] thus *Select Psalmes*   33 Triumph;] triumph'd
A18, Select Psalmes   40 thee] the *Ash 38*   one] an *A18*   42 the]
thee *Ash 38*

Cælum

Cœlum Britanicum:

A
MASQUE
AT
WHITE-HALL
IN THE BANQVET-
TING-HOVSE, ON SHROVE-
TVESDAY-NIGHT, THE
18. of *February*, 1633.

Non habeo ingenium; Cæsar sed jussit: habebo.
Cur me posse negem, posse quod ille putat?

LONDON:
Printed for *Thomas Walkley,* and are to be sold
at his Shop neare *White-Hall.*
1634.

Title-page, first édition
(British Museum, Shelfmark C.34.C.8)

THE
DESCRIPTION
OF THE SCÆNE.

THe first thing that presented it selfe to the sight, was a
rich Ornament, that enclosed the Scæne; in the upper
part of which, were great branches of Foliage growing out
of leaves and huskes, with a Coronîce at the top; and in the
midst was placed a large compartiment composed of Groteske 5
worke, wherein were Harpies with wings and Lions clawes,
and their hinder parts converted into leaves and branches:
over all was a broken Frontispice, wrought with scrowles and
masque heads of Children; and within this a Table adorn'd
with a lesser Compartiment, with this Inscription, *COELVM* 10
BRITANNICVM. The two sides of this Ornament were
thus ordered: First, from the ground arose a square Base-
ment, and on the Plinth stood a great vaze of gold, richly
enchased, and beautified with Sculptures of great Releiue,
with frutages hanging from the upper-part: At the foot of 15
this sate two youths naked, in their naturall colours; each
of these with one arme supported the Vaze; on the cover of
which stood two young women in Draperies, arme in arme;
the one figuring the glory of Princes, and the other Man-
suetude: their other armes bore up an Ovall, in which, to 20
the Kings Majesty was this Imprese, A Lion with an Imperi-
all Crowne on his head; the word, *Animum sub pectore forti*:
On the other side was the like Composition, but the designe
of the Figures varied; and in the Ovall on the top, being
borne up by Nobility and Fecundity, was this Imprese to 25
the Queenes Majesty, A Lilly growing with branches and
leaves, and three lesser Lillies springing out of the Stemme;
the word, *Semper inclita Virtus*: All this Ornament was
heightned with Gold, and for the Invention and various

Coelum Britannicum. For explanation of symbols see p. lx. The text follows
copy *c* of the 1634 edition except where otherwise noted. Variants of spelling and
punctuation in other copies are ordinarily not recorded except where used to
correct *c*.   12 ordered: *adfhptwx*: oreered: *cm*   14 Releiue,] Releine,
34 (*all copies*)

composition,

30 composition, was the newest and most gracious that hath
beene done in this place.

The Curtaine was watchet and a pale yellow in paines,
which flying up on the sudden, discovered the Scæne, repre-
senting old Arches, old Palaces, decayed walls, parts of
35 Temples, Theaters, Basilica's and Therme, with confused
heaps of broken Columnes, Bases, Coronices and Statues,
lying as underground, and altogether resembling the ruines
of some great City of the ancient Romans, or civiliz'd
Brittaines. This strange prospect detain'd the eyes of the
40 Spectators some time, when to a loud Musicke *Mercury*
descends; on the upper part of his Chariot stands a Cocke
in action of crowing: his habit was a Coat of flame colour
girt to him, and a white mantle trimm'd with gold and silver;
upon his head a wreath with small falls of white Feathers,
45 a Caduseus in his hand, and wings at his heeles: being come
to the ground he dismounts and goes up to the State.

Mercury.

FRom the high Senate of the gods, to You
Bright glorious Twins of Love and Majesty,
Before whose Throne three warlike Nations bend
50 Their willing knees, on whose Imperiall browes
The Regall Circle prints no awfull frownes
To fright your Subjects, but whose calmer eyes
Shed joy and safety on their melting hearts
That flow with cheerefull loyall reverence,
55 Come I *Cyllenius*, *Ioves* Ambassadour:
Not, as of old, to whisper amorous tales
Of wanton love, into the glowing eare
Of some choyce beauty in this numerous traine;
Those dayes are fled, the rebell flame is quench'd
60 In heavenly brests, the gods have sworne by Styx
Never to tempt yeelding mortality
To loose embraces. Your exemplar life
Hath not alone transfus'd a zealous heat
Of imitation through your vertuous Court,
65 By whose bright blaze your Pallace is become

30 composition,] composition' *cmpw*: composition·*adfhtx*
adfhtx: Basilita's *cmpw*   46 State. *adfhtx*: State, *cmpw*   35 Basilica's

The

The envy'd patterne of this underworld,
But the aspiring flame hath kindled heaven;
Th'immortall bosomes burne with emulous fires,
Jove rivalls your great vertues, Royall Sir,
And *Iuno*, Madam, your attractive graces;   70
He his wild lusts, her raging jealousies
She layes aside, and through th'Olympique hall,
As yours doth here, their great Example spreads.
And though of old, when youthfull blood conspir'd
With his new Empire, prone to heats of lust,   75
He acted incests, rapes, adulteries
On earthly beauties, which his raging Queene,
Swolne with revengefull fury, turn'd to beasts,
And in despight he retransform'd to Stars,
Till he had fill'd the crowded Firmament   80
With his loose Strumpets, and their spurious race,
Where the eternall records of his shame
Shine to the world in flaming Characters;
When in the Chrystall myrrour of your reigne
He view'd himselfe, he found his loathsome staines;   85
And now, to expiate the infectious guilt
Of those detested luxuries, hee'll chace
Th'infamous lights from their usurped Spheare,
And drowne in the Lethæan flood, their curs'd
Both names and memories. In whose vacant roomes   90
First you succeed, and of the wheeling Orbe
In the most eminent and conspicuous point,
With dazeling beames, and spreading magnitude,
Shine the bright Pole-starre of this Hemispheare.
Next, by your side, in a triumphant Chaire,   95
And crown'd with *Ariadnes* Diadem,
Sits the faire Consort of your heart, and Throne;
Diffus'd about you, with that share of light
As they of vertue have deriv'd from you,
Hee'll fix this Noble traine, of either sexe;   100
So to the Brittish Stars this lower Globe
Shall owe its light, and they alone dispence
To'th'world a pure refined influence.

97 Consort *cmpw*: comfort *adfhtx*

Enter

Enter *Momus* attired in a long, darkish Robe all wrought
105 over with ponyards, Serpents tongues, eyes and eares, his
beard and haire party coloured, and upon his head a wreath
stucke with Feathers, and a Porcupine in the forepart.

Momus.

BY your leave, Mortalls. Goodden Cozen *Hermes*; your
pardon good my Lord Ambassadour: I found the tables
110 of your Armes and Titles, in every Inne betwixt this and
Olympus, where your present expedition is registred, your
nine thousandth nine hundred ninety ninth Legation. I
cannot reach the policy why your Master breeds so few
Statesmen, it suits not with his dignity that in the whole
115 Empyræum there should not be a god fit to send on these
honourable errands but your selfe, who are not yet so carefull
of his honour or your owne, as might become your quality,
when you are itinerant: the Hosts upon the highway cry out
with open mouth upon you for supporting pilfery in your
120 traine; which, though as you are the god of petty Larcinry,
you might protect, yet you know it is directly against the new
orders, and opposes the Reformation in Diameter.

Merc. Peace Rayler, bridle your licentious tongue,
And let this Presence teach you modesty.

125 *Mom.* Let it if it can; in the meane time I will acquaint
it with my condition. Know (gay people) that though your
Poets who enjoy by Patent a particular privilege to draw
downe any of the Deities from Twelfnight till Shrove-
tuesday, at what time there is annually a most familiar enter-
130 course between the two Courts, have as yet never invited
me to these Solemnities, yet it shall appeare by my intrusion
this night, that I am a very considerable Person upon these
occasions, and may most properly assist at such entertain-
ments. My name is *Momus-ap-Somnus-ap-Erebus-ap-Chaos-*
135 *ap-Demogorgon-ap-Eternity.* My Offices and Titles are, The
Supreme Theomastix, Hupercrittique of manners, Protono-
tarie of abuses, Arch-Informer, Dilator Generall, Vniversall
Calumniator, Eternall Plaintiffe, and perpetuall Foreman
of the Grand Inquest. My privileges are an ubiquitary,
140 circumambulatory, speculatory, interrogatory, redargutory

117 or 51: as 34 (*all copies*)

immunity

immunity over all the privy lodgings, behind hangings, dores,
curtaines, through keyholes, chinkes, windowes, about all
Veneriall Lobbies, Skonces or Redoubts, though it bee to
the surprize of a perdu Page or Chambermaid, in, and at all
Courts of civill and criminall judicature, all Counsels, Consul-   145
tations, and Parlamentary Assemblies, where though I am
but a Woollsacke god, and have no vote in the sanction of
new lawes, I have yet a Prærogative of wresting the old to
any whatsoever interpretation, whether it be to the behoofe,
or prejudice, of *Iupiter* his Crowne and Dignity, for, or   150
against the Rights of either house of Patrician or Plebeian
gods. My naturall qualities are to make *Iove* frowne, *Iuno*
powt, *Mars* chafe, *Venus* blush, *Vulcan* glow, *Saturne* quake,
Cynthia pale, *Phœbus* hide his face, and *Mercury* here take his
heeles. My recreations are witty mischiefes, as when *Saturne*   155
guelt his father; the Smith caught his wife and her *Bravo* in
a net of Cobweb-Iron; and *Hebe* through the lubricity of the
pavement tumbling over the Halfpace, presented the Em-
bleme of the forked tree, and discover'd to the tann'd Ethiops
the snowie cliffs of Calabria with the Grotta of Puteolum.   160
But that you may arrive at the perfect knowledge of me
by the familiar illustration of a Bird of mine owne feather,
old *Peter Aretine*, who reduc'd all the Scepters and Myters
of that Age tributary to his wit, was my Parallell; and *Frank
Rablais* suck'd much of my milke too; but your moderne   165
French Hospitall of Oratory, is meere counterfeit, an arrant
Mountebanke, for though fearing no other tortures than his
Sciatica, he discourses of Kings and Queenes with as little
reverence as of Groomes and Chambermaids, yet hee wants
their fang-teeth, and Scorpions taile; I meane that fellow,   170
who to adde to his stature thinkes it a greater grace to dance
on his tiptoes like a Dogge in a doublet, than to walke like
other men on the soles of his feet.

 Merc. No more impertinent Trifeler, you disturbe
The great Affaire with your rude scurrilous chat: 175
What doth the knowledge of your abject state
Concerne *Ioves* solemne Message?

160 Calabria *adfhtx*: Culabria *cmpw*, *Vincent*   165 *Rablais* 51: *Rublais 34*
(*all copies*)   167 tortures *34* (*all copies*): fortunes *40–1772*   168 dis-
courses *1772*: discourse *34* (*all copies*), *40–70*

Mom.

Mom. Sir, by your favour, though you have a more
especiall Commission of employment from *Iupiter*, and a
180 larger entertainment from his Exchequer, yet as a freeborne
god I have the liberty to travell at mine owne charges, with-
out your passe or countenance Legacine; and that it may
appeare a sedulous acute observer, may know as much as a
dull flegmatique Ambassadour, and weares a treble key to
185 unlocke the misterious Cyphers of your darke secrecies, I
will discourse the politique state of heaven to this trimme
Audience.——

At this the Scæne changeth, and in the heaven is discovered
a Spheare, with Starres placed in their severall Images;
190   borne up by a huge naked Figure (onely a peece of Drapery
hanging over his thigh) kneeling, and bowing forwards,
as if the great weight lying on his shoulders opprest him,
upon his head a Crowne, by all which he might easily be
knowne to be *Atlas*.

195 ——You shall understand, that *Iupiter* upon the inspection
of I know not what vertuous Presidents extant (as they say)
here in this Court, but as I more probably ghesse out of the
consideration of the decay of his natural abilities, hath before
a frequent cōvocation of the Superlunary Peers in a solemne
200 Oration recanted, disclaimed, and utterly renounced all the
lascivious extravagancies, and riotous enormities of his fore-
past licentious life, and taken his oath on *Junos* Breviary,
religiously kissing the two-leav'd booke, never to stretch his
limbs more betwixt adulterous sheets, and hath with patheti-
205 call remonstrances exhorted, and under strict penalties en-
joyned a respective conformity in the severall subordinate
Deities; and because the Libertines of Antiquity, the Ribald
Poets, to perpetuate the memory and example of their
triumphs over chastity, to all future imitation, have in their
210 immortall songs celebrated the martyrdome of those Strum-
pets under the persecution of the wives, and devolved to
Posterity the Pedigrees of their whores, bawds, and bastards;
it is therefore by the authority aforesaid enacted, that this
whole Army of Constellations be immediately disbanded and
215 casheerd, so to remove all imputation of impiety from the

212 whores, *adfhtx*: whores *cmpw*

Cœlestiall

Cœlestiall Spirits, and all lustfull influences upon terrestriall
bodies; and consequently that there be an Inquisition erected
to expunge in the Ancient, and suppresse in the moderne
and succeeding Poems and Pamphlets, all past, present, and
future mention of those abjur'd heresies, and to take particu- 220
lar notice of all ensuing incontinences, and punish them in
their high Commission Court. Am not I in election to be a
tall Statesman thinke you, that can repeat a passage at a
Counsell-table thus punctually?

    Merc. I shun in vaine the importunity   225
With which this Snarler vexeth all the gods,
Iove cannot scape him: well, what else from heaven?

    Mom. Heaven! Heaven is no more the place it was; a
cloyster of Carthusians, a Monastery of converted gods,
Iove is growne old and fearefull, apprehends a subversion of 230
his Empire, and doubts lest Fate should introduce a legall
succession in the legitimate heire, by repossessing the Titan-
ian line, and hence springs all this innovation. Wee have
had new orders read in the Presence Chamber, by the Vi-
President of *Pernassus,* too strict to bee observed long. 235
Monopolies are called in, sophistication of wares punished,
and rates imposed on Commodities. Injunctions are gone
out to the Nectar Brewers, for the purging of the heavenly
Beverage of a narcotique weed which hath rendred the Idæaes
confus'd in the Divine intellects, and reducing it to the 240
composition used in *Saturnes* Reigne. Edicts are made for
the restoring of decayed housekeeping, prohibiting the re-
payre of Families to the Metropolis, but this did endanger
an Amazonian mutiny, till the females put on a more mascu-
line resolution of solliciting businesses in their owne persons, 245
and leaving their husbands at home for stallions of hospitality.
Baccus hath commanded all Tavernes to be shut, and no
liquor drawne after tenne at night. *Cupid* must goe no more
so scandalously naked, but is enjoyned to make him breeches
though of his mothers petticotes. *Ganimede* is forbidden 250
the Bedchamber, and must onely minister in publique. The
gods must keepe no Pages, nor Groomes of their Chamber
under the age of 25. and those provided of a competent
stocke of beard. *Pan* may not pipe, nor *Proteus* juggle, but

    222 their *cmpw*: the *adfhtx*

by

255 by especiall permission. *Vulcan* was brought to an Oretenus
and fined, for driving in a plate of Iron into one of the
Sunnes Chariot-wheeles and frost-nailing his horses upon the
fifth of *November* last, for breach of a penall Statute prohibit-
ing worke upon Holydayes, that being the annuall celebra-
260 tion of the Gygantomachy. In briefe, the whole state of the
Hierarchy suffers a totall reformation, especially in the poynt
of reciprocation of conjugall affection. *Venus* hath confest
all her adulteries, and is receiv'd to grace by her husband,
who conscious of the great disparity betwixt her perfections
265 and his deformities, allowes those levities as an equall counter-
poize; but it is the prettiest spectacle to see her stroaking
with her Ivory hand his collied cheekes, and with her snowy
fingers combing his sooty beard. *Iupiter* too beginnes to
learne to lead his owne wife, I left him practising in the
270 milky way; and there is no doubt of an universall obedience,
where the Lawgiver himselfe in his owne person observes his
decrees so punctually; who besides to eternize the memory
of that great example of Matrimoniall union which he derives
from hence, hath on his bedchamber dore, and seeling,
275 fretted with starres in capitall letters, engraven the Inscrip-
tion of *CARLOMARIA*. This is as much I am sure as
either your knowledge or Instructions can direct you to,
which I having in a blunt round tale, without State-formality,
politique inferences, or suspected Rhetoricall elegancies, al-
280 ready delivered, you may now dexteriously proceed to the
second part of your charge, which is the raking of yon
heavenly sparks up in the Embers, or reducing the Ætheriall
lights to their primitive opacity, and grosse darke subsistance;
they are all unrivited from the Spheare, and hang loose in
285 their sockets, where they but attend the waving of your
Caduce, and immediately they reinvest their pristine shapes,
and appeare before you in their owne naturall deformities.

 Merc. Momus thou shalt prevaile, for since thy bold
Intrusion hath inverted my resolves,
290 I must obey necessity, and thus turne
My face, to breath the Thundrers just decree
'Gainst this adulterate Spheare, which first I purge
Of loathsome Monsters, and mis-shapen formes:

267 snowy *adfhtx*: sinowy *cmpw* 281 yon *34 (all copies)*: yonr *40*: your *42–1772*

Downe from her azure concave, thus I charme
The Lyrnean Hydra, the rough unlick'd Beare,   295
The watchfull Dragon, the storme-boading Whale,
The Centaure, the horn'd Goatfish Capricorne,
The Snake-heard Gorgon, and fierce Sagittar:
Divested of your gorgeous starry robes,
Fall from the circling Orbe, and e're you sucke   300
Fresh venome in, measure this happy earth,
Then to the Fens, Caves, Forrests, Deserts, Seas,
Fly, and resume your native qualities.

> *They dance in those monstrous shapes the first Antimaske of*
> *naturall deformity.*   305

Mom. Are not these fine companions, trim playfellowes
for the Deities? yet these and their fellowes have made up
all our conversation for some thousands of yeeres. Doe not
you faire Ladies acknowledge your selves deeply engaged
now to those Poets your servants, that in the height of   310
commendation have rais'd your beauties to a parallell with
such exact proportions, or at least rank'd you in their spruce
society? Hath not the consideration of these Inhabitants
rather frighted your thoughts utterly from the contemplation
of the place? but now that those heavenly Mansions are to 315
be voyd, you that shall hereafter be found unlodged will
become inexcusable; especially since Vertue alone shall be
sufficient title, fine, and rent: yet if there be a Lady not
competently stock'd that way, she shall not on the instant
utterly despaire, if shee carry a sufficient pawne of handsome- 320
nesse; for however the letter of the Law runnes, *Jupiter*
notwithstanding his Age and present austerity, will never
refuse to stampe beauty, and make it currant with his owne
Impression; but to such as are destitute of both, I can afford
but small encouragement. Proceed Cozen *Mercury*, what 325
followes?

Merc. Looke up, and marke where the bright Zodiacke
Hangs like a Belt about the brest of heaven;
On the right shoulder, like a flaming Iewell,
His shell with nine rich Topazes adorn'd,   330

304 monstrous] menstrous *34 (all copies)*   312 proportions, *adfhtx*: prp-
portions, *cmpw*   313 society? *51*: society. *34 (all copies)*   330 shell *51*:
shell, *34 (all copies)*

Lord of this Tropique, sits the skalding Crab:
He, when the Sunne gallops in full careere
His annuall race; his ghastly clawes uprear'd,
Frights at the confines of the torrid Zone,
335 The fiery teame, and proudly stops their course,
Making a solstice, till the fierce Steeds learne
His backward paces, and so retrograde
Poste downe-hill to th'opposed Capricorne.
Thus I depose him from his laughty Throne;
340 Drop from the Sky, into the briny flood,
There teach thy motion to the ebbing Sea,
But let those fires that beautifi'd thy shell
Take humane shapes, and the disorder show
Of thy regressive paces here below.

345 *The second Antimasque is danc'd in retrograde paces, expressing obliquity in motion.*

Mom. This Crab, I confesse, did ill become the heavens;
but there is another that more infests the Earth, and makes
such a solstice in the politer Arts and Sciences, as they have
350 not beene observed for many Ages to have made any sensible
advance: could you but lead the learned squadrons with a
masculine resolution past this point of retrogradation, it were
a benefit to mankinde worthy the power of a god, and to be
payed with Altars; but that not being the worke of this night,
355 you may pursue your purposes: what now succeeds?
Merc. Vice, that unbodied, in the Appetite
Erects his Throne, hath yet, in bestiall shapes,
Branded, by Nature, with the Character
And distinct stampe of some peculiar Ill,
360 Mounted the Sky, and fix'd his Trophies there:
As fawning flattery in the little Dog;
I'th bigger, churlish Murmur; Cowardize
I'th timorous Hare; Ambition in the Eagle;
Rapine and Avarice in th'adventrous Ship
365 That sail'd to Colchos for the golden fleece;
Drunken distemper in the Goblet flowes;
I'th Dart and Scorpion, biting Calumny;
In *Hercules* and the Lion, furious rage;

339 laughty *34 (all copies)*: lofty *51–1772*: haughty *Hazlitt, Ebsworth, Vincent*
Vaine

Vaine Ostentation in *Cassiope*:
All these I to eternall exile doome,   370
But to this place their emblem'd Vices summon,
Clad in those proper Figures, by which best
Their incorporeall nature is exprest.

*The third Antimasque is danc'd of these severall vices, ex-
pressing the deviation from Vertue.*   375

Mom. From henceforth it shall be no more said in the
Proverbe, when you would expresse a riotous Assembly,
That hell, but heaven is broke loose: this was an arrant
Goale-delivery, all the prisons of your great Cities could not
have vomitted more corrupt matter: but Cozen *Cylleneus*, in 380
my judgement it is not safe that these infectious persons
should wander here to the hazard of this Island, they
threatned lesse danger when they were nayl'd to the Firma-
ment: I should conceive it a very discreet course since they
are provided of a tall vessell of their owne ready rigg'd, to 385
embarque them all together in that good Ship call'd the
Argo, and send them to the plantation in *New-England*,
which hath purg'd more virulent humors from the politique
body, then *Guacum* and all the West-Indian druggs have
from the naturall bodies of this kingdome: Can you devise 390
how to dispose them better?

Merc. They cannot breath this pure and temperate Aire
Where Vertue lives, but will with hasty flight,
'Mongst fogs and vapours, seeke unsound abodes.
Fly after them, from your usurped seats,   395
You foule remainders of that viperous brood:
Let not a Starre of the luxurious race
With his loose blaze staine the skyes chrystall face.

All the Starres are quench'd, and the Spheare darkned.

Before the entry of every Antimasque, the Starres in those 400
figures in the Spheare which they were to represent, were
extinct; so as, by the end of the Antimasques in the Spheare
no more Stars were seene.

Mom. Here is a totall Ecclipse of the eighth Spheare,

374 *these cmpw:* those *adfhtx*   375 *the 34 (all copies):* their *51–1772   de-*
viation adfhtx: deviatoin *cmpw*   380 matter: *ahx:* marter: *cdfmptw*

which

405 which neither *Booker*, *Allestre*, nor any of your Prognosticators,
no nor their great Master *Tico* were aware of; but yet in my
opinion there were some innocent, and some generous Con-
stellations, that might have beene reserved for Noble uses:
as the Skales and Sword to adorne the statue of Iustice, since
410 she resides here on Earth onely in Picture and Effigie. The
Eagle had beene a fit present for the Germans, in regard
their Bird hath mew'd most of her feathers lately. The
Dolphin too had beene most welcome to the French, and
then had you but clapt *Perseus* on his *Pegasus*, brandishing
415 his Sword, the Dragon yawning on his backe under the
horses feet, with *Python's* dart through his throat, there had
beene a Divine St. *George* for this Nation: but since you have
improvidently shuffled them altogether, it now rests onely
that wee provide an immediate succession, and to that pur-
420 pose I will instantly proclaime a free Election.

O yes, O yes, O yes,
By the Father of the gods,
and the King of Men,

Whereas we having observed a very commendable practice
425 taken into frequent use by the Princes of these latter Ages,
of perpetuating the memory of their famous enterprizes,
sieges, battels, victories, in Picture, Sculpture, Tapistry,
Embroyderies, and other manifactures, wherewith they have
embellished their publique Palaces, and taken into Our more
430 distinct and serious consideration, the particular Christmas
hangings of the Guard-Chamber of this Court, wherein the
Navall Victory of 88. is to the eternall glory of this Nation
exactly delineated: and whereas We likewise out of a pro-
pheticall imitation of this so laudable custome, did for many
435 thousand yeares before, adorne and beautifie the eighth
roome of Our cælestiall Mansion, commonly called the
Starre-Chamber, with the military adventures, strategems,
atchievements, feats and defeats, performed in Our Owne
person, whilest yet Our Standard was erected, and We a

406 but] bur *34* (*all copies*)   415–16 the horses *cdfmptw*: his horses *ahx*
Python's *adfhtx*: *Pytheus* *cmpw*   420 Election. *40*: Election, *34* (*all copies*)
428 manifactures, *dft*: Manifactures, *ahx*: manifactnres, *cmpw*

Combattant

Combattant in the Amorous Warfare. It hath notwith- 440
standing, after mature deliberation, and long debate, held
first in our owne inscrutable bosome, and afterwards com-
municated with Our Privy Counsell, seemed meet to Our
Omnipotency, for causes to Our selfe best knowne, to un-
furnish and dis-array Our foresaid Starre-Chamber of all 445
those Antient Constellations which have for so many Ages
beene sufficiently notorious, and to admit into their vacant
places, such Persons onely as shall be qualified with exemplar
Vertue and eminent Desert, there to shine in indelible
Characters of glory to all Posterity. It is therefore Our 450
divine will and pleasure, voluntarily, and out of Our owne
free and proper motion, meere grace and speciall favour, by
these presents to specifie and declare to all Our loving
People, that it shall be lawfull for any Person whatsoever,
that conceiveth him or her selfe to be really endued with 455
any Heroicall Vertue or transcendent Merit, worthy so high
a calling and dignity, to bring their severall pleas and pre-
tences before Our Right trusty and Welbeloved Cozen, and
Counsellor, Don *Mercury*, and god *Momus*, &c. Our peculiar
Delegates for that affaire, upon whom We have transferr'd 460
an absolute power to conclude, and determine without
Appeale or Revocation, accordingly as to their wisdomes it
shall in such cases appeare behoovefull and expedient. Given
at Our Palace in *Olympus* the first day of the first month, in
the first yeare of the Reformation.   465

Plutus enters, an old man full of wrinkles, a bald head, a
    thinne white beard, spectacles on his nose, with a buncht
    backe, and attir'd in a Robe of Cloth of gold.

Plutus appeares.

Merc. Who's this appeares?   470
Mom. This is a subterranean Fiend, *Plutus*, in this Dialect
term'd Riches, or the god of gold; a Poyson, hid by Provi-
dence in the bottome of Seas, and Navill of the Earth, from
mans discovery, where if the seeds begunne to sprout above-
ground, the excrescence was carefully guarded by Dragons, 475
yet at last by humane curiosity brought to light, to their

462 Revocation, *cmpw*: Revelation, *adfhtx*   471 subterranean *adfhtx*: sub-
terrauean *cmpw*

                                                        owne

owne destruction; this being the true *Pandora's* box, whence
issued all those mischiefes that now fill the Vniverse.

Plut. That I prevent the message of the gods
480 Thus with my haste, and not attend their summons,
Which ought in Iustice call me to the place
I now require of Right, is not alone
To shew the just precedence that I hold
Before all earthly, next th'immortall Powers;
485 But to exclude the hope of partiall Grace
In all Pretenders, who, since I descend
To equall tryall, must by my example,
Waving your favour, clayme by sole Desert.
If Vertue must inherit, shee's my slave;
490 I lead her captive in a golden chaine,
About the world: She takes her Forme and Being
From my creation; and those barren seeds
That drop from Heaven, if I not cherish them
With my distilling dewes, and fotive heat,
495 They know no vegetation; but expos'd
To blasting winds of freezing Poverty,
Or not shoot forth at all, or budding, wither:
Should I proclaime the daily sacrifice
Brought to my Temples by the toyling rout,
500 Not of the fat and gore of abject Beasts,
But human sweat, and blood powr'd on my Altars,
I might provoke the envy of the gods.
Turne but your eyes and marke the busie world,
Climbing steepe Mountaines for the sparkling stone,
505 Piercing the Center for the shining Ore,
And th'Oceans bosome to rake pearly sands,
Crossing the torrid and the frozen Zones,
'Midst Rocks and swallowing Gulfes, for gainfull trade,
And through opposing swords, fire, murdring Canon,
510 Skaling the walled Towne for precious spoyles.
Plant in the passage to your heavenly seats,
These horrid dangers, and then see who dares
Advance his desperate foot; yet am I sought,
And oft in vaine, through these, and greater hazards;
515 I could discover how your Deities

502 provoke *cmpw*: invoke *adfhtx*   509 through *cpw*: though *adfhmtx*

Are

Are for my sake sleighted, despis'd, abus'd,
Your Temples, Shrines, Altars, and Images
Vncover'd, rifled, rob'd, and disarray'd
By sacrilegious hands: yet is this treasure
To th'golden Mountaine, where I sit ador'd,   520
With superstitious solemne rights convay'd,
And becomes sacred there, the sordid wretch
Not daring touch the consecrated Ore,
Or with prophane hands lessen the bright heape;
But this might draw your anger downe on mortals   525
For rendring me the homage due to you:
Yet what is said may well expresse my power
Too great for Earth, and onely fit for Heaven.
   Now, for your pastime, view the naked root,
Which in the dirty earth, and base mould drown'd,   530
Sends forth this precious Plant, and golden fruit.
You lusty Swaines, that to your grazing flockes
Pipe amorous Roundelayes; you toyling Hinds,
That barbe the fields, and to your merry Teames
Whistle your passions; and you mining Moles,   535
That in the bowels of your mother-Earth
Dwell the eternall burthen of her wombe,
Cease from your labours, when Wealth bids you play,
Sing, dance, and keepe a chearefull holyday.

> *They dance the fourth Antimasque consisting of Countrey*   540
> *people, musique and measures.*

Merc. Plutus, the gods know and confesse your power
Which feeble Vertue seldome can resist;
Stronger then Towers of brasse, or Chastity;
Iove knew you when he courted *Danae*,   545
And *Cupid* weares you on that Arrowes head
That still prevailes. But the gods keepe their Thrones
To enstall Vertue, not her Enemies.
They dread thy force, which even themselves have felt,
Witnesse Mount-Ida, where the Martiall Maid,   550
And frowning *Iuno*, did to mortall eyes
Naked, for gold, their sacred bodies show,
Therefore for ever be from heaven banish'd.

520 ador'd, *51*: ador'd *34 (all copies)*

                                              But

But since with toyle from undiscover'd Worlds
555 Thou art brought hither, where thou first didst breathe
The thirst of Empire, into Regall brests,
And frightedst quiet Peace from her meeke Throne,
Filling the World with tumult, blood, and warre,
Follow the Camps of the contentious earth,
560 And be the Conqu'rers slave, but he that can
Or conquer thee, or give thee Vertues stampe,
Shall shine in heaven a pure immortall Lampe.

Mom. Nay stay, and take my benediction along with you.
I could, being here a Co-Iudge, like others in my place, now
565 that you are condemn'd, either raile at you, or breake jests
upon you, but I rather chuse to loose a word of good counsell,
and entreat you to bee more carefull in your choyce of
company, for you are alwayes found either with Misers, that
not use you at all; or with fooles, that know not how to use
570 you wel: be not hereafter so reserv'd and coy to men of worth
and parts, and so you shall gaine such credit, as at the next
Sessions you may be heard with better successe. But till you
are thus reform'd, I pronounce this positive sentence, That
wheresoever you shall chuse to abide, your society shall adde
575 no credit or reputation to the party, nor your discontinuance,
or totall absence, be matter of disparagement to any man;
and whosoever shall hold a contrary estimation of you, shall
be condemn'd to weare perpetuall Motley, unlesse hee recant
his opinion. Now you may voyd the Court.

580   *Pænia* enters, a woman of a pale colour, large brims of a
hat upon her head, through which her haire started up like
a fury, her Robe was of a darke color full of patches, about
one of her hands was tied a chaine of Iron, to which was
fastned a weighty stone, which shee bore up under her arme.

585   *Pænia enters.*

Merc. What Creature's this?

Mom. The Antipodes to the other, they move like two
Buckets, or as two nayles drive out one another; if Riches
depart, Poverty will enter.

590   *Pov.* I nothing doubt (Great and Immortall Powers)

561 Vertues *34 (all copies)*: Vertuous *40–1772*   566 counsell, *afhx*: couusell,
cdmptw   569 to use *ahx*: to nse *cdfmpt*   571 as at the *cdfmptw*: as the *ahx*
                                                        But that

But that the place, your wisdome hath deny'd
My foe, your Iustice will conferre on me;
Since that which renders him incapable,
Proves a strong plea for me. I could pretend,
Even in these rags, a larger Soverainty   595
Then gaudy Wealth in all his pompe can boast;
For marke how few they are that share the World;
The numerous Armies, and the swarming Ants
That fight and toyle for them, are all my Subjects,
They take my wages, weare my Livery: 600
Invention too and Wit, are both my creatures,
And the whole race of Vertue is my Off-spring;
As many mischiefes issue from my wombe,
And those as mighty, as proceed from gold.
Oft o're his Throne I wave my awfull Scepter,   605
And in the bowels of his state command,
When 'midst his heapes of coyne, and hils of gold,
I pine, and starve the avaritious Foole.
But I decline those titles, and lay clayme
To heaven, by right of Diuine contemplation;   610
Shee is my Darling, I, in my soft lap,
Free from disturbing cares, bargaines, accounts,
Leases, Rents, Stewards, and the feare of theeves,
That vex the rich, nurse her in calme repose,
And with her, all the Vertues speculative,   615
Which, but with me, find no secure retreat.
    For entertainment of this howre, I'll call
A race of people to this place, that live
At Natures charge, and not importune heaven
To chaine the winds up, or keepe backe the stormes,   620
To stay the thunder, or forbid the hayle
To thresh the unreap'd eare; but to all weathers,
Both chilling frost, and skalding Sunne, expose
Their equall face. Come forth, my swarthy traine,
In this faire circle dance, and as you move,   625
Marke, and foretell happy events of Love.

They dance the fifth Antimaske of Gypsies.

Mom. I cannot but wonder that your perpetuall conversa-
tion with Poets and Philosophers hath furnished you with

                                                          no

630 no more Logicke, or that you should thinke to impose upon
us so grosse an inference, as because *Plutus* and you are
contrary, therefore whatsoever is denyed of the one, must be
true of the other; as if it should follow of necessity, because
he is not *Iupiter*, you are. No, I give you to know, I am
635 better vers'd in cavils with the gods, then to swallow such a
fallacie, for though you two cannot bee together in one place,
yet there are many places that may be without you both, and
such is heaven, where neither of you are likely to arrive:
therefore let me advise you to marry your selfe to Content,
640 and beget sage Apothegms, and goodly morall Sentences in
dispraise of Riches, and contempt of the world.

    Merc. Thou dost presume too much, poore needy wretch,
To claime a station in the Firmament,
Because thy humble Cottage, or thy Tub
645 Nurses some lazie or Pedantique virtue
In the cheape Sun-shine, or by shady springs
With roots and pot-hearbs; where thy rigid hand,
Tearing those humane passions from the mind,,
Vpon whose stockes faire blooming vertues flourish,
650 Degradeth Nature, and benummeth sense,
And Gorgon-like, turnes active men to stone.
We not require the dull society
Of your necessitated Temperance,
Or that unnaturall stupidity
655 That knowes nor joy nor sorrow; nor your forc'd
Falsly exalted passive Fortitude
Above the active: This low abject brood,
That fix their seats in mediocrity,
Become your servile minds; but we advance
660 Such vertues onely as admit excesse,
Brave bounteous Acts, Regall Magnificence,
All-seeing Prudence, Magnanimity
That knowes no bound, and that Heroicke vertue
For which Antiquity hath left no name,
665 But patternes onely, such as *Hercules*,
Achilles, Theseus. Backe, to thy loath'd cell,
And when thou seest the new enlightned Spheare,
Study to know but what those Worthies were.

      647 rigid *34 (all copies)*: right *40–1772*

                                    Tiche

Tiche enters, her head bald behind, and one great locke
before, wings at her shoulders, and in her hand a wheele, her 670
upper parts naked, and the skirt of her garment wrought all
over with Crownes, Scepters, Bookes, and such other things
as expresse both her greatest and smallest gifts.

Mom. See where Dame *Fortune* comes, you may know her
by her wheele, and that vaile over her eyes, with which she 675
hopes like a seel'd Pigeon to mount above the Clouds, and
pearch in the eighth Spheare: listen, she begins.

Fort. I come not here (you gods) to plead the Right
By which Antiquity assign'd my Deitie,
Though no peculiar station 'mongst the Stars,   680
Yet generall power to rule their influence,
Or boast the Title of Omnipotent,
Ascrib'd me then, by which I rival'd *Iove*,
Since you have cancell'd all those old records;
But confident in my good cause and merit,   685
Claime a succession in the vacant Orbe.
For since *Astræa* fled to heaven, I sit
Her Deputy on Earth, I hold her skales
And weigh mens Fates out, who have made me blind,
Because themselves want eyes to see my causes,   690
Call me inconstant, 'cause my workes surpasse
The shallow fathom of their human reason;
Yet here, like blinded Iustice, I dispence
With my impartiall hands, their constant lots,
And if desertlesse, impious men engrosse   695
My best rewards, the fault is yours, you gods,
That scant your graces to mortalitie,
And niggards of your good, scarce spare the world
One vertuous, for a thousand wicked men.
It is no error to conferre dignity,   700
But to bestow it on a vicious man;
I gave the dignity, but you made the vice,
Make you men good, and I'le make good men happy.
That *Plutus* is refus'd, dismaies me not,
He is my Drudge, and the externall pompe,   705
In which he deckes the World, proceeds from me,

669 *Tiche afhtx*: *Tiche, cdmpw*   675 over her eyes, *40*: over eyes, *34*
(all copies)

Not

Not him; like Harmony, that not resides
In strings, or notes, but in the hand and voyce.
The revolutions of Empires, States,
710 Scepters, and Crownes, are but my game and sport,
Which as they hang on the events of Warre,
So those depend upon my turning wheele.
    You warlike Squadrons, who in battels joyn'd,
Dispute the Right of Kings, which I decide,
715 Present the modell of that martiall frame,
By which, when Crownes are stak'd, I rule the game.

*They dance the sixth Antimaske, being the representation of
a Battell.*

    Mom. Madam, I should censure you, *pro falso clamore*, for
720 preferring a skandalous cros-bill of recrimination against the
gods, but your blindnesse shall excuse you. Alas! what
would it advantage you, if vertue were as universall as vice
is? it would onely follow, that as the world now exclaimes
upon you for exalting the vicious, it would then raile as fast
725 at you for depressing the vertuous; so they would still keep
their tune, though you chang'd their ditty.
    Merc. The mists, in which future events are wrap'd,
That oft succeed beside the purposes
Of him that workes, his dull eyes not discerning
730 The first great cause, offer'd thy clouded shape
To his enquiring search; so in the darke
The groping world first found thy Deity,
And gave thee rule over contingencies,
Which, to the piercing eye of Providence,
735 Being fix'd and certaine, where past and to come,
Are always present, thou dost disappeare,
Losest thy being, and art not at all.
Be thou then onely a deluding Phantome,
At best a blind guide, leading blinder fooles;
740 Who, would they but survay their mutuall wants,
And helpe each other, there were left no roome
For thy vaine ayd. Wisdome, whose strong-built plots
Leave nought to hazard, mockes thy futile power.
Industrious labour drags thee by the lockes,

737 not at all. *51*: not all. *34* (*all copies*)

Bound

Bound to his toyling Car, and not attending 745
Till thou dispence, reaches his owne reward.
Onely the lazy sluggard yawning lyes
Before thy threshold, gaping for thy dole,
And lickes the easie hand that feeds his sloth.
The shallow, rash, and unadvised man 750
Makes thee his stale, disburdens all the follies
Of his mis-guided actions, on thy shoulders.
Vanish from hence, and seeke those Ideots out
That thy fantasticke god-head hath allow'd,
And rule that giddy superstitious crowd. 755

Hedone, Pleasure, a young woman with a smiling face, in
a light lascivious habit, adorn'd with silver and gold, her
Temples crown'd with a garland of Roses, and over that a
Rainbow circling her head downe to her shoulders.

Hedone enters. 760

Merc. What wanton's this?

Mom. This is the sprightly Lady *Hedone*, a merry game-
ster, this people call her Pleasure.

Plea. The reasons (equall Iudges) here alleag'd
By the dismist Pretenders, all concurre 765
To strengthen my just title to the Spheare.
Honour, or Wealth, or the contempt of both,
Have in themselves no simple reall good,
But as they are the meanes to purchase Pleasure;
The paths that lead to my delicious Palace; 770
They for my sake, I for mine owne am priz'd.
Beyond me nothing is, I am the Gole,
The journeyes end, to which the sweating world,
And wearied Nature travels. For this, the best
And wisest sect of all Philosophers, 775
Made me the seat of supreme happinesse.
And though some, more austere, upon my ruines,
Did to the prejudice of Nature, raise
Some petty low-built vertues, 'twas because
They wanted wings to reach my soaring pitch. 780
Had they beene Princes borne, themselves had prov'd

Of

Of all mankind the most luxurious.
For those delights, which to their low condition
Were obvious, they with greedy appetite
785 Suck'd and devour'd: from offices of State,
From cares of family, children, wife, hopes, feares,
Retir'd, the churlish Cynicke in his Tub
Enjoy'd those pleasures which his tongue defam'd.
Nor am I rank'd 'mongst the superfluous goods;
790 My necessary offices preserve
Each single man, and propogate the kind.
Then am I universall as the light,
Or common Ayre we breathe; and since I am
The generall desire of all mankinde,
795 Civill Felicity must reside in me.
Tell me what rate my choycest pleasures beare,
When for the short delight of a poore draught
Of cheape cold water, great *Lysimachus*
Rendred himselfe slave to the Scythians.
800 Should I the curious structure of my seats,
The art and beauty of my severall objects,
Rehearse at large, your bounties would reserve
For every sense a proper constellation;
But I present their Persons to your eyes.
805   Come forth my subtle Organs of delight,
With changing figures please the curious eye,
And charme the eare with moving Harmonie.

   They dance the seventh Antimaske of the five Senses.

   Merc. Bewitching Syren, guilded rottennesse,
810 Thou hast with cunning artifice display'd
Th'enamel'd outside, and the honied verge
Of the faire cup, where deadly poyson lurkes.
Within, a thousand sorrowes dance the round;
And like a shell, Paine circles thee without,
815 Griefe is the shadow waiting on thy steps,
Which, as thy joyes 'ginne tow'rds their West decline,
Doth to a Gyants spreading forme extend
Thy Dwarfish stature. Thou thy selfe art Paine,
Greedy, intense Desire, and the keene edge
820 Of thy fierce Appetite, oft strangles thee,

                                        And

And cuts thy slender thread; but still the terror
And apprehension of thy hasty end,
Mingles with Gall thy most refined sweets;
Yet thy *Cyrcæan* charmes transforme the world.
Captaines, that have resisted warre and death,   825
Nations, that over Fortune have triumph'd,
Are by thy Magicke made effeminate.
Empires, that knew no limits but the Poles,
Have in thy wanton lap melted away.
Thou wert the Author of the first excesse   830
That drew this reformation on the gods.
Canst thou then dreame, those Powers, that from heaven have
Banish'd th'effect, will there enthrone the cause?
To thy voluptuous Denne, flye Witch, from hence,
There dwell, for ever drown'd in brutish sense.   835

Mom. I concurre, and am growne so weary of these tedious
pleadings, as I'le packe up too and be gone: Besides, I see
a crowd of other suitors pressing hither, I'le stop 'em, take
their petitions and preferre 'em above; and as I came in
bluntly without knocking, and no body bid mee welcome; 840
so I'le depart as abruptly without taking leave, and bid no
bodie farewell.

Merc. These, with forc'd reasons, and strain'd arguments,
Vrge vaine pretences, whilst your Actions plead,
And with a silent importunity   845
Awake the drousy Iustice of the gods
To Crowne your deeds with immortality.
The growing Titles of your Ancestors,
These Nations glorious Acts, joyn'd to the stocke
Of your owne Royall vertues, and the cleare   850
Reflexe they take from th'imitation
Of your fam'd Court, make Honors storie full,
And have to that secure fix'd state advanc'd
Both you and them, to which the labouring world,
Wading through streames of blood, sweats to aspire.   855
Those antient Worthies of these famous Isles,
That long have slept, in fresh and lively shapes
Shall straight appeare, where you shall see your selfe

833 the cause? *51*: th' cause ? *34 (all copies)*   834 hence,] henee, *34 (all copies)*   842 farewell. (*Instead of the period 34 prints a long s with broken top*)
                                                                  Circled

Circled with moderne Heroes, who shall be
860 In Act, what-ever elder times can boast,
Noble, or Great; as they in Prophesie
Were all but what you are. Then shall you see
The sacred hand of bright Eternitie
Mould you to Stars, and fix you in the Spheare.
865 To you, your Royall halfe, to them shee'll joyne
Such of this traine, as with industrious steps
·In the faire prints your vertuous feet have made,
Though with unequall paces, follow you.
This is decreed by *Iove*, which my returne
870 Shall see perform'd; but first behold the rude
And old Abiders here, and in them view
The point from which your full perfections grew.
You naked, antient, wild Inhabitants,
That breath'd this Ayre, and prest this flowery Earth,
875 Come from those shades where dwells eternall night,
And see what wonders Time hath brought to light.

Atlas, and the Spheare vanisheth, and a new Scæne
appeares of mountaines, whose eminent height exceed the
Clouds which past beneath them, the lower parts were wild
880 and woody: out of this place comes forth a more grave Anti-
masque of Picts, the naturall Inhabitants of this Isle, antient
Scots and Irish, these dance a Perica or Marshall dance.

When this Antimasque was past, there began to arise out
of the earth the top of a hill, which by little and little grew
885 to be a huge mountaine that covered all the Scæne; the
under-part of this was wild and craggy, and above somewhat
more pleasant and flourishing: about the middle part of this
Mountaine were seated the three kingdomes of *England*,
Scotland, and *Ireland*; all richly attired in regall habits,
890 appropriated to the severall Nations, with Crownes on their
heads, and each of them bearing the ancient Armes of the
kingdomes they represented: At a distance above these sate
a young man in a white embroidered robe, upon his faire
haire an Olive garland with wings at his shoulders, and
895 holding in his hand a Cornucopia fill'd with corne and fruits,
representing the Genius of these kingdomes.

863 Eternitie] Eternitic *34 (all copies)*

The

The first Song.

GENIVS.

RAise from these rockie cliffs, your heads,
Brave Sonnes, and see where Glory spreads
Her glittering wings, where Majesty
Crown'd with sweet smiles, shoots from her eye   900
Diffusive joy, where Good and Faire,
Vnited sit in Honours chayre.
Call forth your aged Priests, and chrystall streames,
To warme their hearts, and waves in these bright beames.

KINGDOMES.

1. *From your consecrated woods,*   905
Holy Druids.   2. *Silver floods,*
From your channels fring'd with flowers,
3. *Hither move; forsake your bowers*
1. *Strew'd with hallowed Oaken leaves,*
Deck'd with flags and sedgie sheaves,   910
And behold a wonder.   3. *Say,*
What doe your duller eyes survay?

CHORVS of DRVIDS and RIVERS.

We see at once in dead of night
A Sun appeare, and yet a bright
Nooneday, springing from Starre-light.   915

GENIVS.

Looke up, and see the darkned Spheare
Depriv'd of light, her eyes shine there;

CHORVS.

These are more sparkling then those were.

KINGDOMES.

1. *These shed a nobler influence,*
2. *These by a pure intelligence*   920
Of more transcendent Vertue move,
3. *These first feele, then kindle love.*

1.2.   *From the bosomes they inspire,*
       These receive a mutuall fire;
925 1.2.3. *And where their flames impure returne,*
       These can quench as well as burne.

GENIVS.

Here the faire victorious eyes
Make Worth onely Beauties prize,
Here the hand of Vertue tyes
930   *'Bout the heart loves amourous chaine,*
       Captives triumph, Vassals reigne,
       And none live here but the slaine.

CHORVS.

These are th'Hesperian bowers, whose faire trees beare
Rich golden fruit, and yet no Dragon neare.

GENIVS.

935   *Then, from your impris'ning wombe,*
       Which is the cradle and the tombe
       Of British Worthies (faire sonnes) send
       A troope of Heroes, that may lend
       Their hands to ease this loaden grove,
940   *And gather the ripe fruits of love.*

KINGDOMES.

1.2.3. *Open thy stony entrailes wide,*
        And breake old Atlas, *that the pride*
        Of three fam'd kingdomes may be spy'd.

CHORVS.

Pace forth thou mighty British Hercules,
945 *With thy choyce band, for onely thou, and these,*
May revell here, in Loves Hesperides.   .

At this the under-part of the Rocke opens, and out of a
Cave are seene to come the Masquers, richly attired like
ancient Heroes, the Colours yellow, embroydered with silver,
950 their antique Helmes curiously wrought, and great plumes
on the top; before them a troope of young Lords and Noble-

---

923 *bosomes cdfmptw: bosome ahx*

mens

mens sonnes bearing Torches of Virgin-wax, these were
apparelled after the old British fashion in white Coats,
embroydered with silver, girt, and full gathered, cut square
coller'd, and round caps on their heads, with a white feather 955
wreathen about them; first these dance with their lights in
their hands: After which, the Masquers descend into the
roome, and dance their entry.

The dance being past, there appeares in the further part
of the heaven comming downe a pleasant Cloud, bright and 960
transparent, which comming softly downewards before the
upper part of the mountaine, embraceth the Genius, but so
as through it all his body is seene; and then rising againe
with a gentle motion beares up the Genius of the three king-
domes, and being past the Airy Region, piercheth the heavens, 965
and is no more seene: At that instant the Rocke with the
three kingdomes on it sinkes, and is hidden in the earth.
This strange spectacle gave great cause of admiration, but
especially how so huge a machine, and of that great height
could come from under the Stage, which was but six foot 970
high.

The second Song.

KINGDOMES.

1. *HEre are shapes form'd fit for heaven,*
2. *These move gracefully and even,*
3. *Here the Ayre and paces meet*
    So just, as if the skilfull feet 975
    Had strucke the Vials. 1.2.3. *So the Eare*
    Might the tunefull footing heare.

CHORVS.

And had the Musicke silent beene,
The eye a moving tune had seene.

GENIVS.

These must in the unpeopled skie 980
Succeed, and governe Destinie,
Iove is temp'ring purer fire,
And will with brighter flames attire
These glorious lights. I must ascend
And helpe the Worke.

KINGDOMES.

KINGDOMES.

985   1. *We cannot lend*
Heaven so much treasure.   2. *Nor that pay,*
But rendring what it takes away.
3..   *Why should they that here can move*
So well, be ever-fix'd above?

CHORVS.

990 *Or be to one eternall posture ty'd,*
That can into such various figures slide?

GENIVS.

Iove *shall not, to enrich the Skie,*
Beggar the Earth, their Fame shall flye
From hence alone, and in the Spheare
995   *Kindle new Starres, whilst they rest here.*

KINGDOMES.

1.2.3. *How can the shaft stay in the quiver,*
Yet hit the marke?

GENIVS.

                Did not the River
Eridanus, the grace acquire
In Heaven and Earth to flow,
1000   *Above in streames of golden fire,*
In silver waves below?

KINGDOMES.

1.2.3. *But shall not wee, now thou art gone*
Who wert our Nature, wither,
Or breake that triple Vnion
1005   *Which thy soule held together?*

GENIVS.

In Concords pure immortall spring
I will my force renew,
And a more active Vertue bring
At my returne. Adieu.

1010   KINGDOMES Adieu.   CHORVS Adieu.

991 *slide?* 51: *slide.* 34 (*all copies*)   1002 KINGDOMES.] KINGDOMES 34
(*all copies*)

                                        The

The Masquers dance their maine dance; which done, the Scæne againe is varied into a new and pleasant prospect, cleane differing from all the other, the nearest part shewing a delicious garden with severall walkes and perterra's set round with low trees, and on the sides against these walkes, 1015 were fountaines and grots, and in the furthest part a Palace, from whence went high walkes upon Arches, and above them open Tarraces planted with Cypresse trees, and all this together was composed of such Ornaments as might expresse a Princely Villa. 1020

From hence the *Chorus* descending into the roome, goes up to the State.

The third Song.

By the *Chorus* going up to the Queene.

*W*Hilst thus the darlings of the Gods
  From Honours Temple, to the Shrine   1025
Of Beauty, and these sweet abodes
  Of Loue, we guide, let thy Divine
Aspects (Bright Deity) with faire
And Halcyon beames, becalme the Ayre.

We bring Prince Arthur, *or the brave*   1030
  St. George *himselfe (great Queene) to you,*
You'll soone discerne him; and we have
  A Guy, *a* Beavis, *or some true*
Round-Table Knight, as ever fought
For Lady, to each Beauty brought.   1035

Plant in their Martiall hands, Warr's seat,
  Your peacefull pledges of warme snow,
And, if a speaking touch, repeat
  In Loves knowne langvage, tales of woe;
Say, in soft whispers of the Palme,   1040
As Eyes shoot darts, so Lips shed Balme.

For though you seeme like Captives, led
  Jn triumph by the Foe away,

        Yet

 Yet on the Conqu'rers necke you tread,
1045   *And the fierce Victor proves your prey.*
 What heart is then secure from you,
 That can, though vanquish'd, yet subdue?

The Song done they retire, and the Masquers dance the
Revels with the Ladies, which continued a great part of the
1050 night.

The Revels being past, and the Kings Majesty seated
under the State by the Queene; for Conclusion to this
Masque there appeares comming forth from one of the sides,
as moving by a gentle wind, a great Cloud, which arriving
1055 at the middle of the heaven, stayeth; this was of severall
colours, and so great, that it covered the whole Scæne. Out
of the further part of the heaven beginnes to breake forth
two other Clouds, differing in colour and shape; and being
fully discovered there appeared sitting in one of them,
1060 Religion, Truth, and Wisdome. Religion was apparelled in
white, and part of her face was covered with a light vaile,
in one hand a booke, and in the other a flame of fire. Truth
in a Watchet Robe, a Sunne upon her fore-head and bearing
in her hand a Palme. Wisdome in a mantle wrought with
1065 eyes and hands, golden rayes about her head, and *Apollo's*
Cithera in her hand. In the other Cloud sate Concord,
Government, and Reputation. The habit of Concord was
Carnation, bearing in her hand a little faggot of stickes bound
together, and on the top of it a hart, and a garland of corne
1070 on her head: Government was figured in a coat of Armour,
bearing a shield, and on it a *Medusa's* head; upon her head a
plumed helme, and in her right hand a Lance. Reputation, a
young man in a purple robe wrought with gold, and wearing
a laurell wreath on his head. These being come downe in
1075 an equall distance to the middle part of the Ayre, the great
Cloud beganne to breake open, out of which stroke beames of
light; in the midst suspended in the Ayre, sate Eternity on
a Globe, his Garment was long of a light blue, wrought all
over with Stars of gold, and bearing in his hand a Serpent
1080 bent into a circle, with his taile in his mouth. In the firma-

1072 Lance. *ahx*: Lanee. *cdfmptw*   1073 in a purple 40: in purple 34
(*all copies*)

 ment

ment about him, was a troope of fifteene starres, expressing the stellifying of our British Heroes; but one more great and eminent than the rest, which was over his head, figured his Majesty. And in the lower part was seene a farre off the prospect of *Windsor* Castell, the famous seat of the most 1085 honourable Order of the Garter.

The fourth Song.

Eternity, Eusebia, Alethia, Sophia, Homonoia,
Dicæarche, Euphemia.

ETERNITIE.

*B*E *fix'd you rapid Orbes, that beare*
   The changing seasons of the yeare
On your swift wings, and see the old
Decrepit Spheare growne darke and cold;   1090
Nor did Iove *quench her fires, these bright*
Flames, have ecclips'd her sullen light:
This Royall Payre, for whom Fate will
Make Motion cease, and Time stand still;
Since Good is here so perfect, as no Worth   1095
Is left for After-Ages to bring forth.

EVSEBIA.

Mortality cannot with more
Religious zeale, the gods adore.

ALETHIA.

My Truths, from human eyes conceal'd,
Are naked to their sight reveal'd.   1100

SOPHIA.

Nor doe their Actions, from the guide
Of my exactest precepts slide.

HOMONOIA.

And as their owne pure Soules entwin'd,
So are their Subjects hearts combin'd.

                             DICÆARCHE.

1105

DICÆARCHE.

So just, so gentle is their sway,
As it seemes Empire to obay.

EVPHEMIA.

And their faire Fame, like incense hurl'd
On Altars, hath perfum'd the world.
SO. *Wisdome.* AL. *Truth.* EVS. *Pure Adoration.*
1110 HO. *Concord.* DI. *Rule.* EVP. *Cleare Reputation,*

CHORVS.

Crowne this King, this Queene, this Nation.

CHORVS.

Wisdome, Truth, &c.

ETERNITIE.

1115

Brave Spirits, whose adventrous feet
 Have to the Mountaines top aspir'd,
Where faire Desert, and Honour meet,
 Here, from the toyling Presse retir'd,
Secure from all disturbing Evill,
1120 *For ever in my Temple revell.*

With wreathes of Starres circled about,
 Guild all the spacious Firmament,
And smiling on the panting Rout
 That labour in the steepe ascent,
1125 *With your resistlesse influence guide*
Of human change th'incertaine tide.

EVS. ALE. SOP.

But oh you Royall Turtles, shed,
 When you from Earth remove,
On the ripe fruits of your chaste bed,
1130 *Those sacred seeds of Love.*

1105 DICÆARCHE. 40: DICÆARCHES. 34 (all copies) 1110 Concord.] Con-
eord. 34 (all copies) 1121 about,] abont, 34 (all copies) 1123 Rout
adfhtx: Routs cmpw 1124 labour] labonr 34 (all copies) 1130 of]
ef 34 (all copies)

CHORVS.

CHORVS.

Which no Power can but yours dispence,
Since you the patterne beare from hence.

HOM. DIC. EVP.

Then from your fruitfull race shall flow
    Endlesse Succession,
Scepters shall bud, and Lawrels blow   1135
    'Bout their Immortall Throne.

CHORVS.

Propitious Starres shall crowne each birth,
Whilst you rule them, and they the Earth.

The Song ended, the two Clouds, with the persons sitting
on them, ascend; the great Cloud closeth againe, and so 1140
passeth away overthwart the Scæne; leaving behind it nothing
but a sirene Skye. After which, the Masquers dance their
last dance, and the Curtaine was let fall.

The Names of the Masquers.

The Kings Majesty.

Duke of Lenox.
Earle of Devonshire.
Earle of Holland.
Earle of Newport.
Earle of Elgin.
Viscount Grandeson.
Lord Rich.

Lord Feilding. 1145
Lord Digby.
Lord Dungarvin.
Lord Dunluce.
Lord Wharton. 1150
Lord Paget.
Lord Saltine.

The names of the young Lords and Noble-mens Sonnes.

Lord Walden.
Lord Cranborne.
Lord Brackley.
Lord Shandos.
Mr. William Herbert.

Mr. Thomas Howard. 1155
Mr. Thomas Egerton.
Mr. Charles Cavendish.
Mr. Robert Howard.
Mr. Henry Spencer.

1138 *you*] *yon 34 (all copies)*   1156 Cranborne.] Cranborne, *34 (all*
copies)   Egerton.] Egerton, *34 (all copies)*   *copies)*

APPENDIX A

APPENDIX A
POEMS OF UNCERTAIN AUTHORSHIP
The Sparke.

[Perhaps by Sir John Suckling or Walton Poole]

MY first love whom all beauties did adorne:
Firing my heart supprest it with her scorne,
Sun-like to tinder in my brest it lies,
By every sparkle made a sacrifice.
Each wanton eye now kindles my desire,   5
And that is free to all that was entire:
Desiring more, by thee (desire) I lost,
As those that in consumptions hunger most,
And now my wandring thoughts are not confind,
Vnto one woman, but to woman kinde.   10
This for her shape of love, that for her face,
This for her gesture, or some other grace,
And where I none of these doe use to find,
I choose thereby the kernell not the rynd:
And so I hope since my first hopes are gone,   15
To find in many what I lost in one,
And like to Merchants after some great losse,
Trade by retaile, that cannot now ingrosse,
The fault is hers that made me goe astray,
He needs must wander that hath lost his way.   20
Guiltlesse I am shee did this change provoke,
And made that charcoale which to her was oake.
And as a looking glasse from the aspect,
Whilst it is whole, doth but one face reflect,
But being crack't, or broken there are showne,   25
Many halfe faces, which at first were one;
So love vnto my heart did first proffer

The Sparke. Text from 40, collated with Suckling's *Last Remains*, 1659.   *Title:*
The guiltless Inconstant. Suckling   3 Sun-like to] Since like the *Suckling*   5 now
kindles] can kindle *Suckling*   6 all that] all which *Suckling*   8 hunger] linger
Suckling   11 shape of love,] shape I love, *Suckling*   13 *Suckling reads:*
And where that none of all these things I find,   14 thereby] her by *Suckling*
15 hopes are] hope is *Suckling*   18 now ingrosse,] do in gross. *Suckling*
21 did] doth *Suckling*   25 showne,] grown *Suckling*   26 one; 51: one. 40
Suckling reads: Many less faces, where there was but one: 27 proffer] prefer
Suckling

Her

Her image, and there planted none but her,
But since t'was broke and martird by her scorne,
Many lesse faces in her face are borne,   30
Thus like to tynder am I prone to catch
Each falling sparkle, fit for any match.

The Dart.

[Perhaps by William Strode]

OFt when I looke I may descry
   A little face peepe through that eye,
Sure that's the boy which wisely chose
His throne among such beames as those,
Which if his quiver chance to fall,   5
May serve for darts to kill withall.

The mistake.

[Perhaps by Henry Blount]

WHen on faire *Celia* I did spie
   A wounded heart of stone,
The wound had almost made me cry,
   Sure this heart was my owne.

But when I saw it was enthron'd,   5
   In her celestiall brest:
O then I it no longer own'd,
   For mine was ne're so blest.

Yet if in highest heavens doe shine
   Each constant Martyrs heart: 10
Then shee may well give rest to mine,
   That for her sake doth smart.

28 planted] placed *Suckling*   30 her face] her place *Suckling*   31–2
Omitted in Suckling
   The Dart. Text from *40*. See Commentary.   1 descry *51*: descry, *40*
3 chose *51*: chose, *40*   5 fall, *51*: fall: *40*
   The mistake. Text from *40*.   1 spie] spie, *40*: spy *51*   7 own'd,] own'd,, *40*
9 shine *51*: shine, *40*

Where

Where seated in so high a blisse,
    Though wounded it shall live:
Death enters not in Paradise,   15
    The place free life doth give.

Or if the place lesse sacred were,
    Did but her saving eye
Bath my sicke heart in one kind teare,
    Then should I never dye.   20

Slight balmes may heale a slighter sore,
    No medicine lesse divine
Can ever hope for to restore
    A wounded heart like mine.

A divine Love.

[Perhaps by Thomas Carey or Lord Herbert of Cherbury]

1.

VVHy should dul Art, which is wise Natures Ape,
        If she produce a shape
So farre beyond all patternes, that of old,
            Fell from her mold
As thine (admir'd Lucinda) not bring forth   5
An equall wonder, to expresse that worth
        In some new way, that hath
Like her great worke, no print of vulgar path?

2.

Is it because the rapes of Poetry,
        Rifeling the spacious sky   10
Of all his fires, light, beauty, influence,
            Did those dispence
On ayrie creations that surpast
The reall workes of Nature, she at last
        To prove their raptures vaine,   15
Shew'd such a light as Poets could not faine?

18 eye] eye: *40*: eie *51*   22 divine *51*: divine, *40*   23 restore *51*: restore, *40*
A divine Love. Text from *42*; not included in *40*

3. Or

3.

Or is it 'cause the factious wits did vie
    With vaine Idolatry,
Whose Goddesse was supreame, and so had hurld
        Scisme through the world: 20
Whose Priest sung sweetest layes; thou didst appeare
A glorious mysterie, so darke, so cleare,
    As Nature did intend
All should confesse, but none might comprehend?

4.

Perhaps all other beauties share a light   25
    Proportion'd to the sight
Of weake mortality, scatt'ring such loose fires,
    As stirre desires,
And from the braine distill salt amorous rhumes,
Whilst thy immortall flame such drosse consumes,   30
    And from the earthy mold
With purging fires severs the purer gold.

5.

If so, then why in Fames immortall scrowle,
    Doe we their names inroule,
Whose easie hearts, and wanton eyes did sweat,   35
    With sensuall heate?
If Petrarkes unarm'd bosome catch a wound
From a light glance, must Laura be renown'd?
    Or both a glory gaine;
He from ill-govern'd Love, she from Disdaine?   40

6.

Shall he more fam'd in his great Art become,
    For wilfull martyrdome?
Shall she more title gaine, too chaste and faire
        Through his dispaire?
Is Troy more noble 'cause to ashes turn'd,   45
Then Virgin Cities that yet never burn'd?
    Is fire when it consumes
Temples, more fire, then when it melts perfumes?

40 Disdaine ?] Disdaine. *42*: Disdain ? *51*   43 too] to *51*   44 dispaire ?]
dispaire. *42*: dispair? *51*   45 turn'd,] turn'd ? *42*

7. Cause

7.

Cause Venus from the Ocean tooke her forme,
            Must Love needs be a storme: 50
Cause she her wanton shrines in Islands reares,
            Through seas of tearcs,
Ore Rocks, and Gulphs, with our owne sighs for gale,
Must we to Cyprus, or to Paphos sayle?
            Can there no way be given,   55
But a true Hell that leads to her false Heaven?

Vpon the Royall Ship called the Soueraign of the Seas built by Peter Pett Master builder his Father Cap: Phineas Pett Superuisor. 1637

[Probably by Thomas Cary of Tower Hill]

TRiton's *auspicious Sound usher Thy raigne*
      O're the curl'd billowes, Royal SOVERAINE,
Monarchal Ship; whose Fabrick doth outpride
The Pharos, Colosse, *Memphique* Pyramide:
And seemes a moouing Towre, when sprightly gales   5
Quicken the motion, and embreath the sailes.
Wee y *haue heard of* SEAVEN, *now see y* EIGHT
Wonder *at home; of Naual art the height.*
This Britain ARGO *putts down that of* Greece
Be-Deck't with more then one rich Golden Fleece   10
Wrought into Sculptures, *which Emblematize*
Pregnant Conceipt to the more Curious eyes.
Neptune *is proud o'th burden, and doth wonder*
To heare a Fourefold *Fire out-rore* Ioue's *Thunder.*
      Onn then Triumphal Arke, *with* EDGAR's *fame,*   15
      To CHARLES *his* Scepter *add y* Trident's *claime.*

---

52 seas 51: leas 42   56 Heaven?] Heaven. 42
Vpon the Royall Ship, &c. Text from John Payne's engraving, THE TRVE
PORTRAICTVRE OF HIS MA.ties ROYALL SHIP THE SOVERAIGNE OF THE SEAS BVILT
IN THE YEARE 1637. Title from MS. Add. 34217, British Museum.

                                                              To

To a Strumpett :

[Perhaps by Henry Bold]

HAyle thou true modell of a cursed whore
Borne by creation euer to liue poore,
Though cloathd in Jndian silke, or what can bee
Bestowd in riott on thy venery;
Thou eldest daughter to the prince of night,   5
That canst outlye thy father at first sight,
Outscoffe an Ishmaelite, and attempt more
Then all our wicked age hath done before;
Nay when the diuell leaues, thou canst beginne
And teach both him and us new wayes to sinne;   10
Which makes me say that all our former times
Appeare like pictures coppyed by thy Crimes;
Sure thou wert borne euen from the very wombe
Of some ranke Bawd unsavory as a Tombe;
Who carted from all parishes, did sell   15
Forbidden fruites in the high way to Hell:
There didst thou taste all nations that could crowne
Thee with lighte feathers or a silken gowne:
But oh thou beastly surfeit, may they haue
Thee in esteeme as the insatiate graue,   20
And spew thee out of th' Strand, maist thou bee faine
To shelter in the Suburbs of Chick-Lane.
There mayst thou sinne with butchers upon straw,
And still be plagued with Beadles and the Law;
Nere mayst thou gayne a ninepence to sett upp   25
With halfe an ounce, two bottles and a Cupp,
Mayst thou each day upon thy bared feete
Trudge for thy bread and drincke to Turnbull streete,
Creepe to Knockverges, and there learne the thrift
Of raking dunghills, or some poorer shift,   30
And thus at last being torne, turmoyld, and tosst
The patient Gristle of thy nose being lost
May both the Hospitalls grudge and repine
To giue thee one poore plaister to thy Groyne;
And let noe man euer bemoane thy Case   35
That once did know thee in the State of Grace.

To a Strumpett. Text from *H18*; also in *A21*, *A303*, and *Ash 38*   18 lighte
A21, A303, Ash 38: delight, *H18*   silken *A21, A303, Ash 38*: silke *H18*

A Health

A Health to a Mistris.

[Perhaps by Richard Clerke]

TO her whose beautie doth excell
    Story, wee toss these Cupps, and fell
Sobriety, a sacrifice
To the bright luster of her eyes.
Each soule that sipps here is deuine,   5
Her beauty deifies the wine.

A Louers passion.

IS shee not wondrous fayre? but oh I see
  Shee is soe much too fayre, too sweete for me
That I forgett my flames, & a newe fyre
Ha's taught me not to loue, but to admire.
Like to the sun me thinkes I see her face   5
Which I may gase on styll but ne're embrace;
And 'tis heavens pleasure sure, shee should be sent
As pure from earth to heaven, as shee was lent
To vs, and bids vs as we hope for blisse
Not to prophane her with a mortall kisse.   10
Then howe cold growes my loue, & I, howe hott:
Oh howe I loue her, howe I loue her not:
Thus does my ague loue, torment by turnes
That nowe yt freezes, nowe againe yt burnes.

A Health, &c. Text from *A7*; also in *A14, A15, A21, A303, H6*, and *The Academy of Complements*, 1650   2 fell *A21, A303, A15*: sell *A7, A14, Academy of Complements*: fill *H6*

A Louers passion. Text from *S.32, fol. 41ᵛ*, collated with *S.32, fol. 9ᵛ, S14, S17, A19, H31, Ash 38, Ash 47, A30, R84, HM116*. Punctuation partly the editor's. *Title:* A Louers passion. *S14, S17, A19, H31, A30, Ash 38*: On ravisht wᵗʰ his Mʳˢ perfeccons. *S.32, fol. 41ᵛ*: One inamor'd on his mʳˢ perfeccons *S.32, fol. 9ᵛ*: By one thinking on his mʳˢ; *Ash 47*: A Lovers Song *R84*: Vpon a faire Maid yᵗ could not be obtain'd. *HM116*   1 but oh] Oh Bụt *R84*   2 too fayre, too sweete] to fayre, too sweete *S.32, fol. 41ᵛ*: to sweet, to faire, *HM116*   3 That I] I doe *Ash 47*   flames,] flame *A19, Ash 47*   4 Ha's] Hath *H31, A19, S.32, fol. 9ᵛ, A30, Ash 38, Ash 47, R84, HM116*   5 Like to] Just like *S14, S17, A19, A30, Ash 38, Ash 47, R84*: And like *H31*: For like *HM116*   her] yᵗ *HM116*   6 Variants: Which wee should gaze upon but not embrace *S14, R84, S17, A19, H31* ('I should'), *A30, Ash 38* ('wee may'), *HM116* ('I may looke')   7 And 'tis] For 'tis *S14, S17, A19, H31, A30, Ash 38, R84*: T'was *HM116*   8 *HM116 reads:* To them againe, as pure as shee was lent   from earth to heaven,] to heauen againe *S14, S17, A19, H31, A30, Ash 38, R84*: againe to heaven *Ash 47*   11 *HM116 reads:* O then how cold, my loue; ô then how not   I,] O *S14, S17, A19, H31, A30, Ash 38*: eke *Ash 47* [cont. on opposite page]

Of

Of his Mistresse.

I Will not Saint my Cœlia, for shee
More glorious is in her Humanity,
Nor in a heat of Fancy pluck a Starr,
And rob the needy World to fixe Her there.
   These are the subtle raptures of the times,   5
Wherwith the wanton Poet makes his Rhymes
Run high, as doth his Blood; whiles some proud Shee
Pamperd with such new-cookd diuinity
Surfets, belieuing in a pride of Soule
Those Fictions True; so Sinns without controule.   10
   Besides, admitt I could; I might conferr
Praise on my selfe, but not aduantage Her.
Wee prize not Gold made by the Chymick Stone,
As Gold, but for the Transmutation.
Can Angels boast Habituall Purity?   15
Noe: Tis in Them Impeccability;
And therfore not Praise-worthy; they haue nor Will
Nor Power, to Think, much lesse to Practise Ill.
   With Her tis otherwise; for Shee may sinn
Beyond hope of Repentance; & therin   20
Appeares the odds, that, maugre flesh & blood,
Beauty, Temptation, Deuill, Shee is Good.

On the Green Sickness.

Song.

B Right Albion, where the Queene of love
Pressing the pinion of her snow-white Dove
With Siluer harness, or'e thy faire
Region in Trivmph drives her Ivory chaire:
Where now retyr'd shee rests at home   5
In her white frothie bedd, and native fome:

A Louers passion. 13 *HM116 reads:* And thus my Ague Loue torments by
turnes   Thus] Soe *H31, A19, S14, A30, Ash 38, Ash 47*   14 *HM116 reads:*
Sometime it friezeth, y^n againe it burnes   That now] Soe now *S17, A19:* As
now *H31, S14, R84, A30:* Now as *Ash 47*
   Of his Mistresse. Text from *A226*   2 Humanity,] Humanity. *A226*   17
therfore] the'rf *A226*
   On the Green Sickness. Song. Text from *W.* Punctuation partly the editor's.
Title: Againe an other of the same *W.*
917.25

o

Where

Where the graye Morne through mists of lawne
Snowing soft Pearles, shootes an eternall dawne
    On thy Elizian shade: Thou blest
Empire of love and beautie, vnpossest   10
    Chast virgin kingdome, but Create
Mee Monarch of thy free Elective State,
    Lett me Surround with Circling Armes
My beautious Island, and with amorous Charmes
    Mixt with thie flood of Frozen snowe   15
In Crimson streames Ile force the redd Sea flowe.

The Departure.

BY all thy *Glories* willingly I go,
    Yet could have wish'd thee *Constant* in thy *Love*;
        But since thou needs must prove
    Vncertain, as is thy *Beauty*,
    Or as the *Glass*, that shews it thee,   5
My *Hopes* thus soon to overthrow,
Shews thee more fickle, but my *flames* by this
        Are easier quench'd than his,
        VVhom *flattering smiles* betray,
        'Tis tyrannous *delay*   10
        Breeds all this harm,
And makes that *Fire consume*, that should but *warm*.

Till *Time* destroys the Blossoms of thy *Youth*,
Thou art our *Idol*, worship'd at that Rate,
    But who can tell thy *Fate*?   15
Or say that when thy *Beauties* gone,
Thy *Lovers Torch* will still burn on?
I could have serv'd thee with such *truth*
Devoutest *Pilgrims* to their *Saints* do ow,
        Departed long ago;   20
        And at thy ebbing Tide
        Have us'd thee as a *Bride*,
        Who's onely true
'Cause you are *fair*, he loves *himself*, not *you*.
                                    T. C.

The Departure. Text from Thomas Jordan's *Claraphil and Clarinda: in a Forrest of Fancies* [1650?].

                                            APPENDIX B

APPENDIX B
POEMS INCORRECTLY ASCRIBED
TO CAREW IN THE EARLY EDITIONS

TO MY FRIEND,
WILL. D'AVENANT.

[Lines 1–14 by William Habington]

I Crowded 'mongst the first, to see the Stage
  (Inspir'd by thee) strike wonder in our age,
By thy bright fancie dazled: Where each Sceane
Wrought like a charme, and forc't the audience leane
To th'passion of thy Pen, thence Ladyes went   5
(Whose absence Lovers sigh'd for) to repent
Their unkind scorne; And Courtiers, who by art
Made love before, with a converted heart,
To wed those Virgins, whom they woo'd t'abuse;
Both rendred Hymen's pros'lits by thy Muse.   10
   But others who were proofe 'gainst Love, did sit
To learne the subtle Dictats of thy Wit;
And as each profited, tooke his degree,
Master, or Batchelor, in Comedie.
Wee, of th'adult'rate mixture not complaine,   15
But thence more Characters of Vertue gaine;
More pregnant Patternes, of transcendent Worth,
Than barren and insipid Truth brings forth:
So, oft the Bastard nobler fortune meets,
Than the dull Issue of the lawfull sheets.   20

The Enquiry.

[By Robert Herrick]

A Mongst the myrtles as I walk't,
  Love and my sighes thus intertalk't,
Tell me (said I in deepe distresse)
Where may I find my shepheardesse?

To my Friend, &c. Text from *40.*
The Enquiry. Text from *40.*

                                        Thou

Thou foole (said love) knowst thou not this   5
In every thing that's good shee is;
In yonder tulip goe and seeke,
There thou maist find her lip, her cheeke.

In yon ennammel'd pansie by,
There thou shalt have her curious eye;   10
In bloome of peach, in rosie bud,
There wave the streamers of her blood,

In brightest lillies that there stands,
The emblems of her whiter hands.
In yonder rising hill there smells   15
Such sweets as in her bosome dwells.

'Tis true (said I) and thereupon
I went to plucke them one by one
To make of parts a vnion
But on a suddaine all was gone.   20

With that I stopt: said love these be,
(Fond man) resemblances of thee,
And as these flowres, thy joyes shall die
Even in the twinkling of an eye.
    And all thy hopes of her shall wither,   25
    Like these short sweets, thus knit together.

The Primrose.
[by Robert Herrick]

ASke me why I send you here,
    This firstling of the infant yeare:
Aske me why I send to you,
This *Primrose* all bepearl'd with dew.
I strait will whisper in your eares,   5
The sweets of love are wash't with teares.

Aske me why this flower doth shew,
So yellow greene and sickly too:
Aske me why the stalke is weake,
And bending yet it doth not breake;   10
I must tell you these discover,
What doubts and feares are in a lover.

The Enquiry. 9 yon ennammel'd pansie] you ennammel'd pausie *40*   21
stopt:] stopt *40*   The Primrose. Text from *40*

Song.

[by James Shirley]

Would you know what's soft? I dare,
Not bring you to the downe, or aire:
Nor to starres to shew what's bright,
Nor to snow to teach you white.

Nor if you would Musicke heare, 5
Call the orbes to take your eare:
Nor to please your sence bring forth,
Bruised Nard or what's more worth.

Or on food were your thoughts plac't,
Bring you Nectar, for a tast: 10
Would you have all these in one,
Name my mistris, and 'tis done.

The Hue and Cry.

[by James Shirley]

IN loves name you are charg'd hereby,
To make a speedy Hue and Crie,
After a face which t'other day,
Stole my wandring heart away.
To direct you these (in briefe,) 5
Are ready markes to know the theife.
    Her haire a net of beames would prove,
Strong enough to captive *Jove*
In his Eagles shape; Her brow,
Is a comely field of snow. 10
Her eye so rich, so pure a grey,
Every beame creates a day.
And if she but sleepe (not when
The sun sets) 'tis night agen.
In her cheekes are to be seene, 15
Of flowers both the King and Queene,
Thither by the graces led,
And freshly laid in nuptiall bed.

Song. Text from *40*   The Hue and Cry. Text from *40*

On

On whom lips like Nymphes doe waite,
Who deplore their virgin state,   20
Oft they blush, and blush for this,
That they one another kisse,
But observe besides the rest,
You shall know this Fellon best,
By her tongue, for if your eare   25
Once a heavenly musicke heare,
Such as neither Gods nor Men,
But from that voice, shall heare agen
That that is she. O strait surprise,
And bring her unto loves Assize!   30
If you let her goe she may,
Antedate the latter day,
Fate and Philosophy controle,
And leave the world without a soule.

To his Mistris confined.
Song.

[by James Shirley]

O Thinke not Phœbe 'cause a cloud,
* Doth now thy silver brightnes shrowd,*
*   My wandring eye*
Can stoope to common beauties of the Skye.
*   Rather be kind, and this Ecclips,*   5
*   Shall neither hinder eye nor lips,*
*   For wee shall meete,*
Within our hearts and kisse, and none shall see't.

Nor canst thou in thy prison be,
Without some living signe of me;   10
*   When thou dost spye,*
A Sun beame peepe into the roome, 'tis J.
*   For I am hid within a flame,*
*   And thus into thy chamber came,*
*   To let thee see,*   15
In what a marttyredome I burne for thee.

When thou dost touch thy Lute thou mayest,
Thinke on my heart, on which thou plaiest:
                                   When each sad tone,
Vpon the strings doth shew my deeper groane.   20
     When thou dost please, they shall rebound,
     With nimble ayres strucke to the sound,
                              Of thy owne voyce;
O thinke how much I tremble and reioyce.

There's no sad picture that doth dwell,   25
Vpon thy Arras wall, but well
                         Resembles me,
No matter though our age doe not agree,
     Love can make old, as well as time,
     And he that doth but twenty clime,   30
                    If he dare proue,
As true as I, shewes fourescore yeares in love.

The Carver.
To his Mistris.
[Probably by Henry Constable]

A Carver having lov'd too long in vaine,
     Hewd out the portraiture of *Venus* Sunne
In marble rocke: upon the which did raine
     Small drisling drops that from a fount did runne;
Imagining the drops would either weare   5
     His fury out, or quench his living flame:
But when hee saw it bootlesse did appeare,
     He swore the water did augment the same.
So I that seeke in verse to carve thee out,
     Hoping thy beauty will my flame allay,   10
Veiwing my lines impolish't all throughout,
     Find my will rather to my love obey:
That with the Carver I my work doe blame,
     Finding it still th'augmenter of my flame.

The Carver. Text from *40*   4 runne;] runne. *40*   10 allay, *42*:
allay. *40*

To

APPENDIX B

To my Lord Admirall on his late sicknesse, and recovery.

[by Edmund Waller]

VVIth joy like ours, the Thracian youth invade
   Orpheus, returning from th'Elysian shade,
Embrace the Heroe, and his stay implore,
Make it their publike suit he would no more
Desert them so, and for his Spouses sake   5
His vanisht love, tempt the Lethæan Lake,
The Ladies too, the brightest of that time,
Ambitious all his lofty bed to climbe,
Their doubtfull hopes with expectation feed,
Which shall the faire Euridice succeed;   10
Euridice, for whom his numerous moane
Makes listning Trees, and savage Mountaines groane,
Through all the Ayre his sounding strings dilate
Sorrow like that, which touch'd our hearts of late,
Your pining sicknesse, and your restlesse paine,   15
At once the Land affecting, and the Mayne,
When the glad newes that you were Admirall,
Scarce through the Nation spread, 'twas fear'd by all
That our great CHARLES, whose wisdome shines in you
Should be perplexed how to chuse a new: 20
So more then private was the joy and griefe,
That at the worst it gave our soules reliefe,
That in our Age such sense of vertue liv'd,
They joy'd so justly, and so justly griev'd.
    Nature, her fairest light ecclipsed, seemes   25
Her selfe to suffer in these sad extreames,
While not from thine alone thy blood retires,
But from those cheeks which all the world admires.
The stem thus threatned, and the sap, in thee
Droope all the branches of that noble Tree,   30
Their beauties they, and we our love suspend,
Nought can our wishes, save thy health intend;
As Lillies over-charg'd with raine they bend,
Their beauteous heads, and with high heaven contend,
Fold thee within their snowy armes, and cry,   35

To my Lord Admirall, &c. Text from 42; not included in 40.

He

He is too faultlesse, and too young to die:
So like Immortals, round about thee Thay
Sit, that they fright approaching death away.
Who would not languish, by so faire a traine,
To be lamented, and restor'd againe?   40
Or thus with-held, what hasty soule would goe,
Though to the Blest? Ore young Adonis so
Faire Venus mourn'd, and with the precious showre
Of her warme teares cherisht the springing flower.

    The next support, faire hope, of your great name,   45
And second Pillar of that noble frame,
By losse of thee would no advantage have,
But step by step pursues thee to thy grave.

    And now relentlesse Fate about to end
The line, which backward doth so farre extend,   50
That Antique stock, which still the world supplies
With bravest spirits, and with brightest eyes,
Kind Phæbus interposing bade me say,
Such stormes no more shall shake that house, but they
Like Neptune, and his Sea-borne Neece shall be   55
The shining glories of the Land and Sea,
With courage guard, and beauty warme our Age,
And Lovers fill with like Poetique rage.

53 say, Waller's *Poems*, 1645: stay, *42*   54 they Waller's *Poems*, 1645:
say *42*

APPENDIX C

APPENDIX C
THREE LETTERS FROM THOMAS CAREW TO SIR DUDLEY CARLETON
I.
[Public Record Office, S. P. 14/88:67]

Right Honorable my most singul^r. good L^d.

I haue bene thus long in giuing y^r. L^p. account of y^e. success of my business, by reason of my L^d. Carewes absence from this towne, where after I was arriued & had awhile consulted wth. my fath^r. & oth^r.
5 frends, it was thought fitt I should repayre vnto him to y^e. Queenes Court, wch. then wth. y^e. Kings & Princes was at Woodstock; where I deliuered y^r. L^ps. lett^rs. His answeare to me was, y^t. he had allready in that employment a m^r. of artes, whose seauen yeares seruice had not yet deserued to be so displaced, & added, y^t. I being his kinsman might
10 expect from him all those greatest curtesies whatsoeuer, whereunto his neereness of blood did oblige him, wch. I should allwayes finde him readie to performe, but to admitt me into his familie as a seruant, it were a thing (sayde he) farr beneath y^r. qualitie, & wch. my blood could not suffer w^thowt much reluctance. I told him y^t. my comming was not
15 to supplant any man, but y^t. I thought this late addition of hon^r. might haue made those small abilities wch. I had acquired by my trauells & experience in y^r. L^ps. seruice, of vse to his, wch. I did humbly prostitute before his L^p. whoe if he thought not my youth vnworthy so great honor, I should esteeme my self no wayes disparaged by his seruice.
20 He replyed y^t. my languages & whateuer seruiceable partes I had would rust in his seruice for want of vse, & therefore prayed me to propose to my self any oth^r. meanes wherein he might pleasure me, were it y^e. seruice of some oth^r. whoe had more employment, & better meanes of preferment for a Secretarie, or whatsoeuer proiect I could
25 deuise, wherein he promised not only to employe his creditt but his purse if neede were, & so referred me to his returne to London for his answeare to y^r. L^ps. lett^r. at what time he would talke more at large wth. me & my fath^r. abowt this business. This is y^e. issue of my hopes wth. my L^d. Carew nor am I likely to gayne any thing at his return
30 heth^r. from him but fayre wordes & complement.

Y^r. L^ps. lett^rs. to my L^d. of Arrondell, because it was necessarie for me to wayte vppon my L^d. Carew, & could at no time see him but wth. y^e. King from whose side he seldome moueth, I left wth. M^r. Hauers to be deliuered to him, of whome I learned y^t. he was as yet
35 vnfurnished of a Secretarie, wherefore according to y^r. L^ps. instructions

tions my fath^{rs}. councell & my owne inclination I will labour my admittance into his seruice, wherein I haue these hopes, y^e. present vacancie of y^e. place, y^e. reference my fath^r. had to his Grandfath^r. & y^e. knowledge wch. by y^r. L^{ps}. meanes he had of me at Florence, wherein if neede be & if M^r. Chamberlane shall so thinke good I 40 will engage my L^d. Carew, & whereunto I humbly beseech y^r. L^p. to add y^r. effectuall recōmendation, wch. I knowe will be of more power then all my oth^r. pretences, wch. yow will be pleased wth. y^r. most conuenient speede to afforde me, y^t. I may at his returne heth^r. (wch. will be wth. y^e. Kings some 20 dayes hence) meete him wth. y^r. 45 L^{ps}. lett^{rs}. & y^t. I may in case of refusall returne to y^r. seruice y^e. sooner, from wch. I profess (notwthstanding all these fayre shewes of preferrment) as I did wth. much vnwillingness depart, so doe I not wthowt greate affliction discontinue; my thoughts of th^r. prop^r. & regular motion not aspiring higher then the orbe of y^r. L^{ps}. seruice, 50 this irregul^r. being caused by y^r. self whoe are my *primum mobile*, for I euer accounted it hon^r. enough for me to *correre la fortuna del mio Sig^{re}*. nor did I euer ayme at at [*sic*] greater happiness then to be held as I will allways rest

Y^r. L^{ps}.   55
Most humbly deuoted
London this 2 of   to y^r. seruice
Septemb^r *1616*.   Tho: Carew.
[*Endorsed by Carew*:]
To the Right Honble. my most sigul^r. [*sic*]
good L^d. S^r. Dudley Carleton Knight   60
L. Ambassad^r. for his Matie. wth. the
States of y^e. Vnited Prouinces of
y^e. Low Countreyes at the /
                Haghe
[*Endorsed by Carleton*:]   65
Tom: Carew the
2^d of 7^{ber} *1616*.

II.
[Public Record Office, S. P. 14/88:77]

Right Honble. my most singul^r. good L^d.

Since my last to y^r. L^p. of ye 2^d of this p̄nt my L^d. Carewes repayre to towne gaue me occasion to attend his resolution, at his lodging, wch. he deliuered wth. much passion protesting y^t. he did not therefore refuse me because he had no intent to take care or charge of me for I 5 should vppon any occasion be assured of y^e. contrary, but meerely for y^t. he should haue no employment for me, & therefore prayed me, since he tendred herein my owne good more then his particul^r. interest to surcease this suite & preuayle my self of him in an oth^r. kinde; to
                                                y^e.

10 yᵉ. same effect was his excuse to my fathʳ., so as yᵗ. string hath fayled, but as there was euer more appearance, so doe I conceaue better hope of good success wᵗʰ. my Lᵈ. of Arondell; & yᵉ. rathʳ. because my Lᵈ. Carew hath so willingly engaged himself in my behalf, & promiseth to deale very effectually for mc, but chiefly when I shall haue yʳ. Lᵖˢ.
15 recommendations wᶜʰ. I dayly expect:

Allthough I know yʳ. Lᵖ. hath very particulʳ. aduertisments of all yᵉ. occurrents here, yet because other mens fayth can not saue me, as neythʳ. thʳ. penns discharge my duty, I will be bold to giue yʳ. Lᵖ. notice of what I haue obserued or learned since my arriuall.

20   My Lᵈ. Roos tooke his leaue this morning of yᵉ. King but goes not yet these tenn dayes, his brauery entertaynes both Court & citty wᵗʰ. discourse, his golden liueries are so frequent in yᵉ. streetes, yᵗ. it is thought they haue thʳ. seuerall walkes, & are duly relieued by Sigʳ. Diegoes appoyntment; he came this day to yᵉ. Court attended wᵗʰ.
25 10 or 12 Gent. 8 pages very richly accoutred in suites of 80/ᡰⁱ a peece, & some 20 staffiers all in gold lace, Sigʳ. Diego protested yᵗ. all yᵉ. liueryes (for euery man hath two suites) cost 2500/ᡰⁱ ster: besides my Lᵈ. giueth to 20 Gent. yᵗ. attend him 50/ᡰⁱ a man to equippe themselfes for the voyage, he hath wᵗʰ. him 3 Secretaries Mʳ. Gold-
30 burrough whome yʳ. Lᵖ. knew in Italy is one & Duncomb a second, & two Chaplaines. There goe wᵗʰ. him 12 Gent: en compagnon, amongst yᵉ. rest Sʳ. Ed: Sommersett, Sʳ. Richard Lumley newly knighted for yᵉ. voyage, Mʳ. Giles Bridges, & Mʳ. Tho: Hopton, they imbarke at Portsmouth & thence goe by sea to Lisbon. Sigʳ.
35 Diego leaues my Lᵈ. at yᵉ. seaside

My Lᵈ. Dingwell is returned from Venice, hath seene France & Italy & brought home a chayne of 2000/ scudi, wᶜʰ. is all yᵉ. effect of his iourney.

Mʳ. Albert Morton hath taken his leaue of yᵉ. K. & doth wᵗʰⁱⁿ
40 15 dayes take his iourney for Heidelbergh, his waye vnless he bee comāanded to the contrary (he sayes) shall lye by yᵉ. Haghe.

Sʳ. Ed: Cecill arriued here on Sonday last & went this morning wᵗʰ. my Lᵈ. Roos to kiss yᵉ. Kˢ. handes.

My Lady Winwood hath bene lately at yᵉ. point of death, & is not
45 yet past danger. Mʳ. Kansfield told me yᵗ. he left Mʳˢ. Anne Wood now my Lady Harrington (whome yʳ. Lᵖˢ. knowes) irrecouerably sick, so as he peremptorily sayde she was by yᵗ. time deade.

I was told by a Gent: of good creditt that there is lately happened a greate breach betwene yᵉ new-created Viscount Villiars & Mʳ. Secretary
50 Winwood wᶜʰ. is likely much to impayre Mʳ. Secretaryes credit wᵗʰ. his Maᵗʸ. & cast all at least yᵉ. gaynefull employment vppon Sʳ. Tho: Lakes. yᵉ. occasions of thʳ. particulʳ. disgusts I can not yet learne.

Sigʳ.

Sig^r. Diego & Duncomb haue bene very busy at y^e. Exchange in compounding in th^r. L^{ds}. name wth. y^e. Spanish Merchants for a shipp of th^{rs}. lately taken in Spayne, whereof y^t. King is determined 55 to make a present to my L^d. Roos, & wch. he is bound to restore, but y^e. merchants offer my L^d. for composition or rath^r. a gratuitie 5000/^{li}. this money wth. y^e. 5000/^{li} extraordinary he hath from y^e. King & 6^{li} per diem since the first of May, considering my L^d. goes to Lisbon by sea & shall from thence be defrayed to Madrid will wth. 60 little addition discharge his voyage.

But y^t. I should be to iniurious to y^r. L^{ps}. leysure I would add y^e. prīnt discourses of my L^d. Cooke but they are so various & so vncertayne y^t. they serue only to *rompre la teste*, only y^e. more popul^r. & generall bruite hath giuen him a Barronry in lieu of his Chief Justiceshipp, 65 wherewth. it had inuested M^r. Record^r. Mountague, but he for being too corrupt is now supplanted, & y^e *aura popularis* hath conferd y^t. hon^r. on Baron Tanfield.

These enclosed M^r. Attorney Grāls Secretary recomēended to my address this morning   70

It is thought Viscount Villiars & S^r. John Deckam of y^e. Dutchie office shall shortly be preferd to y^e. Counsell table.

M^r. Shireburn perswades me to attempt Viscount Villiers seruice (who hath only M^r. Packer a man though well skild in home businesses yet alltogeth^r. ignorant of forrayne) but as I haue no waye open 75 to him, so haue I no appetite if I fayle in my present proiect, to hazard a third repulse, howsoeuer I shall gouerne my self according to y^r. L^{ps}. lett^{rs}. wch. wth. y^r. recomēendation to my L^d. of Arondell I doe wth. greate deuotion attend.

Thus I in all humilitie take leaue & Rest   80
                                    Y^r. L^{ps}.

London this 11th Most humbly de-
of 7^{ber} 1616 st^o. vet.   uoted to y^r. seruice
[*Not endorsed by Carew.*   Tho: Carew/
Endorsed by Carleton:]
Tom Carew the   85
11th of 7^{ber}
     1616

III.
[Public Record Office, S. P. 14/88:87]

Right Honble. my most singul^r. good L^d.

But that I could not lett this messenger goe emptie I should not haue giuen y^r. L^p. the trouble of these lines at this time, not hauing any thing worth y^r. L^{ps}. knowledge, nor being able as yet to resolue
                                                                                                    yow

5 yow of y^e. effect of my business; by reason of my L^d. of Arondells indefinite answeare, whereby he holdes me in suspence though not wthowt hope of good success, for he protesteth y^t. if he can by any meanes satisfie the pretences of two competitors, whoe are wth. dayly importunitie recommended vnto him from his hon^{ble}. & especiall good

10 frendes (w^{ch} (he sayes) he will endeauour & hopes to effect) he will then wth. all willingnes embrace my seruice, y^e. tender whereof he takes very kindly; thus much he hath professed vnto my L^d. Carew whoe made the first ouerture, to M^r. Shireborn, whoe in y^r. L^{ps}. name seconded y^t. recom̃endation, & to my self, crauing besides a

15 fortnights respite, wch. doth wthin these fewe dayes expire, in y^e. meane time my L^d. Carew doth promise to omitt no occasion or argument of persuasion, so as if y^r. L^{ps}. recommendatory lett^{rs}. (wch. would very oportunely arriue in this coniuncture, & y^e. attending whereof may happily be occasion of My L^d. of Arondells delaye) should meete wth.

20 these circumstances I might well hope this business would sort to y^e. wished issue. I haue in this interstice had leysure to see my sister Grandmoth^r. & oth^r. my frends in Kent, whoe remember th^r. most affectionate seruices to y^r. L^p. & my Lady, I came down yesterday & will on Monday returne to London, at what time the King will be

25 there when it is expected y^e. resolution abowt my L^d. Chief Justice, & many oth^r. businesses will be taken, of y^e. effect whereof I will be bold to aduertise y^r. L^p.

My L^d. Rosses com̃oration here is vppon new businesses prolongued, y^e. negotiation whereof will allsoe lengthen his residence in Spayne,

30 he hath taken a second leaue of y^e. King (at what time M^r. Giles Bridges was knighted) but departeth not yet these 8 dayes.

Not hauing wherewth. to giue y^r. L^p. farth^r. trouble I humbly take leaue [&] rest

Y^r. L^{ps}.

35 Tunstall this   Most humbly deuoted
20th of 7^{ber} 1616 st^o. vet: to y^r. seruice
                            Tho: Carew.

[*Endorsed by Carew*:]
To the Right Honble. my most sĩg^{lr}.
good L^d. S^r. Dudley Carleton

40 Knight L^d. Amb^r. for his Matie.
wth. the States of the vnited Prou^{es}.
of the Low Contreyes at the/
                    Haghe

[*Endorsed by Carleton*:]
Tom Carew ye 20th of
45 7^{ber}. 1616.

APPENDIX D

APPENDIX D
POEMS AND LETTERS
ADDRESSED TO CAREW

Aurelian Tounsend to Tho : Carew
vpon the death of the King
of Sweden.

I Had, and haue a purpose to be kind
  To thee Tom Carew, for where meritts binde,
My court of conscience will a right decree
To one that bringes no aduocate nor fee.
  I loue thy personn which being large and tall,   5
Containes a speritt that full mans it all;
  I loue thy witt, that chooses to be sweete
Rather then sharpe, therefore in Lirique feete
Steales to thy mistris; letting others write
Rough footed Satires that in kissing bite.   10
  I loue thy Celia if shee did infuse
That fire into thee which begott thy Muse,
  And all thy louers that with listening eares
Sipp in and relish thy Ambrosian teares,
Which as they fell like manna on the Herse   15
Of deuine *Donne*, feeding vs all in verse,
So when the windes from euery corner bring
The too true nuse of the dead conquering king,
Lett our land waters meeting by consent
The showres desending from the Firmament,   20
Make a new floode; one whose teare swelling face
Clos'd in an arke of fatall Cyprisse, place
Gustauus bodie, wound about with bayes;
And while a constant gale of sighes conueyes
This world of wonder to the muses hill,   25
Each sacred swann in his immortall bill

Aurelian Tounsend to Tho: Carew, &c. Text from *S.23*; punctuation partly
the editor's. Also in *R2* and in *W* (lines 36–58 only).   *Title:* Aurelian
Townsends elegie on yͤ death of yͤ King of Sweden sent to T: Carewe. *R2*
12 which] that *R2*   16 *S.23 reads:* of of deuine *Donne* feeding vs all in verse
21 teare *R2*: teares *S.23*   23 wound] round *R2*

Shall

Shall beare his name, in wittnesse of that wracke
His snowe white plumes transformd to sable black.
His sword shall like a fierie piller stand,
Or like that graspt in the angrie Angells hand,　　　　　30
Before his Herse, needing no other light
But what hee gaue it to make day of night.
Prinses ambitius of renoune shall still
Striue for his spures to helpe them vp the hill.
His gloryus gauntletts shall vnquestiond lye,　　　　　35
Till handes are found fitt for a monarchie.
Minerua may without hir gorgon com
To beare his sheld, the shield of Christendom:
And the Sunn rising to his daly taske
Would showe the brighter if hee wore his caske.　　　　40
Lett solem silence and darke night be there
Making a morner of the Hemisphere.
And when vpon Pernassus double toppe
His corpes is come lett the Prosession stopp;
And sleeping, in the Muses cradell lay　　　　　　　45
This child of Honor, till at peepe of day
Fame like a Phenix from his ashes rise
Courting this new borne bird of Paradice;
And when each spring to his exhausted head
Is back retyr'd, if out of slime be bredd　　　　　　50
Any foule monster ouer chargd with gall,
One beame of his will make that Pithon fall;
For though this Lyon can no more prescribe
Detraction bounds, then that of Judas tribe,
If in the toyle of tongues his feareles name　　　　　55
Be cought by such as would perplex his fame,
A mouse may free him from those Aspes that lye
Hissing in holes till they truthbitten dye.

27 that] yᵉ *R2*　　　28 transformd *R2*: transforme *S.23*　　　30 the angrie]
th' angry *R2*　　40 showe] shine *R2, W*　　42 the] our *R2, W*　　44 lett]
let, let *R2*　　46 This child of Honor,] the child of honour! *W*　　48 this]
yᵉ *R2*　　49 spring] sprinke *R2*　　52 beame *R2, W*: drame *S.23*　　that
W: tha *S.23*: yᵉ *R2*

Vpon T. C. *having the P.*

TRoth, *Tom.* I must confess I much admire
   Thy water should find passage through the fire:
For fire and water never could agree,
These now by nature have some sympathie:
Sure then his way he forces; for all know   5
The *French* ne'r grants a passage to his foe.
If it be so, his valor I must praise,
That being the weaker, yet can force his ways;
And wish that to his valor he had strength,
That he might drive the fire quite out at length: 10
For (troth) as yet the fire gets the day,
For evermore the water runs away.

                                I. S.

To *Tho : Carew.*

(1)

Vpon my conscience whenso e're thou dy'st
  (Though in the black, the mourning time of Lent)
There will be seene, in Kings-street (where thou ly'st)
  More triumphs, than in dayes of Parl'ament.

(2)

How glad, and gaudy then will Lovers be?   5
  For ev'ry Lover that can Verses read,
Hath beene so injur'd by thy Muse, and thee,
  Ten Thousand, Thousand times, he wish'd thee dead.

(3)

Not but thy verses are as smooth, and high,
  As Glory, Love, or Wine, from Wit can rayse;   10
But now the Devill take such destinie!
  What should commend them, turnes to their disprayse.

Vpon T. C., &c. Text from *The Last Remains of S* John Suckling,* 1659.
  To Tho: Carew. Text from *Madagascar; with other Poems. By W. Davenant,*
1638.

(4)

Thy Wit's chiefe Virtue, is become its Vice;
For ev'ry Beauty thou hast rays'd so high,
That now course-Faces carry such a price,   15
As must undoe a Lover, if he buy.

(5)

Scarce any of the Sex, admits commerce;
It shames mee much to urge this in a Friend;
But more, that they should so mistake thy Verse,
Which meant to conquer, whom it did commend.   20

Ad Thomam Carew, apud J. C.
cum Davenantii Poëmatis.

TEque meum, cùm triste fuit mihi tempus, amorem,
   Officiis dico demeruisse tuis:
Meque tuum, si fortè occasio detur, amorem,
   Officiis dices demeruisse meis.
Si placet, interea, hoc grandis non grande Poetæ,   5
   Ingenii dignum munus habeto tui.

To Tho : Carew.

NO Lute, or lover durst contend with Thee
   Hadst added to thy Loue but *Charity.*
           CP. [Clement Paman]

Ad Thomam Carew, &c. Text from Clement Barksdale's *Nympha Libethris: or the Cotswold Muse, Presenting some extempore Verses to the Imitation of yong Scholars,* 1651.   *Title:* Poëmatis.] Poëmatiis. *Nympha Libethris*   5 grandis] graudis *Nympha Libethris*
To Tho: Carew. Text from MS. Rawl. Poet. 147, Bodleian Library.   1 or lover] *corrected from* nor lover MS.

Two

Two Letters from Sir John Suckling

I

[From *Fragmenta Aurea*, 1646]

A Letter to a Friend to diswade him from marrying a Widow which he formerly had been in Love with, and quitted.

AT this time when no hot Planet fires the blood, and when the *Lunaticks* of *Bedlam* themselves are trusted abroad; that you should run mad, is (*Sir*) not so much a subject for your friends *pitty*, as their *wonder*. 'Tis true, *Love* is a *natural distemper*, a kind of *Small Pocks*: Every one either hath had it, or is to expect it, & the sooner the better.

Thus far you are excused: But having been well cured of a *Fever*, to court a *Relapse*, to make *Love* the *second time* in the *same Place*, is (not to flatter you) neither better nor worse then to fall into a *Quagmire* by *chance*, and ride into it afterwards on *purpose*. 'Tis not *love* (*Tom*) that doth the mischief, but *constancy*, for *Love* is of the nature of a *burning-glasse*, which kept still in one place, *fireth*: changed often, it doth *nothing*: a kind of *glowing-Coal*, which with shifting from hand to hand a man easily endures. But then to *marry*! (*Tom*) Why thou hadst better to live *honest*. *Love* thou knowst is *blind*, what will he do when he hath *Fetters* on thinkest thou?

Dost thou know what *marriage* is? 'Tis *curing* of *Love* the *dearest way*, or waking a *loosing Gamester* out of a *winning dream*: and after a long expectation of a strange *banquet*, a presentation of a *homely meal*. Alas!

An Answer to the Letter.

CEase to *wonder* (honest *Jack*) and give me leave to *pitty thee*, who labourest to condemn that which thou confessest *natural*, and the *sooner* had, the *better*. 5

Thus far there needs no *excuse*, unlesse it be on *thy* behalf, who stilest *second thoughts* (which are by all allowed the *Best*) a *relapse*, and talkest of a *quagmire* where no man ever 10 stuck fast, and accusest *constancy* of *mischief* in what is *natural*, and *advisedly undertaken*.

'Tis confest that *Love* changed often doth nothing; nay 'tis nothing: 15 for *Love* and *change* are incompatible: but where it is kept fixt to its first object, though it *burn* not, yet it *warms* and *cherisheth*, so as it needs no *transplantation*, or *change* of *soyl* to 20 make it fruitful: and certainly if *Love* be *natural*, to *marry* is the best *Recipe* for living honest.

Yes, I know what *mariage* is, and know you know it not, by terming it 25 the *dearest way* of *curing Love*: for certainly·there goes more charge to the keeping of a *Stable full* of *horses*, then *one* onely *Steed*: and much of vanity is therein besides: when, be the 30 errand what it will, this *one Steed* shall serve your turn as well as twenty more. Oh! if you could serve your *Steed* so!

Marriage turns pleasing *Dreams* to 35

18 that] that that *Fragmenta Aurea*

(*Tom*)

(*Tom*) *Love seeds* when it runs up to
Matrimony, and is good for nothing.
Like some *Fruit-trees*, it must be
transplanted if thou wouldst have it
40 active, and bring forth any thing.

Thou now perchance hast vowed
all that can be vowed to any *one face*,
and thinkst thou hast left nothing un-
said to it: do but make *love* to *another*,
45 and if thou art not suddenly furnisht
with *new-language*, and *fresh oathes*,
I will conclude *Cupid* hath used thee
worse then ever he did any of his
train.

50 After all this, to marry a *Widow*, a
kind of *chew'd-meat*! What a fantasti-
cal stomack hast thou, that canst not
eat of a dish til another man hath
cut of it? who would wash after an-
55 other, when he might have fresh
water enough for asking?

Life is sometimes a long-journey:
to be tyed to ride upon one beast still,
and that half-tyr'd to thy hand too!
60 Think upon that (*Tom*.)

Well; If thou must needs *marry* (as
who can tell to what height thou hast
sinned? Let it be a *Maid*, and no
Widow: (for as a modern Author
65 hath wittily resolved in this case) 'tis
better (if a man must be in Prison) to
lie in a private room then in the hole.

70

75

80

ravishing *Realities* which out-doe
what *Fancy* or *expectation* can frame
unto themselves.

That *Love* doth *seed* when it runs
into *Matrimony*, is undoubted *truth*;
how else should it *increase* and *multi-
ply*, which is its greatest *blessing*.

'Tis not the want of *Love*, nor
Cupids fault, if every day afford not
new-language, and *new-waies* of ex-
pressing affection: it rather may be
caused through an *excesse* of *joy*,
which oftentimes strikes *dumb*.

These things considered I will
marry, nay, and to prove the second
Paradox false, I'le marry a *Widow*,
who is rather the *chewer*, then *thing
chewed*. How strangely fantastical is
he who will be an hour in plucking on
a *strait-boot*, when he may be forth-
with furnisht with enough that will
come on easily, and do him as much
credit, and better service? *Wine*
when *first-broacht*, drinks not half so
well as after a while *drawing*. Would
you not think him a mad man who
whilst he might fair & easily ride on
the *beaten-road-way*, should trouble
himself with *breaking up of gaps*? a
well wayed horse will safely convay
thee to thy journeys end, when an *un-
backt Filly* may by chance give thee
a fall: 'Tis *Prince*-like to marry a
Widow, for 'tis to have a *Taster*.

Tis true, *life* may prove a *long-
journey*; and so believe me it must do,
A *very long one* too, before the *Beast*
you talke of prove *tyr'd*. Think you
upon that (*Jack*.)

Thus, *Jack*, thou seest my wel-
tane resolution of *marrying*, and that
a *Widow*, not a *maid*; to which I am
much induced out of what *Pythagoras*
saith (in his *2da Sect. cuniculorum*)
that *it is better lying in the hole, then
sitting in the Stocks.*

36 *Love seeds*] *Love-seeds Fragmenta Aurea* 50 marry a] marry *Fragmenta
Aurea*

II [From

II

[From *The Last Remains of S͏ʳ John Suckling,* 1659]

To T. C.

Though writing be as tedious to me, as no doubt reading will be
to thee, yet considering that I shall drive that trade thou speak'st
of to the *Indies,* and for my Beads and Rattles have a return of Gold
and Pearl; I am content for thy sake, and in private thus to do penance
in a sheet.   5

Know then, Dear *Carew,* that at Eleven last night, flowing as much
with Love as thou hast ebbed, thy Letter found me out. I read, con-
sidered, and admired, and did conclude at last, That *Horseley* Air did
excel the Waters of the *Bath;* just so much as Love is a more noble
disease then the Pox.   10

No wonder if the Countesses think time lost, till they be there:
Who would not be where such Cures flow! The care thou hast of
me, that I should traffick right, draws me by way of Gratitude to
perswade thee to bottle up some of that, and send it hither to Town;
thy returns will be quicker then those to the *Indies,* nor need'st thou   15
fear a vent, since the disease is Epedemical.

One thing more, who knows (wouldst thou be curious in the search)
but thou maist finde an Air of contrary Virtue about thy House, which
may, as this destroyes, so that create Affection; if thou couldst,

> The *Lady of* High-gate *then should embrace*   20
> The *disease of the Stomach, and the word of disgrace.*
> > Gredeline *and* Grass-green
> > *Shall sometimes be seen*
> > *Its Arms to in-twine*
> > *About the* Woodbine.   25

In honest Prose thus: We would carry our selves first, and then
our Friends manage all the little Loves at Court, make more *Tower*
work, and be the Duke of *B.* of our Age, which without it, we shall
never be. Think on't therefore, and be assured, That if thou joyn'st
me in the Patent with thee, in the height of all my greatness I will   30
be thine, all but what belongs to *Desdemonna,* which is just as I mean,
to venture at thy Horse-race Saturday come seven-night.

J. S.

23 *seen*] seen. *Last Remains*

COMMENTARY

3. *The Spring.* The paradox of burgeoning earth and unhappy lover is developed variously in Petrarch's sonnet 'Zefiro torna, e 'l bel tempo rimena'; Desportes's *Complainte* (*Les Premières Œuvres*, 1600, pp. 115 ff.); Thomas Morley, *Madrigalls to Foure Voyces . . . the First Booke*, 1594, Madrigal I (Fellowes, *English Madrigal Verse*, p. 125); Thomas Weelkes, *Madrigals*, 1597, Madrigal VII (Fellowes, p. 210); Drummond of Hawthornden's Sonnet XVII (ed. Kastner, i. 21). But the most immediate reminiscences are from Ronsard; see below.

1. The opening words and lines 19–21 echo, perhaps unconsciously, Ronsard's *Amourette*, from *Le Second Livre des Amours* (*Œuvres*, 1609, pp. 185–6):

> Or' que l'hyuer roidit la glace épesse,
> Rechaufons nous ma gentille Maistresse,
> Non accroupis pres le fouyer cendreux,
> Mais aux plaisirs des combats amoureux.

3. Candies. Coats with ice. Cf. *Timon of Athens*, iv. iii. 225–6, and Drayton, *Quest of Cinthia* (*Poems*, 1627, p. 137):

> those frosts that Winter brings,
> Which candy every greene.

6–7. For 'sacred birth' Hazlitt and Ebsworth adopted the easier manuscript reading 'second birth', which has been more recently followed by Mr. Norman Ault in his textually careful *Treasury of Unfamiliar Lyrics*. But 'sacred' is readily defensible and far richer in suggestion. Sir Thomas Browne writes (*Pseudodoxia Epidemica*, v. xxiii. 3): 'Though useless unto us, and rather of molestation, we commonly refrain from killing Swallows, and esteem it unlucky to destroy them: whether herein there be not a Pagan relique, we have some reason to doubt. For we read in Elian, that these birds were sacred unto the *Penates* or household gods of the ancients, and therefore were preserved. The same they also honoured as the nuncio's of the spring; and we find in Athenæus that the Rhodians had a solemn song to welcome in the Swallow.' Conrad Gesner (*Historiæ Animalium Lib. III. qui est de Auium natura*, 1585, pp. 549–50) mentions that the swallow remains in her nest all winter as though dead, and revives in the spring; this is to be accounted a great marvel, 'ac imaginem resurrectionis nostrorum corporum'.

13. Now all things smile. Cf. Virgil, *Eclog.* vii. 55: 'Omnia nunc rident'; Petrarch, *Zefiro torna*, line 5: 'Ridono i prati e 'l ciel si rasserena'; Ronsard, *Second Livre des Amours*, xxvii, line 8 (ed. cit., p. 150): 'Et toute chose rire en la saison nouvelle.'

13–24. Cf. the conclusion of the Ronsard poem just cited:

> Icy la bergerette en tournant son fuseau
> Desgoise ses amours, & là le pastoureau
> Respond à sa chanson, icy toute chose aime:

Tout parle de l'amour, tout s'en veut enflammer:
Seulement vostre cœur froid d'vne glace extreme
Demeure opiniastre & ne veut point aimer.

Also, from *Sonnets pour Hélène*, ii. lxviii, lines 5–8 (ed. cit., p. 294):

Mais ton corps nonchalant reuesche & rigoureux,
Qui iamais en son cœur le feu d'Amour n'assemble,
En ce beau mois de May, malgré tes ans ressemble,
O perte de ieunesse! à l'Hyuer froidureux.

4. To *A. L. Perswasions to love.* The title 'An Admonition to coy acquain-
tance' in *Ash 47* points for the modern reader the anticipation of Marvell's
To His Coy Mistress. Carew's poem consists of an original introduction
(lines 1–26), a transitional couplet (27–8), and for the rest a free translation
of Marino's canzone *Belleza caduca* (*La Lira*, 1625, Parte Seconda, pp. 84–8).
That the introductory verses may originally have stood as a separate piece is
indicated by the fact that *A21*, *HM116*, and one of the two versions in *A303*
conclude the poem at line 26. The manuscripts exhibit numerous variants,
suggesting that the piece as a whole received long and careful polishing. There
is no evidence on which to identify the lady addressed.

29–35. With this passage Carew begins translating. Compare the original
in Marino, *Belleza caduca*, lines 1–7:

Beltà del sommo Sole
Raggio no, ma baleno
Trà noi risplender suole,
Ma subito vien meno,
Quasi instabil sereno
Di verno, ò pioggia estiua,
Quanto più cara altrui più fuggitiua.

5. **37–48.** In *HL* these lines appear separately, in an autograph musical
setting by Henry Lawes:

Those Curious Locks soe Aptly twynde,
whose Eu'rye hayre a soule does bynde,
will Change their Abren hue, & grow
Cold, & whyte, as winters snow;
y^t Eye wch now is Cupids nest,
will prove his graue as for ye Rest,
in chin, lip, cheeke, or nose,
nor lillye shalbe found, nor Rose;
what will then becom of all,
those whom now you servants call,
like Swallowes when yor suṁers done,
they'le flye & seeke some warmer suñ.

A7 also reproduces these lines as a separate poem.

6. **81–4.** Expanded from the final two lines of *Belleza caduca:*

Cogli cogli il tuo fiore,
Che quasi in vn sol punto, e nasce, e more.

Thomas Randolph uses a similar conceit (*Amyntas*, iv. ix. 38–40):

> How like the hearb Solstitiall is a lover,
> Now borne, now dead again, he buds, sprouts forth,
> Flourishes, ripens, withers in a minute.

—a passage which, as Parry points out in his edition of Randolph, is from Plautus (*Pseudolus*, 38–9).

6. *Lips and Eyes*. Translated from Marino's sonnet, 'Lite degli Occhi e della Bocca' (*Poesie Varie*, ed. Croce, 1913, p. 83):

> Avean lite di pregio e di bellezza,
> in quel volto gentil, gli occhi e la bocca.
> —Da noi—gli occhi dicean—primier si scocca
> l'acuto stral, ch'ogni diamante spezza.—
> La bocca poi:—Da me l'alta dolcezza
> del parlar, del baciar piove e trabocca.—
> Allor gli occhi, piangendo:—E da noi fiocca
> di vive perle oriental ricchezza.—
> Rise la bocca, e, disserrando quelle
> porte d'un bel rubino in duo diviso,
> disse ridente a l'umidette stelle:
> —Or sia giudice Amor, dove il bel viso
> discopra al paragon perle più belle:
> ne le lagrime vostre o nel mio riso?—

In omitting the excrescent *concetti* of lines 10 and 11 Carew shows his usual care for logical unity. His poem is translated into Greek elegiacs by H. Stubbe, *Deliciæ Poetarum Anglicanorum in Græcum versæ*, 1658.

6. *A divine Mistris*. For the first six lines Henry Lawes's autograph setting of the poem in *HL* substitutes the following four:

> all yᵉ workes of Nature are
> defectiue, but my cruell fayre
> was made by Handes farr more divine,
> for she hath Eurye beautyous lyne.

7. 9–10. How likeness creates love is explained by Pico della Mirandola in *A Platonick Discourse upon Love*, tr. by Thomas Stanley (1651), ii. iii: 'Secondly, there is alwayes some convenience and resemblance betwixt the desirer, and desired: Every thing delights, and preserves it self by that, which by natural affinity is most conformable to it; by its contrary is griev'd, and consum'd. Love is not betwixt things unlike; Repugnance of two opposite natures is natural hate. Hate is a repugnance with knowledge.' Compare Donne, *Elegie III*, line 23: 'Likeness glues Love'.

7. *SONG. A beautifull Mistris*. This is a translation of the following poem by Marino (*La Lira*, 1625, Parte Terza, p. 86):

> Per la sua Donna.
>
> *SE quando è chiaro il Cielo*
> *Scopre il viso costei, tinto di scorno*
> *Offusca il Sole, & abbarbaglia il giorno* [.]

Se quando copre il mondo oscuro velo
Volge i begli occhi intorno,
Fà rischiarare, e rotte
Le tenebre sparir, fuggir la notte.
Così discaccia, e sgombra
La luce insieme, e l'ombra.

The version of Carew's lyric set by Henry Lawes, in *HL* and *E20*, and later printed in Lawes's and Playford's collections, omits line 6.

8. *A cruell Mistris.*

1. Wee read of Kings and Gods. The story or stories referred to are hard to identify with certainty. The reference does not exactly fit the miraculous pitcher of Baucis and Philemon (Ovid, *Metamorphoses*, viii. 668–80), since that was filled not with water but with wine. Plutarch, in his *Artaxerxes*, v. i, writes of that monarch that 'once when some were offering him one thing, some another, as he was on a progress, a certain poor labourer, having got nothing at hand to bring him, ran to the river side, and, taking up water in his hands, offered it to him; with which Artaxerxes was so well pleased that he sent him a goblet of gold and a thousand darics'. Another incident of similar purport occurs later in the same *Life*.

13–14. Th' Assyrian King. Nebuchadnezzar, who, however, was no Assyrian. See Daniel iii.

17–18. Of such a Goddesse. The conceit may have been suggested by Torquato Tasso, who in two of his poems 'Assomiglia la condizione de la sua donna a quella de colui ch'arse il tempio di Diana Efesia' (*Rime*, ed. Angelo Solerti, 1898, ii, pp. 159–61).

8. *SONG. Murdring beautie.*

6. murderers. Compare Shakespeare, *As You Like It*, iii. v. 19: 'Lie not, to say mine eyes are murtherers.' It is possible, as suggested by Schelling (*A Book of Seventeenth Century Lyrics*, 1899, p. 254), that Carew is employing the word in its meaning of a small cannon or mortar.

9. *My mistris commanding me to returne her letters.* The poem is probably autobiographical, though the subject, and a few of the details in its treatment, may have been suggested to Carew in the following sonnet by Desportes (*Les Premières Œuvres*, Paris, 1600, fol. 71ʳ):

Lettres, le seul repos de mon ame agitee,
  Helas! il le faut donc me separer de vous:
  Et que par la rigueur d'vn iniuste courroux
  Ma plus belle richesse ainsi me soit ostee.
Ha! ie mourray plustost, & ma dextre indontee
  Flechira par mon sang le Ciel traistre & ialoux,
  Que ie m'aille priuant d'vn bien qui m'est si doux:
  Non, ie n'en feray rien, la chance en est iettee.
Il le faut toutesfois, elle les veut rauoir,
  Et de luy resister ie n'ay cœur ny pouuoir,
  A tout ce qu'elle veut mon ame est trop contrainte.

O Beauté sans arrest, mais trop ferme en rigueur,
Tien, repren tes papiers & ton amitié fainte,
Et me rens mon repos, ma franchise & mon cœur.

1–4. The simile of the merchant who sacrifices his cargo to save his ship
makes its first discoverable appearance in Aeschylus, *Agamemnon*, 1008–13;
it recurs in Aristotle, *Nicomachean Ethics*, 1110ª 8–11.

33 ff. In the story of his fatal encounter, Carew may have had in mind the
sonnet ('Era il giorno ch'al sol si scoloraro') in which Petrarch tells of having
fallen in love with Laura. Spenser, *Amoretti*, xii, has a similar tale to deliver,
but with the unjust conqueror no longer Love, as in Petrarch, but (as in
Carew) the lady herself.

11. 78. other trifeling hearts. Cf. Donne, *The Broken Heart*, lines 9–10:

> Ah, what a trifle is a heart,
>   If once into loves hands it come!

11. *Secresie protested.*

5–6. Silent as the night. Cf. Catullus, vii. 7–8:

> aut quam sidera multa, cum tacet nox,
> furtivos hominum vident amores.

12–16. The idea is borrowed from Donne, *The Dampe*, lines 1–4. See
Introduction, pp. liii–liv.

11. *A prayer to the Wind.* The theme is from Petrarch:

> Ite, caldi sospiri, al freddo core;
>   Rompete il ghiaccio che pietà contende;
>   E se prego mortale al ciel s'intende,
> Morte o mercè sia fine al mio dolore.

William Cartwright's *Absence* (*Comedies, Tragi-Comedies, With other Poems*,
1651, p. 248) closely resembles Carew's poem. The many manuscript
versions of *A prayer to the Wind* and a printed version in *Poems: written by
Wil. Shake-speare. Gent.*, 1640, exhibit great diversity; they are mostly
shorter than the standard text, though after line 6 *Poems: written by Wil.
Shake-speare* (with *S14* in substantial agreement) interpolates four lines:

> Taste her lippe, and then confesse,
> If *Arabia* doe possesse;
> Or that hony *Hybla* Hill,
> Sweets like those which thence distill.

Henry Lawes's musical setting, in *HL* and *Dx*, consists of three six-line
stanzas, substituting for lines 9–24 the couplet:

> haueing gainde so rich a fee
> doe an Other boone for me

—a substitution also found in *D2* and *S14*; at the same point *HM116*
substitutes:

> Tast her lipps & then confesse
> If Arabia doth possesse

Or ye Hybla honor'd hill
Sweet like these y^t thence distill
Hauing got so rich a fee,
Do an other boone for mee

D2, *S14*, and *HM116* agree in omitting lines 5–6 and 27–8. Which of these variants may represent reshapings, which preliminary versions of the poem, can only be guessed at.

12. *Mediocritie in love rejected. SONG.* The theme is that of many poets: cf. Petrarch's 'Morte o mercè sia fine al mio dolore', quoted in the note preceding. Torquato Tasso, in one of his *Rime amorose estravaganti*, 'Persuade la sua donna ad essere o in tutto crudele o in tutto pia' (ed. Solerti, 1898, ii. 355). Ben Jonson's lyric *The Dreame* begins, 'Or Scorne, or pittie on me take' (*Vnder-woods*, 1640, p. 177). A probable imitation of Carew is Sidney Godolphin's *Song*, 'Or love mee lesse, or love mee more' (*Poems of Sidney Godolphin*, ed. William Dighton, 1931, p. 8). A closer imitation is Charles Webbe's 'More Love or more disdain I crave', set by Henry Purcell and published in Banister and Low's *New Ayres and Dialogues*, 1678, pp. 36–7. Richard Lovelace employs the same theme (*Poems*, ed. Wilkinson, 1925, ii. 88):

A La Bourbon.

Done moy plus de pitiè ou plus de Cre-aultè, car sans ce Ie ne puis pas Viure, ne morir.

I.

Divine Destroyer pitty me no more,
  Or else more pitty me;
Give me more Love, Ah quickly give me more,
  Or else more Cruelty!

The source of Lovelace's French motto is not known.

    13. 8. Danaë was the mother of Perseus by Zeus, who came to her in the form of a shower of gold.

13. *Good counsel to a young Maid. SONG.*

    15. *Calenture.* A burning fever. The *Oxford English Dictionary* gives examples of the figurative sense (as here) from Nashe, Donne, and Jeremy Taylor.

14. *To my Mistris sitting by a Rivers side. AN EDDY.* This poem is founded directly upon a passage in Donne's *Elegie VI* (lines 21–34):

When I behold a streame, which, from the spring,
Doth with doubtfull melodious murmuring,
Or in a speechlesse slumber, calmely ride
Her wedded channels bosome, and then chide
And bend her browes, and swell if any bough
Do but stoop downe, or kisse her upmost brow;

Yet, if her often gnawing kisses winne
The traiterous banke to gape, and let her in,
She rusheth violently, and doth divorce
Her from her native, and her long-kept course,
And rores, and braves it, and in gallant scorne,
In flattering eddies promising retorne,
She flouts the channell, who thenceforth is drie;
Then say I; that is shee, and this am I.

A similar conceit appears in Samuel Daniel's *Musophilus* (*The Whole Workes*, 1623, p. 91 of second pagination). Carew uses the figure again in praising the deceased Earl of Anglesey (p. 70, lines 59–62).

15. *SONG.* Conquest by flight.

4. Cf. p. 40, line 9: 'blasting sighes'.

15. *SONG.* *To my inconstant Mistris.* The theme is that of Catullus, viii. 12–19, and Propertius, iii. xxv.

16. *SONG.* *Perswasions to enjoy.* The sophistical argument had already been presented more succinctly by Ronsard (*Sonnets pour Hélène*, ii. xxxii, in *Œuvres*, 1609, p. 276):

> Si la beauté se perd, fais en part de bonne heure,
> Tandis qu'en son Printemps tu la vois fleuronner:
> Si elle ne se perd, ne crain point de donner
> A tes amis le bien qui tousiours te demeure.

1. *the quick spirits in your eye.* 'Spirit', explains Burton, 'is a most subtle vapour, which is expressed from the *blood*, and the instrument of the soul, to perform all his actions; a common tie or *medium* betwixt the body and the soul, as some will have it; or, as *Paracelsus*, a fourth soul of itself. . . . Of these spirits there be three kinds, . . . *natural, vital, animal*.' (*Anatomy of Melancholy*, Part I, Sect. I, Mem. II, Subs. II.) Carew's 'quick' spirits here represent, specifically, the *vital spirits*, 'made in the heart of the *natural*, which by the arteries are transported to all the other parts: if these *spirits* cease, then life ceaseth, as in a *syncope* or swooning'.

17. *Ingratefull beauty threatned.* These lines were translated into Latin elegiacs by Henry Jacob, a fellow of Carew's college, Merton, and published by him in PHILOLOGIÆ *ANAKAΛΥΠΤΗ'PION Oratione celebratum Inaugurali, Quam publice habuit ad Oxonio-Mertonenses* HENRICUS IACOBIUS, 1652, p. 47. For the theme compare Propertius, ii. xi. 1–4:

> Scribant de te alii vel sis ignota licebit:
>   Laudet qui sterili semina ponit humo.
> Omnia, crede mihi, tecum uno munera lecto
>   Auferet extremi funeris atra dies. . . .

6. ympt. 'Imp' is a term of falconry, meaning to graft or repair a wing with feathers (*O.E.D.*).

7–8. Jacob, in his Latin version, relates the 'killing power' to that of Siren and of Basilisk; though it is by no means obvious that Carew ever saw the translation, these ideas may have been present in his own mind:

> Sirenem loqueris? cernis Basiliscon? at illa
> Arma ministrantem me fateare reum.

18. 17–18. Wise Poets. Compare Pico della Mirandola, *A Platonick Discourse upon Love*, tr. by Thomas Stanley (1651), i. vii: 'The ancient Ethnick Theologians, who cast Poetical vails over the face of their mysteries, express these three natures by other names.'

18. *Disdaine returned.*

13–20. Among the notes prepared by Joseph Haslewood for a projected edition of Carew (now in the possession of Mr. C. H. Wilkinson) is the following comment on this passage: 'q. Did our Author afterwards extend his poem, and thereby weaken the effect? The last stanza is not of the same highly poetic turn with the above, which were printed in his life time'—i.e. in Walter Porter's *Madrigales and Ayres*, 1632. This final stanza is often omitted by anthologists, with whom the previous lines are a favourite selection.

19. power. Here in the sense of supernatural being; *S14*, *A303*, *A7*, and *Ash 38* read 'God'.

19. *A Looking-Glasse.* This poem is in its first six lines nearly identical with another, *On his Mistres lookeinge in a glasse*, printed from manuscript on page 132. Since the 1640 *Poems*, which include the present poem but not that on page 132, appeared posthumously, we cannot be sure which of the continuations Carew might have preferred. With his treatment of the theme cf. Marino's *La Donna allo Specchio* (ed. Croce, 1913, p. 78) and Randolph's *To one admiring her selfe in a Looking-Glasse* (*Poems*, 1638, pp. 92–3).

10–12. The same conceit occurs in Marino's poem, lines 5–8:

> Ecco, ma per mio peggio, or s'innamora
> di se medesma al chiaro specchio avante;
> e, fatta mia rival, quel bel sembiante,
> ch'io solo amo ed adoro, ama ed adora.

13–15. Cf. *To A. D. unreasonable distrustfull of her owne beauty*, lines 21–4 (p. 84), and the note on that passage.

19. *An Elegie on the La: Pen: sent to my Mistresse out of* France. This lady's name was given as Pennington by Davies, Hazlitt, and Ebsworth; her true identity appears, however, as 'Lady Peniston' in *R2*, *S14*, and *HM198*, and was first published by Vincent, who writes: 'This lady was Martha, the fourth of the nine daughters of Sir Thomas Temple by his wife Esther . . . Martha married Sir Thomas Peniston of Leigh, Sussex, and died January 4, 1620' (a slip for 14 January 1619/20). 'The elegy was, therefore, composed while Carew was attending Lord Herbert of Cherbury, in Paris.' Lady Peniston was buried in the parish church of Stowe, Buckinghamshire, which was the Temples' family seat; upon one side of her sculptured monument is this inscription:

S THOMAS PENYSTON BARONETT, IN TESTIMONIE OF HIS TRVE AFFECTION,
VNTO THE VERTVOVS LADY HIS WIFE; MARTHA, LADY PENYSTON;
ERECTED THIS MONVMENT TO HIR MEMORIE.
DAVGHTER VNTO S THOMAS TEMPLE· KNIGHT & BARONETT;
SHE DIED THE XIIII· OF IANVARY M·DC·XIX· ATT THE AGE OF XXV·
ONE CHILDE SHE HAD IN THIS CHVRCH LYINGE ALSO INTERRED·

And on the other side appear the following verses:

SHVT IN THIS SEPVLCHRE LYES
THE ASHES OF FAIRE PENYSTON, WHO LOV'D
BY THE MOST WORTHY OF HIR TIME, REMOV'D
TO HEAV'N, SO TO DRAW VP HIR LOVERS EYES
TO THE DIVINE BEAWTIE OF THAT DEITIE, WHEREIN
SHE MAY LOVE ALL THAT LOVE HIR, AND NOT SINNE

This inscription, like Carew's poem, should be read in the light of Lady Peniston's reputation. She was the mistress (in succession to Venetia Stanley) of Richard Sackville, third Earl of Dorset; the affair 'was much talked of abroad and my Lord was condemned for it' (see V. Sackville-West, *Knole and the Sackvilles*, 1922, p. 58; *The Diary of the Lady Anne Clifford*, ed. V. Sackville-West, 1923, pp. 101–10). According to the *Diary*, the Earl paid his last visit 'to my Lady *Penniston's* at her Mother's lodgings in the Strand' on 29 November 1619. The scandal was perhaps open before Carew left England, and he very likely heard subsequent reports; hence the apparently ironic ambiguities in his Elegy, which despite its threnodic trappings is essentially a 'witty' love-lyric.

2. The 'cruell doome' is to be related to the 'alterations in my Mistresse' which inspired the poem on pp. 24–5.

20. 15–16 Cf. Donne, *A Funerall Elegie*, lines 11–12:

Can these memorials, ragges of paper, give
Life to that name, by which name they must live?

And Waller, *To Mr. Henry Lawes, Who Had Then Set a Song of Mine, in the Year 1635*, lines 1–2:

Verse makes heroic virtue live;
But you can life to verses give.

21. 74. blubbred. For Carew the word did not have its present 'low' flavour. Cf. Drummond of Hawthornden (ed. Kastner, ii. 215):

The woefull Marie midst a blubbred band
Of weeping virgines . . ..

And, later, Matthew Prior's lyric beginning 'Dear Cloe, how blubb'red is that pretty face' (ed. Waller, p. 77).

22. *To my Mistresse in absence.*

6. but a carkasse. Cf. *An Excuse of absence* (p. 131), lines 3–4.
9–10. Closely paralleled by Lovelace, *To Lucasta, Going beyond the Seas* (ed. Wilkinson, ii. 15):

Above the highest sphere wee meet
Unseene, unknowne, and greet as Angels greet.

Mr. Wilkinson points out the resemblance to Randolph's *A Platonick Elegie*.
Compare also the speeches of Melidoro, the Platonic lover, in Walter Montagu's
The Shepheard's Paradise, 1659 (written 1632–3), p. 89:

> *Meli.* We *Camena* are arived at Love's supreamest region, where there
> is all serenity and evennesse; there's not a breath of wind to ruffle this our
> smoothnesse: and from thence we look down on others, that are gon no
> higher then the second region yet, where's allwaies roughnesse and stormes
> that blow against them.

Similarly, Donne's *Extasie* and *A Valediction: forbidding mourning*, lines
13–24. For Carew, however, this sublime mingling of souls is not the ulti-
mate object, even ostensibly, but rather a means to

> cheat the lag, and lingring houres,
> Making our bitter absence sweet,
> Till soules, and bodyes both, may meet.

23. *To her in absence. A SHIP.*

1. a troubled sea of griefes. Cf. Catullus, lxiv. 62 and lxv. 4; Virgil,
Aeneid, viii. 19.

15. your armes, which are my port. Cf. Aurelian Townshend, 'Though
regions farr devided', in *Poems and Masks*, ed. Chambers, p. 19:

> Those armes, wherin wide open
> Loues fleete was wont to putt.

23. SONG. Eternitie of love protested.

24. 15–16. Probably a reminiscence of the fabled lamp mentioned by
Donne, *Epithalamion* ('Thou art repriv'd old yeare'), lines 215–16:

> Now, as in Tullias tombe, one lampe burnt cleare,
> Unchang'd for fifteene hundred yeare . . .

'They had a precious composition for lamps, amongst the ancients, reserved
especially for tombs, which kept light for many hundreds of years.' Donne,
Sermon preached on Christmas Day 1621 (ed. Alford, v. 55).

25. *Good counsell to a young Maid.* *D4* appends a quotation from Catullus
(lxii. 45–7):

> Sic virgo, dum intacta manet, tum cara suis; sed
> cum castum amisit polluto corpore florem;
> Nec pueris iucunda manet, nec grata puellis.

For lines 13–18 cf. also Catullus, lxiv. 143–8:

> Iam iam nulla viro iuranti femina credat,
> nulla viri speret sermones esse fideles;
> quis dum aliquid cupiens animus praegestit apisci,
> nil metuunt iurare, nihil promittere parcunt:
> sed simul ac cupidae mentis satiata libidost,
> dicta nihil metuere, nihil periuria curant.

26. *To* T. H. *a Lady resembling my Mistresse.* Both ladies remain un-identified.

27. 16–27. Cf. two passages in Donne: *Elegie X* ('The Dreame'), lines 1–6:

> Image of her whom I love, more then she,
> Whose faire impression in my faithfull heart,
> Makes mee her *Medall*, and makes her love mee,
> As Kings do coynes, to which their stamps impart
> The value: goe, and take my heart from hence,
> Which now is growne too great and good for me:

and *Of the Progresse of the Soule. The second Anniversary*, lines 223–5:

> she whose rich beauty lent
> Mintage to other beauties, for they went
> • But for so much as they were like to her.

27. *To Saxham.* Little Saxham, near Bury, was the seat of Sir John Crofts (1563–1628), knighted in Ireland in 1599, whose son William was created Lord Crofts of Saxham in 1656. Another son, John Crofts (baptized at Toddington, Beds., on 20 Dec. 1598), accompanied Carew to France with Lord Herbert of Cherbury in 1619—Herbert describes him as 'one of my principal gentlemen, and afterwards made the King's Cup-bearer'—and Carew's con-tinuously close relations with the family are shown by the poems connected with its members (see pages 30, 56, 59, 79, 83, and 114). The mansion, according to Nichols (*Progresses of James the First*, iii. 587 n.), was 'probably built in the reign of Henry the Seventh. Lord Crofts added a grand apartment for the reception of Charles the Second; but the whole was pulled down in 1771, though it is said to have appeared as sound then as at its first erection. Some stained-glass was removed to the Church.' A map dated 1638 is repro-duced in S.H.A.H., *Little Saxham Parish Registers, 1559 to 1850*, Wood-bridge, 1901, which states that the manor remained in the possession of the Crofts family until 1789, when it was sold to Lord Cornwallis. Of the hall, adds the writer, there is 'not even a ruin. There is nothing but a moat in the middle of a field enclosing nothing. Just outside the moat are cottages and farm buildings, some of which may represent the old stables.' Augustine Page, in *A Supplement to the Suffolk Traveller*, 1844, p. 685, recalls that 'The Hall was one of those picturesque, brick embattled, manor houses, with towers, irregular gables, finials, and clusters of ornamental chimneys, the style of which prevails in an inferior degree in the neighbouring Hall of Westow'.

Vincent points out the probability that 'before composing this address to Saxham, Carew had somewhat carefully studied Ben Jonson's address to Penshurst'. The ultimate influence of Martial (iii. lviii) is apparent in both poems.

28. 11. 'Sterve . . . in Dutch is to dye, though we commonly use it for a thing *dead*, either by hunger or cold': Sir Francis Kynaston, *The Loves of Troilus and Cresseid*, 1796 (written about 1635), Commentary, p. 5. The *O.E.D.* records transitive uses of *sterve* or *starve* in a similar sense from Shakespeare, *Two Gentlemen*, iv. iv. 159, and Milton, *Paradise Lost*, ii. 600.

17–18. The abundant game mentioned by Carew would probably have come from the extensive warren which was part of the manor. 'The measure of this in the 1638 map is about 220 acres, including a wood of 61 acres. That wood is still there. . . . It is now known as the old Warren wood.' (*Little Saxham Parish Registers*, p. 235, which quotes from Bailey's *Dictionary*, 1763, s.v. 'Warren': 'a franchise or privileged place by prescription or grant to keep beasts and fowls of warren, as conies, hares, partridges and pheasants.')

18. Volarie. An aviary.

21. Partiridge. The first *i* may be due to a misprint, though the *O.E.D.* cites analogous forms (perterych, parteriche, partoriches, parterige) as late as 1550.

47–8. Cf. Ben Jonson, *To Penshurst*:

> Here no man tells my cups; nor, standing by,
> A waiter, doth my gluttony envy.

Carew's version misses Jonson's distinctively personal humour.

29. *Vpon a Ribband.*

1. This silken wreath, which circles in mine arme. Cf. Donne, *The Funerall*, line 3: 'That subtile wreath of haire, which crowns my arme'; and *The Relique.* Ebsworth, to forestall a possible ambiguity, prints 'circles-in'.

Bracelets of hair or silk were a common token of favour; Puget de la Serre's *The Secretary in Fashion*, 1640, pp. 130–1, contains model letters from a gallant requesting 'new chaines, by demanding a Bracelet of your Haire', and from the lady granting the request.

19. the Center. According to Ptolemaic astronomy, the earth.

30. *To the King at his entrance into* Saxham, *by Master* Io. Crofts. On 12 February 1619/20 Chamberlain wrote to Sir Dudley Carleton that King James and his Court 'pass the time merrily at Newmarket, and the running. Masque ranges all over the Country where there be fit subjects to entertain it, as lately they have been at Sir John Crofts' near Bury, and in requital those Ladies have invited them to a Masque of their own invention, all those fair sisters being summoned for the purpose, so that on Thursday next the King, Prince, and all the Court go thither a Shroving.' (Nichols, *Progresses of James the First*, iii. 587.) Again on 16 February 1621/2 Chamberlain reports that the King is 'still at Newmarket, but expected here within ten or twelve days. He is to go next week a Shroving to Sir John Crofts. That Lady and her daughter Cecily have been much at Newmarket of late.' (Nichols, iv. 752–3.) Sir John Crofts had entertained the King with a masque the previous December; in March the King spoke of 'lying reports abroad' that he was married to Sir John Crofts's daughter—probably meaning Cecilia (*Calendars of State Papers, Domestic*, 22 Dec. 1621 and 19 March 1622). It was for one of the royal visits that Carew's verses were written, to be recited by John Crofts, Cecilia's brother. At the time of the King's earliest visit John Crofts, though still in Herbert's service with the Paris embassy, was temporarily in England (see p. xxxii).

17–18. See Exodus xii. 7.

31. *Vpon the sicknesse of* (E. S.). E. S. is perhaps Elizabeth Sheldon, daughter of Thomas Sheldon of Hoby, Leicestershire, whom Carew helped to woo for Christopher Villiers, created Earl of Anglesey on 18 April 1623. In his Elegy addressed to the Countess upon the Earl's death in 1630 (p. 69), Carew recalls his services as an emissary in the courtship; and the reference in the present poem (lines 16–17) to the 'fruit . . . / Which Princes have desir'd to taste' apparently supports the identification.

15. this goodly tree. Cf. Marino, *In morte della Sig. N. Rouera*, lines 12–13 (*La Lira*, 1625, Parte Terza, p. 142):

> *Inuido Ciel, perche sterpar sì presto*
> *L'arbor gentil?*

32. 32. panting. Producing gusts of air by fanning. The *O.E.D.* does not cite the word in this exact meaning, though it records such partly figurative uses as Donne's 'And bellows pant below, which them do move' (*Satyre II*, line 16) and Pope's 'The dying gales that pant upon the trees' (*Eloisa to Abelard*, line 159). C. L. Powell, in *Modern Language Review*, xi (1916), 287, prefers the more commonplace 'painted', a reading found in *S14* and in the first of two copies in *D8*.

35. balmie sweat. Cf. *Vpon a Mole in Celias bosome* (p. 113), line 10: 'A rowling file of Balmy sweat'. Both passages echo Donne's *Elegie VIII*— 'As the sweet sweat of Roses in a Still', &c.

36. her hairie Coronet. Imitated from Donne, *Elegie XIX* ('Going to Bed'), lines 15–16:

> Off with that wyerie Coronet and shew
> The haiery Diademe which on you doth grow.

40. a Canopie. Cf. *The second Rapture* (p. 103), line 11.
42. Calenture. A fever. Cf. p. 13, line 15, and the relevant note.

32. *A New-yeares Sacrifice. To* Lucinda. In *W* dated '1632'—i.e. 1633, New Style. Lucinda is the famous Lucy, Countess of Carlisle (1599–1660), to whom Carew refers under the same name in his poem *To the New-yeare, for the Countesse of Carlile* (p. 91). A daughter of the ninth Earl of Northumberland, she became in 1617 the second wife of James Hay, one of King James's favourites and first Earl of Carlisle (died March 1636). At the court of Charles she was admired for beauty and wit; poems were addressed to her by Waller, Davenant, Cartwright, Suckling, Herrick, and Voiture, and Sir Toby Matthews wrote an enthusiastic prose 'Character' (first published in *A Collection of Letters, made by Sᵣ Tobie Mathews Kᵗ*, 1660). Suckling wrote a dialogue *Vpon my Lady Carliles walking in Hampton-Court garden* (*Fragmenta Aurea*, 1646, pp. 26–7) with himself and T. C.—almost certainly Thomas Carew—as speakers; this is as follows:

Thom.

Idst thou not find the place inspir'd,
And flow'rs as if they had desir'd
No other Sun, start from their beds,
And for a sight steal out their heads?

Heardst thou not musick when she talk't?
And didst not find that as she walkt
She threw rare perfumes all about
Such as bean-blossoms newly out,
Or chafed spices give?—

J. S.

I must confesse those perfumes (*Tom*)
I did not smell; nor found that from
Her passing by, ought sprung up new,
The flow'rs had all their birth from you;
For I pass't o're the self same walk,
And did not find one single stalk
Of any thing that was to bring
This unknown after after spring.

Thom.

Dull and insensible, could'st see
A thing so near a Deity
Move up and down, and feel no change?

J. S.

None, and so great, were alike strange,
I had my Thoughts, but not your way,
All are not born (Sir) to the Bay;
Alas! *Tom*, I am flesh and blood,
And was consulting how I could
In spite of masks and hoods descry
The parts deni'd unto the eye;
I was undoing all she wore,
And had she walkt but one turn more,
Eve in her first state had not been
More naked, or more plainly seen.

Thom.

'T was well for thee she left the place,
There is great danger in that face;
But had'st thou view'd her legg and thigh,
And upon that discovery
Search't after parts that are more dear
(As Fancy seldom stops so near)
No time or age had ever seen
So lost a thing as thou hadst been.

'Amongst men', wrote Sir Toby Matthews, 'her person is both considered and admired; and her Wit, being most eminent, among the rest of her great abilities, She affects the conversation of the persons, who are most famed for it' (*A Collection of Letters*, fol. A5ʳ). 'A nobler, nor more intelligent friendship', wrote Strafford on 5 November 1640, 'did I never meet with in all my life'

(Whitaker, *Life of Sir George Radcliffe*, p. 221). Her portrait was four times painted by Van Dyck.

33. 18. *the involved Serpent of the yeare.* The Egyptian symbol of endless time as a snake devouring its own tail is one of the emblems included in Ripa's *Iconologia*, 1611, p. 152. Cf. Marino, *Buone feste. Al Signor Giulio Coccapani* (*La Lira*, 1625, Parte Terza, p. 249):

> *Anno, che quasi Serpe attorno intorno*
> *Mordi te stesso, onde rinasci, e godi,*

and Drummond of Hawthornden, *Song II*, lines 79–80 (ed. Kastner, i. 67):

> *Bee but the same which vnder* Saturnes *Raigne*
> *Did the serpenting* Seasons *enterchaine.*

34. *SONG.* To her againe, she burning in a Feaver.

4. *she now is fire.* The reading of 1640 hardly makes sense, and the second 'that was' is most readily explainable as due to miscopying from the earlier part of the line. Hazlitt was the first to follow the manuscript reading, from *H17*.

10. The 'and', which was dropped in 1640, is needed metrically, and also helps to smooth the construction. *Gods* is, of course, possessive, not plural. *He* refers to *Love* in the preceding line.

35. *Vpon the Kings sicknesse.* Vincent's conjecture, on internal evidence, that this poem refers not to Charles I's attack of small-pox in 1633 but to the fatal illness of James I in 1625 is corroborated by the catalogue in *S.23*, which lists it as 'when k: James was sicke'.

18. *sober, strong, and young.* Three adjectives equally inappropriate to James. Except that Carew might be expected to indulge in hyperbolic flattery, they would furnish strong evidence for identifying 'the King' as Charles.

19–20. An echo of James's own statement in *The trew Law of free Monarchies* (King James I, *Workes*, 1616, p. 204): 'The King towards his people is rightly compared to a father of children, and to a head of a body composed of diuers members: . . . And as there is euer hope of curing any diseased member by the direction of the head, as long as it is whole; but by the contrary, if it be troubled, all the members are partakers of that paine, so is it betwixt the Prince and his people.'

35–6. 29–38. *That ruddie morning beame.* Prince Charles, aged twenty-four (born 19 November 1600).

36. *SONG.* To a Lady not yet enjoy'd by her Husband.

36. 1–4. The idea of these lines—that of hearts mingling by interchange of spirits through the eyes—is expanded and clarified by Castiglione in the Third Book of *The Courtier* (tr. Hoby, Everyman's Library, p. 247): 'For those lively spirits that issue out at the eyes, because they are engendred nigh the hart, entring in like case into the eyes that they are levelled at, like a shaft to the pricke, naturally pearce to the hart, as to their resting place and there are at rest with those other spirits: and with the most subtill and fine nature of bloud which they carrie with them, infect the bloude about the hart, where

they are come to, and warme it: and make it like unto themselves, and apt to receive the imprinting of the image, which they have carried away with them. . . . The eyes therefore lye lurking like souldiers in war, . . . and as soone as he [the lover] is at hand, the eyes shoote, and like sorcerers bewitch, and especially when by a right line they send their glistering beames into the eyes of the wight beloved, at the time when they doe the like, because the spirites meete together, and in that sweete encounter the one taketh the others nature and qualitie.' Compare Carew's '*If the quick spirits in your eye*' (p. 16), his *Song. Celia singing* (p. 39), *An Hymeneall Dialogue* (p. 66), and the relevant notes.

3. With Carew's '*pure wreathe of eye-beames*' compare Donne, *The Extasie*, lines 7–8, upon which Carew's phrase may be modelled:

> Our eye-beames twisted, and did thred
> Our eyes, upon one double string.

5. Gesner (*Historiæ Animalium Liber III. qui est de Auium natura*, 1585, p. 171) says that eagles test their young by forcing them to gaze steadfastly at the sun; those that flinch are driven from the nest. He cites numerous classical precedents for the story, a commonplace of Renaissance poets. Carew uses the image again in his poem *To Ben. Iohnson*, lines 11–12 (p. 64).

13. *A Dragon kept the golden fruit.* Giordano Bruno writes, in his *Spaccio de la Bestia Trionfante* (*Opere Italiane*, ed. Gentile, Bari, 1927, ii. 61–2): 'Rispose Apolline: . . . le poma d'oro saranno la beltade, il drago sarà la fierezza, Giasone sarà l'amante.' The reference in Bruno is to the expedition of the Argonauts; Carew must have known the passage, since he made the *Spaccio* the pattern for his *Coelum Britannicum* in 1634. Otherwise the golden apples of the Hesperides, carried off in one of Hercules' twelve labours, furnish a more natural reference for the lines.

37. SONG. The willing Prisoner to his Mistris. The willing prisoner is a conventional enough figure. Compare Propertius, i. vi. 27–8:

> Multi longinquo periere in amore libenter,
> in quorum numero me quoque terra tegat.

Also Thomas Bateson, *The Second Set of Madrigales*, 1618, No. XXVII (Fellowes, *English Madrigal Verse*, p. 23):

> Her hair the net of golden wire,
>> Wherein my heart, led by my wandering eyes,
>> So fast entangled is that in no wise
> It can nor will again retire;
>> But rather will in that sweet bondage die,
>> Than break one hair to gain her liberty.

Compare also Drummond of Hawthornden, *Sonnet IV* (ed. Kastner, i. 5):

> Faire is my Yoke, though grieuous bee my Paines,
> Sweet are my Wounds, although they deeply smart,
> My Bit is Gold, though shortned bee the Raines,
> My Bondage braue, though I may not depart.

Of similar opinion are Spenser, *Amoretti*, lxv; Daniel, *Delia*, xiv. But the first two stanzas of Carew's poem are close enough to a Chançon by Pontus de

Tyard (*Œuvres poetiques*, 1573, fol. ciij^{r-v} of second foliation) to suggest specific copying:

> *Plaise à qui plaire peut, & louë qui voudra*
> *La liberté, qu'il à loing d'Amoureuse guerre:*
> *Quand à moy, le doux nœud dont Amour mon cueur serre,*
> *Me plaist tant, que iamais il ne se dissoudra. . . .*
>   *Quand à moy ie seray comblé d'assez grand hœur*
> *De louer les doux yeux de ma docte maistresse,*
> *Veoir sa gaye beauté, & dans sa blonde tresse*
> *Les lacs d'or, dont Amour tient enlacé mon cueur.*

37. *A flye that flew into my Mistris her eye.* This poem, with the signature 'Cary', is recorded by Grierson (*Poems of Donne*, ii, p. ci) as being included in the 'Phillipps' MS., which he gives convincing reasons for dating between 1619 and 1623. It must thus be included among the earlier of Carew's poems. In the manuscript anthologies, where it is one of the most popular, variant readings are extremely numerous but individually unimportant. With Carew's treatment of the theme—a favourite from Petrarch's time to his own—compare Guarini's Madrigal XXXVII (*Rime*, 1598, p. 76):

Core in Farfalla.

> *Vna Farfalla cupida, e vagante*
> *Fatt' è il mio cor amante;*
> *Che và, quasi per gioco,*
> *Scherzando intorno al foco*
> *Di due begli occhi, e tante uolte, e tante*
> *Vola, e riuola, e fugge, e torna, e gira;*
> *Che ne l'amato lume*
> *Lascierà con la vita al fin le piume.*
> *Ma chi di ciò sospira,*
> *Sospira à torto. ardor caro, e felice*
> *Morrà Farfalla, e sorgerà fenice.*

Where the theme is a cliché, the points of difference are of more interest than the similarities. In Carew the poetic Farfalla gives place to the common fly, and there is no overt symbolism; what attracts him is the ingenuity of the theme itself, which he develops with elegant precision and the lightest possible touch of pathos.

15–16. Cf. Ovid, *Metamorphoses*, ii. 319–32.

38. *SONG. Celia singing.* Some manuscripts say that Celia was singing 'in a Gallery at Yorke house' (*HM116*, *H31*, *A30*, *E24*, *R1*, and *Ash 36*); others that her song was addressed 'to her lute in Arundel garden' (*A118* and *A221*). The Duke's Gallery at York House contained a collection of statues and paintings, including nineteen Titians, which the Duke of Buckingham had bought from Rubens. If Arundel garden was the scene, the 'statues' mentioned by Carew were the Arundel marbles, part of the collection made by Thomas Howard, second Earl of Arundel (1585?–1646), and afterwards presented by his grandson, the sixth Duke of Norfolk, to the University of Oxford.

3–4. Cf. Lovelace, *A Dialogue. Lute and Voice* (ed. Wilkinson, ii. 148):

> *V.* Touch thy soft Lute, and in each gentle thread,
>   The *Lyon* and the *Panther* Captive lead.

Carew's Boar and Panther are hardly to be conceived as statues; they may stand hyperbolically for the less ferocious beasts of a deer-park. Cf. Jean Puget de la Serre's account of 'les nouuelles magnificences du Palais de Sainct-James' in his *Histoire de l'Entree de la Reyne Mere dv Roy Tres-Crestien, dans la Grande-Bretagne,* 1639, fol. Kᵛ: 'Ce Jardin est borné d'vn costé d'vne longue gallerie couuerte & grillee par le deuant, ou l'on peut admirer toutes les plus rares merueilles de l'Italie, en vn grand nombre de statues de pierre, & de bronse; . . . Ces deux Jardins sont limitez d'vn grand Parc, a diuerses allées, toutes couuertes de l'ombrage d'vn nombre infiny de chesnes. . . . Ce parc est remply de bestes sauuages, toutesfois, comme c'est le lieu ordinaire de la promenade des Dames de la Court, leurs douceurs les ont tellement apriuoisees, qu'elles se rendent toutes a la force de leurs appas, plustost qu'a la poursuitte des chiens.' In any case the poem implies a comparison of Celia's music to that of Orpheus, whose song was said to move trees, beasts, and stones; cf. Ovid, *Metamorphoses,* xi. 1–2.

39. SONG. *Celia* singing. In Playford's *Select Ayres and Dialogues, The Second Book,* 1669, p. 29, Henry Lawes's setting of this poem is headed: '*Vpon the Hearing* Mrs. MARY KNIGHT *Sing*'. This lady, a singer and actress, was a favourite of Charles II's; Pepys, on 4 September 1668, resolved that he must endeavour to hear her. The alternative title (doubtless supplied by Playford) is thus of no help in identifying Celia.

1–4. For the entry of Love's dart through the eyes Burton expounds the accepted theory (*Anatomy of Melancholy,* Part III, Sect. II, Mem. II, Subs. II): 'But the most familiar and usual cause of Love is that which comes by sight, which conveys those admirable rays of beauty and pleasing graces to the heart.' Cf. Pico della Mirandola, *A Platonick Discourse upon Love,* tr. Thomas Stanley (1651), ii. vi: 'The desire of this Beauty is Love; arising onely from one knowing faculty, the Sight: & that gave *Plotinus*[1] (*Ennead* 3. lib. 5. 3.) occasion to derive ἔρως *Love,* from ὅρασις *Sight.*'

13. After this line *The Academy of Complements,* 1650, interpolates:

> And Sol is mounted on his way,

thus filling out (though flatly) a second nine-line stanza metrically parallel to lines 1–9.

39. *SONG.* To one that desired to know my Mistris. Cf. Donne, *The Curse*:

> Who ever guesses, thinks, or dreames he knowes
>   Who is my mistris, wither by this curse . . ..

The similarity does not extend beyond that of theme.

40. *In the person of a Lady to her inconstant servant.* Torquato Tasso has three madrigals on a similar subject, written 'Ad istanza di una gentildonna'

---

[1] Printed *Plotonius.*

(*Rime*, ed. Solerti, 1898, pp. 460–1). Thomas Randolph has verses of *A Wronged Mistresse to a False Seruant* (ed. G. Thorn-Drury, pp. 162–3), and Richard Lovelace elaborates the situation in his poem *A forsaken Lady to her false Servant that is disdained by his new Mistris* (ed. Wilkinson, ii. 32).

9. Bepal'd with blasting sighes. Cf. p. 15, lines 3–4.

41. *Truce in Love entreated.* Analogues are numerous; cf. the poem 'Love if a God thou art', ascribed to Donne (ed. Grierson, i. 448). But Carew apparently based his poem on the following sonnet by Desportes (*Amours d'Hippolyte*, X, in *Les Premières Œuvres*, Paris, 1600, p. 75ᵛ) or upon a model common to both:

> Amour, qui vois mon cœur à tes piés abbatu,
> Tu le vois tout couuert de sagettes mortelles,
> Pourquoy donc sans profit en pers-tu de nouuelles ?
> Puis que ie suis à toy pourquoy me poursuis-tu ?
> Si tu veux, courageux, esprouuer ta vertu,
> Décoche tous ces traits sur les ames rebelles,
> Sans blesser, trop cruel, ceux qui te sont fidelles,
> Et qui sous ton enseigne ont si bien combatu.
> Quand tu tires sur moy tu fais breches sur breches:
> Donc sans les perdre ainsi, garde ces belles fleches:
> Pour guerroyer les Dieux, & m'accorde la paix.
> Ah ! i'entens bien que c'est, Amour veut que ie meure:
> Ie mourray, mais au moins ce confort me demeure,
> Que la mort de moy seul luy couste mille traits.

4–6. Cf. Ovid, *Amores*, i. ii. 22: 'Nec tibi laus, armis victus inermis ero.' The inglorious conquest reappears in Petrarch ('Era il giorno', lines 9–14) in a form nearer Carew's:

> Trovommi Amor del tutto disarmato,
> Et aperta la via per gli occhi al core,
> Che di lagrime son fatti uscio e varco.
> Però, al mio parer, non li fu onore
> Ferir me de saetta in quello stato,
> A voi armata non mostrar pur l'arco.

41. *To my Rivall.* See note on the next poem.

11. stroake. Soothe, flatter, propitiate.

42. *Boldnesse in love.* In *Holborn-Drollery*, 1673, the first eight lines of this poem are joined with the verses *To my Rivall* (p. 41), and the curious synthesis is rounded off with an extra couplet, which can hardly be of Carew's composition:

> Cease Rival then, and thou'lt descry
> Thou art the blushing Morn, the Planet I.

The property of the marigold (Latin *solsequium*) of opening when the sun shines is a poetic commonplace. Cf. Shakespeare, *Winter's Tale*, IV. iv. 105: 'The marigold, that goes to bed wi' the sun.'

42. A Pastorall Dialogue.

  5–16. Cf. *The willing Prisoner to his Mistris* (p. 37).

44. 41. thy faire grove. Probably imitated from Ben Jonson: 'By that tall Grove, your haire' (*An Elegie*, in *Vnder-woods*, 1640, p. 189). Carew's phrase, with the 'golden mountaine' of line 35, was in turn copied by Robert Heath (*Clarastella*, 1650, p. 16):

> May this fair grove then never fade!
> Or be by blasting time decaid!
> May age ne'r hoar that lovely hair,
> Or leave that golden mountain bare!

Cf. Randolph, *In Anguem, qui Lycorin dormientem amplexus est*, English version (ed. Thorn-Drury, p. 32):

> Hence he slides
> Up to her lockes, and through her tresses glides,
> Her yellow tresses; dazel'd to behold
> A glistring grove, an intire wood of Gold.

And Henry Vaughan, *In Amicum fœneratorem* (ed. Martin, i. 44):

> Rove in their *Amber-tresses*, and unfold
> That glist'ring grove, the Curled wood of gold.

  49–50. Cf. Shakespeare, *Romeo and Juliet*, ii. ii. 92–3:

> At lovers' perjuries,
> They say, Jove laughs.

Also Ovid, *Ars amatoria*, i. 633: 'Iuppiter ex alto periuria ridet amantum', and Tibullus, III. vi. 49–50: 'periuria ridet amantum | Iuppiter'.

44. *Griefe ingrost*. Ingrost: 'Collected from various quarters, amassed in large quantity' (*O.E.D.*). In *A118* and *A221* this poem appears in the following fragmentary form:

> His perplexed loue.
> If she must still denye
> Weepe not but dye
> For my faire will not giue
> Loue enough to let me liue,
> Nor dart from her faire eye
> Scorne enough to make me dye:
> Then let me weepe alone till her kind breath,
> Or blow my teares a way or speake my death.

It is at least possible that the poem was developed from such a nucleus, though the illogical 'For' at line 3 of the fragment shows miscopying or faulty memory.

  45. 13–16. Cf. *Mediocritie in love rejected* (p. 12).

45. A Pastorall Dialogue. In general conception and a few details this poem shows the influence of *Romeo and Juliet*, iii. v. 1–36, which also portrays the reluctant parting of lovers at dawn.

46. *Red, and white Roses*. Translated and expanded from the following lyric by Joannes Bonefonius (*Pancharis*, xxvi, in *Delitiæ C. Poetarum Gallorum*, 1609, i. 674):

> En flores tibi mitto discolores,
> Pallentemque rosam, & rosam rubentem.
> Illam cùm aspicies; miselli amantis
> Puta pallidulos videre vultus.
> Cùm tueberis hanc rubore tinctam,
> Putes igne rubens cor intueri.

In his expansion of the poem Carew has incorporated some details from a similar lyric by Marino (*La Lira*, 1625, Parte Terza, p. 81):

> Fiori donati.

> *Qualhora in questi fiori,*
> *Vn candido, vn vermiglio,*
> *Volgo la mente, e'l ciglio,*
> *Del bel sen, de' begli occhi, ond' io sospiro,*
> *E le neui, e le fiamme inun vi miro.*
> *Miroui ancora del mio core essangue*
> *E l'innocenza, e'l sangue,*
> *O caro don di cara Donna in cui*
> *Io siamo espressi, & ella,*
> *L'vn fedel, l'altra bella.*[1]

47. *To my Cousin* (C. R.) *marrying my Lady* (A.). 'The said Sir *Walt. Raleigh*', writes Anthony Wood (*Athenæ Oxonienses*, 1691, col. 374), 'left behind him a Son named *Carew Raleigh* . . . [who] became a Gent. Com. of *Wadham* coll. in 1620. aged 16. but proved quite different in Spirit from his Father. Afterwards he was Gent. of the Privy Chamber to *K. Ch.* I. who honoured him with a kind token at his leaving *Hampton Court*, when he was jugled into the Isle of *Wight*, cringed afterwards to the Men in Power. . . . I have seen also some Sonnets of his composition, and certain ingenious discourses, but whether ever printed I know not. . . . Sir *Hen. Wotton* gives him the Character of *a Gentleman of dextrous abilities* . . .; and so by others he is with honour mentioned; but far, god wot, was he from his Fathers parts, either as to the Sword or Pen. He was buried in his Fathers grave in the month of *Decemb.* (or thereabouts,) *an.* 1666. leaving Issue behind him a Daughter.' Born in 1605, Carew Ralegh was Sir Walter's second son; Richard Carew of Antony was his godfather. The 'Cousin' of the title has some remote justification: Carew Ralegh's maternal grandmother was Anne Carew, daughter of Sir Nicholas Carew (d. 1539) of Beddington in Surrey; the Carews of Beddington were a younger branch of the family, settled there from the time of Edward III (see *Dictionary of National Biography*, ix. 56). In 1629 Carew Ralegh obtained the manor of East Horsley in Surrey from the Earl of Southampton; a visit there by Thomas Carew is mentioned in one of Suckling's letters: 'I . . . did conclude at last, That *Horseley* Air did excel the Waters of the *Bath*; just so much as Love is a more noble disease then the

---

[1] In line 4 the original reads 'beglio'. The *inun* (printed solid) of line 5 becomes *non* in the next edition, 1629.

Pox' (see p. 213). Carew Ralegh was made a Gentleman of the Privy Chamber in 1635. His verses beginning 'Careless of Love, and free from Fears', set by Henry Lawes, were published in *Ayres and Dialogues, The First Booke*, 1653. He married Philippa, second wife and widow of the wealthy Sir Anthony Ashley, Clerk of the Privy Council, who had died in 1627, aged 76 (*D.N.B.*). I have not been able to discover the date of the wedding.

10. *Semele*. Destroyed by beholding the full majesty of her lover Jove, which Juno had tricked her into demanding that she might see. Cf. Ovid, *Metamorphoses*, iii. 259–309.

49. *A Rapture*. This, the most famous of Carew's poems, was probably written 'In wisdomes nonage, and unriper yeares', as we are told in *The Great Assises Holden in Parnassus by Apollo and his assessours*, 1645. Its influence is manifest in such lyrics as Cleveland's *To Chloris: A Rapture*, Randolph's *A Pastorall Courtship* (which shows close parallels), and Cartwright's *Song of Dalliance*. Its relation to another work, *The Tragedy of Nero, Newly Written*, published anonymously in 1624 and reprinted in 1633, which contains in one of the speeches of Petronius lines very similar to parts of *A Rapture*, is less easy to establish. Vincent assumed that Carew imitated the play; to me it appears more likely that the passage in *Nero*, a verse-drama full of echoes from the courtly poets, was composed with Carew's work fresh in the author's mind. The speech in question is as follows:

> . . . Death, the grim knaue, but leades you to the doore,
> Where entred once, all curious pleasures come
> To meete, and welcome you.
> A troupe of beauteous Ladies from whose eyes,
> Loue, thousand arrowes, thousand graces shootes;
> Puts forth their faire hands to you, and inuites
> To their greene arbours and close shadowed walks,[1]
> Whence, banisht is the roughnesse of our yeeres:
> Onely the west wind blowes; Ith euer Spring,
> And euer Sommer: There the laden bowes
> Offer their tempting burdens to your hand,
> Doubtfull your eye, or tast inuiting more:
> There euery man his owne desires enioyes;
> Faire *Lucrece* lies, by lusty *Tarquins* side,
> And wooes him now againe to rauish her.
> Nor vs, (though *Romane*) *Lais* will refuse,
> To *Corinth* any man may goe; no maske,
> No enuious garment doth those beauties hide,
> Which *Nature* made, so mouing, to be spide,
> But in bright Christall, which doth supply all,
> And white transparent vailes they are attyr'd,
> Through which the pure snow vnderneath doth shine;
> (Can it be snowe, from whence such flames arise?)
> Mingled with that faire company, shall we
> On bankes of *Violets*, and of *Hiacinths*

[1] walks, 1633: walles, 1624.

Of loues deuising, sit, and gently sport,
And all the while melodious Musique heare,
And Poets songs, that Musique farre exceed
The old *Anacreon*[1] crown'd with smyling flowers,
And amorous *Sapho*, on her Lesbian Lute
Beauties sweet Scarres, and *Cupids* godhead sing.

(*The Tragedy of Nero, Newly Written*, 1624, fol. G4ᵛ.) This is just the sort
of thing one would expect to obtain from the impressionistic re-creation of *A
Rapture* at the hand of a second-rate poet. It is easy to see how Carew's

No curtaine there, though of transparant lawne,
Shall be before thy virgin-treasure drawne

and his 'Thy bared snow, and thy unbraded gold' should have impressed the
dramatist sufficiently to result in the 'white transparent vailes' and the 'pure
snow' of the speech; it is harder to imagine how the reverse process could ever
have taken place. If, then, the speech was patterned after *A Rapture*, the
latter must be dated before 1624. As his own principal models Carew pro-
bably took Donne's *Elegie XIX* ('Going to Bed'), the second of the *Basia* of
Johannes Secundus, and—especially in his denunciation of Tyrant Honour—
the chorus 'O bella età dell' oro' from Torquato Tasso's *Aminta*, Act I.

3. Cf. Donne, *The Dampe*, lines 11–12:

First kill th'enormous Gyant, your *Disdaine*,
And let th'enchantresse *Honor*, next be slaine.

Also Daniel, *A Pastorall*, translated from the chorus by Tasso mentioned
above (*Delia*, in *The Whole Workes*, 1623, pp. 178–9 of second pagination):

But onely for that name,
That Idle name of wind:
That Idoll of deceit, that empty sound
Call'd HONOR, which became
Thy tyran of the minde:
And so torments our Nature without ground,
Was not yet vainly found:
Nor yet sad griefes imparts
Amidst the sweet delights
Of ioyfull amorous wights.
Nor were his hard lawes knowne to free-borne hearts.
But golden lawes like these
Which nature wrote. *That's lawfull which doth please.*

10. the grim Swisse. Cf. Donne's

The grim eight-foot-high iron-bound serving-man,
That oft names God in oathes, and onely than,
He that to barre the first gate, doth as wide
As the great Rhodian Colossus stride,

of *Elegie IV* ('The Perfume').

[1] Printed *Anaicean* in both 1624 and 1633.

11. *Only tame fooles.* The 'Only to tame fooles' of the 1640 text is bad metrically. The emendation is supported by all eleven manuscript copies collated.

19–20. Echoed by Randolph, *Upon Love fondly refus'd for Conscience sake,* lines 11–14:

> It was not love, but love transform'd to vice
> Ravish'd by envious Avarice,
> Made women first impropriate; all were free,
> Inclosures mans Inventions be.

Cf. Cleveland, *To the State of Love or the Senses' Festival,* line 28: 'I now impale her in mine arms.'

50. 27. *our close Ivy twines.* Cf. Catullus, lxi. 34–5; Donne, *Elegie XII* ('His parting from her'), line 59: 'Let our armes clasp like Ivy.'

52 ff. A. F. Allison (*Review of English Studies,* xxxiii (1947), 34 ff.) points out an echo of Carew's 'amorous languishment' in Crashaw's *On a prayer booke sent to Mrs. M. R.,* line 63: 'Amorous Languishments, Luminous trances', and shows that lines 81–117 in Crashaw's poem draw heavily on Carew's lines 55–62 and 131–4.

51. 75–6. Cf. Donne, *Elegie VIII* ('The Comparison'), lines 35–8:

> Then like the Chymicks masculine equall fire,
> Which in the Lymbecks warme wombe doth inspire
> Into th'earths worthlesse durt a soule of gold,
> Such cherishing heat her best lov'd part doth hold.

81. ff. For the nautical imagery cf. Donne, *Elegie XVIII* ('Loves Progress'), lines 42–70.

52. 115. *The Roman Lucrece.* In the celebrated legend, a paragon of matronly virtue. But '*Aretine's Lucretia* sold her Maiden-head a thousand times before she was twenty-four years old' (Burton, *Anatomy of Melancholy,* Part III, Sect. II, Mem. I, Subs. II, with marginal reference to one of the Dialogues). In a letter to Malatesta, on the topic 'Abbasso l'onore e viva la vergogna!', Aretino writes in similar strain: 'Che vi parse di Lucrezia? non fu ella matta a tôr consiglio da lui [l'onore]? Era una galantaria il beccarsi la stretta datale da messer Tarquinio, e vivere.' (*Il Primo Libro delle Lettere,* cccx, ed. Fausto Nicolini, Bari, 1913, p. 376.)

116. Aretino composed sonnets to accompany sixteen engravings made by Marcantonio Raimondi for Giulio Romano. Cf. Randolph, *The Muses Looking-glasse* (with *Poems,* 1638), p. 32:

> Within Sir is a Glasse, that by reflexion
> Doth shew the image of all sorts of pleasures
> That ever yet were acted, more variety
> Then *Aretines* pictures.

And Eldred Revett, *Poems,* 1657, p. 7:

> As they from Posture into posture grew,
> Their bodies in all *Aretines* they threw.

117. *Lais.* The famous courtesan of Corinth.

119–20. Echoed by Randolph, *In Anguem, qui Lycorin dormientem amplexus est*, English version (ed. Thorn-Drury, p. 32):

> Downe slips he and about each limbe he hurles
> His wanton body into numerous curles.

125. The Grecian Dame. Penelope, faithful wife of Ulysses.

131–3. The story of Daphne, pursued by Apollo and changed to a bay-tree, is told by Ovid, *Metamorphoses*, i. 452–567. Carew specifically echoes line 551: 'Pes modo tam velox pigris radicibus haeret'.

139–42. Cf. *A divine Love*, lines 37–44 (p. 189). To Laura, wife of Count Hugues de Sade, Petrarch addressed his sonnets.

53. 146. Loves Exchequer. A figure borrowed from Donne, *Elegie XVIII* ('Loves Progress'), lines 91–4:

> Rich Nature hath in women wisely made
> Two purses, and their mouths aversely laid:
> They then, which to the lower tribute owe,
> That way which that Exchequer looks, must go.

153. Cf. Donne, *Elegie III* ('Change'), lines 10–14:

> Women are made for men, not him, nor mee.
> Foxes and goats; all beasts change when they please,
> Shall women, more hot, wily, wild then these,
> Be bound to one man, and did Nature then
> Idly make them apter to'endure then men?

165–6. Parodied by Cleveland, *News from Newcastle*, lines 21–2:

> The moderate value of our guiltless ore
> Makes no man atheist, nor no woman whore.

Ebsworth rewrote the couplet, with the following result:

> This goblin 'Honour', whom the world enshrined,
> Should make men Atheists, and not women kind?

53. *Epitaph on the Lady* Mary Villers. The identity of the child upon whose death this and the two following epitaphs were written presents a puzzle. In the register of the church of St. Martin in the Fields (*Harleian Society Publications*, lxvi (1936), 53) there occurs among the baptisms the following entry:

Marcii 1627 et 1628.

13 Maria Villers fa. Christopheri Villers Comitus [*sic*] Angliseae et Dom'e Elizabethe ux' eius

And among the burials one finds (p. 253):

1630

Aug. 4 Domina Maria Vilers filia Christoferi Villers nuper Comitis Anglisae et Dominae Elizabethae, in chancella

Since the Earl and Countess of Anglesey were Carew's patrons it would be natural for him to commemorate their daughter's death; he has an Elegy on the death of the Earl (p. 69), and it is reasonable to think that the verses

Vpon the sicknesse of (E. S.) (p. 31) had to do with the Countess, born Elizabeth
Sheldon. The difficulty arises from Carew's declaration, in lines 3–4, that

> The Parents that first gave her birth,
> And their sad Friends, lay'd her in earth

—a statement inconsistent with the fact that the Earl of Anglesey had already
died, on 3 April 1630. The word 'Parents' is apparently used here in its
normal modern sense. One must conclude either that Carew was employing
extreme poetic licence or that the Lady Mary Villiers of the poem is still to
be sought.

54. *An other.* The purest Soule, &c.

5–10. C. L. Powell (*Modern Language Review*, xi (1916), 286–7) declares
that 'a considerable stretch of the imagination is required to make anything of
these lines', and proposes an alternative version from *H*17:

> the substance was too pure, the frame
> so glorious, that thether came
> Tenn thousand Cupids, bringing along
> a grace on Each winge, that did throng
> for place there, till they all opprest
> the seate in which they thought to rest.

It is quite possible that this manuscript version is one of Carew's own composi-
tion rather than that of scribal corruptors and correctors; but even so, the
printed version must be considered a revision for the better both in sense and
in sound. The idea of the 'clayie tenement' as a 'weake mold' is spoiled by
referring to it two lines later as 'the frame | so glorious'; and the harshness of
'Tenn thousand Cupids, bringing along' is only partially mitigated by Mr.
Powell's misquoting 'bringing' as 'bearing'. The fatal inadequacy of body to
soul is a theme of wide occurrence; Carew turns to it again in the Epitaph on
Maria Wentworth (p. 56), lines 4–6. Compare the more heroic lines by
Dryden (*Absalom and Achitophel*, i. 156–8):

> A fiery Soul, which working out its way,
> Fretted the Pigmy Body to decay:
> And o'r informed the Tenement of Clay.

11. Modell. In the archaic sense of 'mould'. Shakespeare uses the word
in a similar image (*Henry V*, ii, Prologue, 16–17):

> O England! model to thy inward greatness,
> Like little body with a mighty heart.

54. *An other.* This little Vault, &c.

13–16. With Carew's image of Love disarmed at the tomb compare
Ronsard's *Elegie* on Marie (*Le Second Livre des Amours*, in *Œuvres*, 1609,
p. 202):

> Ce iour Amour perdit ses flammes & ses traicts.
> Esteignit son flambeau, rompit toutes ses armes
> Les ietta sur la tombe, & l'arrousa de larmes.

55. *Epitaph on the Lady S.* This lady, identified in *W* as 'the Lady Psalter', was Mary, first wife of Sir William Salter of Iver, Bucks. Her fine monument, on the north side of the sanctuary in the parish church of St. Peter, Iver, depicts the lady rising out of her coffin at the Last Day, with the inscription:

> TO THE HONORED MEMORIE
> OF THE TRVLY VERTVOVS AND RELIGIOVS LADY, MARY
> SALTER·THE BELOVED CONSORT OF·S^R WILLIAM SALTER
> KNIGHT, ON OF HIS MA^{TIS} CARVERS IN ORDINARY, DAVGHTER
> OF THOMAS SHERLAND·OF WELSHALL IN SVFFOLKE ESQ^R:
> AND ANNE·DAVGHTER OF IVDGE YELVERTON BY MARY
> CATESBY·OF WHISTON IN NORTHAMPTON SHIRE
>
> *Qui obijt 24 Apr: 1631.*
> *Ætat: suæ 30.*
>
> HEER TH'EARTHLY MANSION OF A HE'VENLY MINDE
> A WORTHY MATRONS MORTAL PART IS SHRIN'D
> MORE MIGHT BE SAYD, IF ANIE TOMBE OR STONE
> WERE LARGE ENOVGH FOR HER INSCRIPTION
> BVT WORDS ARE BOOTLES, MORE ELOGIA'S HVRLD
> VPON HER HEARSE ARE VAINE, FOR SO THE WORLD
> LIKE A VAINE=GLORIVS GAIMSTER; SHOVLD BVT BOAST
> NOT WHAT IT NOW HATH, BVT HOW MVCH 'THATH LOST
> AND MAKING HER LOSS KNOW'N·WOVLD CAVSE MEN FEARE
> T'WAS GREATER FARR THEN VERT'V'S BANK COVLD BEAR

Both Sir William Salter (d. 1643) and his father Sir Edward, a Master in Chancery, were Carvers in Ordinary to the King, and would thus have been in daily association with Carew in his office of Sewer. For the Salter family see W. H. Ward and K. S. Block, *A History of the Manor and Parish of Iver*, 1933.

3. musicall sweet tunes. With this metaphor compare Lovelace, *Orpheus to Beasts. Song:*

> Oh could you view .the Melodie
> Of ev'ry grace,
> And Musick of her face . . ..

Mr. C. H. Wilkinson (*Poems of Lovelace*, i. 30–1) cites parallels from Randolph, Cleveland, and Byron. Carew's idea is a familiar one with the Platonists: 'Beauty in general is a *Harmony resulting from several things proportionably concurring to constitute a third*; . . . This is Beauty in the largest sence, the same with Harmony; whence God is said to have framed the World with musical harmonious temperament.' (Pico della Mirandola, *A Platonick Discourse upon Love*, tr. by Thomas Stanley (1651), II. v, vi.) Cf. Sir Thomas Browne, *Religio Medici*, Part II, Sect. IX: 'There is music even in the beauty, and the silent note which Cupid strikes, far sweeter than the sound of an instrument; for there is music wherever there is harmony, order, or proportion; and thus far we may maintain the music of the spheres.'

11–15. With this list of gems and their qualities compare a much longer catalogue by Drayton in *The Muses Elizium, The ninth Nimphall*, lines 101 ff.

(ed. Hebel, iii. 319–20). Contemporary lore relating to gems is fully set forth in Anselmi Boetii de Boodt, *Gemmarum et Lapidum Historia*, Hanoviae, [? 1609]; their medical properties in Ioannis de Laet, *De Gemmis et Lapidibus Libri Duo*, Lugduni Batavorum, 1647. See also Pliny, *Naturalis Historia*, xxxvii, and *Sapientissimi et Excellentissimi Pselli de lapidum virtutibus libellus*, ed. P. J. Maussacus, Tolosae, 1615.

11. the constant Diamond. 'Creditur Adamas . . . constantiam, victoriam animique fortitudinem efficere. Proditur etiam iram comprimere, coniugum-que amorem fouere' (De Boodt, p. 62). The diamond might also be called constant because difficult to break: 'Ἀντίκα ὁ Ἀδάμας . . . κραταιός τέ ἐστιν καὶ δύσθραυστος' (Psellus, pp. 346–7).

the wise Chrysolite. The virtues ascribed to chrysolite are similar to those of 'Tophaze, that doth save | The braines calme temper' (lines 14–15); the stones are similar, and were often not discriminated. De Boodt (p. 104) says that chrysolite mitigates anger, wards off nightmares, and prevents lunatic fits.

12. The devout Saphyre. 'Si circa cordis arterias pendeat, . . . hominem continentem efficere dicitur, sacerdotibus & ecclesiasticis personis qui casti-tatem vouerunt ob id ad gestandum vtilissima censetur' (De Boodt, p. 94; he adds that St. Jerome thought that it had the power 'iram Dei mitigare', and that it was in classical times sacred to Phoebus). Drayton, loc. cit., speaks of

that celestiall colored stone
The Saphyre, heavenly wholly.

12–13. Emrauld apt to write | Records of Memory. 'Memoriam etiam firmare, ac visum reficere & recreare à multis creditur' (De Boodt, p. 100).

13. cheerefull Agat. Though the agate possessed a variety of salutary qualities, such as strengthening the sight and heart, guarding against fevers, and combating the venom of serpents, vipers, and scorpions, none of the sources examined is of much help in justifying or explaining Carew's 'cheere-full'—possibly a misreading for 'carefull'. Drayton's catalogue, with greater traditional justification, includes 'The cheerfull Ruby'.

13–14. grave | And serious Onyx. De Boodt reports that 'alii collo suspensam onychem tristitiam & timorē, aliaq3 melancholica symptomata excitare scribant' (pp. 123–4).

15. witty Amathist. C. L. Powell (*Modern Language Review*, xi (1916), p. 287) proposed the manuscript 'whiter', from *H17*, as a better reading. But this is to miss the whole point of the passage, since Carew assigns to each gem a characteristic virtue which was embodied in Lady Salter. Moreover, 'witty' is quite in accord with the tradition. 'Putatur gestatus ebrietatem pro-hibere. . .. Addunt alii malas cogitationes prohibere, fœlix ingenium, vigi-lantiam ac industriam efficere' (De Boodt, p. 83).

16–17. For Aaron's ephod, with its twelve precious stones, see Exodus xxviii. 17–21.

18–19. One only Pearle. The reference is to Matthew xiii. 45–6.

56. *Maria Wentworth*. This was the second daughter of Sir Thomas Went-worth, created Earl of Cleveland in 1626; she died in January 1632/3, at the

age of eighteen, and was buried with considerable magnificence in the Church of St. George, Toddington, Bedfordshire. Her tomb, by the west wall of the north transept, is still preserved, with Carew's first six stanzas inscribed, not quite correctly, upon it; the sculptor has portrayed her seated, with a sewing-basket. Local tradition says that she died from pricking her finger while sewing on Sunday. The inscription is as follows:

> MARIA WENTWORTH ILLVSTRISS: THOMÆ COMIT[S]
> CLEVELAND FILIA PRÆMORTVÆ PRIMA ANIMAM
> VIRGINEAM EXHALAVIT IANVAR.
> AN[O] DNI: MDCXXXII. ÆTAT: SVÆ XVIII.
>
> AND HERE Y[E] PRETIOVS DVST IS LAYDE,
> WHOSE PVRELIE TEMPERED CLAY WAS MADE
> SO FINE, THAT IT Y[E] GVEST BETRAYD.
>
> ELSE, Y[E] SOVLE GREW SO FAST WITHIN,
> IT BROKE Y[E] OVTWARD SHELL OF SINNE,
> AND SO WAS HATCH'D A CHERVBIN.
>
> IN HEIGHT IT SOAR'D TO GOD ABOVE,
> IN DEPTH IT DID TO KNOWLEDGE MOVE,
> AND SPREAD IN BREADTH IN GENERALL LOVE.
>
> BEFORE, A PIOVS DVTIE SHIN'D
> TO PARENTS, CVRTESIE BEHINDE,
> ON EITHER SIDE, AN EQVALL MINDE.
>
> GOOD TO Y[E] POORE, TO KINDRED DEARE,
> TO SERVANTS KINDE, TO FRIENDSHIPP CLEARE,
> TO NOTHING BVT HERSELFE SEVERE.
>
> SOE THOVGH A VIRGIN, YET A BRIDE
> TO EVERIE GRACE, SHE IVSTIFIED
> A CHAST POLIGAMIE, AND DYED.

See W. L. Rutton, 'The Monument in Toddington Church, Beds., to Lady Maria Wentworth', in *Reliquary and Illustrated Archæologist*, January 1901; and Joseph Hight Blundell, *Toddington: Its Annals and People*, 1925. That Carew should have furnished an epitaph is probably due to the fact that Maria Wentworth's mother was Anne, daughter of Sir John Crofts of Saxham; for Anne Wentworth, Maria's younger sister, Carew was to compose a 'Hymeneall Song' in 1638 upon the occasion of her marriage to Lord Lovelace (p. 114), and he had been a friend of her uncle John Crofts since 1619 at latest, when the two were together in the service of Lord Herbert of Cherbury.

4–6. *And so was hatch'd.* The conceit is Donne's; compare *Of the Progresse of the Soule. The Second Anniversary*, lines 183–4 (ed. Grierson, i. 256):

> This to thy Soule allow,
> Thinke thy shell broke, thinke thy Soule hatch'd but now.

But both are far outdistanced by Cleveland, with his 'Hatch him whom Nature poached but half a man' (*Rupertismus*, line 107, in *Poems*, ed. Berdan, p. 134). Carew had already used the idea of the spirit's proving too much for the frail body in the second of his epitaphs on the Lady Mary Villiers (p. 54).

57. On the Duke of *Buckingham*. The favourite of James and Charles, assassinated at Portsmouth by John Felton on 23 August 1628, and buried 10 September in Henry VII's Chapel, Westminster Abbey. 'A pretentious and inartistic monument was subsequently erected above his grave by his widow' (*D.N.B.*). The widow was Katharine Manners, daughter of the Earl of Rutland. Carew was to write a similar elegy on Buckingham's brother, the Earl of Anglesey, in 1630 (p. 69).

59. Foure Songs. These songs, together with the two following, perhaps belong to the same entertainment or play as the *Prologue* and *Epilogue* (pp. 127–8) which according to *W* were attached 'to a Play presented before the King and Queene, att an Entertanement of them by the Lord Chamberlaine in Whitehall hall'. Fleay (*A Biographical Chronicle of the English Drama*, 1559–1642, 1891, ii. 239) notices a disguised lover and rescued lady in Shirley's *Arcadia*, or again any of the songs *except* that of the 'Lover in the disguise of an Amazon' could be satisfactorily worked into Thomas Killigrew's early play *The Prisoners*; but it seems more likely that the text of the 'Entertanement', except for thèse fragments, has not been preserved. Thomas Killigrew dates the performance ('a Masque at Whitehall') in 1633; see the succeeding note, and cf. Alfred Harbage, *Thomas Killigrew*, 1930, pp. 57–8.

The first of *Iealousie*. Dialogue. This song was included by Thomas Killigrew in his play *Cicilia and Clorinda, or Love in Arms*, written in 1649–50 and published in 1664. 'This Chorus', explains Killigrew in a note dated from Venice, August 1651, 'was written by M. *Thomas Carew*, Cup-bearer to *Charles* the First; and sung in a Masque at *White-hall*, *Anno* 1633. And I presume to make use of it here, because in the first design, 'twas writ at my request upon a dispute held betwixt Mistress *Cicilia Crofts* and my self, where he was present; she being then Maid of Honour: this I have set down, lest any man should believe me so foolish as to steal such a Poem from so famous an Author; or so vain as to pretend the making of it my self; and those that are not satisfied with this Apology, and this Song in this place; I am always ready to give them a worse of mine own' (*Cicilia and Clorinda*, Part II, Act v, sc. ii, in *Comedies, and Tragedies, written by Thomas Killigrew*, 1664, p. 309). Horace Walpole, in the *Anecdotes of Painting*, reports a tradition that Van Dyck's portrait of Carew and Killigrew (see Frontispiece) was painted to commemorate the dispute. 'At Leicester-house is a double portrait, bought by the late prince of Wales of Mr. Bagnols. It represents two of the wits of that time, T. Carew, of the privy chamber to Charles I. and a poet, and Henry [i.e. Thomas] Killigrew. They had a remarkable dispute before Mrs. Cecilia Crofts, sister of the lord Crofts, to which Vertue supposed this picture alluded, as in a play called The wanderer was a song against jealousy, written on the same occasion' (*The Works of Horatio Walpole*, 1798, iii. 222–3). But the portrait could hardly have any connexion with the poem: it bears the date 1638, and the dispute on jealousy could not have taken place in 1638 in the presence of Cecilia Crofts because that lady (who became Killigrew's wife on 29 June, 1636—Carew's poem written for that occasion appears at page 79) died on 1 January, 1637/8.

5–17. The pedigree of Jealousy, as given by Carew, is not wholly clear. Compare Daniel's *Complaint of Rosamond* (*The Whole Workes*, 1623, p. 133 of second pagination):

> O Iealousie, daughter of Enuie and Loue,
> Most wayward issue of a gentle Sire.

And Burton (*Anatomy of Melancholy*, Part III, Sect. II, Mem. III, Subs. I): 'Though *Hercules de Saxonia, cap. 3. Tract de melanch.* will exclude fear from Love Melancholy, yet I am otherwise persuaded. . . . 'Tis full of fear, anxiety, doubt, care, peevishness, suspicion, it turns a man into a woman, which made *Hesiod* belike, put Fear and Paleness *Venus'* daughters,

> —Marti clypeos atque arma secanti
> Alma Venus peperit Pallorem, unaque Timorem:

because fear and love are still linked together.' What Carew really does is to give two alternative genealogies, the first in lines 5–6 and the second, which is quite separate from the first and inconsistent with it, in lines 12–17.

7. *the third Spheare.* According to Ptolemaic astronomy, that of Venus, above the spheres of the Moon and Mercury.

60. 23–42. With this passage compare Burton, *Anatomy of Melancholy*, Part III, Sect. II, Mem. I, Subs. II: ''Tis a happy state this indeed, when the fountain is blessed (saith *Solomon, Prov.* 5. 10.). . . .. But this love of ours is immoderate, inordinate, and not to be comprehended in any bounds. It will not contain itself within the union of marriage, or apply to one object, but is a wandering, extravagant, a domineering, a boundless, an irrefragable, a destructive passion: sometimes this burning lust rageth after marriage, and then it is properly called *Jealousy.*'

60. *Feminine Honour.* The ordeal here referred to, a part of ordinary criminal procedure in medieval England and Germany, consisted in the accused person's walking barefoot over nine red-hot ploughshares. Queen Emma, mother of Edward the Confessor, is said to have vindicated herself by this means from an unjust accusation of adultery. See Freeman, *Norman Conquest*, 1877, ii. 585–7. Carew may have recalled the story from his brief legal studies at the Middle Temple, or he could have heard it from John Selden, in whose *Table-Talk* it occurs (ed. Arber, 1898, pp. 112–13).

61. 19. *Vaine Honour!* Compare Carew's denunciation of Honour in *A Rapture*, p. 49, lines 3–20.

61. Separation of Lovers.

5. *Though Love enter by the sight.* See p. 36, lines 1–4; p. 39, lines 1–4; and the notes on those passages.

62. Incommunicabilitie of Love. Vincent notes that this poem 'is based upon

Donne's Confined Love'. The theme is set in the first stanza of Donne's poem (ed. Grierson, i. 36):

> Some man unworthy to be possessor
> Of old or new love, himselfe being false or weake,
> Thought his paine and shame would be lesser,
> If on womankind he might his anger wreake,
> And thence a law did grow,
> One might but one man know;
> But are other creatures so?

The poems have otherwise nothing in common.

8. *Loves twinn'd-flame, his forked dart.* Cf. Ovid, *Metamorphoses*, i. 466–71.
16–18. A variant of the famous sophism known as Buridan's Ass, after the nominalist philosopher to whom it was ascribed. The same sophism is stated by Dante, *Paradiso*, iv. 1–6.

63. *Another.* A Lady rescued, &c. In *W* the title is given as 'The Princess Song.'

64. To Ben. Iohnson. Jonson's play *The New Inne* was upon its first performance, early in 1629, hissed from the stage; he published it in 1631 as 'The New Inne. Or, The light Heart. A Comoedy. As it was neuer acted, but most negligently play'd, by some, the Kings Seruants. And more squeamishly beheld, and censured by others, the Kings Subiects. 1629. Now, at last, set at liberty to the Readers, his Maties Seruants, and Subiects, to be iudg'd. 1631. By the Author, B. Ionson.' At the end of the volume he affixed a sixty-line poem headed 'The iust indignation the Author tooke at the vulgar censure of his Play, by some malicious spectators, begat this following Ode to himselfe.':

> Come leaue the lothed stage,
> And the more lothsome age:
> Where pride, and impudence (in faction knit)
> Vsurpe the chaire of wit!
> Indicting, and arraigning euery day
> Something they call a Play. . . .

The response to this attack on popular taste was immediate, in the form of satirical rejoinders by Jonson's ill-wishers and indignant defences by his young disciples. Carew's reply was more discriminating than either; though a glowing tribute to Jonson's greatness, it could hardly have made entirely pleasant reading for its recipient.

11–12. all thy Eaglets. The eagle tested the legitimacy of its young by their ability to look steadfastly at the sun. Cf. p. 36, line 5, and the note.

65. 18. By Citie-custome, or by *Gavell-kind*. An echo of Carew's legal studies. Cf. Giles Jacob, *A New Law-Dictionary*, 1729, s.v. 'Custom of London': 'By the *Custom of London*, when a Citizen and Freeman dies, his Goods and Chattels shall be divided into three Parts; the Wife to have one Part; the Executors another, to discharge Legacies, &c. and the Children unprovided for the other third Part. 2 *Danv. Abr.* 311, 312.' And John

Doderidge, *The Vse of the Law* (with *The Lawyers Light*), 1629, p. 32: '. . . the custome of *Kent*, that euery male of equall degree of Childhood, Brotherhood or kindred, shall inherit equally, as daughters shall being Parceners . . . is called *Gauel* kind'. So John Donne, *Sermon XXXII* (*Works*, ed. Alford, ii. 61): 'Heirs of heaven, which is not a gavel-kind, every son, every man alike; but it is an universal primogeniture'.

26. *thy ytch of praise.* James Howell mentions an occasion, real or imaginary, upon which Carew repeated this criticism of Jonson (*Epistolæ Ho-Elianæ*, ed. Joseph Jacobs, 1890, pp. 403–4; Book II, Letter XIII):

I was invited yesternight to a solemn Supper, by *B. J.* . . . there was good company, excellent cheer, choice wines, and jovial welcome: One thing interven'd, which almost spoil'd the relish of the rest, that *B.* began to engross all the discourse, to vapour extremely of himself, and, by vilifying others, to magnify his own *Muse.* *T. Ca.* buzz'd me in the ear, that tho' *Ben.* had barrell'd up a great deal of knowledge, yet it seems he had not read the *Ethiques*, which, among other precepts of Morality, forbid self-commendation, declaring it to be an ill-favour'd solecism in good manners.

The letter is dated from Westminster 5 April 1636.

31. *a Goodwin.* The dangerous Goodwin Sands, seven miles off Ramsgate.

46. *Th'abortive off-spring.* Compare Jonson, *Timber: or Discoveries*, 1641, p. 127: 'The common Rymers powre forth Verses, such as they are, (*ex tempore*) but there never come from them one Sense, worth the life of a Day.' In this whole passage Carew is simply echoing Jonson's own teaching and practice, itself grounded in Horace.

48. *Virge.* 'An area subject to the jurisdiction of the Lord High Steward, defined as extending to a distance of twelve miles round the King's court' (*O.E.D.*).

66. *An Hymeneall Dialogue.*

6. *For though your voyce the ayre did breake.* The peculiar phrasing of this line, which was printed corruptly in 1640, is paralleled in Thomas Stanley's *Speaking and Kissing*, line 1 (*Poems*, 1653, p. 35): 'The air which thy smooth voice doth break', and by Waller, *Of Mrs. Arden*, lines 1–2:

Behold, and listen, while the Fair
Breaks in sweet Sounds the willing Air.

13–14. *that mutual change | Of soules.* Castiglione declares (*The Courtier*, tr. Hoby, Everyman's ed., p. 247) that when lovers are in each other's presence 'the spirites meete together, and in that sweete encounter the one taketh the others nature and qualitie'. Cf. p. 36, lines 1–4, and the note.

67. *Obsequies to the Lady* ANNE HAY. This lady was a distant cousin of Thomas Carew; hence the 'engag'd kindred' of line 71. Sir Edmund Denny of Cheshunt, Herts., King's Remembrancer to Henry VII and Baron of the Exchequer, who died in 1520, had two sons and three daughters, one of whom, Martha, married Sir Wymond Carew of Antony; she was Thomas Carew's grandmother. Sir Anthony Denny, younger son of Sir Edmund, was the father of Edward Denny, created Earl of Norwich 24 October 1626,

whose daughter Honora became on 6 January 1608 the first wife of James Hay, afterwards first Earl of Carlisle; she died in 1614 (*D.N.B.*). The death of their daughter, the Lady Anne, is mentioned as occurring 'yesternight, of an imposthume that she had in her head', in a letter from Mr. Beaulieu to Sir Thomas Puckering from London, 18 Nov. 1629 (*The Court and Times of Charles I*, 1848, ii. 43; noted by I. A. Shapiro in *Notes and Queries*, vol. 196 (1951), pp. 7–8). Her stepmother was the famous Lucy, Countess of Carlisle, second wife of the Earl, addressed by Carew in the poems on pp. 32 and 91.

1–3. The lines are paralleled by Pope in his elegy *On General Henry Withers*, lines 5–6:

> For thee the hardy vet'ran drops a tear,
> And the gay courtier feels the sigh sincere

—a couplet thus criticized by Dr. Johnson: 'The third couplet is more happy; the value expressed for him by different sorts of men raises him to esteem; there is yet something of the common cant of superficial satirists, who suppose that the insincerity of a courtier destroys all his sensations, and that he is equally a dissembler to the living and the dead' (*Lives of the Poets*, ed. G. B. Hill, 1905, iii. 266–7).

25–8. as once *Apelles*. In Pliny's version of the story (*Natural History*, xxxv. 36) the painter was Zeuxis; but the name of Apelles was often substituted in the retelling, perhaps by association with his famous Aphrodite Anadyomene. Cf. Randolph, *The Character of a Perfect Woman*, lines 1–4 (ed. Thorn-Drury, p. 165):

> Apelles curious eye must gaze upon
> all beauties, and from choice of all make one;
> Thais must lend a lipp, Lais a Cheeke,
> then for a browe we must Oenone seeke.

Cleveland re-phrases neatly (*Rupertismus*, lines 77–8):

> Such was the painter's brief for Venus' face;
> Item, an eye from Jane; a lip from Grace.

68. 36. St. Catherine of Siena (1347–80), who wrote *The Book of Divine Doctrine*, was noted for the strictness of her life. St. Clara (1194–1253) was a friend of St. Francis and founded the Franciscan nuns, the 'poor Clares'. For forty years she was Abbess of St. Damian's; the rule for nuns which she devised was approved by the Pope two days before her death.

69. *To the Countesse of* Anglesie. Christopher Villiers, youngest brother of George, first Duke of Buckingham, shared in that favourite's rise to greatness under James and Charles; on 18 April 1623 he was elevated to the peerage as Baron Villiers of Daventry, co. Northampton, and Earl of Anglesey. He married Elizabeth, daughter of Thomas Sheldon, of Hoby, Leicestershire; from lines 72–3 of the present poem we learn that Carew acted as an intermediary or messenger in the courtship. The 'Lady Mary Villers' of the three poems on pages 53 and 54 may have been their daughter, just as the 'E. S.' of the poem on page 31 may represent Elizabeth Sheldon. The Earl of Anglesey died 3 April 1630.

8. old *Æsons* bath. Aeson, father of Jason, was restored to youth by Medea's magic arts; see Ovid, *Metamorphoses*, vii. 162–293.

23. you surfet on your griefe. Compare Shakespeare, *Two Gentlemen*, iii. i. 218–19:

> O, I have fed upon this woe already,
> And now excess of it will make me surfeit.

26. my gratitude. Important evidence that Carew had received the patronage of the Earl and Countess.

70. 33. stately Pillars. Compare p. 122, lines 19–20; also Lord Herbert of Cherbury, *A Description*, lines 57–8 (ed. Moore Smith, p. 4):

> Two Alabaster Pillars stand,
> To warn all passage from that Land.

So Lovelace, *The Triumphs of Philamore and Amoret* (ed. Wilkinson, ii. 158):

> Fixt and unmov'd on's *Pillars* he doth stay,
> And Joy transforms him his own Statua.

And Robert Heath, *Clarastella*, 1650, pp. 62–3 (*A Pastoral Protest of Love*):

> By those moving columns bear
> This Globe and the lov'd frame uprear.

54. proud revenge. I am unable to find any analogy or reason for the 'prevenge' of the 1640 text. The extra *p* was probably due to the influence of 'proud' just preceding.

59 ff. like a quiet Eddie. Cf. Carew's previous use of this figure, p. 14.

71. 79. great *Buckingham*. Assassinated 23 August 1628; see Carew's two Elegies, pp. 57 and 58.

81. Looke up, and meet their beames. Cf. Donne, *Of the Progresse of the Soule. The second Anniversary*, lines 65–6:

> Look upward; that's towards her, whose happy state
> We now lament not, but congratulate.

86. the Trophies of your conquering eye. Echoed from Daniel, *Delia*, x:

> Vpon the prostrate spoyle of that poore hart
> That serues a Trophy to her conquering eies.

The Countess's second husband was the Hon. Benjamin Weston (Burke, *Extinct Peerage*, 1883, p. 560).

71. An Elegie upon the death of the Deane of Pauls, Dr. Iohn Donne. Donne died on 31 March 1631; Carew's *Elegie* was first printed, among the 'Elegies upon the Author', in *Poems, by J. D. with Elegies on the Authors Death. London. Printed by M. F. for Iohn Marriot, and are to be sold at his shop in St Dunstans Church-yard in Fleet-street. 1633*. An address of 'The Printer to the Reader' on fol. *A2* declares that 'whereas it hath pleased some, who had studyed and did admire him, to offer to the memory of the Author, not long after his decease, I have thought I should do you service in presenting them unto you now; . . . you shall finde them in the end . . . as an attestation for their sakes that knew not so much before, to let them see how much honour was attributed to this worthy man, by those that are capable to give it'.

Carew's poem, on p. 385, is preceded by others signed *H. K.*, *Tho: Browne.*, *Edw. Hyde.*, *Dr.* C. B. *of* O., Hen. Valentine., Iz. Wa.; and followed by verses signed *Sir Lucius Carie*, M*ʳ*. Mayne *of Christ-Church in Oxford*, *Arth. Wilson*, M*ʳ* R. B., *Endy: Porter.* The first and third of these pieces had appeared unsigned at the end of *Deaths Duell*, 1632. The *Poems*, 1635, add verses by Daniel Darnelly, Sidney Godolphin, and I. Chudleigh; Tho. Browne's verses are omitted. The poems in the 1639 edition are the same as those of 1635. The present *Elegie* in Carew's *Poems*, 1640, appears in a text differing in many details from that of the three editions of Donne mentioned; Grierson noted of Carew's *Elegie* in his edition of Donne (ii. 257) that 'the 1633 text is so much better that it seems probable that the poem was printed in 1640 from an early, unrevised version'. With this impression I concur, and have accordingly used for this edition the 1633 text rather than that of 1640.

A single manuscript version, in *S.23*, agrees most often with the 1633 readings.

Carew's poem seems to have been written a considerable period before its publication; it is referred to by Aurelian Townshend in his verses to Carew on the death of Gustavus Adolphus in 1632 (see p. 207, lines 14–16) and by Lord Herbert of Cherbury in his own *Elegy for Doctor Dunn*, lines 47–51:

> Having deliver'd now, what praises are,
> It rests that I should to the world declare
> Thy praises, *DUNN*, whom I so lov'd alive,
> That with my witty *Carew* I should strive
> To celebrate thee dead.

Other elegies in the 1633 volume seem to echo Carew's ideas and phraseology. Moreover, Carew's opening lines, if they are to be taken literally, must have been written before other elegies had appeared.

4. The meaning which Carew gives to 'dowe-bak't' in this passage is clarified by Donne's own use of the word in *A Letter to the Lady Carey, and Mʳˢ Essex Riche, from Amyens*, lines 16–21:

> Others whom wee call vertuous, are not so
> In their whole substance, but, their vertues grow
> But in their humours, and at seasons show.
>
> For when through tastlesse flat humilitie
> In dow bak'd men some harmelessenes we see,
> 'Tis but his *flegme* that 's *Vertuous*, and not Hee.

5. uncisor'd. The 1640 text has 'uncizard'. Though Ebsworth prints 'unsizar'd', there can be little doubt that 'unscissor'd' (i.e. with uncut hair) represents the proper interpretation; cf. *To my Friend G. N. From Wrest*, line 64 (p. 88): 'curl'd uncizard *Bacchus*'.

72. 25–8. A similar figure is used by Donne, *To Mʳ Rowland Woodward* lines 3–6 (ed. Grierson, i. 185):

> So 'affects my muse now, a chast fallownesse;
> Since shee to few, yet to too many 'hath showne
> How love-song weeds, and Satyrique thornes are growne
> Where seeds of better Arts, were early sown.

73. 59–60. Cf. p. 75, lines 11–12.

77–8. A reminiscence of Shakespeare, *1 Henry IV*, i. i. 2–3:

> Find we a time for frighted peace to pant,
> And breathe short-winded accents of new broils.

74. 87. I will not draw the envy. The emendation 'thee' for 'the' is proposed by Grierson, *Poems of Donne*, ii. 257. But 'thee' would be, I think, inconsistent with the meaning of the passage as a whole. Carew refuses to catalogue all Donne's perfections, not because such a catalogue would make men envy Donne, but because he wishes to leave part of the privilege of praising and lamenting Donne to other poets, who would else be envious of himself. The lines which follow serve to elaborate the meaning suggested: 'Let others carve the rest . . ..'

98. See the biographies of Donne by Izaak Walton and Sir Edmund Gosse.

74. *In answer of an Elegiacall Letter*, &c. Aurelian Townshend, whose masques and poems (with the notable exception of the 'Elegiacall Letter' addressed to Carew; see p. 207) were first collected by Sir Edmund Chambers in 1912, succeeded Ben Jonson as a writer of masques for Inigo Jones; he is the author of *Albions Triumph*, presented by the King and his gentlemen on 8 January 1631/2, and *Tempe Restord*, with which the Queen and her ladies entertained the gentlemen on 14 February following. As late as 1638, when he joined Carew and others in contributing commendatory verses to Lord Cary's translation of *Romulus and Tarquin*, he seems to have moved prosperously in court circles, but in 1642 he was described by the Earl of Pembroke as 'a poore & pocky Poett. . . . Aurelian would be glad to sell an 100 verses now at sixepence a peice, 50 shillinges an 100 verses' (Chambers, *Aurelian Townshend's Poems and Masks*, 1912, p. xxiv).

Gustavus Adolphus was killed at Lützen on 6 November 1632; 'Aurelian Townsends elegie' on the subject, 'sent to T: Carewe', accompanies the present poem in *R2*, *W* (imperfect), and *S.23*, and was first printed by G. C. Moore Smith, from *S.23*, in *Modern Language Review*, xii (1917), p. 422. With it may be compared the ten elegies published in the Third Part of the *Swedish Intelligencer* in 1633. In Baron North's *A Forest Promiscuous of Several Seasons Productions*, 1659, p. 72, there likewise appears 'An Incentive to our Poets upon the Death of the victorious King of Swedeland'.

2. thy *Barbican*. Townshend is known to have lived for ten years before 1632 in the parish of St. Giles, Cripplegate, of which the Barbican is a part (Chambers, op. cit., pp. xvi–xvii). Carew is playing on the name, in its meaning of watch-tower.

75. 12. Cf. p. 73, lines 58–60.

24. the Knight o' th' Sun. Favourite hero of Don Quixote's friend Master Nicholas the barber, the Cavallero del Febo was the principal character of Diego Ortuñez de Calahorra's famous romance, the *Espejo de Principes y Cavalleros* (1562; continued by Pedro de la Sierra, 1581, and Marcos Martinez, 1589; translated into English as *The Mirrour of Princely deedes and knighthood* and published in several volumes 1580–1601; translated into

French as *L'Admirable Histoire du Chevalier du Soleil*, 1620–6). Cf. Over-bury's character of 'A Very Woman' (*Works*, ed. Rimbault, p. 49): 'she loves her glasse, and the Knight of the Sun for lying'.

26. Annals. Here, as in the '*Cæsars* yeares' of line 28, Carew probably has in mind the *Annales* of Tacitus.

76. 54. Chambers writes: 'Carew's reference at the end of his poem to *The Shepherd's Paradise* has led his editors to suggest that Townshend may have been the author of that tedious pastoral, wherein Henrietta Maria played at court during January, 1633, and provoked a criticism in Prynne's *Histriomastix* (1633), which more than anything led to the clipping of Prynne's ears. But Carew's words do not really bear out any such interpreta-tion, and a reference by Suckling in *A Session of the Poets* fully confirms the printer's statement in the 1659 edition of the play that the author was Walter Montagu' (*Aurelian Townshend's Poems and Masks*, pp. xxii–xxiii). This interpretation is strengthened by the consideration that the description which follows is not at all appropriate to *The Shepheard's Paradise. A Comedy ... Written by W. Mountague*, 1659, but fits exactly Townshend's masque *Tempe Restord*.

61–88. Townshend's 'misterious fable' in *Tempe Restord* tells of Circe and her enchantments, which in the end surrender to the power of 'divine Beauty', a role enacted by the Queen.

62–3. Cf. Pope, *Essay on Man*, ii. 107–8:

> On life's vast ocean diversely we sail,
> Reason the card, but Passion is the gale.

Warton declares that Pope was 'a great reader' of Carew, Crashaw, and Herbert (cf. p. li). The present commentary notes a second apparent echo by Pope, from *Obsequies to the Lady Anne Hay*, lines 1–3 (p. 67), as well as Pope's obvious quotation, in *The Dunciad*, i. 55–6, from 'Aske me no more', line 4 (p. 102).

83–8. The entry of Henrietta Maria, here referred to, is thus described in detail by Townshend:

'In the midst of the ayre the eight *Spheares* in rich habites were seated on a Cloud. . . . To the Musicke of these Spheares there appear'd two other Clouds descending, & in them were discovered eight Stars; these being come to the middle Region of the skie, another greater Cloud came downe aboue them; Which by little and little descending, discovered other glister-ing Stars to the number of sixe: and aboue all in a Chariot of gold-smithes workes richly adorned with precious Iemmes, sat divine Beauty, over whose head, appear'd a brightnesse, full of small starres that inviron'd the top of the Chariot, striking a light round about it. . . . When divine Beauty and her attendants were lighted, that great Cloud that bare them flyes vp againe, leaving the Chariot standing on the Earth.

'This sight altogether was for the difficulty of the Ingining and number of the persons the greatest that hath beene seene here in our time . . . the Queenes Maiesties [habit] was in a garment of watchet Sattine with Stars of silver imbrodered and imbost from the ground, and on her head a Crowne of Stars. . . .' (*Tempe Restord*, pp. 10–11.)

77. 94–100. For the alternative point of view, compare Ben Jonson, *An Epistle to a Friend, to perswade him to the Warres* (*Vnder-woods*, 1640, p. 184):

> Wake, friend from forth thy Lethargie: the Drum
> Beates brave, and loude in *Europe*, and bids come
> All that dare rowse: or are not loth to quit
> Their vitious ease, and be o'rewhelm'd with it.

Of the 'vitious ease' here manifested by Carew, W. J. Courthope writes: 'Such lines are sufficient in themselves to explain the overthrow of the Cavaliers within twelve years at Marston Moor' (*A History of English Poetry*, 1903, iii. 244).

77. *Vpon Master* W. Mountague *his returne from travell.* In *HL* an excerpt consisting of lines 13–24 has been set to music by Henry Lawes.

Walter Montagu (1603?–77) was the second son of Sir Henry Montagu, first Earl of Manchester. He began his picturesque career as a diplomatic agent for the Duke of Buckingham in France and Italy, and ended it as Abbot of St. Martin's, near Pontoise. Though he enjoyed the friendship of Queen Henrietta Maria, his position at court was rendered precarious by his leaning towards Roman Catholicism. It is impossible to specify with which of the returns to England from his numerous sojourns on the Continent the present poem has to do; *D.N.B.* mentions one 'permanent' homecoming in 1633, or again the occasion may be that mentioned in Garrard's letter on 1 March 1635 (*The Earl of Strafforde's Letters and Dispatches*, ed. Knowler, i. 373): 'Our *French* Cavaliers are come home. . . . on the Eve of the Queen's Mask, came the Lord *Dunluce* and *Wat Mountague*. Mr. *Mountague* is well received by the King and Queen; he attended also the Lord Treasurer, with whom, and with every body else, it is now presumed he is upon very good Terms. He hath Wit and good Abilities, God send him to use them well.' He left England in the same year 'a declared Papist', and on his next coming, in 1637, was more coldly received.

78. 21–2. For seven days each winter, says Ovid, the Halcyon (Alcyone) broods upon her nest, which floats on the surface of the sea; and during that time all the winds are chained up (*Metam.* xi. 744–8).

35–6. The antecedent of *him* in line 35 is Æolus; of *him* in line 36, Boreas.

39. we of *Delphos*. Carew could justifiably address Montagu as a fellow devotee of Apollo and the Muses. In 1633 Montagu's pastoral *The Shepheard's Paradise* was played by the Queen and her ladies, and he was later to furnish commendatory verses to Edwin Benlowes's *Theophila, or Love's Sacrifice*, 1652. He also published *Miscellanea Spiritualia: or Devout Essaies*, 1648, and *The Accomplish'd Woman*, a translation from the French, 1656.

78. *To Master* W. Mountague. The legal phraseology of this poem (cf. p. 65, line 18) is pointed by its title in the catalogue of *S.23*: 'A writt of Ne exeat regno agaynst mr Walter Mountague going to trauyle.'

79. *On the Mariage of* T. K. *and* C. C., &c. T. K. is Thomas Killigrew

(1612–83), Page of Honour to Charles I, later Resident in Venice for Charles II, and author of many plays (published in folio, 1664). C. C. (as the title 'vpon mʳˢ Cicille Croftes' in *S.23* corroborates) is Cecilia Crofts, Maid of Honour to Queen Henrietta Maria and daughter of Carew's friend and host Sir John Crofts of Saxham. In 1633 Carew, Killigrew, and Cecilia Crofts were associated in the dispute which resulted in Carew's dialogue *Of Iealousie* (p. 59). The following entries, made by Killigrew in his family Bible, furnish a brief history of the marriage:

> I was maried to my First wife Ms Cissillia Croftes of Saxˢame in Suffoke at Otlands apone Sent Peiteres day being the 29 of Juene 1636. Tho Killigrew

> My suenne Harrey Killigrew was borrn apoen Esterday following being the 9 of Aprill and Sunday 1637. Tho. Killigrew

> My wife diede apoen Nue Yeares day after being the 1 of Januarey and apone a Monday 1637/38 nue stiell in London and lies berried in Westminster Abbey. Tho. Killigrew.

(See R. N. Worth, *Miscellanea Genealogica et Heraldica*, New Series, i. 370; and Alfred Harbage, *Thomas Killigrew*, 1930, p. 65.)

1–8. The idea of the sun's hiding his face before the lady's beauty is a cliché; compare Carew's song *A beautiful Mistris* (p. 7), itself translated from Marino.

80. 31. the fight of Love. Cf. Propertius, ii. i. 44–5:

> Enumerat miles vulnera, pastor oves;
> Nos contra angusto versantes proelia lecto.

And Kynaston, *Leoline and Sydanis*, 1642, p. 10:

> Though *Venus* in Loves wars hath domination,
> Sworne enemy to every Maidenhead,
> And Soveraigne of the acts of generation,
> Whose skirmishes are fought in the field bed. . . .

33. Wee'le strew no nuts. Cf. Catullus, lxi. 124–8.

81. *For a Picture where a Queen Laments over the Tombe of a slaine Knight.* It is barely possible that the picture was that of 'a lamenting stooping woman, wrapt all in white', by Bresciano, which Vanderdoort described as being at Whitehall 'In the King's Long Gallery towards the Orchard' (Vertue, *A Catalogue and Description of King Charles the First's Capital Collection*, 1757, p. 132). Poems of this genre were more popular on the Continent than in England; Marino published a whole *Galeria*.

81. *To a Lady that desired I would love her.* This poem is more complex in stanza and deliberate in pace than is usual in Carew; it is assigned tentatively to Lord Herbert of Cherbury, on grounds of style and verbal correspondence, in G. C. Moore Smith's edition of Lord Herbert's *Poems* (1923, pp. 122, 169). But there is no compelling reason for questioning Carew's authorship; he uses an even more elaborate stanza in the lines *Vpon my Lord Chiefe Iustice* immediately following, and the analytical, meditative mood, though admittedly one often met with in Lord Herbert, is certainly not unknown in Carew as well. Moreover, these verses occur in the 'good' earlier section of Carew's *Poems*, 1640, which must furnish the only external evidence of their authorship; they have not been discovered in any of the manuscript miscellanies examined.

82. 11. Then. Professor Moore Smith cites several examples of a similar use of "Then' in Lord Herbert's poems; but this is surely unconvincing evidence of Herbert's authorship, seeing that these examples can be matched twice over from Carew's unquestioned work (cf. p. 12, line 29; p. 13, line 13; p. 15, line 15; p. 16, line 5; &c.).

29–30. With these two lines Professor Moore Smith justly parallels the beginning of a nameless poem by Lord Herbert (*Poems*, 1923, p. 97), remarking that the similarity 'shows either identity of authorship or borrowing on one side or the other':

> Innumerable Beauties, thou white haire
> Spredde forth like to a Region of the Aire. . . .

Compare also (for the 'calme') Lovelace, *To Amarantha, That she would dishevell her haire* (ed. Wilkinson, 1925, ii. 18):

> Let it flye as unconfin'd
> As it 's calme Ravisher, the winde.

83. *Vpon my Lord Chiefe Iustice.* Of Sir John Finch, Baron Finch of Fordwich, who became Lord Chief Justice of Common Pleas on 16 October 1634, Lord Campbell writes that he was 'one of the worst characters in English history' (*Lives of the Lord Chancellors and Keepers of the Great Seal*, ii. 542). Carew doubtless saw the more amiable aspects of Finch's personality; in 1634 this Lord Chief Justice took a principal part in arranging the spectacular Masque presented by the four Inns of Court, and in 1637 he is mentioned as 'the best Courtier of them all' (Knowler, *Strafforde's Letters and Dispatches*, ii. 85). As a Justice he was prejudiced in favour of the royal prerogative. The A. W. of his 'election' was Lady Anne Wentworth, a niece of Carew's friend John Crofts; the present poem must have been written between 1634 and 1638, when she became the wife of Lord Lovelace. The verses which Carew supplied for her wedding appear at p. 114.

84. 22–3. Astraea, goddess of justice, was the last of the deities to abandon the earth in the sinful Age of Iron. See Ovid, *Metamorphoses*, i. 150.

28. A cliché reproved by Quarles, *Emblemes*, 1635, p. 37 (1. ix):

> And you, more braine-sick Lovers, that can prize
> A wanton smile before eternall Ioyes;
> That know no heav'n but in your Mistresse eyes. . . .

84. *To* A. D. *unreasonable distrustfull of her owne beauty.* Though Ebsworth prints 'A[nn] D[oris]', the lady seems unidentifiable. In *HL* lines 23–34 are set by Henry Lawes.

21–4. Carew's conceit of the pining lover as the true mirror of beauty had already been used by Daniel in *Delia*, Sonnet XXXIIII (*The Whole Workes*, 1623, p. 165 of second pagination):

> Why doost thou DELIA credit so thy glasse,
> Gazing thy beauty deign'd thee by the skies:
> And doest not rather looke on him (alas)
> Whose state best shewes the force of mu[r]dering eies? . . .
> Then leaue thy glasse, and gaze thy selfe on me,
> That Mirror shewes what power is in thy face. . . .

Compare also Spenser, *Amoretti*, xlv ('Leaue lady in your glasse of christall clene').

21. specular stone. Here, apparently, only a mirror. In Donne (*The Undertaking*, line 6; and 'Honour is so sublime perfection', lines 28–30) the term refers perhaps to crystal-gazing, or more likely to a transparent *specularis lapis* mentioned by Pliny (*Natural History*, xxxvi. 45).

85. 35. If then Love flow from Beautie. A Platonic thesis carefully elaborated by Pico della Mirandola; see Thomas Stanley's translation (1651) of his *Platonick Discourse upon Love*.

86. 65–6. no such Indian foole. It is apparently to these verses that Suckling alludes in his letter to T. C. (p. 213): 'I shall drive that trade thou speak'st of to the *Indies*, and for my Beads and Rattles have a return of Gold and Pearl.' Cf. Drayton, *Of his Ladies not comming to London*, lines 101–3 (ed. Hebel, iii. 205):

> And be more foolish then the *Indians* are
> For Bells, for Knives, for Glasses, and such ware,
> To sell their Pearle and Gold.

86. *To my friend* G. N. *from* Wrest. For G. N.'s identity there is no external evidence; the verses show that his first name was 'Ghib' or Gilbert (line 1), that he had been engaged in hunting at the time the poem was written (lines 108–9), and that he had been Carew's comrade in arms (line 110) on Charles's expedition to Berwick in May and June of 1639 (lines 2–8). Ebsworth's identification of G. N. as Gilbert Neville—an identification mentioned by Vincent with some scepticism—is apparently pure guess-work; there seems to be no record of any Gilbert Neville who might have been associated with Carew. Carew's connexion with one branch of the Neville family is shown by the lines on the green sickness which he wrote for Mary and Katherine Neville (pp. 113 and 129; see also the poem on p. 194); these young ladies, however, had no brother Gilbert. Though certainty is not possible on the evidence available, G. N. might plausibly be identified as Gilbert North, who like Carew served Charles I as a gentleman of the privy chamber. The fourth son of Sir John North, who was killed in Flanders in 1597, Gilbert North was educated at Eton and Cambridge, where he was admitted as fellow commoner at Caius College on 16 June 1612, aged fifteen. His elder brothers were Dudley, third Baron North; Sir John North, K.B.; and Roger North, navigator and associate of Sir Walter Ralegh. His availability as recipient of the present poem at about the time it was written is proved by a list, preserved in the Public Record Office (L.C. 5/134, p. 340), of twelve 'Gent of the priuy Chamber appointed to beare the Canopy at S^t

Georges feast at Windsor in Octob. 1639', where his name is the first to appear.

Carew was writing from Wrest Park, in Bedfordshire, a manor 'in the possession of the De Greys, earls of Kent, and their descendants for over six hundred years' (*Victoria History of the County of Bedfordshire*, 1908, ii. 326). The manor, with the title of Earl of Kent, had passed in 1631 to Anthony de Grey, who died in 1643. Like the lines *To Saxham* (p. 27), this poem shows the influence of Martial (III. lviii) and of Jonson's ode *To Penshurst*; compare especially, from the latter:

> Thou art not, PENSHURST, built to envious show,
> Of touch, or marble; nor canst boast a row
> Of polish'd pillars, or a roofe of gold: . . .
> Thou joy'st in better markes, of soyle, of ayre,
> Of wood, of water: therein thou art faire.

2–8. A reference to the rigours of the Scottish expedition of 1639; Charles's forces got as far north as Berwick-on-Tweed, near which they encamped in great discomfort.

6. *Favonius*. The west wind (otherwise called Zephyrus), associated with spring.

9–10. Carew uses the same figure to translate Psalm 104, verses 13–15 (p. 140).

87. 23. Of carved Marble, Touch, or Porpherie. This little catalogue was richly varied by different authors. Cf. the quotation from Jonson, *To Penshurst*, given above; Donne, *A Funerall Elegie*, line 3: 'Alas, what's Marble, Jeat, or Porphyrie'; Drummond, *To the Memory of [John, Earl of Lauderdale]* (ed. Kastner, ii. 193):

> and heere in iet,
> Gold, Brasse, Touch, Porpherie, the Parian stone,

and Drummond, *Rose* (ed. Kastner, ii. 202):

> Though Marble, Porphyry, and mourning Touch.

Touch: 'Short for *touchstone*; . . . *esp.* applied to black marble or some similar black stone used in monumental work. *Obs.*' (*O.E.D.*).

88. 57. *Amalthea*. A nymph who fed Zeus with the milk of a goat; he rewarded her with a horn of the animal, on which he bestowed the power of producing whatever its possessor desired.

85. the barren Spheare. The eighth sphere, which according to Ptolemaic astronomy contained the fixed stars.

93–4. On Vertumnus, Roman god of the changing seasons and their fruits, see Propertius, IV. ii; for his wooing of Pomona, see Ovid, *Metamorphoses*, xiv. 623 ff.

89. 109. th'embleme of warre. Ebsworth emends, mistakenly, to 'emblems'. The emblem of war is the 'pursuit' or chase mentioned in the preceding line, not the animals hunted. Castilione (*The Courtier*, tr. Hoby, Everyman's Library, p. 41) calls hunting 'one of the chiefest' of gentlemanly exercises because 'it hath a certaine likenesse with warre'.

89. *A New-yeares gift. To the King.* The concluding lines show that this poem is probably to be dated 1 January 1630/1; Charles had made peace with Spain in 1629 and with France in 1630.

7. the whiter stone. Cf. Catullus, lxviii. 147–8:

> Quare illud satis est, si nobis is datur unus,
> Quem lapide illa, dies, candidiore notat.

16. captivitie. Figuratively, 'The servitude or subjection of the reason, will, or affections.' *O.E.D.*, which cites Addison, *Cato*, III. i:

> The strong, the brave, the virtuous, the wise
> Sink in the soft captivity together.

90. 26. From budding starres to Suns full blowne. Carew employs the same striking image in the third of his epitaphs on the Lady Mary Villiers (p. 54, lines 9–10).

33. *Byfront.* Janus, two-faced god of the year. The doors of his temple, in the Roman Forum, were closed only in time of peace.

90. *To the Queene.* The title in *H4*, 'The Preist's, to the Queene', suggests that the present lines were intended to be sung or recited at some masque or other entertainment. The presentation of Henrietta Maria as goddess of virtuous love is similar to that in Aurelian Townshend's masque *Tempe Restord*, 1631, which, however, contains no chorus of priests.

12. Compare *A Rapture*, lines 111–14 (p. 52).

91. 23. O free them then. There is no clear antecedent for 'them'; but the necessity of assuming that some preceding lines have been dropped can be avoided by taking the reference as being a general one to all the subjects of Love's 'prophaner' kingdom, liberated and purified by the great Commandress.

91. *To the New-yeare, for the Countesse of* Carlile. This poem, undated, accompanies the new-year's verses *To the Queene* in *H4*; see Carew's other poem addressed to the Countess (p. 32) and the accompanying note. The present poem is to be dated not later than 1 January 1631/2, since the 'royall Goth' of line 16 is pretty obviously Gustavus Adolphus, killed in that year.

7. No attire. The 'No tyre' of 1640 is bad metrically. 'No rich tire', the reading of the 1670 and 1772 editions, supplies the needed syllable; but the present reading, that of *H4*, is more probably what Carew intended.

92. 22. bright *Apollo's* tree. The laurel, used to crown victors in the Pythian games.

92. *To my Honoured friend, Master* Thomas May, *upon his Comedie*, The Heire. These lines, the first published by Carew, were prefixed to *The Heire an excellent comedie. As it was lately Acted by the Company of the Reuels. Written by T. M. Gent.*, 1622. A second edition appeared eleven years later: *The Heire. A Comedie. As it was Acted by the Company of the Revels. 1620, 1633*; for this edition the text of Carew's poem was revised in a few details of wording, and the numerous careless errors of the 1622 printing were corrected. Thomas May (1595–1650) is best known as a translator of Lucan, Martial, and Virgil and as historian of the Long Parliament; his personal reputation has suffered at the hands of later writers who did not like the political bias expressed in the *History*. Clarendon (*Life*, 1759, i. 35) mentions him as a member of the brilliant circle which, in the 1620s, included Carew also.

2. a private Stage. The Company of the Revels performed ordinarily at Blackfriars.

93. 18–20. The story of Apollo and Daphne may be read in Ovid, *Metamorphoses*, i. 452–567. Cf. *A Rapture*, lines 131–9 (p. 52).

39. to scant. The reading of the 1633 edition, 'too scant', shows the sense probably intended by Carew. 'Too . . . . Stressed form of To *prep.*, which in the 16th c. began to be spelt *too*,' *O.E.D.*

93. *To my worthy friend Master* Geo. Sands. These verses appeared in the second edition of Sandys's translation of the Psalms, *A Paraphrase vpon the Divine Poems*, 1638, where they were preceded by commendatory verses signed Falkland and Henry King and followed by others signed Dudley Digges, Francis Wiatt, Henry Rainsford, Edward [*sic*] Waller, and Wintoure Grant. The colophon is dated 1637; the first edition, containing the commendatory verses of only Digges and Falkland, had appeared in 1636.

> The dainty *Sands* that hath to English done
> Smooth sliding *Ovid*   (Drayton)

is remembered to-day principally for his translation of the *Metamorphoses*, completed in 1626.

94. 14. dance. Cf. 2 Samuel vi. 13–14, David's dancing before the Ark of God as it was brought to Jerusalem.

28. I have restored the capital for 'Faire' as in 1638 ('faire' 1640), since 'the first Faire' is God. Cf. Spenser's *Hymne of Heavenly Beauty*, and *Amoretti*, lxxix, which speaks of

> that fayre Spirit, from whom al true
> and perfect beauty did at first proceed.
> He onely fayre, and what he fayre hath made,
> all other fayre lyke flowres vntymely fade.

Drummond's *An Hymne of the Fairest Faire* relates to 'the Nature, Atributes, and Workes of God' (ed. Kastner, ii. 37). Burton (*Anatomy of Melancholy*, Part III, Sect. IV, Mem. I, Subs. I) develops the idea more fully: 'Amongst all those Divine Attributes that God doth vindicate to himself, . . . his Beauty is not the least. . . . *I am amazed*, saith *Austin, when I look up to Heaven, and behold the beauty of the Stars, the beauty of Angels, Principalities, Powers, who can express it? who can sufficiently commend, or set out this beauty which appears in us? so fair a body, so fair a face, eyes, nose, cheeks, chin, brows, all fair and lovely to behold, besides the beauty of the soul, which cannot be discerned. If we so labour, and be so much affected, with the comeliness of creatures, how should we be ravished with that admirable lustre of God himself?* If ordinary beauty have such a prerogative and power, . . . how shall this divine form ravish our souls, which is the fountain and quintessence of all beauty? *Cœlum pulchrum, sed pulchrior cœli fabricator*; if Heaven be so fair, the Sun so fair, how much fairer shall he be that made them fair?'

95. *To my much honoured friend,* Henry *Lord* Cary. Carew's verses were pre-fixed to the second edition of Lord Cary's translation from Malvezzi, published in 1638 with title as follows: *Romulus and Tarquin First Written in Italian By the Marquis Virgilio Malvezzi: And now taught English; by H. L.ᵈ Cary of Lepingtō the second Edition.* Carew's poem follows verses signed Jo. Suckling, and precedes others by W. Davenant, A. Tounshend, Tho. Wortley ('Impri-mantur ... Jan. 22. 1637.'), and Robert Stapylton ('Imprimatur ... Jan. 26. 1637.'). The first edition, 1637, contains no commendatory verses. Henry, Lord Cary of Leppington, was the eldest son of the first Earl of Monmouth, and succeeded to his father's title in 1639. Born in 1596, he studied at Exeter College, Oxford, from 1611 to 1613, and spent three years thereafter on the Continent in travel and the acquisition of languages. At the creation of Charles as Prince of Wales on 4 November 1616 (an occasion upon which Carew distinguished himself for the 'cost and bravery' of his own array) he was made a Knight of the Bath. He may have seen Carew previously in Italy or France. After 1620 he lived in retirement in the country among his books (*D.N.B.*). *Romulus and Tarquin*, his first published work, is a translation from *Il Romulo* and *Il Tarquinio Superbo*, by Vergilio, Marquis de Malvezzi (1599–1654), political commentaries on the classical legends.

6. *teach him speake vulgar Italian.* Perhaps an echo of the 'now taught English' of Cary's title.

8. Pietro Bembo (1470–1547), Cardinal, scholar, and editor of Petrarch, was noted as a purist.

9. Benedetto Varchi (1503–65), Florentine historian and humanist, took a prominent part in the controversy surrounding the establishment of Tuscan as the standard literary dialect of Italy.

the *Crusca.* The Accademia della Crusca or Furfuratorum was founded at Florence in 1582; its great dictionary, the *Vocabulario della Crusca,* appeared in 1612.

95. *To my worthy Friend,* M. D'avenant, *Vpon his Excellent Play,* The Iust Italian. Carew's verses, following others signed *Will. Hopkins,* appeared in *The Iust Italian. Lately presented in the priuate house at Blacke Friers, By his Maiesties Seruants,* 1630. The play was licensed by Herbert on 2 October 1629 (Adams, *Dramatic Records of Sir Henry Herbert,* 1917, p. 32). As one may gather from the present verses, the production was a failure. Carew's attack on popular taste is reminiscent of Jonson's strictures in *The Case is Altered,* II. vii.

96. 6. *controule.* 'To challenge, find fault with, censure, reprehend, object to (a thing). *Obs.*' (*O.E.D.*). The word is of frequent occurrence, in this sense, in Donne.

24. *Red Bull, and Cockpit flight.* The site of the Red Bull theatre is now covered by Woodbridge Street; 'frequent allusions to this house, mostly dis-paraging, are to be found in the contemporary dramatists, who refer to it much in the same strain as did the burlesque writers of thirty years ago to the old Victoria' (Baker, *History of the London Stage,* 1904, p. 15). The Cockpit was a private theatre in Drury Lane; the company from the Red Bull fre-quently performed there.

97. *To the Reader of Master* William Davenant's *Play.* These lines were printed with *The Witts* in 1636; the only commendatory verses in the volume, they immediately follow a dedication to Endymion Porter. *The Witts* was licensed on 19 January 1633/4 and performed before the court and at Black-friars shortly afterwards; of its reception Sir Henry Herbert records: '*The Witts* was acted on tusday night the 28 January, 1633, at Court, before the Kinge and Queene. Well likt. It had a various fate on the stage, and at court, though the kinge commended the language, but dislikt the plott and characters.' Herbert had refused to approve the play, as morally objectionable, and had issued the licence only after intervention by the King. (Adams, *Dramatic Records of Sir Henry Herbert*, 1917, pp. 22, 35, 54.)

1–6. It hath beene said. By Horace, *Epistles*, II. ii. 58–64; Ben Jonson, Prologue to *Epicoene* and Prologue to *The New Inne*. Of Jonson's lines, compare especially the Prologue to *Epicoene*, lines 8–9, 16–18:

> Our wishes, like to those make public feasts,
> Are not to please the cook's taste but the guests'. . . .
> For, to present all custard, or all tart,
> And have no other meats to bear a part,
> Or to want bread, and salt, were but coarse art.

Jonson returns to the figure in the *Ode to Himself* printed with *The New Inne* in 1631. The same idea, with specific acknowledgement to Horace, occurs in Burton, *Anatomy of Melancholy*, 'Democritus to the Reader' (Bohn's Library ed., i. 25): 'There's naught so peevish as men's judgements, yet this is some comfort, *ut palata, sic judicia*, our censures are as various as our palates. . . . Our writings are as so many dishes, our readers guests, our books like beauty, that which one admires, another rejects; so are we approved as men's fancies are inclined.' See also Suckling's Epilogue to *Aglaura* and Prologue to *The Goblins*. The fastidiousness which made Carew reject this common attitude is a strong element in all his writing.

98. To *Will. Davenant* my Friend. In *Madagascar; with other Poems. By W. Davenant*, 1638 ('*Imprimatur*, Matth. Clay Feb. 26. 1637.'), this poem follows one signed Endimion Porter and two signed I. Suckling, and precedes one signed William Habington, with which it was confused in the 1640 *Poems* (see p. 195). Davenant returned Carew's compliment in the lines *To Tho: Carew* (see p. 209), which were printed in the 1638 volume.

19–20. That bastards are often better than legitimate offspring is stated by Euripides, *Andromache* 638 (cf. Drayton, *Poly-Olbion*, Song I; ed. Hebel, iv. 19), and is developed in some detail by Robert Burton in *The Anatomy of Melancholy*, Part II, Sect. III, Mem. II. The first of the 'Problemes' in Donne's *Iuuenilia*, printed 1633, is concerned with the question, 'Why haue Bastards best Fortune?'

98. *The Comparison.* The first ten lines of this poem are printed in *Wits Recreations*, 1640 (fol. D3^{r-v}) and are there followed by

> *The Answer.*
> If earth doth never change, nor move,
> There's nought of earth, sure in thy love,

> Sith heavenly bodies with each one,
> Concur in generation,
> And wanting gravitie are light,
> Or in a borrowed lustre bright;
> If meteors and each falling star
> Of heavenly matter framed are:
> Earth hath my mistrisse, but sure thine
> All heavenly is, though not divine.

99. 11–12. Compare Lord Herbert of Cherbury, *To her Hair*, lines 1–2 (ed. Moore Smith, p. 37):

> Black beamy hairs, which so seem to arise
> From the extraction of those eyes.

Donne had long since rebuked such poetic extravagances (Letter *To the Countesse of Salisbury. August. 1614*, lines 3–7):

> now when the Sunne
> Growne stale, is to so low a value runne,
> That his disshevel'd beames and scattered fires
> Serve but for Ladies Periwigs and Tyres
> In lovers Sonnets. . . .

99. *The Complement.* G. C. Moore Smith in his edition of Lord Herbert of Cherbury's poems, p. 140, comments on the similarity to Lord Herbert's *A Description*. Both poems appear to draw on Marino's sonnet, 'Durante il bagno' (*Poesie Varie*, ed. Croce, 1913, p. 77; see Frank J. Warnke, in *Studies in the Renaissance*, ii (1955), 166–7). But Carew's pattern of alternate praise and qualification, in which he differs from both Marino and Lord Herbert, is set by Propertius, ii. iii. 9–22.

3. *By thine eyes the tempting booke.* Hazlitt prints, on manuscript authority (*H6*), 'that crystall brooke'. But cf. Drayton, *Piers Gaveston*, line 228 (ed. Hebel, i. 165): 'Mine eyes his booke, my bosome was his bed.'

100. 16. *None can parte their whit and red.* This is the reading of nearly all the manuscripts; the feeble 'None can paint them whit and red' of 1640 would be hard to defend. The editor of 1651, evidently surmising that something was wrong with the line, changed 'them' to 'their'.

101. 43–8. Cf. Lord Herbert, *A Description*, lines 55–60:

> At th' entrance of which hidden Treasure,
> Happy making above measure,
> Two Alabaster Pillars stand,
> To warn all passage from that Land;
> At foot whereof engraved is,
> The sad *Non Ultra* of Mans Bliss.

65–6. Vincent points out the similarity of this conclusion to the following lines of a lyric ('I love thee not for sacred chastity') attributed to Marlowe:

> I love thee not for voice or slender small:
> But wilt thou know wherefore? fair sweet, for all.

(Marlowe, *Works*, ed. Bullen, iii. 246.)

102. *On sight of a Gentlewomans face in the water.*
5–8. For this stanza, *W, S14,* and *D8* read,

> Noe windes, but louers sighes drawe nigh
> To trouble theis gladd streames
> On which nor Starr, nor the worlds eye
> Did euer dart such beames.

The version set by Henry Lawes in *HL* is similar, except that for 'nor Starr'
it reads 'noe starr'.

102. A Song. What looks like an early draft of this poem, one of Carew's
best known in his own day and now, appears in *A23*:

> Aske mee no more where Joue bestowes
> When June is past, the damaske Rose
> For on yor Cheekes and lips they bee
> Fresher then on anie tree.

> Aske mee no more where those starres light
> That downewards fall in darke of night,
> For in yor Eyes they sitt and theare
> Fixed become, as in their spheare.

> Aske mee no more where Nightingale
> When June is past puts forth her tale,
> For in yor sweete deuidinge throate
> Shee winters and keepes warme her note.

> Nor aske mee whether East or west,
> The Phoenix builds her spiced nest
> For vnto yo^u shee allwaies flies,
> And in yor fragrant bosome lies.

Another version, in *D2*, rearranges the stanzas and expands the concluding one
with an extra couplet:

> Cant 28.
> Aske me noe more whither doth stray
>   the golden atomes of the day
>   for in pure loue the heauens prepare
>   that powder to enrich thy haire.
> Aske me noe more whither doth hast
>   the nightingale when May is past
>   for in thy sweet devideing throate
>   she winters & keepes warme her note.
> Aske me noe more where Joue bestowes
>   when June is gone, the flameing rose
>   for in thy beauties orient deepe
>   all flowers as in their causes meete.
> Aske me noe more where East or west
>   the Phenix builds her spicie nest

for now to aged ashes growne
she to thy haires is lately flowne
And to preserve her race now runne
craues there a shadow from the sunne.

E24 agrees generally with the standard text, but with the stanzas rearranged
2, 3, 1, 4, 5, and concludes with the additional stanza (cf. p. 99, lines 21–4):

Aske me no more whither north or south
Those vapours fly, come from thy mouth
ffor vnto heauen they fly from hence
And there become Joues francensense.

Ash 47, which follows the same arrangement, also concludes with this stanza,
in the form:

Aske me no more whether North or South
These vapours come ffrom out thy mouth
ffor vnto heaven they are sent ffrom hence
And there are made Joves ffrankinsense.

A30, S14, S17, H35, S.32, Dx, and *HM116* also arrange the stanzas 2, 3,
1, 4, 5; in *Ash 38* the order is 2, 4, 3, 1, 5. In *Poems: by Wil. Shake-speare,*
1640, where the lines are printed without stanzaic division, they follow the
traditional order.

A Latin rendering by Arthur Johnston appears in *Arturi Ionstoni Scoti
Medici Regii Poemata omnia*, Middelburg, 1642, as 'Ad Dominam, ex Anglico'
(reprinted in *Musa Latina Aberdonensis*, 1895, ii. 202); the stanzaic order 2,
3, 1, 4, 5 indicates that Johnston translated from a manuscript version.
Parodies and satirical adaptations (some of them including the cancelled sixth
stanza, thus suggesting that it must have attained wide currency) appeared from
time to time throughout the century: e.g. ten stanzas in MS. Add. 28009
beginning, 'Ask mee no more who twas would preach'; or, from *H18,*

On Lesbia:

Aske me noe more whether doth stray
the sooty night when it is day.
it Cloathes my Lesbia, dyes her skinne
as blacke without as shees within:

Aske me noe more where the Scrichowle
when day is come her Hubbubs howle,
in her harsh throate, whose noyse appalls
worse then tenn Irish funeralls;

Aske me noe more whither doe hye
the drowzy flyes when winters nighe,
They all take up their resting place
in the vast pock-holes of her face:

Aske me noe more where you shall finde
the stinke that Gundamor left behinde;
That horrid steame, that stinke uncouth
flew from his breech into her mouth:

Aske me noe more where Lust and pride,
where Messaline where hell abide;
Hell's twixt her leggs, and in her breast
base Lust and pride haue built their neast:

Aske me noe more whither I must
when this fraile flesh must lye with dust,
Sure not to hell, for there will shee
bee too, and we shall nere agree.

In *A30* Carew's poem is followed by 'The answeare' ('I'le tell you true
whereon doth light') and 'A Moderating Answeare to both:' ('Ile tell you of
another sun'). These and similar verses, mostly political or personal in theme,
appear in *H18*, *Ash 38*, *Wit Restored*, *Merry Drollery*, *Rump Songs*, Thomas
Jordon's *Royal Arbor of Loyal Poesy*, and *Westminster Drollery*. Kynaston's
lines *On concealment of her beauty* appear to be based on Carew's poem; for
later echoes cf. Tennyson's song 'Ask me no more' from *The Princess*, Part VI,
and Franklin P. Adams, in *The New Yorker*, 12 March 1938, p. 27.

3–4. Carew's conceit must be understood in relation to the four causes
distinguished by Aristotle, *Physica*, ii. 3: the material cause (as bronze for a
statue), the formal (as the relation 2 : 1 in the octave), the efficient (as a man
is cause of his children), and the purposive (as health is the cause of walking
about). It is the concept of formal cause which is here applicable; in the lady's
beauty Carew sees the very essence or idea of roses.

Pope uses Carew's phrase in *The Dunciad*, i. 55–6:

Here she beholds the Chaos dark and deep,
Where nameless Somethings in their Causes sleep.

Johnston translates the whole stanza thus:

Ne rogites, quo Flora rosas ableget, ab Arcto
Sol ubi declives in Noton urget equos.
Hae tibi se sistunt; tu mille rosaria mundo
Sufficis, et florum semina mille foves.

103. 11. *dividing.* Descanting or quavering melodiously. Cf. *Romeo and
Juliet*, III. v. 29–30:

Some say the lark makes sweet division;
This doth not so, for she divideth us.

13–16. With the conceit of this stanza compare Lord Herbert of Cherbury,
An Ode upon a Question moved, Whether Love should continue for ever?, lines
133–6 (ed. Moore Smith, p. 66):

This said, in her up-lifted face,
Her eyes which did that beauty crown,
Were like two starrs, that having faln down,
Look up again to find their place.

Of Carew's version and Lord Herbert's, George Williamson remarks (*The
Donne Tradition*, 1930, p. 206): 'The difference is apparent. Both are

Metaphysical, but Herbert's is more subtly and mysteriously so—Jonson has intervened to make Carew's image less difficult and more commonplace; it certainly is not so beautiful as Herbert's, and it does not make so fine a discovery of emotion. In these differences one can see the influence of Jonson which draws Carew out to the *fringe* of the Donne tradition.'

103. *The second Rapture.*

7 ff. Compare Thomas Randolph, *The Muses Looking-Glasse* (with *Poems*), 1638, p. 28 ('Acolastus *a voluptuous Epicure*'):

> Give me a *Venus* hardly yet fifteene,
> Fresh, plump, and active . . ..

And Robert Heath, a conscientious imitator of Carew:

> I'l have a young plump amorous Queen,
> Ripe though she be not yet fifteen.

('Refrigerium', in *Occasional Poems* (with *Clarastella*), 1650, p. 26.) Carew's own 'wench', like Shakespeare's Juliet, is younger still. Ebsworth, who is particularly shocked by the 'about thirteene', proposes to read, 'a wench *above* thirteen', though it is hard to see how that would really much help matters.

104. *The tinder.* A poem of a very popular strain; the Ovidian archetype appears in *Amores*, ii. iv:

> . . . Candida me capiet, capiet me flava puella,
> Est etiam in fusco grata colore venus.

Cf. Marino, *Amore incostante, al Sig. Marcello Sacchetti* (*La Lira*, 1625, Parte Terza, pp. 87–92):

> *CHI vuol veder, MARCELLO,*
> *Protheo d'Amor nouello,*
> *Nouel Camaleonte,*
> *A me giri la fronte. . . .*
>
> *Ogni beltà, ch'io veggia,*
> *Il cor mi tiranneggia.*
> *D'ogni cortese sguardo*
> *Subito auampo, & ardo.*
> *Lasso, ch'à poco a poco*
> *Son fatto esca continua ad ogni foco.*
>
> *Quante forme repente*
> *Offre l'occhio a la mente*
> *Tante son lacci, & hami*
> *Perch' io viè più sempr' ami.*
> *Hor per vna languisco*
> *Hor per altra mi struggo, e'ncenerisco. . . .*

Donne's *The Indifferent* belongs to the same tradition.

105. A Song. The title 'Peregrine' in *A21* probably indicates a melody to which these verses might be sung. In *Parnassus Biceps* the poem is improperly combined with part of a song beginning, 'Keepe on your maske, and

COMMENTARY 267

hide your eye', by William Strode. See Strode's *Poetical Works*, ed. Dobell, pp. 3–6.

7–8. *Come then and kill me.* With this refrain compare *Coelum Britannicum*, lines 931–2 (p. 178).

106. *To the Painter.* The first eleven lines of this poem are perhaps imitated from the beginning of a sonnet (*Sur son pourtrait à I. De-Cour, peintre du Roy*) by Desportes, printed in the *Premières Œuvres*, Paris, 1600, pp. 294^{r-v}:

> *Tu t'abuses* DE-COVR, *pensant representer*
> *Du* CHASTEAVNEVF *d'Amour la Deesse immortelle:*
> *Le Ciel peintre sçauant l'a pourtraitte si belle,*
> *Que son diuin tableau ne se peut imiter.*
> *Comment sans t'esblouir pourras-tu supporter*
> *De ses yeux flamboyans la planete iumelle?*
> *Quelle couleur peindra sa couleur naturelle,*
> *Et les graces qu'on voit sur son front voleter?*

Once well started on his own poem, Carew ignores Desportes's final six lines.

107. *Loves Courtship.* A shorter version appears in *Wits Interpreter*, 1655, as follows:

> *To* Cœlia.
>
> RIse lovely *Cœlia* and be kinde,
>   Let my desires freedome finde,
> And wee'l make the Gods confess
> Mortalls enjoy some happiness.
>   Sit thee down.
> *Cupid* hath but one bow, yet can I spie
> A thousand *Cupid's* in thy eie;
>   Nor may the God behold our bliss,
>   For sure thine eyes doe dark'n his,
>   If thou fearest,
> That hee'l betray thee with his light,
> Let me eclipse thee with his sight,
>   And whilst I shade thee from his eye,
>   Oh! let me hear thee gently cry,
>   I yeild.

6–10. Cf. *Love's Labour's Lost*, IV. iii. 117–20:

> Thou for whom e'en Jove would swear
> Juno but an Ethiop were;
> And deny himself for Jove,
> Turning mortal for thy love.

9. *Thee his immortall Queene to make.* The reading 'immortall' is from a manuscript formerly in the possession of Mr. P. J. Dobell and collated by him; the poem is there ascribed to 'Corbet'. The present text has been altered from the 'mortall Queene' of 1640 and most manuscripts, because it appears to me that 'immortall' is necessary to establish properly the antithesis expressed

in lines 9 and 10. The meaning is that Mars will either make Celia his queen in heaven or live as her husband on earth; to read 'mortall Queene' would give 'mortall' either a meaning at variance with that of the passage as a whole or else no significance at all. The emendation has the additional advantage of regularizing the metre.

108. *On a Damaske rose sticking vpon a Ladies breast.* Carew's poem may owe something to Joannes Bonefonius's lyric (*Pancharis* xiii, in *Delitiæ C. Poetarum Gallorum*, 1609, i. 666–7) beginning:

> Ergo, floscule tu meæ Puellæ
> Hoc florente sinu vsque conquiesces?
> Ergo tu Dominæ meæ papillis
> Beatus nimis insidebis vsque?
> O si, floscule, mî tua liceret
> Istâ sorte frui, & meæ puellæ
> Incubare sinu, atque desidere
> Hos inter globulos papillularum
> Non sic lentus inersque conquiescam,
> Non sic insideam otiosus vsque;
> Sed toto spatio inquietus errem
> Et feram sinui, feramque collo
> Mille basia, mille & huic & illi
> Impingam globulo osculationes. . . .

The theme, a popular one, was capable of varied treatment. Compare Herrick, *Upon the Roses in Julias bosome*; Habington, *To Roses in the bosome of Castara*; Edward Sherburne, *Violets in Thaumantia's Bosome.*

12. a god devine. The manuscripts and the first three editions read 'a good devine'; the present reading first appears in Herringman's edition, 1670. Support for the emendation is furnished by *The Comparison*, lines 13–14 (p. 99), which repeats the present idea almost verbatim:

> Thy lips congealed Nectar are, and such
> As but a Deitie, there's none dare touch.

Against the tautology of 'god devine' must be set the incongruity of 'good devine' (i.e. virtuous clergyman) in the present context.

109. *The protestation, a Sonnet.* The title 'Ciacono' in *A7* has obvious reference to the musical setting. These graceful but thoroughly conventional lines are composed in a style old-fashioned by Carew's day. Compare the following stanzas from a poem published in *The Paradyse of daynty deuises*, 1576 ('Being Forsaken of His Friend He Complaineth. By E. S.'), ed. Rollins, p. 47:

> The grasse me thinks should growe in skie
> The starres, vnto the yearth cleaue faste:
> The water streame should passe awrie,
> The winds should leue their strēgt of blast.
> The Sonne and Moone by one assent,
> Should bothe forsake the firmament.

> The fishe in ayer should flie with finne,
> The foules in floud should bryng forth fry
> All thyngs me thinks should erst beginne,
> To take their course vnnaturally.
> Afore my frende should alter so,
> Without a cause to bee my foe. . . .

Donne similarly refurbished a hackneyed theme in *The Baite*.

109. *The tooth-ach cured by a kisse.* In *814* ascribed to 'Ro: Ellice'.

110. 5–12. Vincent points out a possible relationship between these lines and Donne's *An Anatomie of the World*. *The first Anniversary*, lines 91–4:

> There is no health; Physitians say that wee,
> At best, enjoy but a neutralitie.
> And can there bee worse sicknesse, then to know
> That we are never well, nor can be so?

13–14. That Angell. A reference to John v. 2–4. Compare Cleveland, *To Julia to Expedite Her Promise*, lines 52–4 (ed. Berdan, p. 72):

> Else pious Julia, angel-wise,
> Moves the Bethesda of her trickling eyes
> To cure the spittle world of maladies.

113. *On Mistris N. to the greene sicknesse.* This and the five poems succeeding were not published until 1642. The *Mistris N.* of the title is expanded in *W* to Mrs. *K. N.*; *A118* and *A221* give the title more fully as 'The retired blood exhorted to returne in yᵉ cheekes of yᵉ pale sisters Mʳⁱˢ Katherine, and Mʳⁱˢ Mary Nevill'. These ladies were probably the daughters of Sir Henry Neville of Billingbear, Berkshire, who died in 1629 (see *D.N.B.*). Katherine Neville became in 1640 the second wife of Sir Thomas Lunsford (1610?–53?); Mary married 'a man of the name of Borell' (Vincent). Their aunts Katherine and Mary Neville, daughters of the better-known Sir Henry Neville, courtier and diplomatist (1564–1615), are less likely to have been, chronology considered, the ladies addressed by Carew. Green sickness is an old name, still sometimes used, for chlorosis, 'an anaemic disease of young women'.

1. Stay coward blood. The figure may have been suggested by *Romeo and Juliet*, v. iii. 94–6:

> Thou art not conquer'd; beauty's ensign yet
> Is crimson in thy lips and in thy cheeks,
> And death's pale flag is not advanced there.

113. *Vpon a Mole in* Celias *bosome.* W. J. Courthope singles out this poem for especial denunciation (*A History of English Poetry*, 1903, iii. 244–5): 'A poet of this order found his proper materials in subjects like those cultivated by the Alexandrian epigrammatists. . . . On these he spends all the pains that an ingenious carver gives to the sculpture of heads out of cherry-stones; and too often the result is repulsive in proportion as the pettiness and commonplace of the thought is brought into relief by the pains spent in elaborating it. . . .

The mole in Celia's bosom is a metamorphosed bee—an idea which is worked out with a nauseous minuteness of detail.' The detail to which Courthope probably objected most strongly—the 'rowling file of Balmy sweat' in line 10—is echoed and softened from Donne's *Elegie VIII* ('The Comparison'):

> As the sweet sweat of Roses in a Still,
> As that which from chaf'd muskats pores doth trill,
> As the Almighty Balme of th'early East,
> Such are the sweat drops of my Mistris breast,
> And on her necke her skin such lustre sets,
> They seeme no sweat drops, but pearle coronets.

5. close. 'Private, secluded, snug. *arch.* or *Obs.*' *O.E.D.*, which quotes *Britain's Ida* (1628): 'From a close bower this dainty musique flow'd.'

114. 20. the Bees Honey, and her sting. Cf. Torquato Tasso, *Rime e Prose*, Venice, 1583, p. 53:

> Ne i vostri dolci baci
> De l'api è il dolce mele,
> E vi è il morso de l'api anco crudele.
> Dunque addolcito e punto
> Da voi parto in un punto.

Also Guarini, *Rime*, 1598, p. 94 (Madrigal LXXIII, 'Baciate labra'):

> ... *E chi vi bacia senta*
> *De l'ape ch'io prouai dolce, e crudele*
> *L'ago nel core, e ne la bocca il mele.*

Tasso's lyric was adapted by Drummond in his madrigal *Of a Kisse* (ed. Kastner, i. 113).

114. An Hymeneall Song on the Nuptials of the Lady *Ann Wentworth*, and the Lord *Louelace*. Lady Anne Wentworth, to whom Richard Lovelace dedicated *Lucasta* in 1649, was the daughter and presumptive heiress of Thomas Wentworth, first Earl of Cleveland; according to her 'Nativity' in MS. Ashmole 243, fol. 168ᵛ (Bodleian Library), she was born on 20 July 1623. At some time between 1634 and 1638 she attracted the admiring eye of Sir John Finch, Baron Finch of Fordwich, the Lord Chief Justice (see Carew's poem on that subject, p. 83); but she was won by John Lovelace, second Baron Lovelace of Hurley (1616–70). The marriage licence, issued from the Bishop of London's office, reads as follows: 'Lovelace, the Right Hon. John, Lord Baron, of Hurley, in co. Berks, bachelor, 22, at own disposal, and the Hon. Lady Anne Wentworth, daughter of the Right Hon. Thomas, Earl of Cleveland, spinster, 15, and with her father's consent, alleged by Mr. William Witton, clerk, chaplain to said Earl of Cleveland—at St. Bennet, Paul's Wharf, Chelsea, Middlesex, or St. Giles-in-the-Fields. 9 July, 1638.' (Joseph Foster, *London Marriage Licences, 1521–1869*, p. 861.) Carew's particular interest in the wedding probably arose from the fact that Lady Anne Wentworth's mother was Anne Crofts of Saxham, sister of his friend John Crofts; she had died on the 1st of January preceding.

115. 21–4. The sphere of Venus was third of the eight concentric spheres on

COMMENTARY

which the heavenly bodies were thought to move. Each of these bodies had its governing Intelligence, and each exerted specific influence over human destiny.

25–7. *they do move | The wheele.* Cf. Pico della Mirandola, *A Platonick Discourse upon Love*, tr. Thomas Stanley (1651), ii. xvii: 'Venus *is said to command Fate*. The order and concatenation of causes and effects in this sensible World, called Fate, depends on the order of the Intelligible World, Providence. Hence Platonists place Providence, (the ordering of Ideas) in the first Minde, depending upon God its ultimate end, to which it leads all other things. Thus *Venus* being the order of those Ideas whereon Fate, the Worlds order, depends, commands it.'

115. *A married Woman.* This grave little essay may represent youthful work suggested by Overbury's *A Wife* (1614) and the several imitations which followed it.

116. 11. habituall vertues. For the full statement see Aristotle, *Nicomachean Ethics*, ii. 1–4.

116. *Loves Force.* This is closely related in subject and treatment to the poem preceding, and probably dates from the same period.

1. the first ruder Age. Carew's conception is reminiscent of Lucretius, v. 925 ff.

4. Full-summ'd. Cf. Drayton, *Ideas Mirrour*, Amour 3, lines 9–10 (ed. Hebel, i. 99):

> But now their plumes full sumd with sweet desire,
> To shew their kinde, began to clime the skies.

The term is applied in falconry to a bird whose feathers are fully grown.

8. Food from the Oake, or the next Acorne-heape. Cf. Lucretius, v. 939–40:

> Glandiferas inter curabant corpora quercus
> Plerumque.

121. To his mistris. This and the two poems following were first printed in the edition of 1651.

122. In praise of his Mistris.
19. fair Pillars. Cf. p. 70, line 33, and the note.

123. To *Celia*, upon Love's Vbiquity.
7. a Ball with fire and powder fild. Cf. p. 85, line 47.
15–16. An echo of Horace's 'Caelum non animum mutant qui trans mare currunt' (*Epistulae*, i. xi. 27).
20–6. Cf. *To her in absence. A SHIP.* (p. 23.)
124. 35–40. The compass image occurs in Donne, *A Valediction: forbidding mourning*, lines 21–36; in Jonson's *An Epistle to Master Iohn Selden*, lines 31–3; and in *An Excuse of absence* (p. 131), which Carew translated from Guarini.

127. The prologue to a Play. This Prologue and the Epilogue following were first printed by W. C. Hazlitt in 1870. For possible date and occasion see the six songs beginning on p. 59, and the appended note.

127. The Epilogue to the same Play.

1–14. Carew echoes the Platonic doctrine of the alternation of opposites developed in the *Phaedo*.

128. 9. Tartar. 'An old cant name for a strolling vagabond, a thief, a beggar' (*O.E.D.*).

129. To M^ris^ Katherine Nevill on her greene sicknesse. A companion-piece to the poem on page 113, and (in *W*) to that on page 194. Ascribed to 'Tho Cary' in *A118*. First printed (anonymously) in *Musarum Deliciæ*, 1655.

1. White innocence. Cf. Donne, *Of the Progresse of the Soule. The second Anniversary*, line 114: 'They reinvest thee in white innocence.'

129. To his mistresse retiring in affection. Ascribed in *A118* to 'Tho: Cary', in *A221* to 'Tho: Carew'. First printed by W. C. Hazlitt.

130. 7–8. Cf. p. 7, line 9, and the note.

12. Cf. Catullus, lxxii. 7–8:

> Quis potis est? inquis. quod amantem iniuria talis
> Cogit amare magis, sed bene velle minus.

130. To a Friend. Ascribed to 'Mr Carew' in *Ash 38*. First printed in Bliss's edition of Wood's *Athenæ Oxonienses*, 1815.

131. A Ladies prayer to Cupid. Ascribed to 'T: C.' in *C*; in *R2* accompanies other poems by Carew. First printed (anonymously) in *The Academy of Complements*, 1650. A translation from Guarini's Madrigal CIX (*Rime*, 1598, p. 112^v^):

> Donna accorta.
>
> *Se vuoi ch'io torni a le tue fiamme, Amore,*
> *Non far idolo il core*
> *Ne di fredda vecchiezza,*
> *Ne d'incostante, e pazza giouanezza.*
> *Dammi, se puoi, Signore*
> *Cor saggio in bel sembiante,*
> *Canuto amore in non canuto amante.*

Drummond of Hawthornden adapted the same madrigal in his poem *Lillas Prayer* (ed. Kastner, i. 117).

131. An Excuse of absence. Ascribed to 'T: C.' in *C*; in *R2* accompanies other poems by Carew. First printed by W. C. Hazlitt. Based on Guarini's Madrigal XCVI (*Rime*, 1598, p. 105^v^):

> *Con voi sempre son io*
> *Agitato, ma fermo;*
> *E se'l meno v'inuolo, il più vi lasso.*
> *Son simile al compasso,*
> *Ch'vn piede in voi quasi mio centro i'fermo,*
> *L'altro patisce di [fortuna] i giri,*
> *Ma non può far, che 'ntorno à voi non giri.*

132. On his Mistres lookeing in a glasse. Ascribed in *C* to 'T: Ca:', in *H6* to 'Th: C:'. First printed by W. C. Hazlitt. The first six lines are almost exactly the same as those of *A Looking-Glasse* (p. 19).

133. A Translation of Certain Psalmes. Carew's translation of Psalm 137 was included anonymously in Henry Lawes's *Select Psalmes of a New Translation*, 1655; it was reprinted, from manuscript, in Bliss's edition of *Athenæ Oxonienses*, 1815, and thence in Carew's *Works*, 1824. The other psalms were first printed by W. C. Hazlitt in 1870.

151. *Coelum Britannicum.*

Of the circumstances which impelled Thomas Carew to furnish in 1633–4 a masque for production by Inigo Jones, nothing is known beyond what is implied by the couplet on the title-page, from Ausonius (ed. Peiper, I. iv. 11–12): all unskilled as he is, he has received Caesar's command, and will obey. Aurelian Townshend had offered a similar apology for *Albions Triumph* in 1631—'I was as loath to be brought vpon the Stage as an vnhansom Man is to see himselfe in a great Glasse. But my Excuse, and Glory is, The King commanded, and I obeyed.' But whether Carew's invitation originated with Charles or with Jones does not greatly matter. By 1633 his reputation as poet and wit was firmly established, and though no dramatist, he would be a fair choice to help in filling the place, as supplier of masques, vacated by Ben Jonson three years before. The present work is first heard of in a letter from Garrard to Strafford on 9 January 1633/4: 'There are two Masques in Hand, the first of the Inns of Court, which is to be presented on *Candlemas-day*; the other the King presents the Queen with on *Shrove-Tuesday* at Night: High Expences, they speak of 20000 *l.* that it will cost the Men of the Law. Oh that they would once give over these Things, or lay them aside for a Time, and bend all their Endeavours to make the King Rich! For it gives me no Satisfaction, who am but a looker on, to see a rich Commonwealth, a rich People, and the Crown poor. God direct them to remedy this quickly.' (*Strafforde's Letters and Dispatches*, 1739, i. 177.) In the same letter Garrard mentions that on Twelfth Night the Queen 'feasted the King at *Somerset-house*, and presented him with a Play, newly studied, long since printed, *The Faithful Shepherdess*, which the King's Players acted in the Robes she and her Ladies acted their Pastoral in the last Year'. The 'very stately and solemn masque' projected by Charles, one learns from a report of the Venetian ambassador (*Cal. S.P. Ven., 1632–6*, p. 190), was intended to provide a return for this entertainment; and the obligation was nobly discharged. 'On Shrovetusday night, the 18 of February, 1633,' records Sir Henry Herbert, 'the Kinge dancte his Masque, accompanied with 11 lords, and attended with 10 pages. It was the noblest masque of my time to this day, the best poetrye, best scenes, and the best habitts. The kinge and queene were very well pleasd with my service, and the Q. was pleasd to tell mee before the king, "Pour les habits, elle n'avoit jamais rien vue de si brave." ' (*Dramatic Records of Sir Henry Herbert*, ed. Adams, 1917, p. 55.) This tribute to the brilliant effect of the *Coelum Britannicum* is especially notable because the production could hardly have escaped comparison with that of Shirley's *Triumph of Peace*, sumptuously presented by the gentlemen of the Inns of Court twice in the fortnight preceding. Garrard, however, found the *Coelum Britannicum* itself not so remarkable as the improved management of the house at its presentation: 'On *Shrove-Tuesday* at Night, the King and the Lords performed their Masque. The Templers were all invited and well placed, they have found a new way of letting them in by a turning Chair, besides they let in none but such as have Tickets sent them beforehand, so that now the keeping of the Door is no trouble, the King intends to have this Masque again in the *Easter* Holydays.' (*Strafforde's Letters and Dispatches*, i. 207: 27 Feb. 1633/4.) Sir Humphrey Mildmay, who was likewise present, records in his Diary only: '18°: a fayre day & att nighte was performed his Ma^s: Masque of Lordes etc. att Whitehall'; his record of expenditures for this date records that 'for the Masque of his Ma' he had to pay sixpence (MS. Harl. 454, fols. 5^v, 178^r).

An itemized account of the 'perticuler paiements and Disbursements for and concerning Masqueing Apparel & other attyre for his Majestie & others for the Masque performed on Shrove tuesday the 18th of February 1633' is preserved at the Public Record Office (Audit Office, 3/910, fols. 25^r–26^v); it has been printed by Reyher, *Les Masques anglais*, pp. 516–18, and by Percy Simpson and C. F. Bell, *Designs by Inigo Jones*, pp. 17–19. This shows a total disbursement of £141. 12s. 5d. on costumes, most of the amount going for the 'rich Masqueing suite for his Majesties royall person of aurora Cullor and white sattin enbroidered with silver'. There are preserved nineteen designs for the production, drawn by Inigo Jones (Simpson and Bell, op. cit., pp. 83–8). Apparently the work was produced only once—or twice, if the King's desire (mentioned by Garrard) for a second performance after Easter was carried out. In B.M. MS. Harl. 4931, fol. 28, there appears an outline of the plot, with the marginal notes, in a different hand, 'An: 1638./' and 'This was acted in Germany, before ye Earle of Arundel, w^n he went to Vienna in behalf of ye Paulsgraue.' But this information is probably incorrect. William Crowne, in his *True Relation* of Arundel's journey, which had taken place in 1636, mentions two dramatic pieces presented before Arundel while abroad, the first 'a kinde of Comedy by young Scollers in masking attire' at Vienna (p. 23) and the second an allegorical drama, on the subject of peace, at Prague (pp. 33–7). But neither of these productions could very easily have been *Coelum Britannicum*; and indeed it is hard to imagine a piece less suited for presentation outside the court for which it was originally intended. Brotanek (*Die englischen Maskenspiele*, p. 206 n.) reasonably suggests that the author of the note in MS. Harl. 4931 has confused the allegory of *Coelum Britannicum* with that of the play seen at Prague, as reported by Crowne. The outline, which reads as follows, is nevertheless interesting for its expansion and clarification of a few ideas merely implied in the published text.

An: 1638./

The Designe.

This was acted in Germany, before ye Earle of Arundel, w^n he went to Vienna in behalf of ye Paulsgraue.

The Scene is a Globe supported by Atlas, the Hemisphere beautifyed with Starres. Mercury descends to their Ma:^{ties} declaring the resolution of the Gods to purge the Heauens of those Constellations w:^{ch} antiquity had

fixed there, as eternall Registers of their Luxuryes w:^ch they renounce and
intend a reformation in Conformity to their Ma:^tes exemplar Court, made
such by the sedulous imitacōn of the vnparełled Coniugall Loue and other
heroicall vertues of soe Royall Presidents. To him Momus is ioyned with
intent (as he is feigned a preuiledged Scoffer) to interweaue with the more
serious passages a continued thred of mirth. The disbanded Starres fall
into three antimasques: the first expresseth naturall deformity, Emblem'd
in the Beare, Hydra and other Monsters, the second obliquity in motion,
in a dance of retrograde paces referring to ye Crabbe, ye third a deuiation
from vertue in ye seuerall vices proper to distinct Starres. Momus pro-
claimes ye Bands & Riches, Pouerty, Pleasure [&] Fortune plead right of
Succession to ye vacant Heauens, each attended by his Antimasque, The
first of Ploughmen and Sheaphards and miners treading to rurall musique
wth a Cornucopia and other Country Lasses, such morrises or other rustique
measures as are vsuall at their Sheepsharings and haruest homes, as ye
inexhausted fountaines of wealth: The second of Gypseis, ye third of ye 5.
senses as ye seates of all pleasure, The fourth (because though all Estates
haue an immediate dependance on fortune, yet ye Euents of warre begett
ye greatest reuolutions) Of a scirmachye or vmbratique fight performed
by Souldiers to Martiall Musique. Their seuerall reasons are refuted, and
they, (that ye dramatique and mimique part may be equally mixed suc-
cessiuely alternate their paces and dances, Mercury hauing reserued ye
instauration of ye Heauens for his Ma^ty and those selected Spirits w:^ch
he had dignifyed with ye glory of wayting vpon his perfections soe to
appropriate to their Sphere ye title of Cœlum Britannicum calles out ye last
antimasque of Pictes and other nations anciently inhabiting this Island
Atlas ariseth out of ye earth transformed into a rocky mountaine in ye midst
whereof are seated 3 persones representing 3 Kingdomes on ye topp, their
Genius, vpon ye stage a Chorus of Druides and Riuers. They sing ye Rock
breakes, ye mayne Masquers are discouered in a Caue they issue and dance
their entry, w:^ch finished ye genius ascends singing, ye 3 Kingdomes and
Chorus below alternatiuely answering. The mayne dance succeedes w:^ch
ended Eternity is discouered sitting on a sphere, illustrated with yt accesse
of life w:^ch his ma:^ty in ye most glorious place & forme with ye rest of ye
stellified Masquers are supposed to impart. On ye one side Eusebia,
Alethia[,] Sophia, on ye other Homonoia, Dicæarche, Euphemia, pendant
in ye ayre sing ye Assumption & good night./

The hand in which this outline is transcribed has not been identified. It is
not Carew's.

In general conception, and in many of its details, *Coelum Britannicum* is
based directly on Giordano Bruno's philosophic dialogue (itself derived from
Lucian), the *Spaccio de la Bestia Trionfante*, published in 1584 with a
dedication to Sir Philip Sidney. Carew has handled the material of his
original with considerable skill, cleverly twisting the conclusion of Bruno's
philosophic action so as to compliment the King and Queen, and lightening
the ethical burden with topical quips. The *Spaccio* consists of three dialogues,
with Sophia, Saulino, and Mercury as *interlocutori*; these discuss the recent

revolutionary changes in heaven. Jupiter, now in his old age and exhausted with the dissipations of youth, has determined upon reform for himself and his court; mortals have become lax in their worship of the gods, and he fears his throne is insecure. But the state of heaven itself is not such as to induce reverence in men or virtue in his fellow gods; the stars and constellations are all records of the lusts and misdeeds of himself and the other inhabitants of Olympus. Heaven must be swept clean of these shocking mementoes, and symbols of virtue must take their place, prudence replacing the Dragon, wisdom Cepheus, &c.; false claimants to stellification must be turned away and rival virtues weighed against one another. In the discussion of these problems the god Momus, sceptical and sharp-tongued, has a role similar to that assigned him in *Coelum Britannicum*, and in a few of the speeches of Momus and the other characters it is obvious that Carew had a copy of Bruno's work before him as he wrote.[1]

Scenically and architecturally *Coelum Britannicum* shows close relationship to several Italian and French productions. The nature of this background is variously indicated by Brotanek, *Die englischen Maskenspiele*, 1902; Reyher, *Les Masques anglais*, 1909; Simpson and Bell, *Designs by Inigo Jones for Masques and Plays at Court*, 1924; Enid Welsford, *The Court Masque*, 1927; and Allardyce Nicoll, *Stuart Masques and the Renaissance Stage*, 1938. Many of Inigo Jones's designs and drawings for the production are reproduced by Simpson and Bell, and a few others by Allardyce Nicoll; the latter also provides data on the mechanics of the staging, much of it deduced from continental practice as reported in Sabbatini's *Pratica di fabricar scene e machine ne' teatri*, 1638. The mechanisms explained include the cloud machine and the great mountain which rose up and afterwards sank into the earth. *Coelum Britannicum* was particularly well designed to show off Jones's mechanical and artistic genius, and it may have been he rather than Carew who wrote the detailed prose descriptions connecting the episodes.

The details of the symbolism correspond in most respects with those given in *Iconologia, o vero descrittione d'imagini delle virtu', vitij, Affetti, Passioni humane, Corpi celesti, Mondo e sue parti. Opera di Cesare Ripa Perugino . . . Fatica necessaria ad Oratori, Predicatori, Poeti, Formatori d'Emblemi*, 1611. Where the description in Carew is scanty, it is probable that the fuller details may be safely filled in from Ripa.

The music for the masque is ascribed by Langbaine to Henry Lawes; Grove thinks it probable that through writing music for *Coelum Britannicum* Lawes met the Earl of Bridgewater (whose sons were masquers) and that this led to Ludlow and *Comus*. There is, however, no real evidence that Lawes was the composer, and the only surviving music which might have been used for the masque consists of three pieces, a 'Country Dance' by William Lawes in Playford's *Court Ayres*, 1655 (cf. p. 167, lines 540–1: *'the fourth Antimasque consisting of Countrey people, musique and measures'*), a tune in B.M. MS. Add. 10444 called 'The Gypsies' (cf. p. 169, line 627: *'They dance the fifth Antimaske of Gypsies'*) which probably belongs either to *Coelum Britannicum* or to Jonson's *Gypsies Metamorphosed*, and in the same manuscript another

---

[1] The indebtedness to Bruno was first pointed out in an article on Carew by Robert Adamson in the ninth edition of the *Encyclopaedia Britannica*, published 1875–89.

tune, headed 'The Shepheards Masque', which might conceivably represent (rather than the tune by William Lawes already mentioned) the accompaniment for the fourth antimasque. Ebsworth took the statement at the end of the *Poems*, 1640, that 'The Songs and Dialogues of this Booke were set with apt Tunes to them, by Mr. *Henry Lawes*, one of His Majesties Musitians', as referring to *Coelum Britannicum* immediately preceding; but the statement is almost certainly to be understood rather in relation to the *Poems* as a whole, and it was taken in this sense by the editors of 1651 and 1670, who repeated the information on the general title-page. Mr. Percy M. Young, who has made a special study of the masque music of the period, has suggested to me that William rather than Henry Lawes is most likely to have composed the *Coelum Britannicum* music; he adds that the ascription of the music to Henry Lawes by such authorities as Grove, Pulver, and W. W. Greg is apparently to be derived from Rimbault, who in his *History of Dramatic Music in England to the Death of Purcell* ascribed the setting to Henry Lawes on the evidence furnished by 'detached pieces in Playford's various publications'.

153. 20–4. an Ovall. Inigo Jones's sketch shows 'A lion rampant to right, the head, turned three-quarters towards the spectator, wearing an imperial crown' (Simpson and Bell, *Designs by Inigo Jones*, p. 83).

154. 33. the Scæne. Simpson and Bell record four drawings by Inigo Jones, two of them certainly intended for the present scene and two doubtful. The first of the drawings shows 'Four (or five?) wings on each side of the stage. They represent the remains of ancient buildings standing on boulders. The two pairs nearest the spectator are ruins of the Corinthian order; the next pair, of huge arched structures; the fourth wing on the left consists of three tall Corinthian columns like those of the Temple of Jupiter Stator, that facing it on the right is a pillar with a piece of pediment; behind this is part of an amphitheatre, and facing it on the left a formless mass of masonry.' (*Designs by Inigo Jones*, p. 83.) This drawing, like many of the others, is 'splashed with scene-painters' distemper'.

155. 103. influence. In astrology, 'The supposed flowing or streaming from the stars or heavens of an etherial fluid acting upon the character and destiny of men, and affecting sublunary things generally' (*O.E.D.*).

156. 104. Enter *Momus*. Inigo Jones's sketch shows 'Bust only, three-quarters to left. . . . Lank beard and hair. Wreath of upstanding feathers with porcupine's quills in front. Doublet powdered with daggers and darts.' (Simpson and Bell, op. cit., p. 85.) The 'haire party coloured' is referred to, in the course of a description of Discordia, by Ripa (*Iconologia*, 1611, p. 121): 'La varietà de' colori significa la diuersità de gl'animi, come s'è detto, però l'Ariosto scrisse.

'La conobbe al vestir di color cento.'

108. Goodden. Elliptical for 'Good even'; or 'God give you good even'; the expression was 'used at any time after noon' (*O.E.D.*).

113. reach. To succeed in understanding or comprehending (*O.E.D.*).

122. in Diameter. Diametrically (*O.E.D.*).

157. 143. Skonces or Redoubts. A sconce is a small fort or earthwork; a redoubt is also a type of fortification. Carew continues the military figure in the 'perdu Page or Chambermaid' of line 144; 'perdu' was applied to a

sentinel placed in an extremely hazardous position. The *O.E.D.* interprets the present instance of the word to mean 'Lying out, passing the night out of bed'. This passage is the only example given of the word in that meaning.

156. For the story of Mars and Venus trapped by Vulcan see Ovid, *Metamorphoses*, iv. 169–89—a passage itself drawn from the minstrel's narrative in the eighth book of the *Odyssey*. The 'Cobweb-Iron' echoes lines 178–9:

> Non illud opus tenuissima vincant
> Stamina, non summo quae pendet aranea tigno.

160. Calabria. Vincent, who printed from one of the copies resembling *cmpw*, writes: 'The mis-spelling of some proper names, when it seems to be intentional (e.g. . . . . "Culabria" for "Calabria"), has been retained.' I do not retain the misspellings because I do not understand the intention, if it existed. Compare line 165 below, where all copies of 1634 misspell '*Rablais*' as '*Rublais*'. Vincent here corrects to 'Rabelais'.

163. old *Peter Aretine*. See *A Rapture*, line 116 (p. 52) and the note.

165–73. The 'moderne French Hospitall of Oratory', as E. E. Duncan-Jones shows in *Modern Language Review*, xlvi (1951), 439–40, is very likely the noted stylist J.-L. Guez de Balzac, whose *Lettres* (1624) express opinions of English sovereigns which are prudently omitted in the English translation of 1634; he also writes about his sciatica. James Howell condemns Balzac in a letter '*To Sir* J. S. *at* Leeds-Castle', dated 25 July 1625 (*Epistolae Ho-Elianae*, ed. Joseph Jacobs, 1890, pp. 18–19).

158. 191–4. *Atlas*. Inigo Jones's sketch portrays him 'Whole length, kneeling on his left knee, facing the spectator, his head turned three-quarters to right. He is bearded and wears a crown of spikes; drapery covers his back and right knee. With both hands he supports a huge sphere resting on his shoulders.' (*Designs by Inigo Jones*, p. 85.)

199. frequent. In great numbers, crowded (*O.E.D.*).

159. 228 ff. This passage is derived directly from Bruno, *Spaccio de la Bestia Trionfante*, Dialogo Primo; *Opere Italiane*, 1927, ii. 28–9:

'Sof. Pensa al suo giorno del giudizio, perché il termine de gli o piú o meno o a punto trentasei mila anni, come è publicato, è prossimo; dove la revoluzion de l'anno del mondo minaccia, ch'un altro Celio vegna a repigliar il domino e per la virtú del cangiamento ch'apporta il moto de la trepidazione, e per la varia, e non piú vista, né udita relazione ed abitudine di pianeti. Teme che il fato disponga, che l'ereditaria successione non sia come quella della precedente grande mondana revoluzione, ma molto varia e diversa, cracchieno quantosivoglia gli pronosticanti astrologi ed altri divinatori.'

233 ff. With the various celestial reforms compare the contemporary measures mentioned by Garrard in his letter to Strafford on 9 January 1633/4 (*Strafforde's Letters and Dispatches*, 1739, i. 176): 'We have very plausible Things done of late. The Book called the Declaration of the King's for rectifying of Taverns, Ordinaries, Bakers, Osteries, is newly come forth. I'll say no more of it, your Agent here will send it your Lordship. All Back Doors to Taverns on the *Thames* are commanded to be shut up, only the *Bear*

at the Bridge-Foot is exempted, by Reason of the Passage to *Greenwich*.
To encourage Gentlemen to live more willingly in the Country, all Game
Fowl, as Pheasant, Partridges, Ducks, as also Hares are by Proclamation for-
bidden to be dressed or eaten in any Inns, and Butchers are forbidden to be
Graziers.' A number of royal proclamations from about this date are directed
against 'sophistication', or adulteration, of wares: e.g. on 12 January 1632/3,
'A Proclamation prohibiting the makeing up of Girdles, Belts, Hangers and
other Wares for Mens wearing, or for War Service with Brass Buckles' (in
imitation of iron); 16 April 1633, 'A Proclamation for the preventing of
Frauds and Deceipts used in Drapery'. Wood attributes the wave of reform,
in part at least, to Attorney-General Noy, of whose death in 1634 he writes:
'As his Majesty was somewhat troubled at his loss, and the Clergy more, so
the generality of the Commons rejoyced. The Vintners drank carouses, in
hopes to dress meat again and sell Tobaco, Beer, &c. which by a sullen
capricio, *Noy* restrained them from. The Players also for whom he had done
no kindness, did, the next Term after his decease, make him the subject of a
merry Comedy, stiled *A projector lately dead*, &c.' (*Athenæ Oxonienses*,
1691, i. 507.)

237–41. Cf. the royal proclamation of 13 October 1633 'for preuenting
of the abuses growing by the vnordered Retailing of Tobacco', which provided
that no tobacco-seller might deal in wine, spirits, or beer.

247 ff. Carew modifies the order and some details of the points of reforma-
tion as given by Bruno, *Spaccio*, Dialogo Primo (*Opere Italiane*, 1927,
ii. 31–3):

'Sof. . . . Ha ordinato al suo fabro Vulcano, che non lavore de giorni di
festa; ha comandato a Bacco che non faccia comparir la sua corte, e non
permetta debaccare le sue Evanti, fuor che nel tempo di carnasciale, e nelle
feste principali de l'anno, solamente dopo cena, appresso il tramontar del
sole, e non senza sua speciale ed espressa licenza. . . . Ha vietato a Cupido
d'andar piú vagando, in presenza degli uomini, eroi e dei, cossí sbracato,
come ha di costume; ed ingiontoli che non offenda oltre la vista de Celicoli,
mostrando le natiche per la via lattea, ed Olimpico senato: ma che vada per
l'avenire vestito almeno da la cintura a basso. . . . Quel Ganimede . . . al
presente credo che, se non ha altra virtute che quella che è quasi persa, è
da temere che da paggio di Giove non debba aver a favore di farsi come
scudiero a Marte. . . . Ha imposto a tutti gli dei di non aver paggi o cubi-
cularii di minore etade che di vinticinque anni.'

160. 255. Oretenus. From *ore tenus*, by word of mouth; cf. *Strafforde's
Letters and Dispatches*, i. 165 (6 Dec. 1633): 'One *Bowyer*, a lying shameless
Fellow, was brought *ore tenus* into the *Star Chamber* for abusing the
Archbishop of *Canterbury*.' Hence, as a nonce-word, the legal proceedings
so conducted.

257–60. In Bruno the purification of Heaven is itself appropriately
assigned to the feast of the Gigantomachy: 'Nel giorno dunque, che nel cielo
si celebra la festa de la Gigantoteomachia (segno de la guerra continua e
senza triegua alcuna, che fa l'anima contra gli vizii e disordinati affetti),
vuole effettuar e definir questo padre quello che per qualche spacio di tempo

avanti avea proposto e determinato' (Epistola Esplicatoria; Bruno, *Opere Italiane*, 1927, ii. 13).

161. 295. the rough unlick'd Beare. Pliny, *Natural History*, viii. 126, says that bears when first born are formless masses of flesh, which the mother gradually licks into shape. Cf. Bruno: 'Togliemo via dal cielo de l'animo nostro l'Orsa della difformità' (*Spaccio*, Dialogo Primo; *Opere Italiane*, 1927, ii. 55).

297. Goatfish Capricorne. The figure of Capricornus is traditionally represented with its fore part like a goat and its hind part like a fish.

327–38. Cf. Donne, *An Anatomie of the World. The first Anniversary*, lines 263–7:

> They have impal'd within a Zodiake
> The free-borne Sun, and keepe twelve Signes awake
> To watch his steps; the Goat and Crab controule,
> And fright him backe, who else to either Pole
> (Did not these Tropiques fetter him) might runne.

162. 361–9. Condensed with some freedom from the longer allegorical catalogue in Bruno (*Spaccio*, Dialogo Primo, in *Opere Italiane*, 1927, ii. 55–6): 'la Saetta de la detrazione, . . . il Cane de la murmurazione, la Canicola de l'adulazione. . . . l'Ercole de la violenza, . . . la Cassiopea de la vanità, . . . l'Aquila de l'arroganza, . . . la Lepre del vano timore. . . . l'Argo-nave de l'avarizia, la Tazza de l'insobrietà, . . . il Scorpio de la frode, . . . il Leone de la Tirannia . . .'

163. 387. *New-England.* With Carew's opinion compare that of the Privy Council, which three days after the production of *Coelum Britannicum* took anxious note of 'the frequent transportation of greate nombers of his majesties Subiects out of this Kingdome to the Plantation called New England (whom divers persons knowe to be ill affected, and discontented, aswell with the Civill as Ecclesiasticall Gouerment) are observed to resorte thither, wherby such confusion and disorder is alreadie growne there, especially in poynt of Religion, as besides the ruine of the said Plantation, cannot but highly tend to the Scandall both of the Church and State here'. Ten ships laden with emigrants and supplies, it was noted, were preparing to sail from London; a warrant was issued to prevent their departure. (*Acts of the Privy Council of England*, Colonial Series, i. 199–200.)

389. The resin of the tropical shrub guaiacum has medicinal properties. Cf. Jonson, *Volpone*, ii. ii. 150–3.

164. 405. *Booker, Allestre.* John Booker (1602–67) had recently made a great reputation by predicting from a solar eclipse the deaths of Gustavus Adolphus and the Elector Palatine. His almanac, the *Telescopium Uranium*, first appeared in 1631, and later he was appointed licenser of 'mathematical' or astrological books. There are interesting reminiscences of him in *Mr. William Lilly's History of His Life and Times*, 1715 (written *c.* 1668), pp. 28–9. Richard Allestree, self-termed 'Contemplator in Siderali Scientia', was a native of Derby and a cousin of Dr. Richard Allestree the royalist divine. His almanacs appeared from 1624 to 1643.

406. their great Master *Tico.* Tycho Brahe, the celebrated Danish astronomer (1546–1601).

430–3. A reference to the ten great tapestry hangings ('700 ells of Arras') made by Francis Spering of Haarlem, after designs by Cornelius Vroom, for Lord Howard of Effingham, sold to King James in 1616 for £1,628, and afterwards hung in the House of Lords. They perished in the great fire of 1834. See *The Tapestry Hangings of the House of Lords: Representing the several Engagements between the English and Spanish Fleets, In the ever memorable Year* MDLXXXVIII . . . *By John Pine, Engraver*, 1739, and *Lord Howard of Effingham and the Spanish Armada . . . with the engravings of the hangings of the House of Lords*, Roxburghe Club, 1919.

435–6. The 'eighth roome' or sphere in the Ptolemaic system was that of the fixed stars. The 'Starre-Chamber' was an apartment in the royal palace of Westminster, so called (according to Stow) 'because the roof thereof is decked with the likeness of Stars gilt'; it gave its name to the notorious Court of Star-chamber.

165. 466. *Plutus.* The classical god is substituted for the Ricchezza of Bruno and of Ripa. The *Iconologia*, p. 460, describes Ricchezza as 'Donna vecchia, cieca, & vestita di panno d'oro'.

166. 479 ff. In Carew the speeches of Plutus, Poenia, Tyche, and Hedone replace a debate between Ricchezza, Povertà, and Fortuna in Bruno's *Dialogo Secondo* of the *Spaccio de la Bestia Trionfante*, and Carew has used the speech of Ricchezza (Bruno, *Opere Italiane*, 1927, ii. 98–101) as a model for that of Plutus. Marino's long canzone *L'Oro* (*La Lira*, 1625, Parte Seconda, pp. 120–5) also contains most of the arguments used by Carew.

167. 534. barbe. To mow.

168. 580 ff. *Poenia.* Poverty is described in a manner similar to Carew's, and the details of the description allegorically interpreted, by Ripa, *Iconologia*, 1611, pp. 433–5, which on several points cites the *Plutus* of Aristophanes. Some of the arguments in favour of Poverty, and the answers to them, Carew summarizes from the long discussion in Bruno:

'Sof. Non sí tosto la Povertà vedde la Ricchezza, sua nemica, esclusa, che con una piú che povera grazia si fece innante; e disse che per quella raggione, che facea la Ricchezza indegna di quel loco, lei ne dovea essere stimata degnissima, per esser contraria a colei. A cui rispose Momo:— Povertà, Povertà, tu non sareste al tutto Povertà, se non fussi ancora povera d'argumenti, sillogismi e buone consequenze. Non per questo, o misera, che siete contrarie, séguita che tu debbi essere investita di quello che lei è dispogliata o priva, e tu debbi essere quel tanto che lei non è: come, verbigrazia (poi che bisógna donartelo ad intendere con essempio), tu devi essere Giove e Momo, perché lei non è Giove né Momo.'

The debate in Bruno is inconclusive (*Opere Italiane*, 1927, ii. 102–12).

171. 676. seel'd. Blindfold—a term of falconry.

678 ff. The episode of Fortune is based in detail upon a much longer version in Bruno (*Opere Italiane*, 1927, ii. 112–15).

173. 756. The episode of Hedone is not represented in Bruno.

762–3. gamester. 'A merry frolicsome person'; or 'One addicted to amorous sport, a lewd person' (*O.E.D.*).

174. 797–9. Lysimachus, one of the generals of Alexander the Great and afterwards King of Thrace, in 291 B.C. attempted to subdue the Getae, but was made prisoner instead. Cf. Plutarch, *Moralia*, 126 E–F: 'Nay, we should recall how Lysimachus among the Getae was constrained by thirst to surrender himself and the army with him as prisoners of war, and afterwards as he drank cold water exclaimed, "My God, for what a brief pleasure have I thrown away great prosperity" ' (Loeb Classical Library ed., ii. 239, 241).

178. 948 ff. the Masquers, richly attired like ancient Heroes. Inigo Jones's drawing of one of these masquers shows 'Helmet with scrolled brim in volutes over brows, topped with curling plumes and aigrette. Square falling collar and cuffs turned back and edged with lace. Peaked cuirass-shaped doublet, decorated with scrollwork, with lions' masks on shoulders. Over-sleeves puffed and ornamented with festoons of ribbon; long sleeves slashed and pulled. Bases reaching to above knees decorated with alternate vertical bands of scrollwork and slashing and pulling. Tights. Shoes with roses. Inscribed, *"collors yellow and siluer" "a trefoile at ye bottom of ye base and ye bases somewhat shorter".* (*Designs by Inigo Jones*, p. 86; Jones has also a more elaborate design for the same costume.) Jones's sketches for one of the 'young Lords and Noblemens sonnes' agree with the description given in the text (*Designs by Inigo Jones*, p. 87).

180. 997–1001. Eridanus was a mythical river of the far west, usually identified with the Po. Phaëthon fell into it when he tried to drive the horses of the Sun, and after this the river-god Eridanus became a constellation. Cf. Bruno, *Spaccio*, Dialogo Terzo (*Opere Italiane*, 1927, ii. 211):

'—Venemo, disse Giove, al fiume Eridano; il quale non so come trattarlo; e che è in terra e che è in cielo, mentre le altre cose, de le quali siamo in proposito, facendosi in cielo, lasciâro la terra. Ma questo e che è qua, e che è là; e che è dentro, e che è fuori; e che è alto, e che è basso; e che ha del celeste, e che ha del terrestre. . . . Sia dunque l'Eridano in cielo, ma non altrimente che per credito ed imaginazione.'

181. 1038–9. The 'speaking touch' is that of the gentlemen's hands, with 'touch' the subject of 'repeat'. Cf. Marlowe, *Hero and Leander*, i. 185: 'These lovers parled by the touch of hands.' Also Lovelace, *In allusion to the French-Song. 'N'entendez vous pas ce language'* (ed. Wilkinson, ii. 117):

The Rheth'rick of my Hand
Woo'd you to understand.

And Lovelace, *Aramantha. A Pastorall* (ed. Wilkinson, ii. 107):

Onely the Rhet'rick of the Palm
Prevailing pleads.

182. 1054 ff. a great Cloud. Drawings for this are described in *Designs by Inigo Jones*, pp. 85–6, 88.

1060. The description of Religion corresponds with that in Ripa's *Iconologia*, 1611, p. 456: 'Donna alla quale, vn sottil velo cuopra il viso, tenga nella destra mano vn Libro, & vna Croce, con la sinistra vna fiamma di fuoco.' The description of Truth (lines 1062–4) is not, however, identical with Ripa's; nor is that of Wisdom (lines 1064–6).

1066. Concord. 'Donna, che tiene in mano vn faschio di verghe stretta-mente legato . . . in capo ancora hauerà vna ghirlanda, per acconciatura vi sarà vna mulachia, & così nelle medaglie antiche si vede scolpita' (Ripa, pp. 90–1).

1070. Government. 'Donna simile à Minerua; nella destra mano tiene vn ramo d'oliuo, col braccio sinistro vno scudo, & nella medesima mano vn dardo & con vn morione in capo' (Ripa, p. 207: 'Governo della Republica').

1077. Eternity. '. . . è vestita tutta di azurro celeste stellato . . . nella destra mano hauerà vn serpe in giro, che si tenga la coda in bocca. . . . Donna, che siede sopra vna sfera celeste' (Ripa, pp. 151–3). The sex of Eternity is changed in *Coelum Britannicum*, perhaps because a male voice was needed for the desired choral effect. For the symbolism of the 'Serpent' cf. p. 33, line 18, and the note.

185. 1156–7. *Lord* Brackley . . . *Mr.* Thomas Egerton. Sons of the Earl of Bridgewater; they played the brothers in Milton's masque of *Comus*, presented at Ludlow Castle later in the same year.

APPENDIX A

POEMS OF UNCERTAIN AUTHORSHIP

186. *The Sparke*. In a manuscript formerly in the possession of Mr. P. J. Dobell, and collated by him, this poem is preceded by the following verses, ascribed to John Gill:

My love hath burnt my heart to tinder,
(Since every sparkling eye doth kindle fire)
Consume it must at length into a sinder,
If Cupids mercy graunt not my desi'r:
Whoe onely (for his blessed favor) cries
Hardne this heart, or else put out those eyes.

The Sparke then follows, as 'The Answer to it', and is signed Walton Poole; it contains the final couplet, which is missing in *The Last Remains of Sʳ John Suckling*. In B.M. MS. Add. 33998 and another manuscript collated by C. L. Powell (*Modern Language Review*, xi (1916), 288) the poem is sub-scribed 'Walter Poole'. Both Gill's verses and *The Sparke* are reminiscent of Carew's *The tinder* (p. 104).

23–30. Cf. Donne, *The broken heart*, lines 29–30:

And now as broken glasses show
A hundred lesser faces . . .

187. *The Dart*. Ascribed to 'W. S.' in *A19*, *A221*, and *S14*; anonymous in other manuscripts. In *A19* and *A221* the lines form part of a poem 46 lines long beginning, 'No marvell if the Sunne's bright eye', which was published as Strode's in Dobell's edition. In *HM198* the same poem is extended to 48 lines; in *E24* it begins with the present 6 lines and runs to 28 lines in all.

284 COMMENTARY

The conceit is a commonplace; cf. Ronsard, *Le Premier Livre des Amours, III,* in *Œuvres,* 1609, p. 2:

> *Entre les rais de sa iumelle flame*
> *Ie veis Amour qui son arc desbandoit,*
> *Et dans mon cœur le brandon espandoit,*
> *Qui des plus froids les mouëlles enflame. . . .*

187. *The mistake.* Ascribed to 'Hen: Blount' in *A303, H35,* and *814;* anonymous in other manuscripts. As Vincent points out, this poem resembles Sir Robert Aytoun's lines 'Upon a Diamond cut in the form of a Heart, set with a Crown above and a bloody dart piercing it, sent to the Poet as a New Year's Gift' (*Poems,* ed. Charles Rogers, 1871, p. 66):

> Thou sent to me a heart—'twas crown'd;
> I thought it had been thine,
> But when I saw it had a wound,
> I knew the heart was mine. . . .

188. *A divine Love.* Included tentatively, on grounds of style, in *The Poems of Lord Herbert of Cherbury,* ed. G. C. Moore Smith, 1923. See Introduction, p. lxvi.

5. Lucinda. Cf. Carew's two poems (pp. 32 and 91) in which the Countess of Carlisle is addressed under this name.

190. Vpon the Royall Ship &c. See Thomas Heywood's *A true Discription of his Majesties royall and most stately Ship called the Soveraign of the Seas, built at Wolwitch in Kent 1637 . . .,* 1637, for a full account of the vessel. The second issue, 1638, notes under 'A briefe Addition to the first Coppy, worthy your observation':

'. . . A second thing of which some especiall notice may bee taken, is, that young Mr. PETER PET the Maister Builder, hath to his great expence and charge, to show that this excellent Fabricke is not to be equall'd in the World agayne: and to give a president to all Forraigne Ship-architecters, how they shall dare to undertake the like, hath lately published her true Effigies or portracture in Sculpture, grav'd by the excellent Artist Mr. IOHN PAINE, dwelling by the posterne gate neere unto Tower-hill, of whose exquisite skill, as well in drawing and painting, as his Art in graving, I am not able to give a Character answerable unto his merit.'

The present verses as they appear on this engraving (which also contains a Latin rendering by Henry Jacob) were reprinted by the present editor in *Modern Language Notes* for April 1941, with evidence for ascribing them not to Carew but to Jacob's friend and Payne's neighbour Thomas Cary of Tower-hill. A version from B.M. MS. Add. 34217 had previously been included in R. G. Howarth's edition of Carew (*Minor Poets of the Seventeenth Century,* Everyman's Library, 1931). Another manuscript copy is listed in *Reports of the Historical Manuscripts Commission,* x. 4, p. 21.

191. To a Strumpett: Ascribed to 'TC' in *A303;* anonymous in other manuscripts. First printed among Carew's poems by R. G. Howarth, 1931. A shorter version is to be found in *Latine Songs, With their English: and Poems. By Henry Bold*, 1685, as follows:

On one Grace C. *an Insatiate Whore.*

GO shameful Model of a Cursed Whore!
Damn'd by Creation ever to be poor!
Tho' Cloth'd in Indian Silk, or what may be,
Consumed on thy matchless Venery.
Thou Eldest Daughter to the Prince of Night,
That can'st out-ly thy Father at first Sight.
Out-Scoff an Ishmaelite and attempt more,
Than all our Wicked Age hath done before.
Nay where the Devil ends, thou can'st begin,
And teach both him and us, new ways to sin;
Making us to conclude that all bad Crimes
Are but thy peices Coppy'd by the times.
Surely thou wert born a Whore from the Womb
Of some Rank Baud, Unsavory's a Tomb.
That Carted from all Parishes did sell
Forbidden Fruit in the high way to Hell.
If 'twere not Sin to Curse, would they might have
Thee in Esteem, as an insatiate Grave!
And when with old age and diseases crost,
(The patient Grissel of thy Nose being lost)
Let every Hospital grudg and repine,
To give thee one poor plaister for thy Groyne.
    And ne're let any Man bemone the Case
    That ever knew thee in the State of *Grace*
                                        (*Cook*)

In *Ash 38* the poem is followed by another 'On that famous (Infamous) whore Grace Cooke'.

192. **A Health to a Mistris.** Ascribed in *A15* to 'R: Clerke.', in *A21* to 'R: C:', in *H6* to 'Th: Car'; anonymous in other manuscripts. Richard Clerke was the subject of *An Elegie on the Death of my loving Friend and Cousen, Mr. Richard Clerke, late of Lincolnes-Inne Gentleman*, which young Abraham Cowley published in the *Poetical Blossomes*, 1633:

... *Hee was adorn'd in yeares though farre more young,*
With learned CICERO's, *or a sweeter Tongue.*
And could dead VIRGIL *heare his lofty straine,*
Hee would condemne his owne to fire againe.

Five poems, including *A Health to a Mistris*, are ascribed to him in *A21*, and he is represented in a few other manuscript collections.

192. **A Louers passion.** In *S.32*, fol. 41ᵛ, ascribed to 'Th: Ca:'; in *S.32*, fol. 9ᵛ, ascribed to 'Tho: Cary.'; in *A19* ascribed to 'W. S.'; anonymous in other manuscripts.

193. *Of his Mistresse.* Found only in *A226*, without ascription. The influence of Donne is apparent.

194. *On the Green Sickness. Song.* In *W* this is a companion-piece to Carew's two other poems on the green sickness (pp. 113 and 129). Like the other pieces in *W* it is unsigned.

APPENDIX B

POEMS INCORRECTLY ASCRIBED TO CAREW IN THE EARLY EDITIONS

195. *To my Friend,* Will D'avenant. The first fourteen lines originally appeared on page [A]7ᵛ of *Madagascar*, 1638, and there form part of a poem which, with eighteen lines on the next page, is signed William Habington. Carew's poem in *Madagascar* (page 98 in the present edition) occupies pages [A]6ᵛ and [A]7ʳ; the six lines on the latter page, which contains the signature 'Thomas Carew', were joined with Habington's lines on [A]7ᵛ to form the nonsensical hybrid printed as Carew's in the *Poems* of 1640 and in the editions derived from that for two centuries.

195. *The Enquiry.* Included by Herrick in *Hesperides*, 1648, with some differences in text, as *Mrs. Eliz. Wheeler, under the name of the lost Shepardesse.*

196. *The Primrose.* Included in *Poems: written by Wil. Shake-speare. Gent.*, 1640, under 'An Addition. . . . By other Gentlemen'; and in Herrick's *Hesperides*, 1648, with some differences in text.

197. *Song.* Claimed by Shirley in his *Poems*, 1646, where in 'A Postscript to the Reader' he complains of 'some indiscreet Collector not acquainted with distributive Justice', by whom some of his compositions had been 'mingled with other mens (some Eminent) conceptions in Print'. Shirley's text differs considerably from that of Carew's *Poems*, 1640.

197. *The Hue and Cry.* First printed in *The Wittie Faire One. A Comedie: By Iames Shirley*, 1633 (Act III, scene i). A revised version, differing considerably from both that of 1633 and that printed among Carew's *Poems*, 1640, is claimed by Shirley in his *Poems*, 1646, under the title 'Loves Hue and Cry'.

198. *To his Mistris confined.* Previously plagiarized by Samuel Pick in *Festum Voluptatis*, 1639. Claimed by Shirley in his *Poems*, 1646, with lines 17–24 omitted.

199. *The Carver. To his Mistris.* Previously printed in Henry Constable's *Diana . . . augmented with diuers Quatorzains of honourable and lerned personages*, 1594 (Decade VI, Sonnet iii).

200. *To my Lord Admirall on his late sicknesse, and recovery.* First printed in Carew's *Poems*, 1642. Included in *The VVorkes of Edmond Waller Esquire*, 1645, and *Poems, &c. written by Mr. Ed. Waller*, 1645. Waller confirmed his authorship by including the lines in his authorized *Poems* of 1668.

APPENDIX C
THREE LETTERS TO SIR DUDLEY CARLETON

For the occasion of these letters see pp. xx-xxv. They were first printed in W. C. Hazlitt's edition of Carew, 1870.

APPENDIX D
POEMS AND LETTERS ADDRESSED TO CAREW

207. Aurelian Tounsend to Tho: Carew &c. First printed by G. C. Moore Smith in *Modern Language Review*, xii (1917), p. 422, from *S.23*. Carew's reply appears on pp. 74-7 of this edition.

210. Ad Thomam Carew. 'J. C.' is probably John Crofts of Saxham; 'Davenantii Poëmatis' probably refers to Davenant's *Madagascar*, 1638.

210. To Tho: Carew. The copious lyrics of Clement Paman, uneven in quality, have yet to be collected from manuscript; one of his poems is printed in Norman Ault's *Seventeenth Century Lyrics*, 1928. Paman was a Cambridge man (B.A. 1632, M.A. 1635), elder brother of the more noted Dr. Henry Paman, F.R.S. The present couplet does not require us to believe that he knew Carew personally.

211. Two letters. Besides these two letters from Suckling there exist two other letters addressed by Lucius Cary, second Viscount Falkland, to a 'noble Cosin' who, it has been asserted, may have been Thomas Carew. These are printed in full, from S.P. 16/534: 112, Public Record Office, by Kurt Weber in his *Lucius Cary, Second Viscount Falkland*, 1940, pp. 62-3. Falkland in his first letter compliments his 'cousin' on an 'excellente worke' lately produced and asks for a loan of the manuscript; 'I shall be sure to say more of it, when I haue read it, but the while I must say this, both of it and the great actresse of it, that her action was worthy of it. and it was worthy of hir action, and I beleeue the world can fitt neither of them, but with one another.' With the second note Falkland returns the manuscript and asks to have a copy made; 'it is not twice or thrise reading this peece, that will sufficiently satisfie a well advised reader . . . one of ye fayrest, wittiest & newest widdows of or tyme, my lady Dorothy Sherly longs extreamely to read it'. The editor of the *Cal. S.P. Dom., Charles I, Addenda, 1625–49*, comments (Preface, p. xxi): 'He discusses some work which had evidently lately been acted, and as he speaks of the "actress" of it, it must have been a private masque . . . probably the "Cœlum Brittanicum", produced by Carew at Court just at the time that Lady Dorothy (daughter of the first Earl of Essex) was left a widow.' With the identification of the 'noble Cosin' as Carew Mr. Weber concurs, as 'very likely'. Against it I can urge only one objection, but I think a decisive one: Falkland refers in the first letter to the 'great actresse' and her 'worthy' performance; but no such role is provided in *Coelum Britannicum*, where the only female speaking parts are those of Poenia, Fortune, and Hedone, each of whom delivers only one speech before being dismissed with insults. The evidence points rather to some Queen's masque, with Henrietta Maria the focus of interest, or to such a work as *The Shepheard's Paradise*, by Falkland's noble cousin Walter Montagu, produced by the Queen and her ladies in 1633 with the Queen herself glorified in the dual role of Saphira and Bellesa. Whatever their true reference, the letters are not concerned with any known work by Thomas Carew.

211. *An Answer.* 'Tom's' answer apparently furnished the basis for some verses in *The Vocal Miscellany*, 1734, ii. 31:

SONG XXXIX. *As Celia near a Fountain lay.*

> Tell me not *Celia* once did bless,
> Another Mortal's Arms;
> That cannot make my Passion less,
> Nor mitigate her Charms.
>
> Shall I refuse to quench my Thirst,
> Depending Life to save,
> Because some droughty Shepherd first,
> Has kiss'd the smiling Wave.
>
> No, no; methinks 'tis wondrous great,
> And suits a noble Blood,
> To have in Love, as well as State,
> A Taster to our Food.

The verses also occur, with the title 'An Apology for Loving a Widow', in the Cowper family miscellany (B.M. MS. Add. 28101, fol. 207ᵛ).

213. **2–3.** *that trade thou speak'st of to the* **Indies.** Perhaps a reference to Carew's verses *To A. D. unreasonable distrustfull of her owne beauty*, lines 65–6 (p. 86):

> I'le trade with no such Indian foole as sells
> Gold, Pearles, and pretious stones, for Beads and Bells.

Horseley was the seat of Carew's friend and cousin Carew Ralegh, for whom he wrote the hymeneal verses given on p. 47. '*The disease of the Stomach, and the word of disgrace*' = 'raw' + 'lie', or 'Rawlie' (Ralegh). The same rebus is quoted of Sir Walter Ralegh by John Aubrey (*Brief Lives*, ed. Andrew Clark, 1898, ii. 182).

NOTE ON THE
MUSICAL SETTINGS OF
CAREW'S POEMS

'THE Songs and Dialogues of this Booke', one reads at the end of Carew's *Poems*, 1640, 'were set with apt Tunes to them, by M^r. *Henry Lawes*, one of His Majesties Musitians.' A large number of Henry Lawes's settings are preserved in print and in manuscript, with others by William Lawes, Nicholas Laniere, William Webb, Walter Porter, Roger Hill, Jeremy Savill, Dr. John Wilson, and one Giovanni Giacomo Castoldi da Carravaggio. I have attempted to bring together all the settings of Carew's poetry to appear in print during the seventeenth century, and to these I have been able to add other settings preserved only in manuscript. The printed and manuscript collections from which these are derived are as follows:

Walter Porter, *Madrigales and Ayres*, 1632	(*WP*)
Select Musicall Ayres and Dialogues (Playford), 1652	(*P52*)
Select Musicall Ayres and Dialogues, in Three Bookes (Playford), 1653	(*P53*)
Henry Lawes, *Ayres and Dialogues, The First Booke*, 1653	(*L53*)
„ „ *The Second Book of Ayres, and Dialogues*, 1655	(*L55*)
Select Ayres and Dialogues (Playford), 1659	(*P59*)
Cheerfull Ayres or Ballads, by John Wilson D^r in Musick Professor of the same in the Vniversity of Oxford, 1660	(*JW*)
Select Ayres and Dialogues, The Second Book (Playford), 1669	(*P69*)
John Banister and Thomas Low, *New Ayres and Dialogues*, 1678	(*BL*)
Synopsis of Vocal Musick, by A. B., 1680	(*AB*)
The Banquet of Musick, The Second Book (Playford), 1688	(*P88*)
British Museum, MS. Add. 10337	(*A10*)
„ „ MS. Add. 11608	(*A116*)
„ „ MS. Add. 29396	(*A29*)
„ „ MS. Add. 31432	(*A314*)
„ „ MS. Add. 31434	(*A4*)
„ „ MS. Egerton 2013	(*E20*)
Bodleian Library, MS. Mus. Sch. B. 2	(*Oxf*)
„ „ MS. Don. C. 57 (an early collection of songs, some by Henry Lawes, acquired by the Friends of the Bodleian in May 1937)	(*FB*)
An autograph collection by Henry Lawes (the 'Cooper Smith' MS.) in the possession of Miss N. D. Church, Beaconsfield	(*HL*)
New York Public Library, MS. Drexel 4257 ('John Gamble his booke amen 1–6–5–9')	(*Dx*)

In the following check-list the settings are given alphabetically by first lines of the poems represented; these are not in all cases the first lines of the poems as set.

Admit (thou darling of mine eyes)
    (1) by Henry Lawes, for solo voice. *HL.*
    (2) by Roger Hill, for solo voice with thoroughbass. *P69.*

As *Celia* rested in the shade
    by Henry Lawes, for two voices with thoroughbass. *L53.*

Aske me no more where Iove *bestowes*
    (1) by William Lawes, for solo voice with thoroughbass. *BL, A314* (autograph), *FB, Dx.*
    (2) by Dr. John Wilson, for three voices (cantus primus, cantus secundus, bass). *JW.*
    (3) anonymous, for solo voice with thoroughbass. *FB.*

[Fayre *Doris* breake thy Glasse, it hath perplext]
    An excerpt from this poem, beginning 'Looke sweetest Doris on my Loue sick hart', and ending 'in Smoakinge Insence, to Adore thyne Eyes' (lines 22–34) is set by Henry Lawes, for solo voice with thoroughbass, in *HL.*

Feare not (deare Love) that I'le reveale
    (1) by Henry Lawes, for solo voice with thoroughbass, in *HL* and *FB*; arrangement for three voices (Cantus primus, Cantus secundus, and Bassus) in *L55* and *P59.*
    (2) by William Lawes, for four voices with thoroughbass, in *Oxf.* The manuscript is defective, and includes only the last six lines of the setting, beginning 'Only this meanes'.
    (3) anonymous, for solo voice, in *A10.* This setting is incomplete. The text begins, 'Thinke not, deare loue'.

Gaze not on thy beauties pride
    by Henry Lawes, for solo voice with thoroughbass. *HL, E20.*

Give me more love, or more disdaine
    by Henry Lawes, for solo voice with thoroughbass. *HL, L53, P69.*

Goe thou gentle whispering wind
    by Henry Lawes, for solo voice with thoroughbass. *HL, FB, Dx.*

Happy Youth, that shalt possesse
    by Henry Lawes, for solo voice with thoroughbass. *HL.*

Harke how my Celia, *with the choyce*
    by Henry Lawes, for solo voice with thoroughbass. *E20, FB, HL. E20* contains also a second version with tablature for lute accompaniment.

Hee that loves a Rosie cheeke
    (1) by Walter Porter, for four voices (Canto, Alto, Tenor, Quinto) with additional instrumental part and figured bass. *WP.*
    (2) by Henry Lawes, for solo voice with thoroughbass. *HL, A116, L53, P59, Dx.*

Hence vaine intruder, hast away
by Henry Lawes, for solo voice with thoroughbass. *HL.*

How ill doth he deserve a lovers name
by Henry Lawes, for solo voice with thoroughbass. *HL, A116, A29, Dx.*

I burne, and cruell you, in vaine
by Henry Lawes, for solo voice with thoroughbass. *HL.*

I was foretold, your rebell sex
by Henry Lawes, for solo voice with thoroughbass. *HL, P69.*

If the quick spirits in your eye
(1) by Henry Lawes, for solo voice with thoroughbass. *HL, P52, P53, P59, Dx.*
(2) by Giovanni Giacomo Castoldi da Carravaggio, for three voices (Cantus Primus, Cantus Secundus, and Bassus), under 'Fourteen Italian Songs'. *AB.*

If when the Sun at noone displayes
by Henry Lawes, for solo voice with thoroughbass. *HL, L53, P69, E20.* Ascribed to William Lawes in *E20.*

Ile gaze no more on her bewitching face
by Henry Lawes, for solo voice with thoroughbass. *HL, FB.*

In *Celia's* face a question did arise
(1) by Walter Porter, for three voices (Canto, Tenor, Basso) with added Quinto and figured bass. *WP.*
(2) by Henry Lawes, for solo voice with thoroughbass. *HL.*

In her faire cheekes two pits doe lye
anonymous, for solo voice, in *Dx.*

[In natures peeces still I see]
by Henry Lawes, for solo voice with thoroughbass, in *HL.* The beginning of the text ('all yᵉ workes of Nature are | defectiue, but my cruell fayre') differs from that of the received version; see Commentary, p. 217.

Know *Celia,* (since thou art so proud,)
by Henry Lawes, for solo voice with thoroughbass. *HL, L55.*

Ladyes, flye from Love's smooth tale
by Henry Lawes, for solo voice with thoroughbass. *HL, FB, Dx, P53, P59, P69.*

[Leade the black Bull to slaughter, with the Bore]
An excerpt (lines 13–24) beginning 'Sweetly breathinge vernall Aire' and concluding 'dwell vppon thy Rosye winge' is set by Henry Lawes, for solo voice with thoroughbass, in *HL.*

Let fooles great Cupids *yoake disdaine*
by Henry Lawes, for solo voice with thoroughbass. *HL.*

Marke how the bashfull morne, in vaine
by Nicholas Laniere (?), for solo voice with thoroughbass. Ascribed to Laniere in *P69.* From the heading 'By his Majesty' in *A116,* Gerald

Hayes (*King's Music*, 1937, p. 24) argues in favour of Charles I as composer. Anonymous in *Dx*.

My soule the great Gods prayses sings
by Henry Lawes, for five voices (Cantus primus, Cantus secundus, Contratenor, Tenor, and Bassus) with thoroughbass and instrumental 'Simphonia', in *A4* (autograph).

No more, blind God, for see my heart
(1) by Henry Lawes, for solo voice with thoroughbass. *HL*.
(2) by Jeremy Savill, for solo voice with thoroughbass. *P53, P59*.

No more shall meads be deckt with flowers
by Nicholas Laniere, for solo voice with thoroughbass. *E20, P69, P88*.

Now she burnes as well as I
by Henry Lawes, for solo voice with thoroughbass (as 'Second part' after '*I burne, and cruell you, in vaine*'). *HL*.

Of what mould did nature frame me
by William Webb, for solo voice with thoroughbass. *FB*.

Reade in these Roses, the sad story
by Henry Lawes, for solo voice with thoroughbass. *HL, E20*.

Seeke not to know my love, for shee
(1) by Henry Lawes, for solo voice with thoroughbass. *HL, FB*.
(2) anonymous, for solo voice with thoroughbass. *P69*.

Sitting by the streames that Glide
by Henry Lawes, for five voices (Cantus primus, Cantus secundus, Contratenor, Tenor, and Bassus) with thoroughbass and instrumental 'Simphonia', in *A4* (autograph).

Stand still you floods, doe not deface
by Henry Lawes, for solo voice with thoroughbass. *HL*.

Stay coward blood, and doe not yield
by Henry Lawes, for solo voice with thoroughbass. *HL*.

That flattring Glasse, whose smooth face weares
Anonymous, for solo voice. *E20*.

That lovely spot which thou dost see
by Henry Lawes, for solo voice with thoroughbass. *HL*.

Shep. This mossie bank they prest. *Ny.* That aged Oak
by Henry Lawes, for two voices ('Two *Trebles* or *Tenors*') with thoroughbass. *P69*.

[Thinke not cause men flatt'ring say]
An excerpt (lines 37–48), beginning 'Those Curious Locks soe Aptly twynde' and concluding 'they'le flye & seeke some warmer sun', is set by Henry Lawes, for solo voice with thoroughbass, in *HL*.

Weepe not (my deare) for I shall goe
by Henry Lawes, for solo voice with thoroughbass. *HL, P69*.

Weepe not, nor backward turne your beames
>   by Henry Lawes, for two voices with thoroughbass. *L55*.

When on the Altar of my hand
>   by Henry Lawes, for solo voice with thoroughbass. *HL, L53*. A variant
>   of this setting, with more florid melody, occurs in *FB* with tablature for
>   theorbo accompaniment.

When this Flye liv'd, she us'd to play
>   by Henry Lawes, for solo voice with thoroughbass, in *HL* and *P69*; with
>   tablature for lute accompaniment in *FB*.

When thou, poore excommunicate
>   by Henry Lawes, for solo voice with thoroughbass. *HL, L53*.

When you the Sun-burnt Pilgrim see
>   by Henry Lawes, for solo voice with thoroughbass. *HL*.

Wherefore doe thy sad numbers flow
>   by Henry Lawes, for solo voice. *HL*.

Wonder not though I am blind
>   by Henry Lawes, for solo voice. *HL*.

You that thinke Love can convey
>   by Henry Lawes, for solo voice with thoroughbass. *HL, P69*.

INDEX OF FIRST LINES

INDEX OF FIRST LINES 295

PRINTED IN GREAT BRITAIN
AT THE UNIVERSITY PRESS, OXFORD
BY VIVIAN RIDLER
PRINTER TO THE UNIVERSITY